Rational choice, collective decisions, and social welfare

Rational choice, collective decisions, and social welfare

KOTARO SUZUMURA

The Institute of Economic Research
Hitotsubashi University, Tokyo

CAMBRIDGE UNIVERSITY PRESS

Cambridge
London New York New Rochelle
Melbourne Sydney

CAMBRIDGE UNIVERSITY PRESS
Cambridge, New York, Melbourne, Madrid, Cape Town, Singapore,
São Paulo, Delhi, Dubai, Tokyo

Cambridge University Press
The Edinburgh Building, Cambridge CB2 8RU, UK

Published in the United States of America by Cambridge University Press, New York

www.cambridge.org
Information on this title: www.cambridge.org/9780521122559

First published 1983
This digitally printed version 2009

A catalogue record for this publication is available from the British Library

Library of Congress Cataloguing in Publication data

Suzumura, Kōtarō, 1944–

Rational choice, collective decisions, and social welfare.

Bibliography: p.

Includes index.

1. Social choice. 2. Welfare economics. I. Title.
HB846.8.S96 1983 302′.13 82–22110

ISBN 978-0-521-23862-5 Hardback
ISBN 978-0-521-12255-9 Paperback

Contents

Preface

From the time of its birth, the theory of collective choice and social welfare has led a curious life. Active investigations have come from quite variegated research fields, including economics, political science, moral philosophy, and decision theory, giving depth and breadth to this rapidly developing field. Nevertheless, there are still some who would deny its legitimacy as a branch of the social sciences in general and as a branch of economics in particular. Even the message of a central result thereof, that is, Arrow's celebrated general impossibility theorem, has not been made crystal clear. Indeed, Professor Arrow wrote in his Nobel Prize lecture delivered in 1972 that "[the] philosophical and distributive implications of the paradox of social choice are still not clear. Certainly, there is no simple way out. I hope that others will take this paradox as a challenge rather than as a discouraging barrier." This book, which is an outgrowth of my doctoral dissertation submitted to Hitotsubashi University in 1979, represents a modest attempt to respond to this challenge.

There are four main topics that I discuss in this work. First, I examine the concept of a choice function and the rationalizability thereof in terms of the revealed preference and related axioms. Second, I examine the robustness of the Arrovian impossibility theorems with special emphasis on the choice-functional formulation of social choice theory. Third, I explore the extended sympathy approach in social choice theory, thereby clarifying such concepts as envy and impartiality in this extended conceptual framework. Fourth, I examine the compatibility of the Paretian values and the individual libertarian claims. Throughout this work, I want to shed as much light as I can on the factors that are responsible for the stability of the voluntary association of free individuals. This work, therefore, is not meant to be a survey of the theory of collective choice and social welfare. Those who want to obtain an overview of this field must turn to other sources.

My investigation, which matured into this book, began while I was working at the London School of Economics and Political Science in 1974–6. Substantial portions of my work took shape at the Kyoto Institute of Economic Research in 1976–81, during which time I also made a fruitful visit to Stanford University (1979–80). Many persons helped me en route by their writings as well as by conversations. My special thanks go to

Professors Kenneth Arrow and Amartya Sen, whose seminal works and insightful comments were extremely helpful throughout my study. Thanks are also due Professors Masahiko Aoki, Douglas Blair, Georges Bordes, Peter Coughlin, Bhaskar Dutta, John Fountain, Wulf Gaertner, Steve Goldman, Peter Hammond, Jerry Kelly, Takashi Negishi, Hukukane Nikaido, Prasanta Pattanaik, and David Starrett. Needless to say, they are not responsible for any remaining defects of this work.

Along the way, I have written several papers, which were published in *Economica, International Economic Review, Journal of Economic Theory, Mathematical Social Sciences, Review of Economic Studies*, and the Caen Conference Proceedings entitled *Social Choice and Welfare*. I am grateful to the editors, as well as to the co-authors of some of these papers, for their permission to include here in part (often in a generalized form) the contents of these articles.

Last, but not least, my thanks go to Ms. Ryoko Kasai, Ms. Tomoko Kashima, and Ms. Mana Takai, who typed several versions of this work at the Kyoto Institute of Economic Research.

Kotaro Suzumura

January 4, 1983

CHAPTER 1

Prologue

> [T]he social order is a sacred right which serves as a foundation for all other rights. This right, however, since it comes not by nature, must have been built upon convention. To discover what these conventions are is the matter of our inquiry.
>
> Jean-Jacques Rousseau*

1 The problem of rule selection

In trying to lay the foundations of the new welfare economics, J. R. Hicks brought forward the following problem:

> Although the economic system can be regarded as a mechanism for adjusting means to ends, the ends in question are ordinarily not a single system of ends, but as many independent systems as there are "individuals" in the community. This appears to introduce a hopeless arbitrariness into the testing of efficiency [of any given economic organization]. You cannot take a temperature when you have to use, not one thermometer, but an immense number of different thermometers, working on different principles, and with no necessary correlation between their registrations. How is this difficulty to be overcome? [Hicks, 1939, p. 699]

According to Hicks, there are three possible ways of dealing with this problem:

1. Instead of using the preference scales of the individuals in the community, the investigator may use his own "thermometer," that is, decide for himself what is good or bad for society in judging the relative performances of the alternative economic organizations.†
2. The investigator may seek a method of aggregating the (possibly) conflicting reports of the various thermometers so as to construct an "average" or "social" registration.

* J.-J. Rousseau, *The Social Contract or Principle of Political Right*. In *Social Contract: Essays by Locke, Hume and Rousseau* (with an introduction by Sir Ernest Barker). London: Oxford University Press, 1947, p. 240.

† To avoid awkward wording, the pronoun "he" will often be used in the generic sense to mean "he or she."

3. The investigator may focus attention on those cases in which the difficulty due to the heterogeneity of individual preferences may be circumvented by allowing *hypothetical* compensation payments between gainers and losers.

The first of these methods was rejected by Hicks because of its paternalistic and "unscientific" flavor, whereas the second method was identified with the traditional method of Marshall, Edgeworth, and Pigou, of "weighting" the component parts under the assumption of interpersonal comparability of welfare units, and was likewise rejected on the Robbinsian ground that we had no "scientific" means for interpersonal welfare comparisons. This left only the third method, which Hicks did adopt, and the foundations of the new welfare economics were based on this method.

Soon after removal of the scaffold for construction, however, demolition activity began. The hypothetical compensation principles proposed by Pareto (1909), Barone (1908), and Kaldor (1939), and used extensively by Hicks (1939, 1940), were found to contain grave logical difficulties.[1] The very foundations of the new welfare economics were thereby revealed to be quite shaky. Because Hicks's third method involving the hypothetical compensation principle turned out to be will-o'-the-wisp, we must once again face up to the Hicksian problem of making social judgments in the face of heterogeneous individual preferences.

As a matter of fact, the second method (which Hicks immediately threw away), which involves constructing a rule that aggregates individual preferences, commands more careful scrutiny, because the weighted-sum-of-utilities method is just a particular instance thereof, and the class of possible rules is very broad indeed. It was Arrow (1950, 1963, 1967*a*, 1967*c*) who formalized this preference aggregation problem in a way that was in concordance with the Robbins–Hicks–Allen *ordinalist* approach to individual utility and welfare. His studies had an even more devastating effect on the prior effort to lay the foundations of welfare economics, because Arrow's central conclusion was that *there cannot possibly exist a "rational," "efficient," and "democratic" rule of preference aggregation.* How is this difficulty to be overcome? The following chapters will examine this and related problems.

The first order of business is to further clarify the nature of our problem. We have said that we want to construct a rule that aggregates individual preferences with a view toward forming social judgments regarding the comparative virtues of alternative economic organizations. A point to keep in mind is that this rule selection or system design should in itself be a matter of concern for the individuals in the society. The reason is that an acknowledged rule associates to each possible set of individual preference orderings a social choice procedure for selecting a socially preferred decision out of any set of feasible alternatives. Now, "the principles of practical reasoning for an entity capable of decision are to be decided upon by that entity. Thus the principle of choice for a rational individual is his to make; but, similarly, the principles of social choice must be adopted by the association itself, that is, by the individuals that constitute it" (Rawls, 1968, p. 69). This granted, we seem to be trapped by the prima facie infinite regression: We need a rule for aggregating individual preferences over primitive social states, and this presupposes a higher-order rule for aggregating individual preferences over alternative rules of the first order, and so on ad infinitum. How can we break this impasse?

The clue is found in the fact that it is much easier to propose and then accept or reject an abstract performance criterion of a rule (such as that the outcome generated by a rule should not invidiously favor or disfavor any individual, because otherwise those who feel that their wishes are unfairly treated by the rule will have legitimate resentment against the social decisions thereby arrived at and will fail to be motivated to cooperate with others to attain the socially "best" position identified by that rule), even though preferences among rules (of any order) may be prohibitively difficult to form in the vacuum. Motivated by this simple observation, we proceed as follows.

Let each individual propose the performance criteria that he wishes the rule to satisfy, with the understanding that the rule acknowledged now will be binding on indefinite future contingencies, the peculiarities of which cannot be known in the primordial stage of rule selection. Each individual recognizes that he is required, along with everybody else, to make a firm commitment in advance. Because each individual is deprived of any opportunity to tailor the rule to favor him if it is adopted and to reject the rule if it comes to act to his disadvantage, it is likely that everyone will have every incentive to propose performance criteria of a general nature.[2]

The next step is to single out certain performance criteria from among those that were initially proposed, the selection being made on the basis of unanimous acknowledgment by all individuals. Given this set of unanimously acknowledged criteria, an investigation should then be made to identify those rules for social choice that are thereby qualified.

A point of some importance is that a rule need not necessarily be unanimously acknowledgeable simply because each one of its component axioms elicits agreement among individuals in isolation. As Samuelson (1977, p. 85) observed, the classic phrase "by their fruit must ye know them" applies above all to axiom systems, and the joint effect of a set of individually appealing axioms on a rule might turn out to yield an unappealing rule, one eventually unacceptable to the participating individuals. Even worse, a combination of individually innocent and persuasive axioms might annihilate *all* rules, as Arrow's general impossibility theorem exemplifies.

Let us notice that the message of these paradoxes and logical contradictions need not necessarily be negative. They may serve as signals that force us to reexamine the individual axioms (performance criteria) and, going back one step further, the conceptual framework in which these axioms are phrased. It is to be hoped that we can thereby penetrate to a more appropriate understanding of the factors that are responsible for the institutional stability of voluntary associations of free individuals. This is the central frame of thought that guides us throughout this work.[3]

2 Plan of the book

Following this introductory chapter and its Appendix, which expounds an elementary theory of binary relations, there are seven chapters that constitute the main body of this book. In Chapter 2 we introduce the formal concept of a choice function and the rationality thereof, with a view toward characterizing the concept of a rational choice function in terms of the revealed preference and related axioms. In the main body of the chapter we consider this rationalization problem, which is the choice-functional counterpart of the integrability problem in demand theory, when the domain of a choice function contains all finite subsets taken from the universal set. This restriction is imposed because of the intended application of this theory in the rest of the book. In the Appendix to Chapter 2 we develop a more general theory of a rational choice function.

In Chapter 3 we set about analyzing the problem of the primordial rule selection, and we examine Arrow's general impossibility theorem on the "rational," "efficient," and "democratic" collective choice rules. Special care will be taken here with the robustness of the Arrovian impossibility theorems with respect to the successive weakening of the collective rationality requirement.

In Chapter 4 we focus our attention on a particular class of rules: The simple majority decision rule and its extensions.

Up to this point, our investigation into the structure of a social choice rule makes use only of an informational basis that excludes any form of interpersonal welfare comparisons. In the rest of this book, we examine the effect of widening the informational basis for collective choice. Instead of confining our attention to the *intrapersonally ordinal* and *interpersonally noncomparable* preference orderings by each and every individual, we now ask each individual to put himself in the position of each other individual through the imaginary exchange of circumstances to determine if that is a better or worse position than his actual position. It can hardly be denied that individuals may make, and do make, interpositional comparisons of this type, and this provides us with one operational interpretation of what one may mean by interpersonal comparisons of welfare.

In Chapter 5 we formulate a social choice version of the "equity-as-no-envy" approach of Foley (1967), Varian (1974, 1975, 1976), and others, and in Chapter 6 we examine two versions of the constrained majoritarian social choice rules. Both chapters make extensive use of the interpersonal comparisons of welfare mentioned earlier and try to gauge their effects on the Arrovian impossibility theorems.

In Chapter 7 we examine another class of impossibility theorems and the resolutions thereof. The impossibility theorems in question maintain the incompatibility of democratic values and libertarian claims and assert that unadulterated exercise of libertarian rights, coupled with mechanical use of the Pareto unanimity principle, may disqualify all collective choice rules with unrestricted domain. Two resolution schemes will be presented, the first of which restricts mechanical use of the Pareto unanimity principle, whereas the second restricts the exercise of rights by the impartial principles of justice. It is clear that they differ in their informational requirements as well as in their basic attitudes toward libertarian rights and democratic values. Nevertheless, they seem to share a common general moral: The ultimate guarantee of a minimal level of libertarian rights in a democratic society lies in an attitude whereby individuals respect and care for equal basic liberty and justice for one another in the conflict situation.

Finally, Chapter 8 summarizes the broad implications of our analysis and puts forward several qualifications.

3 Concluding remarks

Before concluding this introductory chapter, two final remarks are necessary regarding terminology. First, in the theory of collective choice and social welfare, the term "individual" may be interpreted flexibly, depending on the context. In some contexts it may mean a human individual, whereas in others it may refer to a nation, a social group within a large committee, a team, and so on. In the main, we shall refer to "individual" as if we mean human individual, but the theory makes good sense under the different interpretations of the term.

Second, a "social state" is a primitive concept of our analysis; it can stand for almost anything that can be construed as the outcome of a social decision process. Depending on the context, it may denote "a set of bills passed and bills failed" (Plott, 1972, p. 84) or "a vector whose components are values of the various particular decisions actually made by the government, such as tax rates, expenditures, antimonopoly policy, and price policies of socialized enterprise" (Arrow, 1963, p. 87) or "a complete description of the amount of each type of commodity in the hands of each individual, the amount of labor to be supplied by each individual, the amount of each productive resource invested in each type of productive activity, and the amounts of various types of collective activity" (Arrow, 1963, p. 17), and so on. It is hoped that the reader will keep in mind this flexibility of interpreting the concept of a social state.

Appendix: Elementary properties of binary relations

1. In the whole body of this book, we shall make extensive use of the theory of binary relations in general, as well as the extension theorems for binary relations in particular. Let us therefore gather some elementary properties of binary relations in a form that is convenient for later reference. The following notation will be used throughout.

$\exists$	existential quantifier ("there exists")
$\forall$	universal quantifier ("for all")
$\rightarrow$	implication ("if ..., then ...")
$\leftrightarrow$	equivalence ("if and only if")
$\sim$	negation ("not")
&	conjunction ("and")
$\vee$	alternation (the inclusive "or")
$=$	identity
$x \in A$	x belongs to (is an element of) A
$x \notin A$	x does not belong to (is not an element of) A
$A \subset B$	A is contained in (is a subset of) B
$A \supset B$	A contains (is a superset of) B
$A \subset\subset B$	A is properly contained in B ($A \subset B$ & $A \neq B$)
$\{x \in A \mid P(x)\}$	set of all $x \in A$ having a property P
$A \cap B$	intersection of A and B (elements belonging to both A and B)
$A \cup B$	union of A and B (elements belonging to either A or B)
$A \times B$	Cartesian product of A and B, namely the set of ordered pairs (x, y) such that $x \in A$ and $y \in B$
$A \setminus B$	set-theoretic difference, namely the set of points x such that $x \in A$ and $x \notin B$
$\mathscr{P}(A)$	power set of A, namely the set of all subsets of A
Z^+	set of all positive integers
$\varnothing$	empty set

Other symbols will be explained when necessity dictates.

2. Let X be the universal set of our discourse. A *binary relation* on X is a proposition (R) such that, for any ordered pair (x, y), where $x, y \in X$, we can unambiguously say that (R) is true or false. The set of all ordered pairs (x, y) that satisfy (R), to be written as R, is then a well-defined subset of $X \times X$. Conversely, given a set $R \subset X \times X$, we can define a binary relation (R) by

$$(R) \text{ is true for } (x, y) \leftrightarrow (x, y) \in R$$

We can thus identify a binary relation on X with a subset of $X \times X$. It is customary to write, for all $x, y \in X$, xRy if and only if $(x, y) \in R$ holds true. In this Appendix (and, indeed, in most of this book) we shall use the set-theoretic notation for the sake of convenience of mathematical operations on a class of binary relations. We shall have more to say on this matter in the final section.

Given a binary relation R on X, we define the *symmetric part* $I(R)$ and the *asymmetric part* $P(R)$ thereof by

$$I(R) = \{(x, y) \in X \times X \mid (x, y) \in R \;\&\; (y, x) \in R\} \tag{A.1}$$

and

$$P(R) = \{(x, y) \in X \times X \mid (x, y) \in R \;\&\; (y, x) \notin R\} \tag{A.2}$$

respectively. Clearly, $I(R) \cap P(R) = \varnothing$ and $I(R) \cup P(R) = R$ hold true for every R.

A notable example of a binary relation is what we call a *weak preference relation* R of an agent, which is defined on a set X of all conceivable options by

$$(x, y) \in R \leftrightarrow \text{According to the agent's view, } x \text{ is at least as good as } y$$

$I(R)$ and $P(R)$ will then denote the *indifference relation* and the *strict preference relation*, respectively, of this agent. To the extent that it may facilitate understanding, we provide interpretations of a variety of properties of a binary relation to be introduced later in terms of a weak preference relation, although these properties can apply to any binary relation we may specify.

3. Let us now enumerate several properties of a binary relation R that have been found relevant in various contexts of social choice theory.[4]

(a) *Completeness*

$$\forall x, y \in X: x \neq y \rightarrow (x, y) \in R \vee (y, x) \in R$$

(b) *Reflexivity*

$$\forall x \in X: (x, x) \in R$$

(c) *Irreflexivity*

$$\forall x \in X: (x, x) \notin R$$

(d) *Transitivity*

$$\forall x, y, z \in X: [(x, y) \in R \,\&\, (y, z) \in R] \rightarrow (x, z) \in R$$

(e) *Quasi transitivity*

$$\forall x, y, z \in X: [(x, y) \in P(R) \,\&\, (y, z) \in P(R)] \rightarrow (x, z) \in P(R)$$

(f) *Triple acyclicity*

$$\forall x, y, z \in X: [(x, y) \in P(R) \,\&\, (y, z) \in P(R)] \rightarrow (z, x) \notin P(R)$$

(g) *Acyclicity*

$$\forall t \in Z^+, \forall x^1, x^2, \ldots, x^t \in X: [\forall \tau \in \{1, 2, \ldots, t-1\}: (x^\tau, x^{\tau+1}) \in P(R)] \rightarrow (x^t, x^1) \notin P(R)$$

(h) *Consistency*

$$\forall t \in Z^+, \forall x^1, x^2, \ldots, x^t \in X: [(x^1, x^2) \in P(R) \,\&\, \forall \tau \in \{2, 3, \ldots, t-1\}: (x^\tau, x^{\tau+1}) \in R] \rightarrow (x^t, x^1) \notin R$$

(i) *Symmetry*

$$\forall x, y \in X: (x, y) \in R \rightarrow (y, x) \in R$$

(j) *Asymmetry*

$$\forall x, y \in X: (x, y) \in R \rightarrow (y, x) \notin R$$

(k) *Equivalence:* R satisfies (b), (d), and (i)
(l) *Ordering:* R satisfies (a), (b), and (d)
(m) *Quasi ordering:* R satisfies (b) and (d)

Consider an agent with a weak preference relation R on the set X of all conceivable options. If he is not like Buridan's ass, whose inability to compare two haystacks resulted in starvation, then R is a complete binary relation. It is also the case that R is reflexive, because every option is at least as good as itself, and the strict preference relation $P(R)$ is irreflexive.

The properties (d) to (h), when they are applied to a weak preference relation R, represent various degrees of the internal coherence of the preference structure. Let us explain their respective meanings as well as their mutual relations.

There are three distinct possibilities of the three-term cycles generated by R. First, we have a situation where we start from one option and climb up the preference ladder three times only to find ourselves in the initial position. If we denote $(u, v) \in P(R)$ by an arrow with two heads from v to u, this three-term cycle can be depicted as in Figure 1.1a. The second

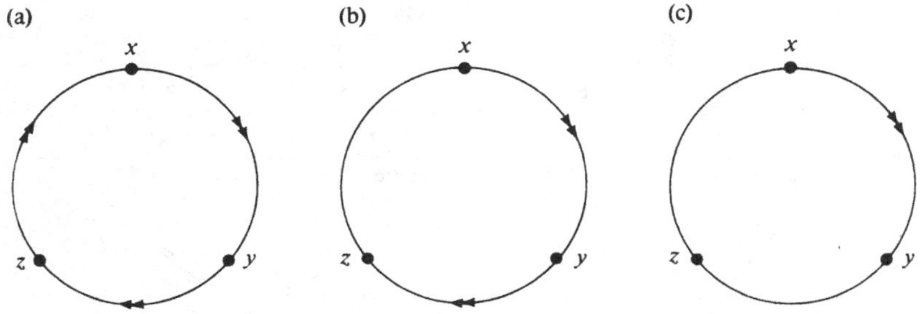

Figure 1.1. Three-term cycles.

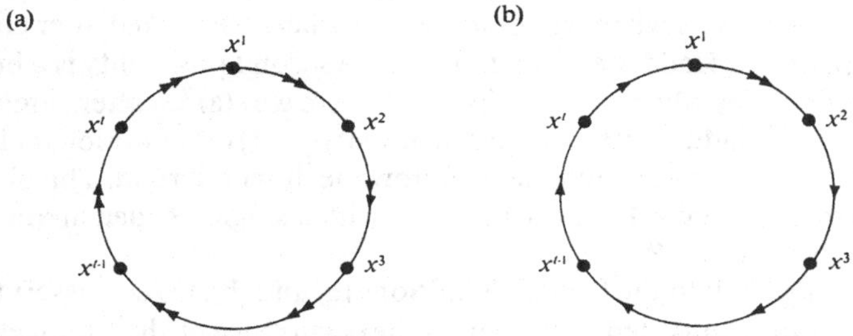

Figure 1.2. t-Term cycles.

possibility is that, starting from one option, we climb up the preference ladder twice and then move to another option on the same preference plateau only to realize that we are back to the initial position. Denoting $(u, v) \in I(R)$ by an arc without arrow connecting u and v, this three-term cycle can be shown as in Figure 1.1b. The third and last possibility is described in Figure 1.1c, where we start from an option and come back to that option again by climbing up the preference ladder once and then moving to another option on the same preference plateau twice. It is easy to verify that these three possibilities exhaust the three-term cycles that R can generate.

Referring back to the definitions (d), (e), and (f), we can easily verify that a transitive R excludes all of these three-term cycles. It can also be seen that a quasi-transitive R excludes the three-term cycles of the types in Figures 1.1a and 1.1b, whereas an acyclic R excludes the three-term cycles of the Figure 1.1a type only.

Going one step further, let us consider two possibilities of the t-term cycles generated by R, where $t \in Z^+$ satisfies $3 \leq t < +\infty$, that are described by Figures 1.2a and 1.2b. The first possibility described in

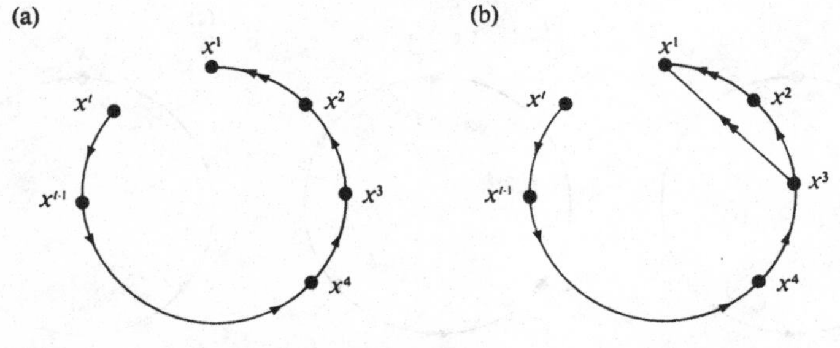

Figure 1.3. Transitivity and t-term coherence.

Figure 1.2a obtains when we come back to where we started after climbing up the preference ladder exactly t times. The second possibility is a bit more subtle. It obtains when we come back to where we started after climbing up the preference ladder just once and then visit $(t-1)$ other options subject to the condition that we should never follow the downhill road. This situation is described in Figure 1.2b, where an arc with a single-headed arrow from v to u denotes $(u, v) \in R$.

Referring back to the formal definitions (g) and (h), we can assert that an acyclic [resp. a consistent] R excludes the occurrence of the t-term cycles of the Figure 1.2a [resp. Figure 1.2b] type for every $t \in Z^+$. Because the t-term cycles of the Figure 1.2a type constitute a special case of the t-term cycles of the Figure 1.2b type, it follows that *consistency implies acyclicity*. It is also clear that *acyclicity implies triple acyclicity*.

How is transitivity, which is the strongest three-term coherence condition, related to the t-term coherence conditions? To answer this question, suppose that R is transitive and assume that we have a preference chain described by Figure 1.3a, where $3 \leq t < +\infty$, so that we have

$$(x^1, x^2) \in P(R) \,\&\, \forall \tau \in \{1, 2, \ldots, t-1\}: (x^\tau, x^{\tau+1}) \in R \tag{A.3}$$

R being transitive, it follows from $(x^1, x^2) \in P(R)$ and $(x^2, x^3) \in R$ that $(x^1, x^3) \in R$. We show that a contradiction ensues if we have $(x^1, x^3) \in I(R)$. Suppose that $(x^2, x^3) \in R$ is in fact $(x^2, x^3) \in P(R)$ [resp. $(x^2, x^3) \in I(R)$]. We then have a three-term cycle of the Figure 1.1b type [resp. the Figure 1.1c type], in contradiction with the assumed transitivity of R. Now that we have $(x^1, x^3) \in P(R)$, we can connect x^1 and x^3 with a double-headed arrow from the latter to the former to obtain Figure 1.3b. Using x^3 in place of x^2 and x^4 in place of x^3, we can repeat the foregoing argument to obtain $(x^1, x^4) \in P(R)$. Proceeding in this way, we can eventually assert that (A.3) entails $(x^1, x^t) \in P(R)$, which in effect excludes the possibility of a t-term

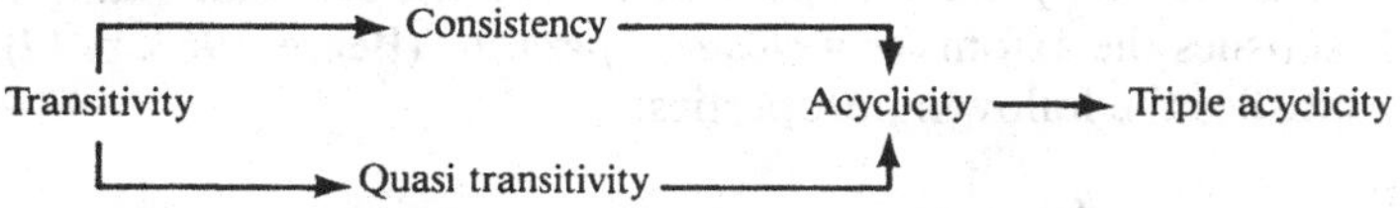

Figure 1.4. Implication network among preference coherence conditions.

cycle of the Figure 1.2b type. We have thus shown that *transitivity implies consistency*. A similar (but simpler) argument can be invoked to assert that *quasi transitivity implies acyclicity*.

For mnemonic convenience, let us summarize the logical relationship that holds among (d), (e), (f), (g), and (h) in Figure 1.4, where a single-headed arrow standing for a logical implication may not be reversed, in general.[5]

Finally, care should be taken with some elementary but useful implications of transitivity. If R is transitive, $I(R)$ as well as $P(R)$ is transitive, and

$$\forall x, y, z \in X: \left\{ \begin{array}{l} (x, y) \in P(R) \ \& \ (y, z) \in I(R) \\ \\ (x, y) \in I(R) \ \& \ (y, z) \in P(R) \end{array} \right\} \rightarrow (x, z) \in P(R) \qquad \text{(A.4)}$$

holds true. The proof of these assertions, which is partly contained in our preceding argument, is left as an exercise.

So much for the internal coherence conditions. The remaining properties (i) to (m) do not seem to require detailed elucidation. However, two remarks might be in order. First, *a binary relation* R *is symmetric if and only if* $R = I(R)$, *and* R *is asymmetric if and only if* $R = P(R)$. Second, *an equivalence* R *divides all options into mutually exclusive subsets, to be called the* R*-equivalence classes, such that* $(x, y) \in R$ *for any* x *and* y *in the same subset, whereas* $(x, y) \notin R$ *and* $(y, x) \notin R$ *if* x *and* y *do not belong to the same subset.*[6]

4. Given two binary relations R^1 and R^2 on X, we define the *composition* thereof by

$$R^1R^2 = \{(x, y) \in X \times X \mid \exists z \in X: (x, z) \in R^1 \ \& \ (z, y) \in R^2\} \qquad \text{(A.5)}$$

which is instrumental in defining the *transitive closure* $T(R)$ of a given binary relation R on X. Defining an infinite sequence of binary relations $(R^{(\tau)})_{\tau=1}^{\infty}$ by

$$R^{(1)} = R, \quad R^{(\tau)} = RR^{(\tau-1)} \quad (\tau \geq 2)$$

let

$$T(R) = \bigcup_{\tau=1}^{\infty} R^{(\tau)} \qquad \text{(A.6)}$$

It is easy to verify that an operator $T(\cdot)$ on the set of all binary relations on X satisfies the axioms of a *closure operation* (Berge, 1963, p. 12); that is, $T(\cdot)$ satisfies the following properties:

(T_1) $T(R) \supset R$

(T_2) $R^1 \supset R^2 \to T(R^1) \supset T(R^2)$

(T_3) $T[T(R)] = T(R)$

(T_4) $T(\varnothing) = \varnothing$

We can readily verify that *R is transitive if and only if $R = T(R)$ holds true.* Therefore, $T(R)$ is a transitive superset of R for any R in view of (T_3). The crucial importance of the transitive closure stems from the following property thereof.

Theorem A (1)
For any binary relation R, $T(R)$ is the smallest transitive superset of R.

Proof: It is easy to see that R is transitive if and only if $RR \subset R$ holds true. Notice also that if R^1, R^1_* and R^2, R^2_* are binary relations on X such that $R^1 \subset R^1_*$ and $R^2 \subset R^2_*$, then $R^1R^2 \subset R^1_* R^2_*$ holds true. In order to establish the assertion of the theorem, let R_* be an arbitrary transitive superset of R. By definition, we have

$$R \subset R_*, \quad R_*R_* \subset R_* \tag{A.7}$$

It then follows that $R^{(2)} = RR \subset R_*R_* \subset R_*$, which implies, in turn, that $R^{(3)} = RR^{(2)} \subset R_*R_* \subset R_*$. Repeating in this way, we obtain

$$\forall \tau \in Z^+ : R^{(\tau)} \subset R_* \tag{A.8}$$

The assertion of the theorem follows from (A.6) and (A.8).[7] ∎

Let R and S be, respectively, a binary relation on X and a subset of X. Let the *restriction* of R on S be defined by

$$R(S) = R \cap (S \times S) \tag{A.9}$$

Of particular interest and importance is the *transitive closure of R on S*, which is defined simply by $T(R(S))$. A crucial fact is that *$T(R(S))$ is an ordering on S if R is complete and reflexive.*

5. Our next order of business is that of introducing the concepts of greatestness and maximality with respect to a given binary relation. Given a binary relation R on X and a subset S of X, we define a subset $\mu_R(S)$ of S by

$$\mu_R(S) = \{x \in X \mid \forall\, y \in S: (x, y) \in R\} \tag{A.10}$$

which is to be called the set of all *R-majorants* of S. We can make use of this set to define the set $G(S, R)$ of all *R-greatest points* of S and the set $\sigma_R(S)$ of all *R-suprema* of S by

$$\begin{aligned} G(S, R) &= S \cap \mu_R(S) \\ &= \{x \in S \mid \forall\, y \in S: (x, y) \in R\} \end{aligned} \tag{A.11}$$

and

$$\sigma_R(S) = \{x \in \mu_R(S) \mid \forall\, y \in \mu_R(S): (y, x) \in R\} \tag{A.12}$$

respectively. Related but distinct from these is the set $M(S, R)$ of all *R-maximal points* of S, which is defined by

$$M(S, R) = \{x \in S \mid \forall\, y \in S: (y, x) \notin P(R)\} \tag{A.13}$$

Theorem A(2)

(a) $S \cap \sigma_R(S) = G(S, R)$, and
(b) $M(S, R) \supset G(S, R)$, the set-theoretic equality being valid if R is complete and reflexive.

Proof of (a): By definition, we have

$$\begin{aligned} S \cap \sigma_R(S) &= S \cap \mu_R(S) \cap \{x \in X \mid \forall\, y \in \mu_R(S): (y, x) \in R\} \\ &= G(S, R) \cap \{x \in X \mid \forall\, y \in \mu_R(S): (y, x) \in R\} \end{aligned}$$

so that it suffices to prove that

$$G(S, R) \subset \{x \in X \mid \forall\, y \in \mu_R(S): (y, x) \in R\} \tag{A.14}$$

If we negate (A.14) and if $G(S, R) \neq \varnothing$, then we must have

$$\exists\, x \in G(S, R), \exists\, y \in \mu_R(S): (y, x) \notin R \tag{A.15}$$

in contradiction with $(y, x) \in R$, which follows from (A.10) and (A.11). If, on the other hand, $G(S, R) = \varnothing$, (A.14) is obviously true. ▮

Proof of (b): Because $(x, y) \in R$ excludes the possibility of $(y, x) \in P(R)$, $M(S, R)$ must be a superset of $G(S, R)$. To complete the proof, we have only to notice that $(y, x) \notin P(R)$ implies $(x, y) \in R$ if R is complete and reflexive. ▮

A simple sufficiency condition for the existence of an R-maximal point is provided by the next theorem.

Theorem A(3)
If R is an acyclic binary relation on X and S is a nonempty finite subset of X, then $M(S,R) \neq \emptyset$.

Proof: We use an induction argument on the number $\#S$ of the elements in S. If $\#S = 1$, the proposition is obviously true. Suppose that the proposition is true when $\#S = k$, and consider the case where $\#S = k+1$. Take any $x_0 \in S$, and let $S_0 = S \setminus \{x_0\}$. By the induction hypothesis there exists an $x^* \in M(S_0, R)$. If $(x_0, x^*) \notin P(R)$, we obtain $x^* \in M(S,R)$, and we are home. Otherwise, $(x_0, x^*) \in P(R)$ should hold true. R being acyclic, $x_0 \neq x^*$. If $x_0 \in M(S,R)$, we are home. Assume, therefore, that $x_0 \notin M(S,R)$. Then there exists an $x_1 \in S$ such that $(x_1, x_0) \in P(R)$. Because R is acyclic, $x_1 \notin \{x_0, x^*\}$. If $x_1 \in M(S,R)$, we are home. If not, we have $(x_2, x_1) \in P(R)$ for some $x_2 \in S$. R being acyclic, $x_2 \notin \{x_1, x_0, x^*\}$. Because S is a finite set, this algorithm must sooner or later lead us to an $x^{**} \in M(S,R)$. ∎

Coupled with Theorem A(2), Theorem A(3) implies that $G(S,R)$ *is nonempty for any nonempty finite set S if R is complete, reflexive, and acyclic.*

6. It is now time to discuss some extension theorems for binary relations that will play indispensable roles in later chapters of this book. As a matter of terminology, let us say that a binary relation R^2 is an *extension* of another binary relation R^1 if and only if we have (i) $R^1 \subset R^2$ and (ii) $P(R^1) \subset P(R^2)$. (Conversely, R^1 is said to be a *subrelation* of R^2 if and only if R^2 is an extension of R^1.) When this is in fact the case, we say that R^1 and R^2 are *compatible* binary relations.

The following classical theorem due to Szpilrajn (1930)[8] specifies a sufficiency condition for the existence of an extension that is an ordering, to be called an *ordering extension*.

Theorem A(4)
A quasi ordering R has an ordering extension R^*.

The proof of this theorem requires an auxiliary proposition called Zorn's lemma. Let R and S be, respectively, a binary relation on X and a nonempty subset of X. We say that the pair (S,R) is *inductive* if every nonempty subset A of S, over which R is complete and reflexive, has an R-supremum in S, namely, $S \cap \sigma_R(A) \neq \emptyset$.

Zorn's lemma
Suppose that R is a quasi ordering on X and (S,R) is inductive. Then there exists an R-maximal point of S.

Although the validity of Zorn's lemma is not intuitively clear, it is demonstrably equivalent to an important *axiom of choice* that is accepted today by most mathematicians.[9]

Proof of Theorem A(4): Let Ω be the collection of all quasi-ordering extensions of R. Ω is nonempty, because $R \in \Omega$. Let Ω' be a subcollection of Ω such that, for any $A, B \in \Omega'$, either $A \supset B$ or $A \subset B$ holds true, and define

$$R_0 = \bigcup_{R' \in \Omega'} R' \tag{A.16}$$

It is clear that $R_0 \in \Omega \cap \sigma_{\supset}(\Omega')$, which implies that $(\Omega, \supset)$ is inductive. In view of the fact that $\supset$ is a quasi ordering on Ω, we can now apply Zorn's lemma to assert the existence of a $\supset$-maximal element in Ω; that is,

$$R^* \in M(\Omega, \supset) \tag{A.17}$$

What remains to be established is completeness and reflexivity of R^*. Suppose, to the contrary, that there are x_0 and y_0 in X satisfying $(x_0, y_0) \notin R^*$ and $(y_0, x_0) \notin R^*$. Let R_1 be defined by

$$\forall x, y \in X: (x, y) \in R_1 \leftrightarrow \begin{cases} (x, y) \in R^* \\ \vee \\ [(x, x_0) \in R^* \ \& \ (y_0, y) \in R^*] \end{cases} \tag{A.18}$$

It is clear that $R^* \subset R_1$. Because $(x_0, y_0) \in R_1$ and $(x_0, y_0) \notin R^*$, it is in fact true that $R^* \subset \subset R_1$. To show transitivity of R_1, let $(x, y) \in R_1$ and $(y, z) \in R_1$. If $(x, y) \in R^*$ and $(y, z) \in R^*$, we have $(x, z) \in R^* \subset R_1$, thanks to transitivity of R^*. If $(x, y) \in R^*$ and $[(y, x_0) \in R^*$ and $(y_0, z) \in R^*]$, we obtain $[(x, x_0) \in R^*$ and $(y_0, z) \in R^*]$, which implies $(x, z) \in R_1$ in view of (A.18). The case where $[(x, x_0) \in R^*$ and $(y_0, y) \in R^*]$ and $(y, z) \in R^*$ can be similarly treated. Finally, the case where

$$[(x, x_0) \in R^* \ \& \ (y_0, y) \in R^*] \ \& \ [(y, x_0) \in R^* \ \& \ (y_0, z) \in R^*] \tag{A.19}$$

can never occur, because (A.19) entails $(y_0, x_0) \in R^*$, a contradiction. Therefore, R_1 is transitive.

To show that R_1 is an extension of R, notice first that $R \subset R^* \subset \subset R_1$. Let $(x, y) \in P(R) \subset P(R^*)$. We then have $(x, y) \in R^*$ and $(y, x) \notin R^*$. If it is true that $[(y, x_0) \in R^*$ and $(y_0, x) \in R^*]$, it follows that $(y_0, x_0) \in R^*$, a contradiction. Therefore, $(y, x) \notin R_1$ is the case, which implies $(x, y) \in P(R_1)$, and hence $P(R) \subset P(R_1)$. It then follows that

$$R_1 \in \Omega, R^* \subset \subset R_1 \tag{A.20}$$

in contradiction of the $\supset$-maximality of R^* in Ω. ▌

R being a quasi ordering is sufficient for the existence of an ordering extension thereof, as is asserted by Szpilrajn's theorem, but it is not necessary. In our analysis of collective choice and social welfare, it is often useful to have an extension theorem that identifies the necessary and sufficient condition for the existence of an ordering extension. Our final theorem in this Appendix provides precisely a condition to that effect.

Theorem A(5)
A binary relation R on X has an ordering extension if and only if it is consistent.

Proof of necessity: If R is not consistent, there exist $z^1, z^2, \ldots, z^t$ in X for some $t \in Z^+$ such that $(z^1, z^2) \in P(R)$, $(z^2, z^3) \in R, \ldots, (z^t, z^1) \in R$. Let R^* be an extension of R. Because $R \subset R^*$ and $P(R) \subset P(R^*)$ by definition, we immediately know that R^* cannot be consistent. A fortiori, R^* cannot be an ordering extension of R. ▌

Proof of sufficiency: Assuming that R is consistent, let a binary relation R_0 be defined by

$$R_0 = \Delta_X \cup T(R) \tag{A.21}$$

where Δ_X is the diagonal binary relation on X to be defined by

$$\Delta_X = \{(x, y) \in X \times X \mid x = y\} \tag{A.22}$$

We show that R_0 is a quasi ordering on X. Reflexivity of R_0 being obvious, we have only to establish transitivity thereof. Let $x, y, z \in X$ be such that $(x, y) \in R_0$ and $(y, z) \in R_0$. If (x, y) as well as (y, z) belongs to $T(R)$, we get $(x, z) \in T(R) \subset R_0$ by virtue of transitivity of $T(R)$. If $(x, y) \in \Delta_X$ [resp. $(y, z) \in \Delta_X$], we have $x = y$ [resp. $y = z$], so that $(x, z) \in R_0$ is implied by $(y, z) \in R_0$ [resp. $(x, y) \in R_0$]. Now that R_0 has turned out to be a quasi ordering, it has an ordering extension R^* by virtue of Theorem A(4). If we can show that R_0 is an extension of R, we are home. By virtue of (A.21), $R \subset R_0$ is obviously true. To show the validity of $P(R) \subset P(R_0)$, take any $(x, y) \in P(R)$. It follows from $(x, y) \in R$ that $(x, y) \in R_0$, so that we have only to prove that $(y, x) \notin R_0$ follows from $(x, y) \in P(R)$. Assume, therefore, that $(y, x) \in R_0$. Clearly, $(y, x) \notin \Delta_X$, because otherwise $(x, y) \in P(R)$ could not have been the case in the first place. It then follows that $(y, x) \in T(R)$. When $(x, y) \in P(R)$ is added to this, we obtain a contradiction with the consistency of R. This completes the proof (Suzumura, 1976*b*, Theorem 3). ▮

7. Let us conclude with a remark on notational convention. Consider an ordering R on a set $X = \{x, y, z\}$ defined by

$$R = \Delta_X \cup \{(x, y), (y, x), (x, z), (y, z)\} \tag{A.23}$$

where $\Delta_X = \{(x, x), (y, y), (z, z)\}$. An equivalent way of representing this ordering, to which we have already referred, is given by

$$xRx,\ yRy,\ zRz,\ xRy,\ yRx,\ xRz,\ yRz \tag{A.24}$$

Still another way of representing R is to express it as

$$R\colon [x, y], z \tag{A.25}$$

The guiding principle here is to arrange alternatives horizontally with the more preferred alternative to the left of the less preferred, indifference among alternatives, if any, being described by embracing them together by square brackets. (Incidentally, parentheses embracing two or more alternatives are used to indicate that there is no restriction whatsoever on the ranking of these alternatives vis-à-vis each other.)

Each method has merit as well as demerit. The method of (A.23) is precise and convenient for theoretical treatment, but it may well become lengthy and clumsy when X is large. The method of (A.24) is concise as far as the pairwise statement is concerned, but in describing the whole structure of an ordering it falls short of the preciseness attained by the first method. The method of (A.25) is by far the most concise, but (unlike the first two methods) it applies only to orderings. In view of these pros and cons, we shall make use of all of them in what follows, depending on the context.

So much for the purely technical preparations. It is now time for our economic analysis of rational choice.

CHAPTER 2

Rational choice and revealed preference

> [T]here is a sense in which the word rationality can be used which renders it legitimate to argue that at least some rationality is assumed before human behaviour has an economic aspect – the sense, namely, in which it is equivalent to "purposive".... [I]t is arguable that if behaviour is not conceived of as purposive, then the conception of the means-end relationships which economics studies has no meaning. So if there were no purposive action, it could be argued that there were no economic phenomena. But to say this is not to say in the least that all purposive action is completely consistent. It may indeed be urged that the more that purposive action becomes conscious of itself, the more it necessarily becomes consistent. But this is not to say that it is necessary to assume *ab initio* that it always is consistent or that the economic generalizations are limited to that, perhaps, tiny section of conduct where all inconsistencies have been resolved.
>
> Lionel Robbins*

0 Introduction

Almost every human act, individual or collective, involves choice under environmental constraints, which we can analyze via a generalization of the pure theory of consumer's behavior. In this analysis we start from the set of all conceivable states. The external environment delimits the range of *available states* without necessarily reducing the range to a single alternative. Those states that could actually be chosen compose a subset of the set of available states. Clearly, the set of available states changes when the external environment undergoes a change, and the choice therefrom will be changed accordingly. We can conceptualize in this way a functional relationship between the *choice set,* namely the set of all chosen states, and the set of available states. The domain of this functional relationship–to be called a *choice function* – is determined by the variability of the external environment. This concept of a choice function clearly corresponds to a demand function in the competitive consumption theory. The purpose of

* L. Robbins, *An Essay on the Nature and Significance of Economic Science,* 2nd edition. London: Macmillan, 1935, p. 93.

this chapter is to introduce a concept of rational choice functions and to characterize it in terms of the revealed preference and related axioms. This problem – to be called the *rationalizability problem* (which is the choice-functional counterpart of the integrability problem in consumption theory) – is of fundamental importance for the theory of choice in general and for the theory of collective choice in particular.

What do we mean by choice being rational? We often hear it said in the literature that what may be termed rational behavior consists of two assumptions:

(a) Confronted with the range of available alternatives, a rational agent will choose those alternatives that bring him to the best attainable position.
(b) The preference ("at least as good as") relation of a rational agent satisfies the strong consistency property to the effect that if alternative x is no less preferred to alternative y, and y to z, then x is no less preferred to z.

Assumption (a) means that the choice of a rational agent is *purposive*, whereas assumption (b) means that the preference ("at least as good as") relation of a rational agent satisfies the logical requirement of transitivity. We could cite numerous sources in the literature to back up this conception of rational choice. Suffice it to quote a passage from Arrow (1967*a*, p. 5): "The idea of transitivity clearly corresponds to some strong feeling of the meaning of consistency in our choice. Economists have traditionally identified the concept of rationality with the notion of choices derivable from an ordering."

Whatever merit this definition may well have as an intuitive conception of rational choice, however, assuming the preference ("at least as good as") relation to be transitive entices strong empirical criticism. There have been a few experimental researches that have suggested that the imperfect discriminatory power of humans leads to nontransitive indifference, hence to a nontransitive "at least as good as" relation, and Armstrong (1948, p. 3) went as far as to maintain the following: "That indifference is not transitive is indisputable, and the world in which it were transitive is indeed unthinkable."[1] Although some counterarguments could be constructed, we should rather like to respond by weakening the traditional conception of rational choice and say that *a choice behavior is rational if it is made in accordance with the optimization of some preference relation, irrespective of whether or not this underlying preference relation is transitive.* This notion of rational choice as optimizing choice goes at least as far back as Robbins (1935), and it has been extensively studied in recent years, most notably by Arrow (1959), Richter (1966, 1971), Wilson (1970), Sen (1971), Plott (1973),

Herzberger (1973), Schwartz (1972, 1976), Blair and associates (1976), and Suzumura (1976*a*, 1977). It is the rational choice function in this sense that we should like to formalize and to characterize in this chapter. Besides being of independent interest and importance, what follows serves as an essential building block in our theory of collective decisions and social welfare.

1 Choice functions and revealed preference

1.1 Choice functions and the concept of rational choice

Our general conceptual framework for the analysis of choice can be modeled after the pure theory of consumer's choice. Let X be a universal set of conceivable states that is fixed throughout our analysis.[2] Let $\mathscr{S}$ be a distinguished nonempty collection of nonempty subsets of X. An intended interpretation is that each and every $S \in \mathscr{S}$ denotes the set of available states that could possibly be presented to the agent under an appropriate specification of the environmental conditions. The pair $(X, \mathscr{S})$ will be called hereafter a *choice space*. A *choice function* on a choice space $(X, \mathscr{S})$ is a function C defined on $\mathscr{S}$ that assigns a nonempty subset (*choice set*) $C(S)$ of S to each and every $S \in \mathscr{S}$. When $x \in C(S)$ and $y \in S$, we say that x is chosen and y could have been chosen from S.

Note that we are allowing $C(S)$ to contain more than one state in S. In order to single out the final choice from S, therefore, some tie-breaking devices have to be applied to $C(S)$. Our analysis in this chapter is devoted only to the first part of this two-stage choice framework.

It is now time we formalize the concept of a rational choice function. We say that a weak preference relation R on the universal set X *rationalizes* (or is a *rationalization* of) a choice function C on $(X, \mathscr{S})$ if and only if, for every $S \in \mathscr{S}$, $C(S)$ consists of the R-greatest points of S, namely,

$$\exists R \subset X \times X, \forall S \in \mathscr{S}: C(S) = G(S, R) \tag{2.1}$$

Whenever a choice function C on $(X, \mathscr{S})$ has a weak preference relation R satisfying (2.1), we say that C is a *rational choice function*. This formalization clearly corresponds to an intuitive idea of rational choice as discussed in the introduction to this chapter, namely, that a choice function is rational if and only if we can construe the choice described by C as a choice in accordance with the optimization of some underlying weak preference relation.

Before setting about characterizing rational choice functions, several remarks seem to be in order.

First, an alternative formalization of rational choice as optimizing choice can be provided by

$$\exists R \subset X \times X, \forall S \in \mathcal{S}: C(S) = M(S, R) \tag{2.2}$$

Let us say that a choice function C is G-rational [resp. M-rational] if there exists a weak preference relation R such that, for all $S \in \mathcal{S}$, $C(S)$ consists of and only of $x^* \in S$ satisfying $(x^*, x) \in R$ [resp. $(x, x^*) \notin P(R)$] for all $x \in S$. Note that both concepts of rationality are deeply rooted in the tradition of economic theory. For instance, a Walras–Hicks consumer in the competitive markets is a G-rational agent, whereas a "planner" seeking a Pareto efficient allocation of resources is an M-rational agent. Note also that *an M-rational choice function is G-rational, but not vice versa, in general.* To verify this assertion, let C on $(X, \mathcal{S})$ be M-rational with an M-rationalization R. We define a binary relation R' on X by

$$\forall x, y \in X: [(x, y) \in R' \leftrightarrow (y, x) \notin P(R)] \tag{2.3}$$

By definition, we then have $M(S, R) = G(S, R')$ for all $S \in \mathcal{S}$, so that C is G-rational with a G-rationalization R'. To negate the validity of the converse, we have only to refer to Example 1 in Appendix B at the end of this chapter.[3] In what follows we shall concentrate on the G-rationality concept, so that whenever we talk about a rational choice function without any qualification, we are referring to a G-rational choice function.

Second, we should like to emphasize that our concept of rationality is nonvacuous in the sense that *not all choice functions are rational.*[4] To substantiate this claim, we can invoke Example 2 in Appendix B.

Third, it is interesting as well as useful to introduce several degrees of rationality in view of the fairly weak nature of our concept of rational choice. Let us say that a choice function is *full rational* if and only if it is rational with an ordering rationalization. The reader will immediately recognize that this concept of full rational choice corresponds precisely to the traditional concept of rational choice defined by (a) and (b) in the introduction to this chapter. Less demandingly, we say that a choice function is *quasi-transitive rational* [resp. *acyclic rational*] if and only if it is rational with a quasi-transitive [resp. acyclic] rationalization. We should like to characterize these rationality concepts in terms of some intuitively transparent axioms on a choice function.

1.2 Axioms of revealed preference and of congruence

To begin with, let us define two revealed preference relations induced by a choice function C on a choice space $(X, \mathcal{S})$ by

$$R_C = \bigcup_{S \in \mathcal{S}} [C(S) \times S] \tag{2.4}$$

and

$$R_C^* = \bigcup_{S \in \mathscr{S}} [C(S) \times \{S \setminus C(S)\}] \tag{2.5}$$

In words, we say that a state x is revealed R_C-preferred to a state y if and only if there exists an $S \in \mathscr{S}$ such that x is chosen and y could have been chosen from S, and x is revealed R_C^*-preferred to y if and only if x is chosen and y could have been chosen *but was actually rejected* from some $S \in \mathscr{S}$.

The potential importance of these revealed preference relations stems from an observation to the following effect. If the choice behavior of an agent is guided systematically by some underlying preferences, that fact will infallibly reveal itself in his actual choices, so that by observing his choices under alternative specifications of environmental conditions, we may possibly reconstruct his underlying preferences. This was indeed the original insight of Samuelson (1938; 1947, Chapter V; 1948; 1950*b*) that propelled him to open the door to the splendid edifice of revealed preference theory for a competitive consumer.

In order to motivate our theory of rational choice functions, let us have a brief look at the classical Samuelson–Houthakker–Richter theory. Consider a competitive economy involving l commodities ($2 \leq l < +\infty$), and let X, $p = (p_1, p_2, \ldots, p_l) \gg 0$, and $M > 0$ denote, respectively, the *commodity space* (the nonnegative orthant of the Euclidean l-space), the *competitive price vector*, and the *income* of our agent.[5] Let $\mathscr{B}$ denote the collection of the *competitive budget sets*, a typical member of which is given by

$$B(p, M) = \{x \in X \mid p \cdot x \leq M\} \tag{2.6}$$

Let h denote the *demand function* of our competitive agent, which is a *single-valued* choice function on the choice space $(X, \mathscr{B})$. Given any $B(p, M) \in \mathscr{B}$, $h(B(p, M)) \in B(p, M)$ stands for the commodity bundle that this agent chooses from the competitive budget set $B(p, M)$.[6] In terms of this h, we can now introduce several choice-consistency conditions due originally to Samuelson (1938; 1947, Chapter V; 1950*b*) and Houthakker (1950).

(i) In his first article (1938) on the revealed preference theory, Samuelson introduced a choice-consistency condition that he later (1950*b*, p. 370) called the *weak axiom of consumer's behavior*, which reads as follows:

$$\exists\, B(p, M) \in \mathscr{B}: \begin{cases} x = h(B(p, M)) \\ \& \\ y \in B(p, M) \setminus \{h(B(p, M))\} \end{cases}$$
$$\rightarrow \forall\, B(p', M') \in \mathscr{B}: [y = h(B(p', M')) \rightarrow x \notin B(p', M')]$$

Suppose, contrary to Samuelson's postulate, that we have two budget sets $B(p^1, M^1)$ and $B(p^2, M^2)$ in $\mathscr{B}$ such that

$$x = h(B(p^1, M^1))$$
$$y \in B(p^1, M^1) \ \& \ y \neq h(B(p^1, M^1))$$
$$y = h(B(p^2, M^2))$$

and

$$x \in B(p^2, M^2)$$

From the first two lines of this stipulation we can presume that our agent prefers x to y, because he chooses x in rejection of y from a budget set that includes x as well as y. We shall then be puzzled by his choice behavior described by the last two lines, because he chooses y from a budget set from which x could have been chosen. Samuelson's postulate excludes such perplexing choice inconsistency and, as such, is quite appealing.

(ii) Houthakker's *semitransitivity axiom* of revealed preference (1950, pp. 162–3) was introduced in terms of a finite sequence of bundles $(x^\tau)_{\tau=1}^{t}$ for some $t \in Z^+$ satisfying

$$\forall \tau \in \{1, 2, \ldots, t\}: x^\tau = h(B(p^\tau, p^\tau \cdot x^\tau)) \tag{2.7}$$

$$\forall \tau \in \{1, 2, \ldots, t-1\}: x^{\tau+1} \in B(p^\tau, p^\tau \cdot x^\tau) \tag{2.8}$$

and

$$\exists \tau \in \{1, 2, \ldots, t-1\}: x^{\tau+1} \neq h(B(p^\tau, p^\tau \cdot x^\tau)) \tag{2.9}$$

Note that, according to (2.7) and (2.8), x^τ presumably can be at least as good as $x^{\tau+1}$ for every $\tau \in \{1, 2, \ldots, t-1\}$, because x^τ is chosen from a budget set that also contains $x^{\tau+1}$. According to (2.9), this chain of revealed preferences should contain at least one *strict* preference. Houthakker's axiom requires in this situation that $x^1 \notin B(p^t, p^t \cdot x^t)$ hold true. This seems to be a reasonable requirement, because otherwise we would have a cyclic revealed preference relations.

What Samuelson (1950*b*, pp. 370–71) called the *strong axiom* is the same requirement as Houthakker's, save for the strengthening of (2.9) into

$$\forall \tau \in \{1, 2, \ldots, t-1\}: x^{\tau+1} \neq h(B(p^\tau, p^\tau \cdot x^\tau)) \tag{2.10}$$

and, as such, is a fortiori reasonable.

Coming back to our general conceptual framework where the focus of our attention is a choice function C on a choice space $(X, \mathscr{S})$, we now generalize Samuelson's and Houthakker's axioms. In this and other contexts the following simple lemma (Suzumura, 1977, p. 286) serves us well.

Lemma 2.1

$$P(R_C) \subset P(R_C^*) \subset R_C^* \subset R_C$$

Proof: We have only to prove that $P(R_C) \subset P(R_C^*)$, the remaining inclusions being valid by definition. If $(x, y) \in P(R_C)$, then we have

$$\exists S \in \mathscr{S}: x \in C(S) \ \& \ y \in S \tag{2.11}$$

and

$$\forall S' \in \mathscr{S}: y \notin C(S') \vee x \notin S' \tag{2.12}$$

If we apply (2.12) to $S' = S$, this, coupled with (2.11), yields

$$\exists S \in \mathscr{S}: x \in C(S) \ \& \ y \in S \setminus C(S) \tag{2.13}$$

and (2.12) implies

$$\forall S' \in \mathscr{S}: y \notin C(S') \vee x \notin S' \vee x \in C(S') \tag{2.14}$$

It follows from (2.13) and (2.14) that $(x, y) \in P(R_C^*)$, as desired. ∎

Let a finite sequence $(x^1, x^2, \ldots, x^t)$ $(t \geq 2)$ in X be called an *H-cycle of order t* if we have $(x^1, x^2) \in R_C^*$, $(x^\tau, x^{\tau+1}) \in R_C$ $(\tau = 2, 3, \ldots, t-1)$, and $(x^t, x^1) \in R_C$. Similarly, a finite sequence $(x^1, x^2, \ldots, x^t)$ $(t \geq 2)$ in X is called an *SH-cycle of order t* if we have $(x^1, x^2) \in R_C$, $(x^\tau, x^{\tau+1}) \in R_C^*$ $(\tau = 2, 3, \ldots, t-1)$, and $(x^t, x^1) \in R_C^*$. In view of Lemma 2.1, it is clear that *an SH-cycle of some order is an H-cycle of the same order*. This being the case, the exclusion of an H-cycle of any order excludes, a fortiori, the existence of an SH-cycle of the same order. We are now ready to introduce the following two revealed preference axioms.

Houthakker's axiom of revealed preference (HOA)
There exists no H-cycle of any order.

Strong axiom of revealed preference (SA)
There exists no SH-cycle of any order.

A moment's reflection should convince the reader that HOA and SA may be equivalently phrased as follows:[7]

$$\text{HOA:} \quad \forall x, y \in X: (x, y) \in T(R_C) \rightarrow (y, x) \notin R_C^*$$

$$\text{SA:} \quad \forall x, y \in X: (x, y) \in T(R_C^*) \rightarrow (y, x) \notin R_C$$

Because $R_C^* \subset T(R_C^*)$ holds true, the following axiom represents a weaker version of SA.

Weak axiom of revealed preference (WA)

$$\forall x, y \in X: (x, y) \in R_C^* \rightarrow (y, x) \notin R_C$$

It should be clear that HOA, SA, and WA represent, respectively, a natural reformulation of Houthakker's semitransitivity axiom, Samuelson's strong postulate, and Samuelson's weak postulate in terms of a choice function C on a choice space $(X, \mathscr{S})$.[8] This observation would also serve to motivate our HOA, SA, and WA.

Along with these lineal descendants of Samuelson–Houthakker postulates, we introduce three further choice-consistency conditions of the revealed preference type that are of crucial importance in the theory of rationalizability.

First, we should like to introduce the congruence axioms due to Richter (1966, 1971) and Sen (1971).

Strong congruence axiom (SCA)

$$\forall S \in \mathscr{S}: [x \in S \ \& \ \{\exists\, y \in C(S): (x, y) \in T(R_C)\}] \rightarrow x \in C(S)$$

Weak congruence axiom (WCA)

$$\forall S \in \mathscr{S}: [x \in S \ \& \ \{\exists\, y \in C(S): (x, y) \in R_C\}] \rightarrow x \in C(S)$$

SCA as well as WCA has strong intuitive appeal. Suppose that C on a choice space $(X, \mathscr{S})$ satisfies SCA [resp. WCA]. It then follows that for every $S \in \mathscr{S}$, an $x \in S$ that is indirectly [resp. directly] revealed R_C-preferred to a $y \in C(S)$ should itself be chosen from S.

Second, we should like to pay attention to an axiom originated by Arrow (1959), which reads as follows:

Arrow's axiom (AA)

$$\forall S_1, S_2 \in \mathscr{S}: S_1 \subset S_2 \rightarrow [S_1 \cap C(S_2) = \varnothing \vee S_1 \cap C(S_2) = C(S_1)]$$

An intuitive interpretation of AA is that if some elements are chosen out of a set $S_2 \in \mathscr{S}$ and then the range of available states is narrowed down to $S_1 \in \mathscr{S}$, but still contains some previously chosen states, no previously unchosen state becomes chosen and no previously chosen state becomes unchosen, which sounds mild and reasonable.

1.3 *Equivalence and implication*

Before setting about examining the rationality contents of the preceding axioms, let us try to put them in order by establishing the logical relationship that holds quite generally among them.

Theorem 2.1

(a) Houthakker's axiom (HOA) and the strong congruence axiom (SCA) are equivalent.
(b) The strong axiom of revealed preference (SA) is implied by Houthakker's axiom (HOA) and implies the weak axiom of revealed preference (WA).
(c) The weak axiom of revealed preference (WA) and the weak congruence axiom (WCA) are equivalent.
(d) The weak axiom of revealed preference (WA) implies Arrow's axiom (AA).

Proof of (a): Suppose that C on a choice space $(X, \mathscr{S})$ satisfies HOA. Let $x, y \in X$ and $S \in \mathscr{S}$ be such that $x \in S$, $(x, y) \in T(R_C)$, $y \in C(S)$, and $x \notin C(S)$. It then follows that $(x, y) \in T(R_C)$ and $(y, x) \in R_C^*$, in contradiction with HOA.

Suppose, conversely, that HOA is violated by C on $(X, \mathscr{S})$, so that $(x, y) \in T(R_C)$ and $(y, x) \in R_C^*$ for some $x, y \in X$. Then there exists an $S \in \mathscr{S}$ such that $x \in S$, $(x, y) \in T(R_C)$, $y \in C(S)$, and $x \notin C(S)$, negating the validity of SCA. ▮

Proof of (b): Obvious by definition. ▮

Proof of (c): Assume that C on $(X, \mathscr{S})$ is such that $x \in S$, $y \in C(S)$, and $(x, y) \in R_C$ hold true for some $S \in \mathscr{S}$. If $x \notin C(S)$ were the case, so that WCA would be violated by this C, we would have $(y, x) \in R_C^*$ and $(x, y) \in R_C$, which negates the validity of WA. Therefore WA implies WCA.

Conversely, suppose that C violates WA, so that $(x, y) \in R_C^*$ and $(y, x) \in R_C$ hold true for some $x, y \in X$. It then follows that there exists an $S \in \mathscr{S}$ such that $y \notin C(S)$ even when $x \in C(S)$, $y \in S$, and $(y, x) \in R_C$. This is a clear violation of WCA. ▮

Proof of (d): Suppose that WA is satisfied by C on $(X, \mathscr{S})$, and take $S_1, S_2 \in \mathscr{S}$ such that $S_1 \subset S_2$ and $S_1 \cap C(S_2) \neq \varnothing$. If it is the case that $S_1 \cap C(S_2) \neq C(S_1)$, negating the validity of AA, either

$$\exists\, x \in X: x \in S_1 \cap C(S_2) \;\&\; x \notin C(S_1) \tag{2.15}$$

or

$$\exists\, y \in X: y \in C(S_1) \;\&\; y \notin S_1 \cap C(S_2) \tag{2.16}$$

must be the case. In the former case [resp. the latter case], we take $z \in C(S_1)$ [resp. $w \in S_1 \cap C(S_2)$] to conclude that $(z, x) \in R_C^*$ and $(x, z) \in R_C$ [resp. $(w, y) \in R_C^*$ and $(y, w) \in R_C$], in contradiction with WA. ▮

Note that no restriction whatsoever is placed on the contents of X as well as of $\mathscr{S}$ in Theorem 2.1, so that the assertion thereof applies to whatever choice function we may care to specify. In this general setting, the converse of (b) and (d) in Theorem 2.1 does not necessarily hold true, as Examples 3–5 in Appendix B establish.

2 Characterization of rational choice functions

2.1 Preliminary remarks on the domain of a choice function

Consider a choice function C on a choice space $(X, \mathscr{S})$. There are three specifications of the family $\mathscr{S}$, to be called the domain of C, that are of interest in the theory of rational choice functions. In increasing order of generality, they may be expressed as follows:

(a) Domain consisting of finite nonempty sets: $\mathscr{S}$ consists of and only of all finite nonempty subsets of X.
(b) Finitely additive domain: For any $S_1, S_2 \in \mathscr{S}$, $S_1 \cup S_2 \in \mathscr{S}$ holds true.[9]
(c) General domain: $\mathscr{S}$ is a specified nonempty collection of nonempty subsets of X.

The domain (c) is by far the weakest restriction on $\mathscr{S}$, and the theory of rational choice functions developed on this minimal domain condition applies to whatever choice situations we may care to specify: Choice of consumers in a competitive or noncompetitive market, of government bureaucracies, of voters, and of whatsoever. However, as Howard (1971, p. xvii) put it, "cold winds blow through unstructured sets," and one may wish to introduce some structural restrictions on $\mathscr{S}$ so as to take in a richer harvest. One obvious candidate is the domain condition (b), which has been exploited in detail by Hansson (1968) and Herzberger (1973), although an exclusive reliance on finite additivity is likely to appear suspect in view of its failure in demand theory and in many other disciplines. Going one step further, Arrow (1959, p. 122) has suggested that "the demand-function point of view would be greatly simplified if the range over which the choice functions are considered to be determined is broadened to include all finite sets," and Sen (1971), Plott (1973), Blair and associates (1976), Schwartz (1976), and many others followed suit.

In the main text we shall be concerned exclusively with the theory of rational choice functions using the domain condition (a) in view of the intended use thereof in later chapters. The corresponding theory under alternative domain conditions will be relegated to Appendix A at the end of this chapter.

2.2 *Characterization of full rationality*

Let $\mathscr{S}_F$ denote the collection of all finite nonempty subsets of X.

Theorem 2.2

A choice function C on a choice space $(X, \mathscr{S}_F)$ is full rational if and only if C satisfies Arrow's axiom (AA).[10]

As an auxiliary step, let us define the *base relation* R^C for C (Arrow, 1959, Definition 2, p. 122; Herzberger, 1973, Definition 14, p. 204):

$$R^C = \{(x, y) \in X \times X \mid x \in C(\{x, y\})\} \tag{2.17}$$

Lemma 2.2

Let C be a choice function on a choice space $(X, \mathscr{S}_F)$. Then

(a) C is rational if and only if R^C is a rationalization of C, and
(b) if C satisfies Arrow's axiom (AA), R^C is an ordering on X.

Proof of (a): Clearly we have only to prove the "only if" part. Let C be rational with a rationalization R. Without loss of generality, we can assume that R is reflexive. Take any $\{x, y\} \in \mathscr{S}_F$. By definition, $C(\{x, y\}) = G(\{x, y\}, R)$ holds true, so that we have

$$\begin{aligned}(x, y) \in R^C &\leftrightarrow x \in C(\{x, y\})\\ &\leftrightarrow x \in G(\{x, y\}, R)\\ &\leftrightarrow (x, y) \in R\end{aligned}$$

Because this is true for any pair set $\{x, y\}$, we have $R^C = R$, as desired. ▮

Proof of (b): The domain of C being $\mathscr{S}_F$, it is clear that R^C is complete and reflexive on X. We have only to prove, therefore, that AA implies transitivity of R^C. Let x, y, and z be such that $(x, y) \in R^C$ and $(y, z) \in R^C$. If $x = y$ or $y = z$ or $x = z$, clearly $(x, z) \in R^C$ is implied. Assume therefore that x, y, and z are all distinct. Let $\{x, y, z\} = S$, and assume that $x \notin C(S)$. If $y \in C(S)$, we obtain $y \in \{x, y\} \cap C(S) \neq \varnothing$, so that AA implies that $\{x, y\} \cap C(S) = C(\{x, y\})$. But this is false, because $x \in C(\{x, y\})$ and $x \notin C(S)$. Therefore, $x \notin C(S)$ implies $y \notin C(S)$. By similar argument we can show that $y \notin C(S)$ implies $z \notin C(S)$. It then follows that $x \notin C(S)$ implies $C(S) = \varnothing$, a contradiction. Therefore, it must be true that $x \in C(S)$. Because $x \in \{x, z\} \cap C(S)$ and AA applies to C, we obtain $x \in C(\{x, z\}) = \{x, z\} \cap C(S)$, so that $(x, z) \in R^C$, as desired. ▮

Proof of Theorem 2.2: If C is full rational, there exists an ordering R on X that satisfies

$$\forall S \in \mathscr{S}_F: C(S) = G(S, R) \tag{2.18}$$

Let $S_1, S_2 \in \mathscr{S}_F$ be such that $S_1 \subset S_2$ and $S_1 \cap C(S_2) \neq \varnothing$. Take any $x \in S_1 \cap C(S_2)$ and $z \in C(S_1)$. Thanks to (2.18), $x \in S_1 \cap C(S_2)$ yields $x \in S_1$ and $(x, y) \in R$ for all $y \in S_2$, which implies $x \in C(S_1)$, in view of $S_1 \subset S_2$. We have thus proved that

$$\forall S_1, S_2 \in \mathscr{S}_F: S_1 \subset S_2 \rightarrow [S_1 \cap C(S_2) = \varnothing \vee S_1 \cap C(S_2) \subset C(S_1)] \tag{2.19}$$

holds true. Thanks again to (2.18), $z \in C(S_1)$ yields $z \in S_1$ and $(z, w) \in R$ for all $w \in S_1$. If it so happens that $z \notin C(S_2)$, then there exists a $v \in S_2$ satisfying $(v, z) \in P(R)$. Take any $u \in S_1 \cap C(S_2)$. We then have $(u, v) \in R$, which, coupled with $(v, z) \in P(R)$, yields $(u, z) \in P(R)$ by virtue of transitivity of R. However, this contradicts $(z, u) \in R$, which follows from $z \in C(S_1)$ and $u \in S_1$. We have thus proved that

$$\forall S_1, S_2 \in \mathscr{S}_F: S_1 \subset S_2 \rightarrow [S_1 \cap C(S_2) = \varnothing \vee S_1 \cap C(S_2) \supset C(S_1)] \tag{2.20}$$

holds true. Coupled with (2.19), (2.20) shows that C satisfies AA, as was to be proved.

We prove next that a choice function satisfying AA is full rational. By virtue of Lemma 2.2, it suffices if we can prove that

$$\forall S \in \mathscr{S}_F: C(S) = G(S, R^C) \tag{2.21}$$

Take any $S \in \mathscr{S}_F$ and let $x \in C(S)$ and $y \in S$. Because $x \in \{x, y\} \cap C(S)$ and C satisfies AA, we have $x \in C(\{x, y\})$, namely, $(x, y) \in R^C$. This being true for every $y \in S$, we are assured that $x \in G(S, R^C)$. Thus, $C(S) \subset G(S, R^C)$ is true for every $S \in \mathscr{S}_F$. To show the converse, let $x \in G(S, R^C)$ and $y \in C(S)$. Because $(x, y) \in R^C$ and $y \in \{x, y\} \cap C(S)$, it follows from $\{x, y\} \cap C(S) = C(\{x, y\})$, which is ensured by AA, that $x \in C(S)$. Thus, $G(S, R^C) \subset C(S)$ holds true for every $S \in \mathscr{S}_F$, completing the proof. ∎

We have thus completely characterized the full rationality of a choice function C on a choice space $(X, \mathscr{S}_F)$ by Arrow's axiom. A natural question that suggests itself is the role played by the revealed preference and congruence axioms in the theory of rational choice functions. Our simple answer may be stated as follows.

Theorem 2.3
Let C be a choice function on a choice space $(X, \mathscr{S}_F)$. Then the following properties of C are mutually equivalent:

FR: Full rationality
HOA: Houthakker's axiom of revealed preference
SA: Strong axiom of revealed preference
WA: Weak axiom of revealed preference
SCA: Strong congruence axiom
WCA: Weak congruence axiom
AA: Arrow's axiom

Proof: Thanks to Theorem 2.1 and Theorem 2.2, we have only to prove that FR implies SCA. Assume, therefore, that C on $(X, \mathscr{S}_F)$ satisfies FR, and let $S \in \mathscr{S}_F$ and $x, y \in X$ be such that $x \in S$, $y \in C(S)$, and $(x, y) \in T(R_C)$. By definition,

$$\exists t \in Z^+, \exists z^1, z^2, \ldots, z^t \in X : \begin{cases} x = z^1 \\ \forall \tau \in \{1, 2, \ldots, t-1\} : (z^\tau, z^{\tau+1}) \in R_C \\ z^t = y \end{cases}$$

holds true, so that we have

$$\exists S_1, S_2, \ldots, S_{t-1} \in \mathscr{S}_F, \forall \tau \in \{1, 2, \ldots, t-1\} : z^\tau \in C(S_\tau) \;\&\; z^{\tau+1} \in S_\tau$$

C being full rational, it then follows that

$$x = z^1, \forall \tau \in \{1, 2, \ldots, t-1\} : (z^\tau, z^{\tau+1}) \in R \;\&\; y = z^t \tag{2.22}$$

where R stands for an ordering that rationalizes C. R being transitive, we observe from (2.22) that $(x, y) \in R$. Coupled with $y \in C(S) = G(S, R)$, we thus have $x \in C(S)$, as desired. ∎

Note that all choice-consistency conditions introduced thus far turn out to be necessary and sufficient for a choice function to be full rational. That leaves us with a question: Under what choice-consistency condition is a choice function necessarily quasi-transitive rational? How about acyclic rationality? To these questions we now turn.

2.3 *Characterization of quasi-transitive rationality and of acyclic rationality: I*

Our first characterization of quasi-transitive rationality and of acyclic rationality makes use of four choice-consistency conditions, the first three of which are weakened versions of Arrow's axiom. Let us begin our analysis with the formal definition and an intuitive interpretation of these conditions.

The first choice-consistency condition, which was introduced by Chernoff (1954) in his seminal work on rational selection of decision functions, reads as follows.

Chernoff's axiom (CA)

$$\forall S_1, S_2 \in \mathscr{S}: S_1 \subset S_2 \rightarrow [S_1 \cap C(S_2) = \varnothing \vee S_1 \cap C(S_2) \subset C(S_1)]$$

This is a very basic requirement of choice consistency, which is necessarily satisfied by any rational choice function,[11] and may be interpreted as follows. Suppose that some states are chosen from a set $S_2 \in \mathscr{S}$, and then the range of available states is somehow narrowed down to $S_1 \in \mathscr{S}$, which still contains some previously chosen states. CA requires that no previously chosen states become unchosen.[12]

Second, we require a condition to the effect that when the range of available states is expanded from $S_1 \in \mathscr{S}$ to $S_2 \in \mathscr{S}$, the choice set from S_2 should never be the *proper* subset of that from S_1.

Superset axiom (SUA)

$$\forall S_1, S_2 \in \mathscr{S}: [S_1 \subset S_2 \;\&\; C(S_2) \subset C(S_1)] \rightarrow C(S_1) = C(S_2)$$

The third choice-consistency condition we now introduce is that of path independence, due to Arrow (1963, p. 120) and Plott (1973).

Path independence α [PI(α)]

$$\forall S_1, S_2 \in \mathscr{S}: C(S_1 \cup S_2) = C(C(S_1) \cup C(S_2))$$

Path independence β [PI(β)]

$$\forall S_1, S_2 \in \mathscr{S}: C(S_1 \cup S_2) = C(C(S_1) \cup S_2)$$

The condition PI(α) requires that we choose over $S = S_1 \cup S_2$ directly or choose over the parts thereof and then choose over the choices made in the first round without changing the ultimate result, whereas the condition PI(β) requires that we proceed in choosing from $S = S_1 \cup S_2$ by comparing the alternatives that have not been in the first-round contest with the "winners" in the first round. Despite their apparent difference, they are in fact equivalent, as the following theorem (Plott, 1973, Theorem 1) asserts.

Theorem 2.4
A choice function C on a choice space $(X, \mathscr{S}_F)$ satisfies the path independence α [PI(α)] if and only if it satisfies the path independence β [PI(β)].

Proof: Assuming that C satisfies PI(α), we first observe that

$$\forall S \in \mathcal{S}_F: C(S) = C(C(S)) \tag{2.23}$$

is thereby implied by taking $S_1 = S_2 = S$. We then obtain

$$\begin{aligned}\forall S_1, S_2 \in \mathcal{S}_F: C(S_1 \cup S_2) &= C(C(S_1) \cup C(S_2)), \quad &\text{by PI}(\alpha)\\ &= C[C(S_1) \cup C(C(S_2))], \quad &\text{by (2.23)}\\ &= C(S_1 \cup C(S_2)), \quad &\text{by PI}(\alpha)\end{aligned}$$

Therefore, PI(β) is implied by PI(α).

Conversely, assume that C satisfies PI(β). We then obtain

$$\begin{aligned}\forall S_1, S_2 \in \mathcal{S}_F: C(S_1 \cup S_2) &= C(C(S_1) \cup S_2), \quad &\text{by PI}(\beta)\\ &= C(C(S_1) \cup C(S_2)), \quad &\text{by PI}(\beta)\end{aligned}$$

so that PI(α) is implied. ∎

Fourth, we introduce a choice-consistency condition that requires that if a given state $x \in S$ is not defeated by any state in S in a *binary* contest, then x must be among the elements chosen from S. Note that this does not prevent an element that x defeats in a binary contest from being chosen along with x.

Generalized Condorcet property (GC)

$$\forall S \in \mathcal{S}: G(S, R^C) \subset C(S)$$

We can now assert the following characterization theorem (Blair et al., 1976, Theorem 1) for a path-independent choice function.[13]

Theorem 2.5

A choice function C on a choice space $(X, \mathcal{S}_F)$ satisfies path independence (PI) if and only if it satisfies Chernoff's axiom (CA) and the superset axiom (SUA).

Proof: Assume that C satisfies PI. To prove that C then satisfies CA, let $S_1, S_2 \in \mathcal{S}_F$ be such that $S_1 \subset S_2$ and $S_1 \cap C(S_2) \neq \varnothing$. Take an $x \in S_1 \cap C(S_2)$. Thanks to PI(α) and $S_2 = (S_2 \setminus S_1) \cup S_1$, we then have $x \in C(C(S_2 \setminus S_1) \cup C(S_1))$. In view of $x \in S_1$, we observe that $x \in C(S_1)$. Therefore, CA is implied by PI, as desired. To prove that PI implies SUA, suppose to the contrary that there exist S_1, $S_2 \in \mathcal{S}_F$ such that $S_1 \subset S_2$, $C(S_1) \supset C(S_2)$, and $C(S_1) \neq C(S_2)$. By virtue of PI(α), we have $C(S_1 \cup S_2) = C(C(S_1) \cup C(S_2))$. $S_1 \subset S_2$ being the case, the left-hand side is equal to $C(S_2)$, and $C(S_1) \supset C(S_2)$ implies that the right-hand side is $C(C(S_1))$, which is equal to $C(S_1)$, thanks to (2.23). Therefore, $C(S_1) = C(S_2)$, a contradiction. Therefore, SUA must be satisfied by this C.

Conversely, we prove that PI follows from CA and SUA. The first step is to show that

$$\forall S_1, S_2 \in \mathscr{S}_F: C(S_1 \cup S_2) \subset C(C(S_1) \cup C(S_2)) \tag{2.24}$$

holds true if C satisfies CA. Take any $S_1, S_2 \in \mathscr{S}_F$ and let $S = S_1 \cup S_2$. By virtue of CA, we have $S_1 \cap C(S) \subset C(S_1)$ and $S_2 \cap C(S) \subset C(S_2)$, so that we obtain

$$C(S) \cap (S_1 \cup S_2) = C(S) \subset C(S_1) \cup C(S_2) \subset S$$

By the second use of CA, it then follows that

$$C(S_1 \cup S_2) \cap [C(S_1) \cup C(S_2)] = C(S_1 \cup S_2) \subset C(C(S_1) \cup C(S_2))$$

establishing (2.24). As a matter of fact, we should have an equality in (2.24) by virtue of SUA, where use is made of $C(S_1) \cup C(S_2) \subset S_1 \cup S_2$. Therefore, PI is implied by CA and SUA. ▮

We can now assert the following characterization theorem (Blair et al., 1976, p. 367) for a quasi-transitive rational choice function.

Theorem 2.6
A choice function C on a choice space $(X, \mathscr{S}_F)$ is quasi-transitive rational if and only if it satisfies Chernoff's axiom (CA), the superset axiom (SUA), and the generalized Condorcet property (GC).

If we take Theorem 2.5 into consideration, Theorem 2.6 follows from the next proposition.

Theorem 2.7
A choice function C on a choice space $(X, \mathscr{S}_F)$ is quasi-transitive rational if and only if it satisfies path independence (PI) and the generalized Condorcet property (GC) (Plott, 1973, Theorems 3 and 4).

Proof: In the first place, we show the sufficiency of PI and GC. Thanks to Lemma 2.2(a), we have only to show that R^C is quasi-transitive and that

$$\forall S \in \mathscr{S}_F: C(S) = G(S, R^C) \tag{2.25}$$

holds true. With a view to establishing (2.25), let us suppose that there exist an $S \in \mathscr{S}_F$ and an $x \in C(S)$ such that $(x, y) \notin R^C$ for some $y \in S$. Thanks to PI, we then have

$$C(S) = C(C(\{x, y\}) \cup C(S \setminus \{x, y\}))$$

which implies that $x \notin C(S)$, a contradiction. Therefore, we should have $C(S) \subset G(S, R^C)$ for all $S \in \mathscr{S}_F$. Taking GC into consideration, we can in fact obtain (2.25). To show quasi transitivity of R^C, let x, y, and z be such that $\{x\} = C(\{x, y\})$ and $\{y\} = C(\{y, z\})$. By virtue of PI, we then have

$$\begin{aligned} C(\{x,z\}) &= C(C(\{x, y\}) \cup \{z\}) \\ &= C(\{x\} \cup C(\{y, z\})) \\ &= C(\{x, y\}) \\ &= \{x\} \end{aligned}$$

as desired.

Second, we show the necessity of PI and GC for C to be quasi-transitive rational. Because (2.25) must hold true in the case where C is quasi-transitive rational, the necessity of GC is obvious. To show the necessity of PI, let $S_1, S_2 \in \mathscr{S}_F$ be chosen arbitrarily. C being quasi-transitive rational, it satisfies CA, so that

$$\forall S_1, S_2 \in \mathscr{S}_F: C(S_1 \cup S_2) \subset C(C(S_1) \cup C(S_2)) \tag{2.26}$$

holds true, as we have shown in the proof of Theorem 2.5. To show that the set-theoretic equality in fact applies in (2.26), take any $x \in C(C(S_1) \cup C(S_2))$. Without loss of generality, we can assume that $x \in C(S_1)$, so that

$$\forall z \in S_1: (x, z) \in R^C \tag{2.27}$$

We also have $(x, z) \in R^C$ for all $z \in C(S_1) \cup C(S_2)$, thanks to the fact that $x \in C(C(S_1) \cup C(S_2))$. In particular, we obtain

$$\forall z \in C(S_2): (x, z) \in R^C \tag{2.28}$$

Suppose now that $x \notin C(S_1 \cup S_2)$. We then have

$$\exists y^1 \in S_1 \cup S_2: (y^1, x) \in P(R^C) \tag{2.29}$$

In view of (2.27), $y^1 \in S_2$ must be the case. This y^1 cannot be in $C(S_2)$, in view of (2.28). Therefore, $y^1 \in S_2 \setminus C(S_2)$ holds true. Then there exists a $y^2 \in S_2$ satisfying $(y^2, y^1) \in P(R^C)$. Taking (2.29) and the quasi transitivity of R^C into consideration, it then follows that $(y^2, x) \in P(R^C)$. In view of (2.28), $y^2 \in S_2 \setminus C(S_2)$ must be the case. Repeating this procedure, we can generate an *infinite* sequence $y^1, y^2, y^3, \ldots$ in a *finite* set S_2, a contradiction. Therefore, we should obtain

$$C(C(S_1) \cup C(S_2)) \subset C(S_1 \cup S_2) \tag{2.30}$$

Coupled with (2.26), (2.30) establishes the necessity of PI. This completes the proof. ∎

If we strike out the superset axiom from the set of characterizing axioms for quasi-transitive rationality given in Theorem 2.6, we obtain the set of characterizing axioms for acyclic rationality.

Theorem 2.8
A choice function C on a choice space $(X, \mathscr{S}_F)$ is acyclic rational if and only if it satisfies Chernoff's axiom (CA) and the generalized Condorcet property (GC) (Blair et al., 1976, Theorem 2).

Proof: Assume that C satisfies CA and GC. In view of Lemma 2.2(a), we have only to prove that

$$\forall S \in \mathscr{S}_F\colon C(S) = G(S, R^C) \tag{2.31}$$

holds true and that R^C is acyclic. Take any $S \in \mathscr{S}_F$ and let $x \in C(S)$. CA then implies that $x \in \{x, y\} \cap C(S) \subset C(\{x, y\})$ for all $y \in S$, which establishes that $C(S) \subset G(S, R^C)$. In combination with GC, this establishes (2.31). To show acyclicity of R^C, suppose $x^1, x^2, \ldots, x^t$ are such that

$$(x^1, x^2), (x^2, x^3), \ldots, (x^{t-1}, x^t) \in P(R^C)$$

namely, that $x^\tau \notin C(\{x^{\tau-1}, x^\tau\})$ for $\tau = 2, 3, \ldots, t$. By CA we then have $x^\tau \notin C(\{x^1, x^2, \ldots, x^t\})$ for $\tau = 2, 3, \ldots, t$. Because $C(\{x^1, x^2, \ldots, x^t\}) \neq \varnothing$, we must have $C(\{x^1, x^2, \ldots, x^t\}) = \{x^1\}$. By another application of CA, $x^1 \in C(\{x^1, x^t\})$, namely, $(x^t, x^1) \notin P(R^C)$, as desired.

To show the converse, assume that (2.31) is true with R^C being acyclic. Clearly GC is satisfied, and we have already noted that CA is a necessary condition for rationality. This completes the proof. ∎

This completes our first characterization of full rationality, quasi-transitive rationality, and acyclic rationality. What remains to be clarified is the axiomatic basis of the concept of rationality per se. The message of the next proposition is that Theorem 2.8 already provides us with such a characterization.

Theorem 2.9
A choice function C on a choice space $(X, \mathscr{S}_F)$ is rational if and only if it is acyclic rational.[14]

Proof: Clearly, it is enough to prove the "only if" part. Suppose, to the contrary, that C has a rationalization R that is not acyclic. Then there exists a finite subset $S = \{z^1, z^2, \ldots, z^t\}$ of X such that

$(z^{\tau}, z^{\tau+1}) \in P(R)$ $(\tau = 1, 2, \ldots, t-1)$ and $(z^t, z^1) \in P(R)$. It then follows that $C(S) = G(S, R) = \varnothing$ for this $S \in \mathscr{S}_F$, which is a contradiction. ▮

2.4 *Characterization of quasi-transitive rationality and of acyclic rationality: II*

Let us now turn to our second characterization of quasi-transitive rationality and of acyclic rationality. A distinctive feature of this alternative approach lies in the fact that the characterization of various rationality concepts can be given in terms of and only of a single revealed preference relation R_C that a choice function C induces.

To prepare for this alternative approach, let us introduce several auxiliary concepts that are due originally to Wilson (1970). Let C and R be a choice function on a general choice space $(X, \mathscr{S})$ and an arbitrary binary relation on X, respectively. For any $x \in X$, let $R(x)$ stand for the *R-upper-contour set* determined by x:

$$R(x) = \{y \in X \mid (y, x) \in R\} \tag{2.32}$$

We say that C on $(X, \mathscr{S})$ is an *R-cut* if and only if

$$\forall S \in \mathscr{S}: C(S) = S \cap \left[\bigcup_{y \in C(S)} R(y)\right] \tag{2.33}$$

holds true. An R-cut will be denoted by C^R_{cu} in what follows.[15]

We say that C on $(X, \mathscr{S})$ is an *R-solution* if and only if

$$\forall S \in \mathscr{S}: C(S) = S \cap \left[\bigcap_{y \in C(S)} R(y)\right] \tag{2.34}$$

holds true. An R-solution will be denoted hereafter by C^R_{so}.[16]

Finally, C on $(X, \mathscr{S})$ is called an *R-core* if and only if

$$\forall S \in \mathscr{S}: C(S) = S \cap \left[\bigcap_{y \in S} R(y)\right] \tag{2.35}$$

holds true. We denote an R-core on $(X, \mathscr{S})$ by C^R_{co}.[17]

We can now put forward the following alternative characterization theorem.

Theorem 2.10
Let C be a choice function on a choice space $(X, \mathscr{S}_F)$.

(a) C is full rational if and only if C is an R_C-cut (i.e., $C = C^{R_C}_{\text{cu}}$).
(b) C is quasi-transitive rational if and only if C is an R_C-solution (i.e., $C = C^{R_C}_{\text{so}}$).
(c) C is acyclic rational if and only if C is an R_C-core (i.e., $C = C^{R_C}_{\text{co}}$).

Proof of (a): Clearly, C being an R_C-cut is equivalent to the weak congruence axiom, so that this assertion follows from Theorem 2.3.[18] ∎

Proof of (b): In the first place, we prove the "if" part. Suppose, therefore, that C is an R_C-solution (i.e., $C = C_{so}^{R_C}$). We have only to show that C satisfies Chernoff's axiom (CA), the superset axiom (SUA), and the generalized Condorcet property (GC) by virtue of Theorem 2.6.

(i) To show that C satisfies CA, let $S_1, S_2 \in \mathscr{S}_F$ and $x \in X$ be such that $S_1 \subset S_2$ and $x \in S_1 \cap C(S_2)$. C being an R_C-solution, $x \notin C(S_1)$ implies that $x \notin S_1$ or $(x, y) \notin R_C$ for some $y \in C(S_1)$. Because $x \in S_1$, the latter must be the case. But $y \in C(S_1) \subset S_1 \subset S_2$ and $x \in C(S_2)$ imply that $(x, y) \in R_C$, a contradiction. Therefore, $S_1 \cap C(S_2) \subset C(S_1)$, and CA holds true.

(ii) To show the validity of SUA, let $S_1 \subset S_2$, $C(S_2) \subset C(S_1)$, and $x \in C(S_1) \setminus C(S_2)$ for some $x \in X$. C being an R_C-solution, $x \in C(S_1)$ and $x \notin C(S_2)$ imply, respectively, that

$$x \in S_1 \ \& \ \forall y \in C(S_1): (x, y) \in R_C \tag{2.36}$$

and

$$x \notin S_2 \vee \exists z \in C(S_2): (x, z) \notin R_C \tag{2.37}$$

Because $x \in S_1 \subset S_2$, (2.37) implies that $(x, z) \notin R_C$ for some $z \in C(S_2) \subset C(S_1)$, which contradicts (2.36). The validity of SUA is thereby established.

(iii) To show that C satisfies GC, let $x \in G(S, R^C)$. Because $R^C \subset R_C$ and $C(S) \subset S$, we then have $x \in S$ and $(x, y) \in R_C$ for all $y \in C(S)$. C being an R_C-solution, we obtain $x \in C(S)$. It then follows that $G(S, R^C) \subset C(S)$, which establishes the validity of GC.

To show the converse, let us assume that

$$\forall S \in \mathscr{S}_F: C(S) = G(S, R^C) \tag{2.38}$$

holds true and that R^C is quasi-transitive. If C is not an R_C-solution, we have

$$\exists S \in \mathscr{S}_F, \exists x \in S \setminus C(S), \forall y \in C(S): (x, y) \in R_C \tag{2.39}$$

In this case we obtain

$$\exists z^1 \in S: (z^1, x) \in P(R^C) \subset P(R_C) \tag{2.40}$$

If $z^1 \in C(S)$, (2.39) and (2.40) are contradictory. On the other hand, if $z^1 \in S \setminus C(S)$,

$$\exists z^2 \in S: (z^2, z^1) \in P(R^C) \subset P(R_C) \tag{2.41}$$

holds true. R^C being quasi-transitive, it follows from (2.40) and (2.41) that $(z^2, x) \in P(R^C) \subset P(R_C)$, which excludes the possibility of $z^2 \in C(S)$, in view of (2.39). Therefore, $z^2 \in S \setminus C(S)$ must be the case. Repeating this procedure, we can generate an *infinite* sequence $z^1, z^2, z^3, \ldots$ in a *finite* set S, a contradiction. Therefore, C should be an R_C-solution, which completes the proof. ∎

Proof of (c): Because $C_{co}^{R_C}(S) = G(S, R_C)$ holds true for every $S \in \mathcal{S}_F$, $C = C_{co}^{R_C}$ ensures that C is rational, with a rationalization R_C. We can now invoke Theorem 2.9 to conclude that C is acyclic rational.

Conversely, suppose that C is rational, with an acyclic rationalization R. Take any $S \in \mathcal{S}_F$ and let $x \in C(S)$. It then follows that $(x, y) \in R_C$ for all $y \in S$, so that $x \in C_{co}^{R_C}(S)$ holds true. Therefore,

$$\forall S \in \mathcal{S}_F: C(S) \subset C_{co}^{R_C}(S) \tag{2.42}$$

is true. To show that the set-theoretic equality in fact applies in (2.42), we take any $S \in \mathcal{S}_F$ and let $x \in C_{co}^{R_C}(S)$. We then obtain

$$\forall y \in S, \exists S_{x,y} \in \mathcal{S}_F: x \in C(S_{x,y}) \ \& \ y \in S_{x,y} \tag{2.43}$$

C being rationalized by R, it follows that $(x, y) \in R$ for all $y \in S$, which implies that $x \in C(S)$, as was to be proved.[19] ∎

2.5 *Summary*

The theory of rational choice functions developed thus far can be summarized for mnemonic convenience as in Figure 2.1, where a double-headed arrow indicates logical equivalence and a single-headed arrow indicates logical implication.

In passing, let us have a brief look at a special case in which the value taken by a choice function C on $(X, \mathcal{S}_F)$ is always a singleton set. To understand the simplification of the theory of rational choice functions rendered by this special feature, we have only to verify that *Arrow's axiom and Chernoff's axiom are equivalent for a single-valued choice function.* To prove this, we have only to show that Chernoff's axiom implies Arrow's axiom in this case. Let S_1 and S_2 in $\mathcal{S}_F$ be such that $S_1 \subset S_2$ and $S_1 \cap C(S_2) \neq \varnothing$. If C satisfies Chernoff's axiom, we have $S_1 \cap C(S_2) \subset C(S_1)$. Both sides of this inclusion relationship being singleton sets, the set-theoretic equality in fact applies, thereby establishing the validity of Arrow's axiom.[20] If we have a second look at Figure 2.1 with this equivalence in mind, we cannot fail to observe that Chernoff's axiom, which is a necessary condition for a choice function C to be rational, turns out to be sufficient for C on $(X, \mathcal{S}_F)$ to be full rational, and all the arrows therein become bidirectional.

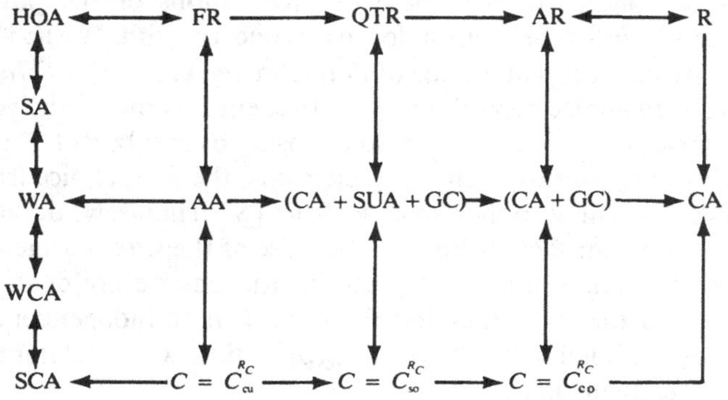

Figure 2.1. Structure of rational choice functions when $\mathscr{S} = \mathscr{S}_F$.

3 Some weaker variants of the choice-consistency conditions

3.1 Weak path independence

In our later analysis of collective decisions and social welfare, we shall have occasions in which some weaker variants of the choice-consistency conditions introduced thus far will play crucial roles. It will facilitate later reference, therefore, if we introduce them now and clarify their mutual relationships.

To begin with, consider the following four weaker variants of the path-independence condition.

Weak path independence $\alpha 1$ [WPI(α1)]

$$\forall S_1, S_2 \in \mathscr{S}: C(S_1 \cup S_2) \supset C(C(S_1) \cup C(S_2))$$

Weak path independence $\alpha 2$ [WPI(α2)]

$$\forall S_1, S_2 \in \mathscr{S}: C(S_1 \cup S_2) \subset C(C(S_1) \cup C(S_2))$$

Weak path independence $\beta 1$ [WPI(β1)]

$$\forall S_1, S_2 \in \mathscr{S}: C(S_1 \cup S_2) \supset C(C(S_1) \cup S_2)$$

Weak path independence $\beta 2$ [WPI(β2)]

$$\forall S_1, S_2 \in \mathscr{S}: C(S_1 \cup S_2) \subset C(C(S_1) \cup S_2)$$

It is clearly the case that each one of [WPI(α1) & WPI(α2)] and [WPI(β1) & WPI(β2)] is equivalent to PI(α) and PI(β), respectively. Why should we be concerned with these decompositions of the path-independence condition? The reason for our concern with WPI(α1) stems from the following observation due to Ferejohn and Grether (1977*a*, p. 21): "[A] satisfactory choice procedure is one that ensures that if the problem of choosing over [S] is broken up into choosing over subsets [S_1 and S_2] and then choosing over the remaining elements, the final choice from this procedure should still be in the choice set from [S]. That is, we do not want to end up in an unsatisfactory position because of the way the agenda was manipulated or because of the way the institutions we are dealing with work." The plea for the remaining three weak path-independence conditions can be provided by the following proposition, which relates them to conditions already justified.

Theorem 2.11
Let C be a choice function on a choice space $(X, \mathscr{S}_F)$. Then

(a) Chernoff's axiom (CA), the weak path independence α2 [WPI(α2)], and the weak path independence β2 [WPI(β2)] are equivalent, and
(b) the weak path independence β1 [WPI(β1)] implies the weak path independence α1 [WPI(α1)].[21]

Proof of (a): To begin with, let us prove that CA and WPI(α2) are equivalent. Assume that WPI(α2) holds true on C, and let S_1, $S_2 \in \mathscr{S}_F$ be such that $S_1 \subset S_2$ and $S_1 \cap C(S_2) \neq \varnothing$. Take an $x \in S_1 \cap C(S_2)$. Thanks to WPI(α2) and $S_2 = (S_2 \setminus S_1) \cup S_1$, we then have $x \in C(C(S_2 \setminus S_1) \cup C(S_1))$. In view of $x \in S_1$, it then follows that $x \in C(S_1)$. Therefore, CA is implied. Conversely, let CA be satisfied by C, and let $S = S_1 \cup S_2 \in \mathscr{S}_F$. By virtue of CA, we have $S_1 \cap C(S) \subset C(S_1)$ and $S_2 \cap C(S) \subset C(S_2)$, so that

$$C(S) \cap (S_1 \cup S_2) = C(S) \subset C(S_1) \cup C(S_2) \subset S$$

By the second use of CA, it then follows that

$$C(S_1 \cup S_2) \cap [C(S_1) \cup C(S_2)] = C(S_1 \cup S_2) \subset C(C(S_1) \cup C(S_2))$$

so that WPI(α2) is implied.

Second, we prove the equivalence between WPI(α2) and WPI(β2). Assume that WPI(β2) is true. We then have

$$\begin{aligned} C(S_1 \cup S_2) &\subset C(C(S_1) \cup S_2) \\ &\subset C(C(S_1) \cup C(S_2)) \end{aligned}$$

for all $S_1, S_2 \in \mathscr{S}_F$, so that WPI($\alpha$2) follows from WPI($\beta$2). Conversely, let WPI($\alpha$2), which is equivalent to CA, be true. Let

$S = S_1 \cup S_2 \in \mathscr{S}_F$. Thanks to CA, $S_1 \cap C(S) \subset C(S_1)$ and $S_2 \cap C(S) \subset C(S_2)$ hold true, which implies that $C(S) \subset C(S_1) \cup C(S_2) \subset S_1 \cup C(S_2) \subset S$. By the second application of CA, we then obtain

$$C(S_1 \cup S_2) \cap [S_1 \cup C(S_2)] \subset C(S_1 \cup C(S_2))$$

the left-hand side of which reduces to $C(S_1 \cup S_2)$. Therefore, WPI(β2) is implied. ▮

Proof of (b): Assume that C satisfies WPI(β1). For every S_1, $S_2 \in \mathscr{S}_F$ we then obtain

$$\begin{aligned} C(S_1 \cup S_2) &\supset C(C(S_1) \cup S_2) \\ &\supset C(C(S_1) \cup C(S_2)) \end{aligned}$$

by applying WPI(β1) twice. Therefore WPI(α1) is implied. ▮

3.2 *Dual Chernoff, Nash, and stability axioms*

Let us introduce three further choice-consistency conditions that are weak but still have bites.

First, we introduce what we call the dual Chernoff condition, which, in combination with Chernoff's axiom, constitutes a decomposition of Arrow's axiom.

Dual Chernoff axiom (DCA)

$$\forall S_1, S_2 \in \mathscr{S}: S_1 \subset S_2 \rightarrow [S_1 \cap C(S_2) = \varnothing \vee S_1 \cap C(S_2) \supset C(S_1)]$$

An intuitive interpretation of DCA can be phrased as follows. Suppose that the winner(s) in a large contest (S_2) participates in a smaller contest (S_1). Then the winner(s) in S_1 must be among the winner(s) in S_2 who happens to participate in S_1.

Second, we call in an axiom of choice consistency that Nash (1950) introduced in his analysis of two-person bargaining problems.[22]

Nash's axiom (NA)

$$\forall S_1, S_2 \in \mathscr{S}: [S_1 \subset S_2 \ \& \ C(S_2) \subset S_1] \rightarrow C(S_1) = C(S_2)$$

An intuitive interpretation of NA goes as follows. If the range of available states is narrowed from S_2 to S_1 but still contains all previously chosen states, the choice from S_1 should be the same as that from S_2, because the states in $S_2 \setminus S_1$ could have been chosen from S_2 *ab initio* but were actually rejected.

Finally, we introduce an axiom that requires that the choice set $C(S)$ obtained by applying a choice mechanism C to S should be invariant under further applications of C to the choice set. Why should this property be of interest? One possible argument goes as follows.[23] If the choice set $C(S)$ contains more than one element, then we have to choose one of these elements at random. This means that there will be no systematic reason to choose one over the other. But if there exists no particular reason to choose one of the elements in $C(S)$ over the other, then we must not be able to divide $C(S)$ further into the "chosen part" $C(C(S))$ and the "rejected part" $C(S) \setminus C(C(S))$ by applying C once more.

Stability axiom (ST)

$$\forall S \in \mathscr{S}: C(S) \in \mathscr{S} \rightarrow C(C(S)) = C(S)$$

The following theorem clarifies how these choice-consistency axioms are related with each other and with previously introduced axioms.

Theorem 2.12
Let C be a choice function on a choice space $(X, \mathscr{S}_F)$. Then

(a) the dual Chernoff axiom (DCA) implies the weak path independence $\beta 1$ [WPI($\beta 1$)], which in turn implies the superset axiom (SUA),[24]
(b) Arrow's axiom (AA) implies Nash's axiom (NA), which in turn implies the superset axiom (SUA),[25] and
(c) Chernoff's axiom (CA) as well as Nash's axiom (NA) implies the stability axiom (ST).[26]

Proof of (a): Assume that C satisfies DCA, and take any S_1, $S_2 \in \mathscr{S}_F$. In view of $C(S_1) \cup S_2 \subset S_1 \cup S_2$, we can use DCA to obtain either

$$C(S_1 \cup S_2) \cap [C(S_1) \cup S_2] = \varnothing \tag{2.44}$$

or

$$C(S_1 \cup S_2) \cap [C(S_1) \cup S_2] \supset C(C(S_1) \cup S_2) \tag{2.45}$$

If the latter alternative is in fact the case, we obtain

$$C(S_1 \cup S_2) \supset C(C(S_1) \cup S_2)$$

so that we are home. Suppose, therefore, that the former alternative is true. Because $S_1 \subset S_1 \cup S_2$, we can again apply DCA to obtain either

$$C(S_1 \cup S_2) \cap S_1 = \varnothing \tag{2.46}$$

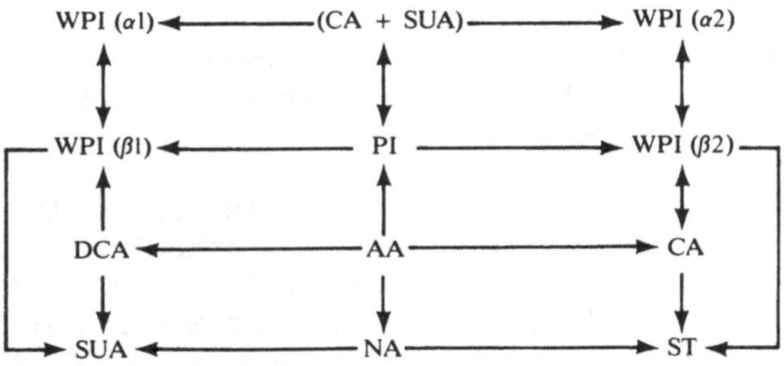

Figure 2.2. Implication network among choice-consistency conditions.

or

$$C(S_1 \cup S_2) \cap S_1 \supset C(S_1) \tag{2.47}$$

It follows from (2.44) that

$$C(S_1 \cup S_2) \cap C(S_1) = C(S_1 \cup S_2) \cap S_2 = \varnothing$$

so that

$$C(S_1 \cup S_2) \subset S_1 \setminus C(S_1) \tag{2.48}$$

Therefore, the validity of (2.46) is negated, and we are led to accept (2.47). But (2.47) and (2.48) are contradictory. Therefore, this case cannot happen.

Assume next that C satisfies WPI($\beta 1$), and let $S_1, S_2 \in \mathscr{S}_F$ be such that $S_1 \subset S_2$ and $C(S_2) \subset C(S_1)$. By virtue of WPI($\beta 1$), we then have

$$C(S_2) = C(S_1 \cup S_2) \supset C\big(C(S_2) \cup S_1\big) = C(S_1)$$

which, coupled with $C(S_2) \subset C(S_1)$, yields $C(S_1) = C(S_2)$, as desired. ▮

Proof of (b): Obvious by definition. ▮

Proof of (c): For any $S \in \mathscr{S}_F$, let $S_1 = C(S)$ and $S_2 = S$. Then $C(C(S)) = C(S)$ follows from CA as well as from NA. ▮

This completes our analysis of the various choice-consistency conditions. In order to facilitate later reference, our main conclusions are summarized in Figure 2.2, where a single-headed arrow denoting logical implication is irreversible in general.[27]

Before closing this section, let us extract a revealed-preference implication of the dual Chernoff axiom of choice consistency that is going to play a vital role later.

Theorem 2.13
Suppose that a choice function C on a choice space $(X, \mathscr{S}_F)$ satisfies the dual Chernoff axiom (DCA). Then a revealed preference relation R_C induced by C is transitive (Bordes, 1976, Theorem 1).

Proof: Assume that C satisfies DCA, and let $x, y, z \in X$ be such that $(x, y) \in R_C$ and $(y, z) \in R_C$ are satisfied. Then there exist $S_1, S_2 \in \mathscr{S}_F$ such that $x \in C(S_1)$, $y \in S_1 \cap C(S_2)$, and $z \in C(S_2)$ hold true. Let $S = S_1 \cup S_2$, which belongs to $\mathscr{S}_F$, and assume that $x \notin C(S)$. If $y \in C(S)$ is the case, then we obtain $y \in S_1 \cap C(S)$ and $S_1 \subset S$. Therefore, DCA ensures $S_1 \cap C(S) \supset C(S_1)$, which contradicts $x \in C(S_1)$ and $x \notin C(S)$, so that $x \notin C(S)$ implies $y \notin C(S)$. We now take any $w \in C(S)$. If $w \in S_1$ [resp. $w \in S_2$] is the case, we obtain $C(S_1) \subset S_1 \cap C(S)$ [resp. $C(S_2) \subset S_2 \cap C(S)$] by virtue of DCA, which contradicts $x \in C(S_1) \setminus C(S)$ [resp. $y \in C(S_2) \setminus C(S)$]. Therefore, $x \in C(S)$ must be the case, which ensures that $(x, z) \in R_C$, as desired. ∎

4 Concluding remarks

According to Herbert Simon, "the term 'rational' has long had in economics a much more specific meaning than its general dictionary signification of 'agreeable to reason; not absurd, preposterous, extravagant, foolish, fanciful, or the like; intelligent, sensible.' As is well known, *the rational man of economics is a maximizer, who will settle for nothing less than the best.*"[28] It is precisely this concept of rationality that we have axiomatically examined in this chapter on the condition that the domain of a choice function consist of and only of nonempty finite subsets of the universal set. Our main results, which are summarized in Figure 2.1, will be used extensively in the subsequent analysis of collective choice and social welfare. In order to examine how much they hinge on the specified domain condition, we put forward Appendix A, where a rationalizability theory on the general domain will be developed.

Before closing this chapter, let us emphasize that our analysis of rational choice functions in no way provides a justification of the traditional concept of rationality as maximality. Quite to the contrary, our analysis is meant to help in tracking down just where the prevailing concept of rational choice comes to conflict with other, arguably more basic requirements on the satisfactoriness of a choice mechanism.

Appendix A: A generalized theory of rationalizability

0. Apart from this introduction, this Appendix consists of three sections. In Section 1 we introduce still further choice-consistency conditions of the revealed preference type and bring them in order vis-à-vis the conditions that are made much use of in the main text. In Section 2 we prove several rationalizability theorems for a choice function with the general domain. Finally, we consider in Section 3 a choice function with the finitely additive domain and examine how the results obtained in Section 2 are thereby affected.

1. Consider a choice function C on a choice space $(X, \mathscr{S})$, where $\mathscr{S}$ is a specified nonempty collection of nonempty subsets of X. Let us say that a finite sequence of sets $(S_1, S_2, \ldots, S_t)$, where $S_\tau \in \mathscr{S}$ $(\tau = 1, 2, \ldots, t)$, is *C-related* if and only if

$$\forall \tau \in \{1, 2, \ldots, t-1\}: S_\tau \cap C(S_{\tau+1}) \neq \varnothing \ \& \ S_t \cap C(S_1) \neq \varnothing$$

holds true. In terms of this auxiliary concept, we can now formulate three choice-consistency axioms due to Hansson (1968) that are arranged in order of increasing strength.

Hansson's version of the weak axiom [WA(H)]
For any C-related pair of sets (S_1, S_2) in $\mathscr{S}$, $S_1 \cap C(S_2) = C(S_1) \cap S_2$ holds true.

Hansson's version of the strong axiom [SA(H)]
For any C-related sequence of sets $(S_1, S_2, \ldots, S_t)$ in $\mathscr{S}$, it is true that $S_\tau \cap C(S_{\tau+1}) = C(S_\tau) \cap S_{\tau+1}$ for *some* $\tau \in \{1, 2, \ldots, t-1\}$.

Hansson's axiom of revealed preference (HAA)
For any C-related sequence of sets $(S_1, S_2, \ldots, S_t)$ in $\mathscr{S}$, it is true that $S_\tau \cap C(S_{\tau+1}) = C(S_\tau) \cap S_{\tau+1}$ for *every* $\tau \in \{1, 2, \ldots, t-1\}$.

These choice-consistency conditions, which admittedly are very abstract, are related to other, now-familiar, choice-consistency conditions of the revealed preference type as follows.

Theorem A(1)
Let C be a choice function on a choice space $(X, \mathscr{S})$. Then

(a) the weak axiom of revealed preference (WA) and Hansson's version of the weak axiom [WA(H)] are equivalent,
(b) the strong axiom of revealed preference (SA) implies Hansson's version of the strong axiom [SA(H)],[29] and
(c) Houthakker's axiom of revealed preference (HOA) and Hansson's axiom of revealed preference (HAA) are equivalent.

Proof of (a): Assume that C satisfies WA, and let (S_1, S_2) be a C-related pair of sets in $\mathscr{S}$. If it so happens that $x \in S_1 \cap C(S_2)$

and $x \notin C(S_1) \cap S_2$ hold true for some $x \in X$, then $(y, x) \in R_C^*$ and $(x, y) \in R_C$ are valid for any $y \in C(S_1) \cap S_2$, so that WA is violated. Therefore, WA implies WA(H). Assume, conversely, that C satisfies WA(H), and let $x, y \in X$ be such that $(x, y) \in R_C^*$ and $(y, x) \in R_C$, negating the validity of WA. Then there exist S_1 and S_2 in $\mathscr{S}$ such that

$$x \in C(S_1), \quad y \in S_1 \setminus C(S_1), \quad x \in S_2, \quad \text{and} \quad y \in C(S_2)$$

It then follows that (S_1, S_2) is a C-related pair of sets in $\mathscr{S}$. Nevertheless, $y \notin C(S_1) \cap S_2$, and $y \in S_1 \cap C(S_2)$, which imply that

$$C(S_1) \cap S_2 \neq S_1 \cap C(S_2)$$

negating the validity of WA(H). Therefore, WA(H) implies WA. ∎

Proof of (b): Suppose that C satisfies SA, and consider any C-related sequence of sets $(S_1, S_2, \ldots, S_t)$ in $\mathscr{S}$. Let us prove that C then satisfies SA(H). If we have

$$S_{t-1} \cap C(S_t) = C(S_{t-1}) \cap S_t$$

there remains nothing to be proved. Suppose, therefore, that $S_{t-1} \cap C(S_t) \neq C(S_{t-1}) \cap S_t$. There are three cases to be considered separately. First, suppose that there exists an $x \in X$ such that

$$x \in C(S_{t-1}) \cap S_t \quad \text{and} \quad x \notin S_{t-1} \cap C(S_t)$$

Take any $y \in S_{t-1} \cap C(S_t)$. [Such a y exists by virtue of the C-relatedness of $(S_1, S_2, \ldots, S_t)$.] Then we obtain $(y, x) \in R_C^*$ and $(x, y) \in R_C$, which contradict SA. Second, suppose that there are x and y in X such that

$$x \in S_{t-1} \cap C(S_t), \quad x \notin C(S_{t-1}) \cap S_t, \quad \text{and} \quad y \in C(S_{t-1}) \cap S_t$$

Once again we have $(y, x) \in R_C^*$ and $(x, y) \in R_C$, in contradiction of SA. Finally, suppose that $C(S_{t-1}) \cap S_t = \varnothing$. $(S_1, S_2, \ldots, S_t)$ being C-related in $\mathscr{S}$, there exists a $z^t \in X$ such that $z^t \in S_{t-1} \cap C(S_t)$. If $z^t \in C(S_{t-1})$, then we obtain

$$z^t \in C(S_{t-1}) \cap C(S_t) \subset C(S_{t-1}) \cap S_t$$

a contradiction. Therefore, $z^t \in S_{t-1} \setminus C(S_{t-1})$. If we have

$$S_{t-2} \cap C(S_{t-1}) = C(S_{t-2}) \cap S_{t-1}$$

there remains nothing further to be proved. Otherwise, we can repeat the preceding argument to obtain a $z^{t-1} \in$

$[S_{t-2} \setminus C(S_{t-2})] \cap C(S_{t-1})$. This algorithm leads us either to

$\exists \tau \in \{1, 2, \ldots, t-1\}$: $S_\tau \cap C(S_{\tau+1}) = C(S_\tau) \cap S_{\tau+1}$

or to the following: There exist $z^2, z^3, \ldots, z^t$ in X such that

$$z^2 \in [S_1 \setminus C(S_1)] \cap C(S_2)$$

$$z^3 \in [S_2 \setminus C(S_2)] \cap C(S_3)$$

$$\vdots$$

$$z^t \in [S_{t-1} \setminus C(S_{t-1})] \cap C(S_t)$$

In the latter case, take a $z^1 \in C(S_1) \cap S_t$. [Note that such a z^1 does exist, thanks to the C-relatedness of $(S_1, S_2, \ldots, S_t)$.] We then obtain $(z^1, z^t) \in T(R_C^*)$ and $(z^t, z^1) \in R_C$, in contradiction to SA. This establishes that SA implies SA(H). ▮

Proof of (c): By virtue of Theorem 2.1(a), we have only to prove that HAA and SCA are equivalent.

Assume first that C satisfies HAA. Let $(x, y) \in T(R_C)$, $x \in S$, and $y \in C(S)$ hold true for some $S \in \mathscr{S}$. Then either (i) $(x, y) \in R_C$ or (ii) there exist $\{z^1, \ldots, z^{t-1}\} \subset X$ and $\{S_1, \ldots, S_t\} \subset \mathscr{S}$ such that $x \in C(S_1)$, $z^\tau \in S_\tau \cap C(S_{\tau+1})$ $(\tau = 1, \ldots, t-1)$, and $y \in S_t$. In case (i), we have $x \in C(S)$, because HAA implies WA, which is equivalent to WCA. In case (ii), taking $x \in S$ and $y \in C(S)$ into consideration, $(S, S_1, \ldots, S_t)$ turns out to be C-related, which yields $S \cap C(S_1) = C(S) \cap S_1$ by virtue of HAA. Thus, $x \in C(S)$. In any case, SCA is implied.

Assume this time that C satisfies SCA. Let a sequence $(S_1, S_2, \ldots, S_t)$ in $\mathscr{S}$ be C-related, and let z^τ and z^t be taken arbitrarily from $S_\tau \cap C(S_{\tau+1})$ and $S_t \cap C(S_1)$, respectively $(\tau = 1, 2, \ldots, t-1)$. It will be shown that $S_1 \cap C(S_2) = C(S_1) \cap S_2$. By definition, we have $z^1 \in S_1$, $(z^1, z^t) \in T(R_C)$, and $z^t \in C(S_1)$, so that SCA entails $z^1 \in C(S_1)$. Noticing that $z^1 \in C(S_2) \subset S_2$, we have $S_1 \cap C(S_2) \subset C(S_1) \cap S_2$. Next let z be an arbitrary point of $C(S_1) \cap S_2$. Then $z \in S_2$, $(z, z^1) \in R_C \subset T(R_C)$, and $z^1 \in C(S_2)$, so that we have $z \in C(S_2)$, thanks to SCA. Thus, we have $C(S_1) \cap S_2 \subset S_1 \cap C(S_2)$, yielding $S_1 \cap C(S_2) = C(S_1) \cap S_2$. In a similar way, we can show that $C(S_\tau) \cap S_{\tau+1} = S_\tau \cap C(S_{\tau+1})$ holds true for any $\tau \in \{1, 2, \ldots, t-1\}$. Thus, HAA is implied. ▮

Another version of the strong axiom of revealed preference has been introduced by Uzawa (1957). Let a binary relation E_C be induced by a choice function C on $(X, \mathscr{S})$ as follows:

$$E_C = \bigcup_{S \in \mathscr{S}} [C(S) \times C(S)]$$

Because $R_C = R_C^* \cup E_C$ holds true by definition, SA can be rephrased as

$$\forall x, y \in X: (x, y) \in T(R_C^*) \rightarrow \begin{cases} (y, x) \notin R_C^* \\ \& \\ (y, x) \notin E_C \end{cases} \tag{A.1}$$

Uzawa's axiom is an apparently weaker version of the contrapositive of (A.1), which reads as follows.

Uzawa's axiom of revealed preference (UA)

$$\forall x, y \in X: [(x, y) \in E_C \rightarrow (y, x) \notin T(R_C^*)]$$

Theorem A(2)
Let C be a choice function on a choice space $(X, \mathcal{S})$. Then C satisfies Uzawa's axiom of revealed preference (UA) if and only if it satisfies the strong axiom of revealed preference (SA).

Proof: Clearly, we have only to prove the "only if" part. Assume, therefore, that SA is false. Then there exist $x, y \in X$ and $S \in \mathcal{S}$ such that $(x, y) \in T(R_C^*)$, $y \in C(S)$, and $x \in S$. If $x \in C(S)$, then we have x, $y \in C(S)$ and $(x, y) \in T(R_C^*)$, so that UA is falsified. If $x \in S \setminus C(S)$, then $(y, x) \in R_C^*$ holds true, which yields $(y, y) \in T(R_C^*)$, in view of $(x, y) \in T(R_C^*)$, $R_C^* \subset T(R_C^*)$, and transitivity of $T(R_C^*)$. In this case, as well, UA is falsified. ∎

We are now fully prepared to present a generalized theory of rationalizability.

2. Quite generally, the following rationalizability theorems are true, and they are arranged in order of decreasing strength.

Theorem A(3)
A choice function C on a choice space $(X, \mathcal{S})$ is full rational if and only if it satisfies Houthakker's axiom of revealed preference (HOA) (Suzumura, 1977).

Proof of necessity: If a choice function C is full rational, with an ordering rationalization R, then

$$\forall S \in \mathcal{S}: C(S) = G(S, R) \tag{A.2}$$

must hold true. Suppose that there exists a sequence $(x^1, x^2, \ldots, x^t)$ $(t \geq 2)$ such that $(x^1, x^2) \in R_C^*$ and $(x^\tau, x^{\tau+1}) \in R_C$ $(\tau = 2, 3, \ldots, t-1)$. Then there exists a sequence $(S_1, S_2, \ldots, S_{t-1})$ in $\mathcal{S}$ such that

$x^1 \in C(S_1)$, $x^2 \in S_1 \setminus C(S_1)$, $x^\tau \in C(S_\tau)$, and $x^{\tau+1} \in S_\tau$ $(\tau = 2, 3, \ldots, t-1)$. Because C is full rational, we then have $(x^1, x^2) \in P(R)$ and $(x^\tau, x^{\tau+1}) \in R$ $(\tau = 2, \ldots, t-1)$, which entail $(x^1, x^t) \in P(R)$, thanks to transitivity of R. But this result clearly excludes the possibility that $(x^t, x^1) \in R_C$, so that there exists no H-cycle of any order whatsoever. ▮

Proof of sufficiency: Let the diagonal Δ_X be defined by

$$\Delta_X = \{(x, y) \in X \times X \mid x = y\} \tag{A.3}$$

and define a binary relation Q by

$$Q = \Delta_X \cup T(R_C) \tag{A.4}$$

It is easy to see that Q is transitive and reflexive. Thanks to Theorem A(4) in the Appendix to Chapter 1, there exists an ordering R that subsumes Q; namely, there exists an ordering R such that

$$Q \subset R \tag{A.5}$$

and

$$P(Q) \subset P(R) \tag{A.6}$$

We are going to show that this R in fact satisfies

$$R_C \subset R \tag{A.7}$$

and

$$P(R_C) \subset P(R) \tag{A.8}$$

The former is obviously true in view of $R_C \subset T(R_C)$, (A.4), and (A.5). To prove the latter, we have only to show that $P(R_C) \subset P(Q)$, thanks to (A.6). Assume that x and y such that $(x, y) \in P(R_C)$, which means $(x, y) \in R_C$ and $(y, x) \notin R_C$. From $(x, y) \in R_C$ it follows that $(x, y) \in Q$. Assume now that $(y, x) \in Q$. Clearly, $(y, x) \notin \Delta_X$; otherwise, we could not have supposed that $(x, y) \in P(R_C)$. It follows that $(y, x) \in T(R_C)$, which, in combination with $(x, y) \in P(R_C) \subset R_C^*$, implies the existence of an H-cycle of some order, a contradiction. Therefore, (A.7) and (A.8) are valid.

Let an $S \in \mathscr{S}$ be chosen, and let $x \in C(S)$. Then, $(x, y) \in R_C$ for all $y \in S$. In view of (A.7), we then have $x \in G(S, R)$. It follows that

$$C(S) \subset G(S, R) \tag{A.9}$$

Next, let $x \in S \setminus C(S)$, and take any $y \in C(S)$, so that $(y, x) \in R_C^*$. If we happen to have $(x, y) \in R_C$, it turns out that (x, y) is an H-cycle of order 2, a contradiction. Therefore, we must have $(x, y) \notin R_C$, which, in view of $(y, x) \in R_C^* \subset R_C$, implies $(y, x) \in P(R_C)$. Thanks to (A.8), we then have $(y, x) \in P(R)$, entailing $x \in S \setminus G(S, R)$. Therefore, we obtain

$$G(S, R) \subset C(S) \tag{A.10}$$

Because (A.9) and (A.10) are valid for any $S \in \mathcal{S}$, we have shown that C is full rational, with an ordering rationalization R. This completes the proof. ∎

Theorem A(4)
A choice function C on a choice space $(X, \mathcal{S})$ is quasi-transitive rational if it satisfies the strong axiom of revealed preference (SA).[30]

Proof: Assume that C satisfies SA, and let a binary relation R be defined by

$$R = \{(x, y) \in X \times X \mid (x, y) \in T(R_C^*) \vee (y, x) \notin T(R_C^*)\} \tag{A.11}$$

which is complete and reflexive. Indeed, if $(x, y) \notin R$ for some x, $y \in X$, then $(x, y) \notin T(R_C^*)$ and $(y, x) \in T(R_C^*)$. It then follows from (A.11) that $(y, x) \in R$, which establishes the completeness as well as reflexivity of R.

Our next task is to prove that $P(R) = T(R_C^*)$ holds true. By definition we have $(x, y) \in P(R)$ if and only if

$$(x, y) \in T(R_C^*) \quad \text{and} \quad (y, x) \notin T(R_C^*) \tag{A.12}$$

We are home if we can show the asymmetry of $T(R_C^*)$. Suppose, to the contrary, that $(x, y) \in T(R_C^*)$ and $(y, x) \in T(R_C^*)$ hold true for some $x, y \in X$. By virtue of transitivity of $T(R_C^*)$, it then follows that $(x, x) \in T(R_C^*)$, in contradiction with UA, which is equivalent to SA. Now that $P(R) = T(R_C^*)$ is true, we are assured that R is quasi-transitive, thanks to transitivity of $T(R_C^*)$.

To complete the proof of the theorem, we prove that

$$\forall S \in \mathcal{S}: C(S) = G(S, R) \tag{A.13}$$

Let an $S \in \mathcal{S}$ be arbitrarily chosen, and let x and y be such that $x \in C(S)$ and $y \in S$. If $y \in S \setminus C(S)$, then $(x, y) \in R_C^* \subset T(R_C^*)$, so that $(x, y) \in R$. If, on the other hand, $y \in C(S)$ is the case, we have $(x, y) \in E_C$, so that $(y, x) \notin T(R_C^*)$ by virtue of UA. Therefore, $(x, y) \in R$ is true in this case as well. Because $(x, y) \in R$ for all $y \in S$, $C(S) \subset G(S, R)$ is true. Conversely, let $x \in G(S, R)$; that is,

$$\forall y \in S: (x, y) \in T(R_C^*) \vee (y, x) \notin T(R_C^*) \tag{A.14}$$

If it is the case that $x \notin C(S)$, then

$$\forall z \in C(S): (z, x) \in R_C^* \subset T(R_C^*) \tag{A.15}$$

holds true, so that we have $(x, x) \in T(R_C^*)$, in view of (A.14) and transitivity of $T(R_C^*)$. But this contradicts UA, hence SA, on C. ▮

Theorem A(5)
A choice function C on a choice space $(X, \mathscr{S})$ is acyclic rational if it satisfies the weak axiom of revealed preference (WA) and R_C^* is acyclic.[31]

Proof: Let a binary relation R_0 on X be defined by

$$R_0 = R_C \cup \{(x, y) \in X \times X \mid (y, x) \notin R_C^*\} \tag{A.16}$$

If $(x, y) \notin R_0$ for some $x, y \in X$, we obtain both of $(x, y) \notin R_C$ and $(y, x) \in R_C^*$. By virtue of WA, we then obtain $(x, y) \notin R_C^*$. It follows that $(y, x) \in R_0$, so that R_0 is complete. Reflexivity of R_0 is ensured by the foregoing proof if only we put $x = y$. To show acyclicity of R_0, notice that

$$\begin{aligned}(x, y) \in P(R_0) &\leftrightarrow (x, y) \in R_0 \ \&\ (y, x) \notin R_C \ \&\ (x, y) \in R_C^* \\ &\rightarrow (x, y) \in R_C^* \ \&\ (y, x) \notin R_C^* \\ &\leftrightarrow (x, y) \in P(R_C^*)\end{aligned}$$

so that acyclicity of R_0 follows from that of R_C^*.

Let a function C_0 be defined on $\mathscr{S}$ by

$$\forall S \in \mathscr{S}: C_0(S) = G(S, R_0) \tag{A.17}$$

We show that $C(S) = C_0(S)$ holds true for all $S \in \mathscr{S}$. Take, therefore, any $S \in \mathscr{S}$, and let $x \in C(S)$. If $x \notin C_0(S)$, then there exists a $y \in S$ such that $(x, y) \notin R_0$, which implies that $(x, y) \notin R_C$. On the other hand, $x \in C(S)$ and $y \in S$ entail $(x, y) \in R_C$, a contradiction. Therefore, $C(S) \subset C_0(S)$. Conversely, let $x \in C_0(S)$ and $x \notin C(S)$. Take any $y \in C(S)$. We then obtain $(y, x) \in R_C^*$, which implies $(x, y) \notin R_C$, by virtue of WA. It follows that $(x, y) \notin R_0$, which contradicts $x \in C_0(S)$. Therefore, $C_0(S) \subset C(S)$, completing the proof. ▮

On examining the proof of Theorem A(5) it will be recognized that acyclicity of R_C^* is used only when we prove acyclicity of R_0, and not otherwise, so that we have established the following theorem en route.

Theorem A(6)
A choice function C on a choice space $(X, \mathscr{S})$ is rational if it satisfies the weak axiom of revealed preference (WA).[32]

According to Theorem A(1)(c) and Theorem A(3), Hansson's axiom of revealed preference (HAA) is necessary and sufficient for a choice function to be full rational. Likewise, Hansson's version of the weak axiom [WA(H)] is sufficient for a choice function to be rational, as the combination of Theorem A(1)(a) and Theorem A(6) establishes. A natural question now emerges. What role does Hansson's version of the strong axiom [SA(H)] play in the theory of rational choice? An answer can be provided via the following theorem.

Theorem A(7)
Let a choice function C on a choice space $(X, \mathscr{S})$ satisfy Hansson's version of the strong axiom [SA(H)]. Then R_C^* is acyclic.[33]

Coupled with Theorem A(5), Theorem A(7) allows us to assert that *a choice function satisfying Hansson's version of the strong axiom is acyclic rational.*

Proof of Theorem A(7): Let C satisfy SA(H), and assume that R_C^* is not acyclic. Then there exists a sequence $(z^1, z^2, \ldots, z^t)$ in X such that $(z^\mu, z^{\mu+1}) \in R_C^*$ $(\mu = 1, 2, \ldots, t-1)$ and $(z^t, z^1) \in R_C^*$. It follows that there exist $S_1, S_2, \ldots, S_t$ in $\mathscr{S}$ satisfying $z^1 \in [S_t \setminus C(S_t)] \cap C(S_1)$, $z^2 \in [S_1 \setminus C(S_1)] \cap C(S_2)$, $z^3 \in [S_2 \setminus C(S_2)] \cap C(S_3), \ldots,$ $z^{t-1} \in [S_{t-2} \setminus C(S_{t-2})] \cap C(S_{t-1})$, and $z^t \in [S_{t-1} \setminus C(S_{t-1})] \cap C(S_t)$. Because $(S_1, S_2, \ldots, S_t)$ is a C-related sequence in $\mathscr{S}$, there exists a $\tau \in \{1, 2, \ldots, t-1\}$ such that

$$S_\tau \cap C(S_{\tau+1}) = C(S_\tau) \cap S_{\tau+1}$$

But then we obtain $z^{\tau+1} \in [S_\tau \setminus C(S_\tau)] \cap C(S_{\tau+1}) \subset S_\tau \cap C(S_{\tau+1}) \subset C(S_\tau)$, a contradiction. ▮

This completes our general theory of rational choice functions. Our main results are summarized in Figure 2.3, where a double-headed arrow indicates logical equivalence and a single-headed arrow indicates logical implication, which is generally irreversible.[34]

3. It may be of some interest to examine how the preceding theory will be simplified by the finite additivity of $\mathscr{S}$. The simplification is great indeed, as the following theorem crystallizes.

Theorem A(8)
Let C be a choice function on a choice space $(X, \mathscr{S})$ such that $\mathscr{S}$ is closed with respect to finite addition. Then C is full rational if and only if it satisfies Arrow's axiom (AA).

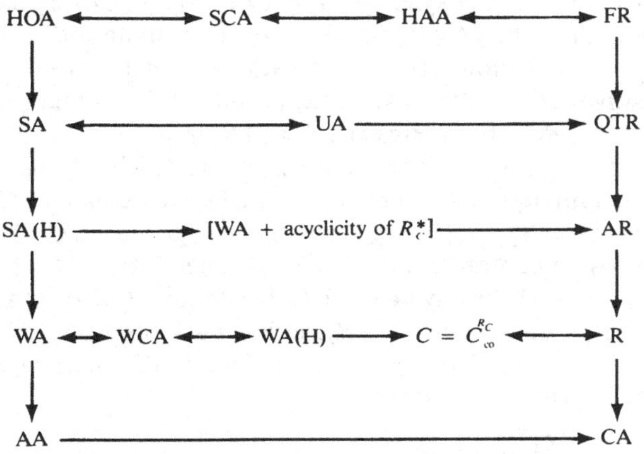

Figure 2.3. Structure of rational choice functions on the general domain.

Proof: Clearly we have only to prove the "if" part, the "only if" part being valid on the general domain.

Step 1: We prove that, given the finite additivity of $\mathscr{S}$, AA implies WA. Suppose, to the contrary, that WA is false. Then there exist $S_1, S_2 \in \mathscr{S}$ and $x, y \in X$ such that

$$x \in C(S_1) \cap S_2 \ \& \ y \in [S_1 \setminus C(S_1)] \cap C(S_2) \tag{A.18}$$

Let $S = S_1 \cup S_2$, which is in $\mathscr{S}$ by finite additivity. Because $C(S) \subset S_1 \cup S_2$ holds true, if it so happens that $S_1 \cap C(S) = \varnothing$, then $S_2 \cap C(S) \neq \varnothing$ must be the case, so that AA implies that $C(S_2) = S_2 \cap C(S)$. In view of (A.18), it then follows that $y \in S_1 \cap C(S)$, a contradiction. Similar contradiction is obtained if we assume that $S_2 \cap C(S) = \varnothing$. AA therefore implies that

$$S_1 \cap C(S) = C(S_1) \tag{A.19}$$

and

$$S_2 \cap C(S) = C(S_2) \tag{A.20}$$

Making intersection of $S_2 \cap C(S)$ and $S_1 \setminus C(S_1)$, we obtain

$$\begin{aligned} S_2 \cap C(S) \cap [S_1 \setminus C(S_1)] &= C(S) \cap S_1 \cap [S_2 \setminus C(S_1)] \\ &= C(S_1) \cap [S_2 \setminus C(S_1)], \qquad \text{from (A.19)} \\ &= \varnothing \end{aligned}$$

and (A.18) and (A.20) yield $y \in S_2 \cap C(S) \cap [S_1 \setminus C(S_1)]$, a contradiction. Therefore, AA implies WA, given the finite additivity of $\mathscr{S}$.

Step 2: We now prove that with $\mathscr{S}$ finitely additive, R_C is transitive if C satisfies AA. Let x, y, and z be such that $(x, y) \in R_C$ and $(y, z) \in R_C$. Then there exist S_1 and S_2 in $\mathscr{S}$ such that $x \in C(S_1)$, $y \in S_1 \cap C(S_2)$, and $z \in S_2$. Let $S = S_1 \cup S_2$, which belongs to $\mathscr{S}$ by finite additivity, and assume that $x \notin C(S)$. If we had $y \in C(S)$, we would have $S_1 \cap C(S) \neq \varnothing$, so that $C(S_1) = S_1 \cap C(S)$ follows from AA, in contradiction to $x \notin C(S)$. Therefore, $x \notin C(S)$ implies that $y \notin C(S)$. Take any $v \in C(S)$. It then follows that $(v, x) \in R_C^*$ and $(v, y) \in R_C^*$. Because $v \in S_1 \cup S_2$, either $v \in S_1$ or $v \in S_2$ is true. In the former case, we obtain $(x, v) \in R_C$, and in the latter case $(y, v) \in R_C$ holds true. Therefore, we obtain

$$x \notin C(S) \rightarrow \begin{cases} [(v, x) \in R_C^* \ \& \ (x, v) \in R_C] \\ \vee \\ [(v, y) \in R_C^* \ \& \ (y, v) \in R_C] \end{cases} \tag{A.21}$$

In view of step 1, WA should be satisfied by our C, so that the conclusion of (A.21) is false. We should therefore have $x \in C(S)$, which implies that $(x, z) \in R_C$, as desired.

Step 3: Let

$$Q = \Delta_X \cup R_C \tag{A.22}$$

where $\Delta_X = \{(x, y) \in X \times X \mid x = y\}$. Thanks to the preceding step 2, Q is a quasi ordering on X, so that Theorem A(4) in the Appendix to Chapter 1 ensures the existence of an ordering R satisfying

$$Q \subset R \tag{A.23}$$

and

$$P(Q) \subset P(R) \tag{A.24}$$

We show that R in fact satisfies

$$R_C \subset R \tag{A.25}$$

and

$$P(R_C) \subset P(R) \tag{A.26}$$

In view of (A.22) and (A.23), it is clear that (A.25) is true. To establish (A.26), let $(x, y) \in P(R_C)$, so that $(x, y) \in R_C$ and $(y, x) \notin R_C$. Thanks to (A.22), we obtain $(x, y) \in Q$. Suppose that $(y, x) \in Q$. Then either $(y, x) \in R_C$ or $x = y$ should be true, both of which contradict

$(x, y) \in P(R_C)$. Therefore, $(y, x) \notin Q$; hence $(x, y) \in P(Q)$. Because (A.24) is true, we then obtain $(x, y) \in P(R)$.

Take any $S \in \mathscr{S}$ and let $x \in C(S)$. It then follows that $(x, y) \in R_C$ holds true for all $y \in S$. In view of (A.25), we then obtain $x \in G(S, R)$. Therefore,

$$C(S) \subset G(S, R) \tag{A.27}$$

Conversely, let $x \in S \setminus C(S)$, and take any $y \in C(S)$. Then we have $(y, x) \in R_C^*$, which implies that $(y, x) \in R_C$. Because C satisfies WA, we must have, from $(y, x) \in R_C^*$, that $(x, y) \notin R_C$, so that we obtain $(y, x) \in P(R_C)$. It then follows from (A.26) that $(y, x) \in P(R)$; hence $x \in S \setminus G(S, R)$. Therefore, we have

$$G(S, R) \subset C(S) \tag{A.28}$$

Because (A.27) and (A.28) are true for any $S \in \mathscr{S}$ and R is an ordering on X, we are home. ∎

It deserves emphasis that the finite additivity of $\mathscr{S}$ changes the theory of rational choice functions rather drastically. Without it, Arrow's axiom does not ensure even the bare rationality (Example 19 in Appendix B), whereas the same axiom is equivalent to full rationality with it [Theorem A(8)]. As a result, all the choice-consistency conditions that appear in Figure 2.3, except $C = C_{co}^{R_C}$ and CA, become equivalent. If, in addition, the value taken by C is always a singleton set, even $C = C_{co}^{R_C}$ and CA turn out to be equivalent to all other choice-consistency conditions, hence to full rationality.

Before concluding this Appendix, let us keep on record another revealed preference implication of Arrow's axiom that will be needed in Chapter 7.

Theorem A(9)
Let C be a choice function on a choice space $(X, \mathscr{S})$ such that $\mathscr{S}$ is closed with respect to finite addition. Then the revealed preference relation R_C^* induced by C is transitive.

Proof: Let $x, y, z \in X$ be such that $(x, y) \in R_C^*$ and $(y, z) \in R_C^*$ hold true. By definition, there exist S_1, $S_2 \in \mathscr{S}$ such that $x \in C(S_1)$, $y \in [S_1 \setminus C(S_1)] \cap C(S_2)$, and $z \in S_2 \setminus C(S_2)$ are satisfied. Letting $S = S_1 \cup S_2$, and proceeding as in the proof of Theorem A(8), we may assert that $x \in C(S)$ holds true. To conclude the proof, assume that $z \in C(S)$ is the case. We then obtain $(z, y) \in R_C$ and $(y, z) \in R_C^*$, which contradicts WA that C satisfies, as we proved in step 1 of the proof of Theorem A(8). We must accept, therefore, that $z \in S \setminus C(S)$ is the case, which establishes that $(x, z) \in R_C^*$ is true, as desired. ∎

Appendix B: Counterexamples

Example 1

Let $X = \{x, y, z\}$, $\mathscr{S} = \{S_1, S_2, S_3\}$, $S_1 = \{x, y\}$, $S_2 = \{x, z\}$, and $S_3 = X$, and let a choice function C on $(X, \mathscr{S})$ be defined by $C(S_1) = S_1$, $C(S_2) = S_2$, and $C(S_3) = \{x\}$. This choice function is G-rational with a G-rationalization $R = \Delta_X \cup \{(x, y), (y, x), (x, z), (z, x)\}$, where $\Delta_X = \{(x, x), (y, y), (z, z)\}$. Assume that this C is M-rational, with an M-rationalization R'. It follows from $C(S_1) = S_1$ that

$$(x, y) \in I(R') \vee [(x, y) \notin R' \ \& \ (y, x) \notin R'] \tag{B.1}$$

and $C(S_2) = S_2$ yields

$$(x, z) \in I(R') \vee [(x, z) \notin R' \ \& \ (z, x) \notin R'] \tag{B.2}$$

Finally, $C(S_3) = \{x\}$ tells us that

$$[(x, y) \in P(R') \vee (z, y) \in P(R')] \ \& \ [(x, z) \in P(R') \vee (y, z) \in P(R')] \tag{B.3}$$

It follows from (B.1), (B.2), and (B.3) that $(z, y) \in P(R')$ and $(y, z) \in P(R')$, a contradiction. Thus, C cannot possibly be M-rational. ∎

Example 2

Let $X = \{x, y, z\}$, $\mathscr{S} = \{S_1, S_2\}$, $S_1 = \{x, y\}$, and $S_2 = X$, and let C on $(X, \mathscr{S})$ be defined by $C(S_1) = \{x\}$ and $C(S_2) = S_2$. Suppose that R happens to be a rationalization of this C. Because $C(S_1) = \{x\}$, we must have $(x, y) \in P(R)$ or $(y, y) \notin R$, and $y \in C(S_2)$ implies that $(y, y) \in R$ and $(y, x) \in R$, a contradiction. ∎

Example 3

Let $X = \{x, y, z\}$, $\mathscr{S} = \{S_1, S_2, S_3\}$, $S_1 = \{x, y\}$, $S_2 = \{y, z\}$, and $S_3 = \{x, z\}$, and let a choice function C on $(X, \mathscr{S})$ be defined by $C(S_1) = S_1$, $C(S_2) = S_2$, and $C(S_3) = \{z\}$. The revealed preference relations R_C and R_C^* induced by this C are

$$R_C = \Delta_X \cup \{(x, y), (y, x), (y, z), (z, y), (z, x)\}$$

and

$$R_C^* = \{(z, x)\}$$

where $\Delta_X = \{(x, x), (y, y), (z, z)\}$. Because $(x, z) \in T(R_C)$ and $(z, x) \in R_C^*$, this C violates Houthakker's axiom. However, the strong axiom of revealed preference is satisfied, because $\{(z, x)\} = T(R_C^*)$ and $(x, z) \notin R_C$. ∎

Example 4
Let $X = \{x, y, z\}$, $\mathscr{S} = \{S_1, S_2, S_3\}$, $S_1 = \{x, y\}$, $S_2 = \{y, z\}$, and $S_3 = \{x, z\}$, and let a choice function C on $(X, \mathscr{S})$ be defined by $C(S_1) = \{x\}$, $C(S_2) = S_2$, and $C(S_3) = \{z\}$. We can easily verify that this C induces the following revealed preference relations:

$$R_C^* = \{(x, y), (z, x)\}$$

and

$$R_C = \Delta_X \cup R_C^* \cup \{(y, z), (z, y)\}$$

where $\Delta_X = \{(x, x), (y, y), (z, z)\}$. It then follows that

$$T(R_C^*) = R_C^* \cup \{(z, y)\}$$

Therefore, we have $(z, y) \in T(R_C^*)$ and $(y, z) \in R_C$, so that this choice function C does not satisfy the strong axiom of revealed preference, even if this C does satisfy the weak axiom. ∎

Example 5
Let $X = \{x, y, z, w\}$, $\mathscr{S} = \{S_1, S_2\}$, $S_1 = \{x, y, z\}$, and $S_2 = \{y, z, w\}$, and let a choice function C on $(X, \mathscr{S})$ be defined by $C(S_1) = \{y\}$ and $C(S_2) = \{z\}$. It is clear that this C vacuously satisfies Arrow's axiom. Nevertheless, C does not satisfy the weak axiom of revealed preference, because $(y, z) \in R_C^*$ and $(z, y) \in R_C^* \subset R_C$ follow from $y \in C(S_1)$, $z \in S_1 \setminus C(S_1)$, $z \in C(S_2)$, and $y \in S_2 \setminus C(S_2)$. ∎

Example 6
Let $X = \{x, y, z\}$, $\mathscr{S} = \{S_1, S_2, \ldots, S_7\}$, $S_1 = \{x\}$, $S_2 = \{y\}$, $S_3 = \{z\}$, $S_4 = \{x, y\}$, $S_5 = \{y, z\}$, $S_6 = \{x, z\}$, and $S_7 = X$, and let C on $(X, \mathscr{S})$ be defined by $C(S_t) = S_t$ $(t = 1, 2, \ldots, 6)$ and $C(S_7) = S_4$. Suppose that this C has a rationalization R. It follows from $C(S_7) = S_4$ that $(z, x) \notin R$ or $(z, y) \notin R$, and $C(S_5) = S_5$ and $C(S_6) = S_6$ yield, respectively, $(z, y) \in R$ and $(z, x) \in R$. This contradiction tells us that C is not rational. However, it is easy, if tedious, to verify that this C satisfies PI (Plott, 1973, p. 1081). ∎

Example 7
Let $X = \{x, y, z\}$, $\mathscr{S} = \{S_1, S_2, S_3\}$, $S_1 = \{x, y\}$, $S_2 = \{y, z\}$, and $S_3 = \{x, z\}$, and let C on $(X, \mathscr{S})$ be defined by $C(S_1) = \{x\}$, $C(S_2) = \{y\}$, and $C(S_3) = \{z\}$. It is easy to verify that a *cyclic* binary relation

$$R = \Delta_X \cup \{(x, y), (y, z), (z, x)\}$$

where $\Delta_X = \{(x, x), (y, y), (z, z)\}$, does rationalize this C, uniquely at that. ∎

Example 8
Let $X = \{x, y, z, w\}$, $\mathscr{S} = \{S_1, S_2, \ldots, S_{15}\}$, $S_1 = \{x\}$, $S_2 = \{y\}$, $S_3 = \{z\}$, $S_4 = \{w\}$, $S_5 = \{x, y\}$, $S_6 = \{x, z\}$, $S_7 = \{x, w\}$, $S_8 = \{y, z\}$, $S_9 = \{y, w\}$, $S_{10} = \{z, w\}$, $S_{11} = \{x, y, z\}$, $S_{12} = \{x, y, w\}$, $S_{13} = \{x, z, w\}$, $S_{14} = \{y, z, w\}$, $S_{15} = X$, $C(S_t) = S_t$ $(t = 1, 2, 3, 4)$, $C(S_5) = C(S_6) = C(S_7) = C(S_{11}) = C(S_{13}) = C(S_{15}) = S_1$, $C(S_8) = S_8$, $C(S_9) = S_2$, $C(S_{10}) = S_3$, $C(S_{12}) = S_7$, and $C(S_{14}) = S_8$. It is easy, if tedious, to verify that this choice function satisfies WPI(α1). It does not satisfy WPI(β1), however, because $C(C(S_{11}) \cup S_9) = S_7 \not\subset C(S_{11} \cup S_9) = C(S_{15}) = S_1$ (Ferejohn and Grether, 1977*a*, p. 23). ▮

Example 9
Let $X = \{x, y, z\}$, $\mathscr{S} = \{S_1, S_2, \ldots, S_7\}$, $S_1 = \{x\}$, $S_2 = \{y\}$, $S_3 = \{z\}$, $S_4 = \{x, y\}$, $S_5 = \{y, z\}$, $S_6 = \{x, z\}$, and $S_7 = X$, and let C on $(X, \mathscr{S})$ be defined by $C(S_t) = S_t$ $(t = 1, 2, \ldots, 5)$, $C(S_6) = S_3$, and $C(S_7) = S_5$. Note that this choice function fails to satisfy DCA, because $S_4 \subset S_7$, $C(S_7) \cap S_4 = \{y\}$, and $C(S_4) = \{x, y\} \supset\supset \{y\}$ hold true. Note, however, that this C satisfies WPI(β1), indeed even PI itself, as we can easily verify. ▮

Example 10
Let $X = \{x, y, z\}$, $\mathscr{S} = \{S_1, S_2, \ldots, S_7\}$, $S_1 = \{x\}$, $S_2 = \{y\}$, $S_3 = \{z\}$, $S_4 = \{x, y\}$, $S_5 = \{y, z\}$, $S_6 = \{x, z\}$, and $S_7 = X$, and let C on $(X, \mathscr{S})$ be defined by $C(S_t) = S_t$ $(t = 1, 2, 3)$, $C(S_4) = C(S_6) = S_1$, and $C(S_5) = C(S_7) = S_5$. This C satisfies SUA, but does not satisfy WPI(β1), because we have

$$C(C(S_4) \cup S_3) = \{x\} \not\subset C(S_3 \cup S_4) = \{y, z\} \quad ▮$$

Example 11
Let $X = \{x, y, z\}$, $\mathscr{S} = \{S_1, S_2, \ldots, S_7\}$, $S_1 = \{x\}$, $S_2 = \{y\}$, $S_3 = \{z\}$, $S_4 = \{x, y\}$, $S_5 = \{y, z\}$, $S_6 = \{x, z\}$, and $S_7 = X$, and let C on $(X, \mathscr{S})$ be such that $C(S_t) = S_t$ $(t = 1, 2, \ldots, 6)$ and $C(S_7) = S_5$. This C satisfies CA as well as NA, but because $S_4 \cap C(S_7) = \{y\} \neq C(S_4) = \{x, y\}$, AA is violated. ▮

Example 12
Let $X = \{x, y, z\}$, $\mathscr{S} = \{S_1, S_2, \ldots, S_7\}$, $S_1 = \{x\}$, $S_2 = \{y\}$, $S_3 = \{z\}$, $S_4 = \{x, y\}$, $S_5 = \{y, z\}$, $S_6 = \{x, z\}$, and $S_7 = X$, and let C on $(X, \mathscr{S})$ be such that $C(S_t) = S_t$ $(t = 1, 2, 3)$, $C(S_4) = C(S_6) = \{x\}$, and $C(S_5) = C(S_7) = \{y\}$. This C satisfies SUA. But NA is violated, because $C(S_7) \subset S_4$ and $C(S_4) \neq C(S_7)$ hold true. Neither is DCA true, because $S_4 \cap C(S_7) = \{y\} \not\supset C(S_4) = \{x\}$ is true. Note also that this C satisfies ST, but it fails to satisfy CA as well as NA. ▮

Example 13
Let $X = \{x, y, z\}$, $\mathscr{S} = \{S_1, S_2, S_3\}$, $S_1 = \{x, y\}$, $S_2 = \{y, z\}$, and $S_3 = \{x, z\}$, and let C on $(X, \mathscr{S})$ be defined by $C(S_1) = \{x\}$, $C(S_2) = S_2$, and $C(S_3) = \{z\}$. It is easy to verify that

$$R_C^* = \{(x, y), (z, x)\}; \quad R_C = \Delta_X \cup R_C^* \cup \{(y, z), (z, y)\}$$

where $\Delta_X = \{(x, x), (y, y), (z, z)\}$, hold true. Because we have

$$T(R_C^*) = R_C^* \cup \{(z, y)\}$$

$(z, y) \in T(R_C^*)$ and $(y, z) \in R_C$ hold true, which implies that this C does not satisfy SA. Note, however, that (S_1, S_2, S_3) is C-related and

$$S_2 \cap C(S_3) = \{z\} = C(S_2) \cap S_3$$

so that this C satisfies SA(H). ▌

Example 14
Let $X = \{x, y, z\}, \mathscr{S} = \{S_1, S_2, \ldots, S_7\}, S_1 = \{x\}, S_2 = \{y\}, S_3 = \{z\}, S_4 = \{x, y\}$, $S_5 = \{x, z\}$, $S_6 = \{y, z\}$, and $S_7 = X$, and let C on $(X, \mathscr{S})$ be such that $C(S_t) = S_t$ $(t = 1, 2, \ldots, 5)$, $C(S_6) = S_3$, and $C(S_7) = S_5$. This C can be rationalized by a complete and quasi-transitive relation

$$R = \Delta_X \cup \{(x, y), (y, x), (x, z), (z, x), (z, y)\}$$

where $\Delta_X = \{(x, x), (y, y), (z, z)\}$. However, we have

$$x, y \in C(S_4), \quad x \in C(S_7), \quad \text{and} \quad y \in S_7 \setminus C(S_7)$$

so that the validity of UA, and hence that of SA by virtue of Theorem A(2), is negated. ▌

Example 15
Let $X = \{x, y, z, u, u^*, v, v^*, w, w^*\}$, $\mathscr{S} = \{S_1, S_2, S_3\}$, $S_1 = \{x, y, u, u^*\}$, $S_2 = \{y, z, v, v^*\}$, and $S_3 = \{x, z, w, w^*\}$, and let C on $(X, \mathscr{S})$ be defined by $C(S_1) = \{x, u^*\}$, $C(S_2) = \{y, v^*\}$, and $C(S_3) = \{z, w^*\}$. It is easy to verify that

$$R_C^* = \{(x, y), (x, u), (u^*, u), (u^*, y), (y, z), (y, v), (v^*, z), (v^*, v), (z, x), (z, w), (w^*, x), (w^*, w)\}$$

holds true. It then follows that $(x, y) \in P(R_C^*)$, $(y, z) \in P(R_C^*)$, and $(z, x) \in P(R_C^*)$, so that R_C^* is not acyclic. This C can be rationalized, however, by the following binary relation:

$$R = P(R) \cup I(R)$$

$$P(R) = \{(u^*, u), (u, y), (v^*, v), (v, z), (w^*, w), (w, x)\}$$

and

$$I(R) = \Delta_X \cup \{(x, u^*), (u^*, x), (u^*, y), (y, u^*), (x, y), (y, x), (x, u), (u, x), (y, v^*), (v^*, y), (y, v), (v, y), (y, z), (z, y), (v^*, z), (z, v^*), (z, w^*), (w^*, z), (z, x), (x, z), (z, w), (w, z), (w^*, x), (x, w^*)\}$$

where $\Delta_X = \{(x, x), (y, y), (z, z), (u, u), (u^*, u^*), (v, v), (v^*, v^*), (w, w), (w^*, w^*)\}$. Note that this R is acyclic, as desired. ∎

Example 16
Let $X = \{x, y, z\}$, $\mathscr{S} = \{S_1, S_2, S_3, S_4\}$, $S_1 = \{x, y\}$, $S_2 = \{y, z\}$, $S_3 = \{x, z\}$, and $S_4 = X$, and let C on $(X, \mathscr{S})$ be such that $C(S_1) = S_1$, $C(S_2) = \{z\}$, $C(S_3) = S_3$, and $C(S_4) = S_3$. Because $x \in C(S_4)$, $y \in S_4 \setminus C(S_4)$, $y \in C(S_1)$, and $x \in S_1$, we obtain $(x, y) \in R_C^*$ and $(y, x) \in R_C$, so that this C does not satisfy WA. Nevertheless, this C has an acyclic rationalization defined by $R = \Delta_X \cup \{(x, y), (y, x), (z, y), (x, z), (z, x)\}$, where $\Delta_X = \{(x, x), (y, y), (z, z)\}$. ∎

Example 17
Let $X = \{x, y, z\}$, $\mathscr{S} = \{S_1, S_2, S_3\}$, $S_1 = \{x, y\}$, $S_2 = \{y, z\}$, and $S_3 = \{x, z\}$, and let C on $(X, \mathscr{S})$ satisfy $C(S_1) = \{x\}$, $C(S_2) = \{y\}$, and $C(S_3) = S_3$. In this case,

$$S_1 \cap C(S_2) = \{y\}, S_2 \cap C(S_3) = \{z\}, S_3 \cap C(S_1) = \{x\},$$
$$C(S_1) \cap S_2 = \varnothing, C(S_2) \cap S_3 = \varnothing$$

so that C does not satisfy SA(H). Note, however, that

$$R_C^* = \{(x, y), (y, z)\}$$
$$R_C = \Delta_X \cup R_C^* \cup \{(x, z), (z, x)\}$$

which implies that WA as well as acyclicity of R_C^* holds true. ∎

Example 18
Let $X = \{x, y, z\}$, $\mathscr{S} = \{S_1, S_2, S_3\}$, $S_1 = \{x, y\}$, $S_2 = \{y, z\}$, and $S_3 = \{x, z\}$, and consider a choice function C that satisfies $C(S_1) = \{x\}$, $C(S_2) = \{y\}$, $C(S_3) = S_3$. This C has a unique rationalization

$$R = \Delta_X \cup \{(x, y), (y, z), (x, z), (z, x)\}$$

where $\Delta_X = \{(x, x), (y, y), (z, z)\}$, which is acyclic but not quasi-transitive. ∎

Example 19
Let $X = \{x, y, z, w\}$, $\mathscr{S} = \{S_1, S_2, S_3\}$, $S_1 = \{x, y, z\}$, $S_2 = \{x, y, w\}$, and $S_3 = \{y, z, w\}$, and consider a choice function C defined by $C(S_1) = \{y\}$, $C(S_2) = \{x\}$, and $C(S_3) = \{y\}$. This C trivially satisfies AA. Suppose that this C has a rationalization R. From $C(S_1) = \{y\}$ we obtain $(y, x) \in R$, and $C(S_3) = \{y\}$ yields $(y, w) \in R$. Because $y \notin C(S_2)$ is the case, we have either $(y, x) \notin R$ or $(y, w) \notin R$, a contradiction. Therefore, Arrow's axiom does not ensure rationality. A fortiori, Chernoff's axiom, which is necessary for a choice function to be rational, is not sufficient. ∎

In view of Lemma 2.1, it is clear that Houthakker's axiom implies that

$$\forall x, y \in X: [(x, y) \in T(R_C) \rightarrow (y, x) \notin P(R_C)]$$

that is, R_C is consistent. Similarly, the strong axiom implies that

$$\forall x, y \in X: [(x, y) \in T(R_C^*) \rightarrow (y, x) \notin P(R_C^*)]$$

that is, R_C^* is consistent.

Example 20
To show that consistency of R_C is not strong enough to imply HOA, let $X = \{x, y, z\}$, $\mathscr{S} = \{S_1, S_2, S_3\}$, $S_1 = \{x, y\}$, $S_2 = \{y, z\}$, $S_3 = \{x, z\}$, and $S_4 = X$, and consider a choice function C defined by $C(S_1) = \{x\}$, $C(S_2) = S_2$, $C(S_3) = S_3$, and $C(S_4) = S_4$. It is easy to verify that

$$R_C = \Delta_X \cup \{(x, y), (y, x), (y, z), (z, y), (x, z), (z, x)\}$$

and

$$R_C^* = \{(x, y)\}$$

where $\Delta_X = \{(x, x), (y, y), (z, z)\}$. Because $(y, x) \in T(R_C)$ and $(x, y) \in R_C^*$, this C does not satisfy HOA. On inspection, we realize that R_C can be inconsistent only if $(x, y) \in P(R_C)$, which requires that $(y, x) \notin R_C$. But this is false. ∎

Example 21
The consistency of R_C^*, which we have shown earlier to be implied by the strong axiom, does not always imply SA. To exemplify this, let $X = \{x, y, z\}$, $\mathscr{S} = \{S_1, S_2, S_3\}$, $S_1 = \{x, y\}$, $S_2 = \{y, z\}$, $S_3 = \{x, z\}$, $C(S_1) = \{x\}$, $C(S_2) = \{y\}$, and $C(S_3) = S_3$. In this case,

$$R_C = \Delta_X \cup R_C^* \cup \{(x, z), (z, x)\}$$

and

$$R_C^* = \{(x, y), (y, z)\}$$

where $\Delta_X = \{(x, x), (y, y), (z, z)\}$. Because $(x, z) \in T(R_C^*)$ and $(z, x) \in R_C$, SA is false. But R_C^* is clearly consistent. ∎

CHAPTER 3

Arrovian impossibility theorems

> There is only one law which by its nature requires unanimous assent. This is the social pact: For the civil association is the most voluntary act in the world; every man having been born free and master of himself, no one else may under any pretext whatever subject him without his consent.... Apart from this original contract, the votes of the greatest number always bind the rest; and this is a consequence of the contract itself.
>
> Jean-Jacques Rousseau*

0 Introduction

Consider a group of individuals characterized by the coexistence of the potential benefit of cooperation within the group, and the conflict with respect to the way the fruit thereof is to be distributed among members. In order that this group may form a cooperative society that is organizationally stable as a voluntary association of free individuals, a prior and binding agreement on the rule for resolving such distributional conflicts as may arise among them in the future seems to be definitely needed. An important and distinctive feature of this problem of rule design is that individuals do not, and indeed cannot, necessarily foresee the issues that may possibly be in dispute, nor do they have full information as to the natural abilities and other personal characteristics of each other. The purpose of this chapter is to consider the problem of rule design paying due attention to this informational constraint.

It was unmistakably Arrow's seminal work (1950, 1963) that initiated a fully articulated study of this problem of rule design. According to his celebrated general impossibility theorem, a set of seemingly reasonable axioms that are meant to crystallize minimal requirements on the "democratic" rule for resolving the conflicting claims of individuals is demonstrably self-contradictory, so that there cannot possibly exist a satisfactory rule. The implication of this striking result is very negative and sweeping indeed. But one should not fail to recognize that Arrow's theorem and related negative

* J.-J. Rousseau, *The Social Contract* (translated and introduced by M. Cranston). Harmondsworth, Middlesex: Penguin Books, 1968, pp. 152–3.

results may well serve as a signal that forces us to reexamine the conceptual framework of the analysis of rule design. Viewed in this way, the thrust of the apparently negative assertions may turn out to be quite positive after all. It is with this prospect in view that we focus our attention on Arrow's theorem and the variants thereof throughout this chapter.

The plan of this chapter is as follows. In Section 1 we formally introduce the concept of a collective choice rule and coin our basic terminology. Arrow's general impossibility theorem is the center of our concern in Section 2, and in Section 3 we discuss several generalizations thereof. In Section 4 we examine the effect of weakening our requirement of collective rationality on the general impossibility theorems, and we go on to explore the impossibility theorems without collective rationality. Finally, in Section 5 we state several qualifications of the analysis presented in this chapter.

1 Collective choice rule

1.1 Basic concepts

Let there be n individuals, $2 \leq n < +\infty$, who gather together to form a society for their mutual benefit without having full information concerning the natural abilities and other relevant personal characteristics of each other. Let these individuals be labeled $i = 1, 2, \ldots, n$, and let $N = \{1, 2, \ldots, n\}$ denote the set of individuals.

By a social state we mean a complete specification of the economic, social, and other features of the world that can possibly affect the welfare of individuals. Let X stand for the set of all conceivable social states that can possibly be realized by the voluntary cooperation of these individuals; it is assumed to contain at least three elements. At each moment, however, only a subset of X will be made available, subject to the specified environmental constraint and the mode of cooperation among individuals. Let $\mathscr{S}$ denote the family of sets of available states. In what follows, we assume that $\mathscr{S}$ consists of and only of finite nonempty subsets of X; that is, $\mathscr{S} = \mathscr{S}_F$ in the notation of Chapter 2. To simplify our notation, however, we shall use $\mathscr{S}$ in place of $\mathscr{S}_F$ throughout the rest of this book. Because a social state is so defined as to be mutually exclusive, only a single state should eventually be chosen from each and every $S \in \mathscr{S}$. We allow a social choice set $C(S)$ from S to contain more than one state in S, but with the understanding that all states in $C(S)$ are socially judged to be equivalent.

It is assumed that the social choice is made in this way: Prior to the realization of the set $S \in \mathscr{S}$ of available states and the profile of individual preference orderings $(R_1, R_2, \ldots, R_n)$, one ordering for each individual, individuals will grope jointly for a rule of social choice – to be called a *collective choice rule* – that is a function F mapping each profile into a social choice function on a choice space $(X, \mathscr{S})$. If an agreement on F is made, then for each realized profile $(R_1, R_2, \ldots, R_n)$ a social choice function $C = F(R_1, R_2, \ldots, R_n)$ will be determined, which in its turn determines a social choice set $C(S)$ for each realized set of available social states $S \in \mathscr{S}$.

An explanation of the reason for this scenario of social choice is in order. Given a set of available states $S \in \mathscr{S}$ and a profile of individual preference orderings $(R_1, R_2, \ldots, R_n)$, it is to the greatest advantage of individual $i \in N$ to let society choose a state in $G(S, R_i)$, and (except possibly in a very rare situation) it will generally be the case that $\bigcap_{i \in N} G(S, R_i) = \varnothing$. Furthermore, it is wasteful (in the sense of being Pareto-inefficient) to choose a state in $\bigcap_{i \in N} \{S \setminus G(S, R_i)\}$. In a "normal" situation, therefore, whatever social state one may nominate as a "reasonable" social choice from the set of available states, almost inevitably there will exist some "favored" individuals and some "unfavored" individuals. Suppose that an unfavored individual resentfully attacks the "unjust" social decision declared against his expressed preference. Would one be forced to rectify the claimed injustice rendered on him? "It depends" should, we think, be the reasoned answer. The social choice would indeed be unjust and should naturally be rectified if the procedure for social choice in the face of interpersonal conflicts of views was regrettably such that it invidiously discriminated for or against any individual according to the ethically irrelevant natural and/or social contingencies associated with him. Therefore, it is a necessary condition for a procedurally just social choice that the rule of social choice be designed in the primordial stage of ignorance where such irrelevant information is prevented from being exploited. Our scenario is an analytical device to implement this necessity.

Formally speaking, a profile is a function from N into the set of all preference orderings on X, and a collective choice rule is a function from the set A of all profiles into the set of all choice functions on a choice space $(X, \mathscr{S})$. For any profile $a \in A$, we occasionally write $a(i)$ $(i \in N)$ as R_i^a and $a = (R_1^a, R_2^a, \ldots, R_n^a)$. Furthermore, a social choice function that a collective choice rule F associates with a profile $a \in A$ will be denoted by $C^a = F(a)$.

Back now to the problem of rule design. We take the point of view that a satisfactory collective choice rule is one that is unanimously accepted by each and every individual. By being unanimously accepted, we mean here that a rule in question satisfies a set of axioms, each component of which succeeds in securing unanimous assent. Our search for a satisfactory collective choice rule thus boils down to characterizing a rule that satisfies such a set of axioms.

1.2 Universality and independence: two basic axioms

There are two basic axioms regarding a rule that we shall maintain throughout this chapter. The first axiom is the requirement of universal applicability of a rule, which reads as follows.

Condition U (unrestricted domain)
The domain of a collective choice rule consists of all logically possible profiles of individual preference orderings.

Why should we require this much robustness of a rule? Is it not an unnecessarily ambitious attempt to seek a universally applicable rule, thereby making the task of the rule designer unreasonably difficult, if in every actual application thereof the individual's de facto preferences are circumscribed rather narrowly by the factors of birth, wealth, social status, education, and other social and natural contingencies? Something must be said to guard the condition U against this criticism.

Our plea goes as follows. Although we have no intention to deny the fact that our preferences are not randomly generated, but are socially conditioned and endogenously circumscribed, we note at the same time that these conditioning endogenous factors are precisely the outcome of the socioeconomic game, the rule of which is precisely the subject matter of our inquiry. Just as in the case of parlor games, the rule of the socioeconomic game must be designed and agreed on prior to commencement of the game. But in the primordial stage of rule design, the fate of the prospective members of the society is hidden behind the Rawlsian "veil of ignorance," so that a rule of the game must be designed in such a way as to be robust enough to satisfy the condition U.

The second axiom we want to discuss here is basically a requirement of informational efficiency of a rule. To motivate this condition, consider a profile $a = (R_1^a, R_2^a, \ldots, R_n^a) \in A$ and a set of available states $S \in \mathscr{S}$. How much detailed information do we need of a in order to choose socially from the set S, paying due attention to individual wishes? It seems to be minimally necessary to collect information about $R_i^a(S) = R_i^a \cap (S \times S)$ for all $i \in N$, namely the ranking of social states in S by each and every individual, if indeed we want to take individual wishes into consideration at all. The axiom in question, which is nothing other than Arrow's requirement of *independence of irrelevant alternatives* (Arrow, 1963, pp. 26–8), declares that these minimal informational inputs are all we need in order to arrive at the proper social choice from S. In view of the transactions costs for information gathering, processing, and transmitting, the practical appeal of this requirement of informational efficiency of the preference aggregation mechanism seems to be fairly substantial. Formally, the axiom can be expressed as follows.

Condition I (independence)
If two profiles $a = (R_1^a, R_2^a, \ldots, R_n^a) \in A$ and $b = (R_1^b, R_2^b, \ldots, R_n^b) \in A$ and an opportunity set $S \in \mathscr{S}$ are such that $R_i^a(S) = R_i^b(S)$ for all $i \in N$, then $C^a(S) = C^b(S)$ holds true, where $C^a = F(a)$ and $C^b = F(b)$.

Condition I is called the independence-of-irrelevant-alternatives axiom because it requires that social choice over a set of "relevant" available alternatives must depend on the individual orderings over only those alternatives, not on any other "irrelevant" alternatives that are not actually available. It seems to us that the most forceful argument in support of this condition is that provided by Arrow, which deserves to be cited in full:

> The essential point of the modern insistence on ordinal utility is the application of Leibniz's principle of the identity of indiscernibles. Only observable differences can be used as a basis for explanation.... The Condition of Independence of Irrelevant Alternatives extends the requirement of observability one step farther. Given the set of alternatives available for society to choose among, it could be expected that, ideally, one could observe all preferences among the available alternatives, but there would be no way to observe preferences among alternatives not feasible for society. [Arrow, 1963, pp. 109–10]

Several remarks on the meaning of this critical condition are in order. First, it is occasionally asserted that it is condition I that excludes the use of information concerning the individual's preference intensities, whatever sense this latter expression may be given. Note, however, that the very concept of a collective choice rule as a function mapping a profile of individual preference *orderings* into a social choice function completes the exclusion of any information other than the ranking of alternatives by individuals.

Second, care should be taken concerning the occasional unfortunate confusions in the literature between condition I and Chernoff's axiom of choice consistency, despite rather obvious contextual differences between them.[1] Note that Nash's axiom of choice consistency is also occasionally referred to as the independence-of-irrelevant-alternatives axiom. In what follows, the independence axiom always refers to the family of the Arrovian requirement.

Our third remark is concerned with the relationship between condition I and the binary variant thereof, which is defined as follows.

Condition BI (binary independence)
If two profiles $a = (R_1^a, R_2^a, \ldots, R_n^a) \in A$ and $b = (R_1^b, R_2^b, \ldots, R_n^b) \in A$ and $x, y \in X$ are such that $R_i^a(\{x, y\}) = R_i^b(\{x, y\})$ for all $i \in N$, then $C^a(\{x, y\}) = C^b(\{x, y\})$ holds true, where $C^a = F(a)$ and $C^b = F(b)$.

Clearly, condition I implies condition BI as a special case, but the converse implication does not hold true in general. We shall show, however, that in the special case, with which Arrow (1963) was concerned, the converse in fact holds true. The proof of this assertion will be given in Section 2.

Last, we note that condition I is, for all its intuitive appeal, a rather stringent simplicity requirement. To bring this fact into relief, we have only to ask the following question: How much can we modify the individual preference orderings without affecting the social choice from $\{x, y\}$? As long as a rule of our concern obeys the condition BI (or, a fortiori, condition I), we can in fact move around any z ($\neq x, y$) as much as we care to indicate without bringing about any change in the social choice from $\{x, y\}$ if only individual preferences are kept intact over $\{x, y\}$. The force of this condition cannot be overemphasized, but it still seems to be a desirable and practically appealing axiom.[2]

2 Arrow's impossibility theorem

2.1 *Collective rationality*

Arrow's seminal work (1950, 1963, 1967*a*, 1967*c*) on the problem of rule design made use of a conceptual framework that is slightly different from ours, and it is worth our while to make clear their relationships.

Instead of our collective choice rule, Arrow talks about a *social welfare function,* by which is meant "a process or rule which, for each [profile] of individual orderings $R_1, \ldots, R_n$ for alternative social states (one ordering for each individual), states a corresponding social ordering of alternative social states, R" (Arrow, 1963, p. 23). He then defines "the [social] choice function [$C(S)$] derived from the social ordering R to be the choice which society would actually make if confronted with a set of alternatives S [through the optimization of R over S]" (Arrow, 1963, p. 26). Viewed from the standpoint of our framework, Arrow's restriction via the concept of a social welfare function on the admissible class of rules can be phrased as follows.

Condition FR (full rationality)
For each profile $a = (R_1^a, R_2^a, \ldots, R_n^a) \in A$, $C^a = F(a)$ should be a full rational choice function.

Intuitively speaking, the condition FR requires that to each profile of individual preference ordering there correspond a collective preference ordering that rationalizes the social choice function. In our judgment, this is the weakest link in the Arrovian theory of social choice, and in due time we shall have to face up to the question Why *collective* rationality? Before coming to that point, however, let us see just where this axiom, coupled with other axioms required by Arrow, brings us. The force of this requirement of collective full rationality can be exemplified by the following theorem, to which we have already alluded.

Theorem 3.1
A full rational collective choice rule satisfies the binary independence condition (BI) if and only if it satisfies the independence condition (I).

Proof: Clearly, we have only to prove that BI implies I if F is full rational. To show this, let $a = (R_1^a, R_2^a, \ldots, R_n^a) \in A$, $b = (R_1^b, R_2^b, \ldots, R_n^b) \in A$, and $S \in \mathscr{S}$ be such that $R_i^a(S) = R_i^b(S)$ for all $i \in N$. We then have $R_i^a(\{x, y\}) = R_i^b(\{x, y\})$ for all $i \in N$ if $\{x, y\}$ is a pair-set contained in S. By virtue of BI, we then have

$$\forall \{x, y\} \subset S: C^a(\{x, y\}) = C^b(\{x, y\}) \tag{3.1}$$

C^h $(h = a, b)$ being full rational, we obtain

$$\forall \{x, y\} \subset S: \{x, y\} \cap C^h(S) = \begin{cases} \varnothing \\ \vee \\ C^h(\{x, y\}) \end{cases} \tag{3.2}$$

where $h = a, b$, in view of Theorem 2.2. It then follows that

$$\begin{aligned} C^h(S) &= C^h(S) \cap \left[\bigcup_{\{x,y\} \subset S} \{x, y\} \right] \\ &= \bigcup_{\{x,y\} \subset S} [C^h(S) \cap \{x, y\}] \\ &= \bigcup_{\substack{\{x,y\} \subset S \\ \{x,y\} \cap C^h(S) \neq \varnothing}} C^h(\{x, y\}) \end{aligned}$$

where $h = a, b$. Taking (3.1) into consideration, we then obtain $C^a(S) = C^b(S)$, as was to be proved. ∎

2.2 *Pareto unanimity principles*

To complete a set of the Arrovian axioms on a satisfactory collective choice rule, we now introduce several versions of Pareto unanimity principles that occupy the central place in the modern theory of welfare economics.[3]

Condition P (Pareto principle)
For every profile $a = (R_1^a, R_2^a, \ldots, R_n^a) \in A$ and every $x, y \in X$, if we have $(x, y) \in \bigcap_{i \in N} P(R_i^a)$, then $[x \in S \rightarrow y \notin C^a(S)]$ holds true for every $S \in \mathscr{S}$, where $C^a = F(a)$.

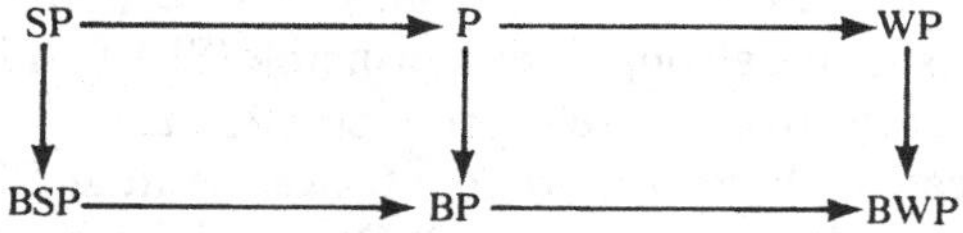

Figure 3.1. Pareto unanimity conditions.

Condition BP (binary Pareto principle)
For every profile $a = (R_1^a, R_2^a, \ldots, R_n^a) \in A$ and every $x, y \in X$, if we have $(x, y) \in \bigcap_{i \in N} P(R_i^a)$, then $\{x\} = C^a(\{x, y\})$ holds true, where $C^a = F(a)$.

Condition SP (strong Pareto principle)
For every profile $a = (R_1^a, R_2^a, \ldots, R_n^a) \in A$ and every $x, y \in X$, if $(x, y) \in P(\bigcap_{i \in N} R_i^a)$, then $[x \in S \rightarrow y \notin C^a(S)]$ for every $S \in \mathscr{S}$, where $C^a = F(a)$.

Condition BSP (binary strong Pareto principle)
For every profile $a = (R_1^a, R_2^a, \ldots, R_n^a) \in A$ and every $x, y \in X$, if $(x, y) \in P(\bigcap_{i \in N} R_i^a)$, then $\{x\} = C^a(\{x, y\})$, where $C^a = F(a)$.

Condition WP (weak Pareto principle)
For every profile $a = (R_1^a, R_2^a, \ldots, R_n^a) \in A$ and every $x, y \in X$, if $(x, y) \in \bigcap_{i \in N} P(R_i^a)$, then $[\{x \in S \;\&\; y \in C^a(S)\} \rightarrow x \in C^a(S)]$ for all $S \in \mathscr{S}$, where $C^a = F(a)$.

Condition BWP (binary weak Pareto principle)
For every profile $a = (R_1^a, R_2^a, \ldots, R_n^a) \in A$ and every $x, y \in X$, if $(x, y) \in \bigcap_{i \in N} P(R_i^a)$, then $x \in C^a(\{x, y\})$, where $C^a = F(a)$.

These conditions naturally decompose into three pairs, the second condition in each pair being a binary variant of the first condition in that pair. Condition P requires that if every individual prefers x to y, then society should not choose y from an opportunity set that contains x. Condition SP weakens the antecedent of condition P, and condition WP weakens the concluding part of condition P, so that the validity of the logical assertions in Figure 3.1 are obviously true, and Theorem 3.2 puts forward a condition that guarantees the reversibility of the vertical arrows therein.

Theorem 3.2

(a) Let F be a collective choice rule that satisfies Chernoff's axiom (CA). Then F satisfies Pareto principle (P) if and only if it satisfies the binary Pareto principle (BP).

(b) Let F be a collective choice rule that satisfies Chernoff's axiom (CA). Then F satisfies the strong Pareto principle (SP) if and only if it satisfies the binary strong Pareto principle (BSP).

(c) Let F be a collective choice rule that satisfies the dual Chernoff axiom (DCA). Then F satisfies the weak Pareto principle (WP) if and only if it satisfies the binary weak Pareto principle (BWP).[4]

Proof: To prove the nontrivial part of (a) and (b), assume that F satisfies BP [resp. BSP], and let $a = (R_1^a, R_2^a, \ldots, R_n^a) \in A$ and x, $y \in X$ be such that $(x, y) \in \bigcap_{i \in N} P(R_i^a)$ [resp. $(x, y) \in P(\bigcap_{i \in N} R_i^a)$]. Let there be an $S \in \mathcal{S}$ such that $x \in S$ and $y \in C^a(S)$, negating that F satisfies P [resp. SP]. By virtue of Chernoff's axiom on C^a, we have

$$\{x, y\} \cap C^a(S) \subset C^a(\{x, y\})$$

the right-hand side of which reduces to $\{x\}$ by virtue of BP [resp. BSP], and the left-hand side contains y by assumption. This contradiction establishes the desired result.

To prove the nontrivial part of (c), assume that F satisfies BWP, and let $a = (R_1^a, R_2^a, \ldots, R_n^a) \in A$ and $x, y \in X$ be such that $(x, y) \in \bigcap_{i \in N} P(R_i^a)$. If F does not satisfy WP, there exists an $S \in \mathcal{S}$ such that $y \in C^a(S)$ and $x \in S \setminus C^a(S)$. Because C^a satisfies the dual Chernoff axiom and $y \in \{x, y\} \cap C^a(S) \neq \varnothing$, we obtain

$$C^a(\{x, y\}) \subset \{x, y\} \cap C^a(S)$$

But this is a contradiction, because BWP implies that $x \in C^a(\{x, y\})$, and we have $\{x, y\} \cap C^a(S) = \{y\}$, establishing the desired result. ∎

In passing, let us note that condition FR and condition P are requirements that apply to any fixed profile of individual preference orderings and, as such, do not involve comparisons between social choice functions corresponding to different profiles. In contrast, condition I is concerned with the responsiveness of the social choice function to the variations in profiles. In Fishburn's terminology (1973), the former class of conditions is called the *intraprofile condition*, and the latter class of conditions is referred to as the *interprofile condition*.

2.3 *Impossibility theorems*

How broad is a class of collective choice rules satisfying Arrovian axioms of unrestricted domain, collective full rationality, independence, and Pareto principle? Full characterization of such a class of rules was conducted by Arrow (1950, 1963), according to which these seemingly mild conditions are in fact demanding enough to annihilate all but a few highly unappealing pathological rules.

Several auxiliary concepts and definitions are in order before we set about presenting Arrow's theorem. Let $\mathscr{V}_N$ denote the family of all nonempty subsets of N. We shall say that a "coalition" $V \in \mathscr{V}_N$ is *decisive* for a rule F on an ordered pair of states $(x, y) \in X \times X$ if and only if

$$(x, y) \in \bigcap_{i \in V} P(R_i^a) \rightarrow \{x\} = C^a(\{x, y\}) \tag{3.3}$$

holds true for every profile $a = (R_1^a, R_2^a, \ldots, R_n^a) \in A$, where $C^a = F(a)$. Likewise, a $V \in \mathscr{V}_N$ is said to be *almost decisive* for a rule F on an ordered pair of states $(x, y) \in X \times X$ if and only if

$$\left[(x, y) \in \bigcap_{i \in V} P(R_i^a) \;\&\; (y, x) \in \bigcap_{i \in N \setminus V} P(R_i^a)\right] \rightarrow \{x\} = C^a(\{x, y\}) \tag{3.4}$$

holds true for every profile $a = (R_1^a, R_2^a, \ldots, R_n^a) \in A$, where $C^a = F(a)$. In words, a group of individuals V is decisive [resp. almost decisive] for (x, y) if and only if they can secure the *unique* choice of x in the binary choice context $\{x, y\}$ by their concerted preference for x against y *whatever preferences individuals outside V may express* [resp. *even if individuals outside V express their concerted preference for y against x*]. Obviously, decisiveness implies almost decisiveness, but not vice versa in general.

Related, but slightly different, is the concept of a blocking coalition, which goes as follows. A $V \in \mathscr{V}_N$ is said to be *blocking* for a rule F on an ordered pair of states $(x, y) \in X \times X$ if and only if

$$(x, y) \in \bigcap_{i \in V} P(R_i^a) \rightarrow x \in C^a(\{x, y\}) \tag{3.5}$$

holds true for every $a \in A$, whereas a $V \in \mathscr{V}_N$ is said to be *almost blocking* for a rule F on an ordered pair of states $(x, y) \in X \times X$ if and only if

$$\left[(x, y) \in \bigcap_{i \in V} P(R_i^a) \;\&\; (y, x) \in \bigcap_{i \in N \setminus V} P(R_i^a)\right] \rightarrow x \in C^a(\{x, y\}) \tag{3.6}$$

holds true for every $a \in A$. In words, a group of individuals V is blocking [resp. almost blocking] for (x, y) if and only if they can block the *unique* choice of y in the binary choice context $\{x, y\}$ by their concerted preference for x against y *whatever preferences individuals outside V may express* [resp. *even if individuals outside V express their concerted preference for y against x*]. It is clear that V being blocking for (x, y) implies V being almost blocking for the same pair, but not necessarily vice versa.

Note that the foregoing concepts of decisiveness, almost decisiveness, blockingness, and almost blockingness are *local* concepts in the sense that they refer to a specified pair of states. Going one step further, let us say that a $V \in \mathscr{V}_N$ is decisive [resp. blocking] for a rule F on a set $S \in \mathscr{S}$ if and only if V is decisive [resp. blocking] for F on every ordered pair $(x, y) \in S \times S$. In particular, if a $V \in \mathscr{V}_N$ is decisive [resp. blocking] for a rule F on the universal set X, we say that V is *globally decisive* [resp. *globally blocking*] for F.

We are now in the stage of defining the concept of the oligarchy and that of the dictator, which are due to Gibbard (1969) and Arrow (1963), respectively. We say that a coalition $V \in \mathscr{V}_N$ is an *oligarchy* for F if and only if (a) V is globally decisive for F and (b) each member of V is globally blocking for F, so that, for every $x, y \in X$ and every $a = (R_1^a, R_2^a, \ldots, R_n^a) \in A$,

$$\begin{cases} (x, y) \in \bigcap_{i \in V} P(R_i^a) \rightarrow \{x\} = C^a(\{x, y\}) \\ \& \\ (x, y) \in \bigcup_{i \in V} P(R_i^a) \rightarrow x \in C^a(\{x, y\}) \end{cases} \tag{3.7}$$

holds true, where $C^a = F(a)$.[5] We say that an individual $i_0 \in N$ is a *dictator* for F if and only if $\{i_0\}$ is globally decisive for F. If a collective choice rule F admits the existence of an oligarchy [resp. a dictator], we say that F is *oligarchic* [resp. *dictatorial*].

The following important lemma establishes that even a single instance of local almost decisiveness [resp. local almost blockingness] cannot surface without implying the global and stronger version thereof if a collective choice rule satisfies several conditions introduced so far.

Lemma 3.1
Assume that $\#X \geq 3$. Let F be a collective choice rule that satisfies unrestricted domain (U), quasi-transitive rationality (QTR), binary independence (BI), and the binary Pareto principle (BP). Then a coalition $V \in \mathscr{V}_N$ that is almost decisive [resp. almost blocking] for F on some $(x, y) \in X \times X$ is globally decisive [resp. globally blocking] for F.

Proof: Let $V \in \mathscr{V}_N$ be an almost decisive coalition for F on $(x, y) \in X \times X$, and take any pair of states $(x^*, y^*) \in X \times X$. We are home (as far as the decisiveness part is concerned) if we can show that V is decisive for F on (x^*, y^*). There are several cases to be treated separately.

Case 1: $\{x, y\} \cap \{x^*, y^*\} = \varnothing$

Consider a profile $a = (R_1^a, R_2^a, \ldots, R_n^a) \in A$ whose restriction on $S = \{x, y, x^*, y^*\}$ is as follows:[6]

$$\begin{aligned} R_i^a(S) \quad &\text{for} \quad i \in V\text{: } x^*, x, y, y^* \\ R_i^a(S) \quad &\text{for} \quad i \in N \setminus V\text{: } y, (x^*, y^*), x \end{aligned} \tag{3.8}$$

By virtue of condition U, F should be able to generate a choice function corresponding to this profile, say $C^a = F(a)$. Thanks to condition BP, we obtain

$$\{x^*\} = C^a(\{x^*, x\}) \tag{3.9}$$

and

$$\{y\} = C^a(\{y^*, y\}) \tag{3.10}$$

whereas V being almost decisive for F on (x, y) implies that

$$\{x\} = C^a(\{x, y\}) \tag{3.11}$$

Successive applications of condition QTR then yield $\{x^*\} = C^a(\{x^*, y^*\})$. Invoking condition BI, we can then assert that V is decisive for F on (x^*, y^*) in this case.

Case 2: $\{x, y\} \cap \{x^*, y^*\}$ is a singleton set

Consider a subcase where $x = x^*$, and choose a profile $b = (R_1^b, R_2^b, \ldots, R_n^b) \in A$ such that

$$\begin{aligned} &R_i^b(S') \quad \text{for} \quad i \in V\text{: } x = x^*, y, y^* \\ &R_i^b(S') \quad \text{for} \quad i \in N \setminus V\text{: } y, (x = x^*, y^*) \end{aligned} \tag{3.12}$$

where $S' = \{x, y, y^*\}$. By virtue of condition BP, we obtain $\{y\} = C^b(\{y, y^*\})$, and almost decisiveness of V for F on (x, y) yields $\{x\} = C^b(\{x, y\})$. Thanks to condition QTR, it then follows that $\{x\} = C^b(\{x, y^*\})$; that is, $\{x^*\} = C^b(\{x^*, y^*\})$, as desired. Three other subcases can be treated similarly.

Case 3: $\{x, y\} = \{x^*, y^*\}$

If $x^* = y$ and $y^* = x$, we take a $z \in X \setminus \{x^*, y^*\}$ and apply the result in case 2 successively. [Such a z does exist by virtue of $\#X \geq 3$.] Explicitly, almost decisiveness of V for F on (x, y) implies decisiveness of V for F on (z, y), and hence almost decisiveness of V for F on (z, y), which in its turn implies that V is decisive (hence almost decisive) for F on (z, y^*). The last assertion then implies that V is decisive for F on (x^*, y^*). If $x^* = x$ and $y^* = y$ are true, then our result in the case where $x^* = y$ and $y^* = x$ can be used twice to conclude the proof-of-decisiveness part of the lemma.

Suppose now that $V \in \mathscr{V}_N$ is almost blocking for F on $(x, y) \in X \times X$, and take any ordered pair of states $(x^*, y^*) \in X \times X$ as before. We have only to indicate where and how the foregoing proof for the decisiveness part should be modified. Consider case 1. Our argument can be exactly the same up to (3.10), but (3.11) should be replaced by

$$x \in C^a(\{x, y\}) \tag{3.13}$$

because V is almost blocking, rather than almost decisive, for F on (x, y). Assume that $\{y^*\} = C^a(\{x^*, y^*\})$ happens to be the case. C^a being quasi-transitive rational, we then obtain $\{y\} = C^a(\{x, y\})$, in contradiction of (3.13). We can then assert that $x^* \in C^a(\{x^*, y^*\})$, which ensures that V is blocking for F on (x^*, y^*), as desired. It would be superfluous to indicate how case 2 and case 3 can be treated. ∎

We are now at the stage of presenting the following:

Theorem 3.3

Assume that $\# X \geq 3$. If a collective choice rule F satisfies unrestricted domain (U), quasi-transitive rationality (QTR), binary independence (BI), and the binary Pareto principle (BP), then there exists an oligarchy for F (Gibbard, 1969; Sen, 1970*b*; Mas-Colell and Sonnenschein, 1972).

Proof: To begin with, note that condition BP implies that the set N of all individuals is globally decisive, so that the family $\mathscr{D}_F$ of all coalitions $V \in \mathscr{V}_N$ that are globally decisive for F is nonempty.

Step 1: We prove that

$$\forall V_1, V_2 \in \mathscr{D}_F: V_1 \cap V_2 \neq \varnothing \ \& \ V_1 \cap V_2 \in \mathscr{D}_F \tag{3.14}$$

Take any $V_1, V_2 \in \mathscr{D}_F$ and three distinct states $x, y, z \in X$. Let $S = \{x, y, z\}$, and consider a profile $a = (R_1^a, R_2^a, \ldots, R_n^a) \in A$, the restriction on S of which reads as follows:

$$\begin{aligned} &R_i^a(S) \quad \text{for} \quad i \in V_1 \cap V_2: x, y, z \\ &R_i^a(S) \quad \text{for} \quad i \in V_1 \setminus V_2: (x, z), y \\ &R_i^a(S) \quad \text{for} \quad i \in V_2 \setminus V_1: y, (x, z) \\ &R_i^a(S) \quad \text{for} \quad i \in N \setminus (V_1 \cup V_2): (x, z), y \end{aligned} \tag{3.15}$$

Because $(x, y) \in \bigcap_{i \in V_1} P(R_i^a)$ and $V_1 \in \mathscr{D}_F$, we have $\{x\} = C^a(\{x, y\})$. Likewise, we obtain $\{y\} = C^a(\{y, z\})$ from $(y, z) \in \bigcap_{i \in V_2} P(R_i^a)$ and $V_2 \in \mathscr{D}_F$. Thanks to quasi-transitive rationality of C^a, it then follows that $\{x\} = C^a(\{x, z\})$. If it so happens that $V_1 \cap V_2 = \varnothing$, then the profile a places no constraint whatsoever on the restricted profile $(R_1^a(\{x,z\}),\ldots,R_n^a(\{x,z\}))$, as is clear from (3.15); yet we have $\{x\} = C^a(\{x,z\})$. This is a clear contradiction of condition BP. Therefore, it should be the case that $V_1 \cap V_2 \neq \emptyset$. Note, then, that $V_1 \cap V_2$ is decisive for F on (x,z), so that it is globally decisive, thanks to Lemma 3.1, namely $V_1 \cap V_2 \in \mathscr{D}_F$.

Step 2: Next we show that $\mathscr{D}_F$ has a unique smallest element.[7] Let $V_1, V_2 \in \mathscr{D}_F$ be the smallest elements of $\mathscr{D}_F$. Because $V_1 \cap V_2 \in \mathscr{D}_F$, by virtue of step 1, the smallestness of V_1 and V_2 is contradicted unless $V_1 = V_2$. This establishes the uniqueness of the smallest element of $\mathscr{D}_F$, assuming that there exists at least one. But the existence is in no dispute, because $\mathscr{D}_F$ is a finite family of finite sets. Let V_0 denote the unique smallest element of $\mathscr{D}_F$.

Step 3: For every $j \in V_0$, we now prove that $\{j\}$ is globally blocking. Take any $j \in V_0$ and fix it for the rest of this step. Take three distinct states $x, y, z \in X$ and consider a profile $a = (R_1^a, R_2^a, \ldots, R_n^a) \in A$ whose restriction on $S = \{x, y, z\}$ is given by

$$\begin{aligned} &R_j^a(S): y, (x,z) \\ &R_i^a(S) \quad \text{for} \quad i \in V_0 \setminus \{j\}: x, y, z \qquad (3.16) \\ &R_i^a(S) \quad \text{for} \quad i \in N \setminus V_0: (x,z), y \end{aligned}$$

V_0 being globally decisive, $(y,z) \in \bigcap_{i \in V_0} P(R_i^a)$ entails $\{y\} = C^a(\{y,z\})$, and we must have $\{x\} \neq C^a(\{x,z\})$, because $V_0 \setminus \{j\} \notin \mathscr{D}_F$, by the smallestness of V_0. If it happens to be the case that $\{x\} = C^a(\{x, y\})$, quasi-transitive rationality of C^a implies that $\{x\} = C^a(\{x,z\})$, a contradiction. Therefore, $y \in C^a(\{x, y\})$ must be the case. Thus, we have shown that

$$\left[(y,x) \in P(R_j^a) \ \& \ (x,y) \in \bigcap_{i \in N \setminus \{j\}} P(R_i^a)\right] \rightarrow y \in C^a(\{x,y\})$$

so that $\{j\}$ is almost blocking for F on (y,x), where we are invoking condition BI. Thanks to Lemma 3.1, we are now assured that $\{j\}$ is globally blocking. V_0 being globally decisive, with $\{j\}$ being globally blocking for every $j \in V_0$, this completes our proof that F has an oligarchy, namely V_0. ∎

This is a rather perplexing result. It shows unambiguously that a set of axioms on a class of admissible rules that seems at first sight to be fairly modest and not unreasonable in fact turns out to be overly demanding and annihilates all rules except for oligarchic rules, which are difficult to accept as the basis of voluntary cooperation of free individuals. Arrow's requirement of collective rationality is in fact stronger than what is assumed in Theorem 3.3, which brings us to a more exacting result.

Theorem 3.4
Assume that $\# X \geq 3$. If a collective choice rule F satisfies the unrestricted domain (U), full rationality (FR), binary independence (BI), and the binary Pareto principle (BP), then F is dictatorial (Arrow, 1950; 1963, Chapter VIII).

Proof: Invoking Theorem 3.3, we can assert that F admits an oligarchy V_0. Take an $i_0 \in V_0$ and three distinct states x, y, z. Let $S = \{x, y, z\}$, and consider a profile $a = (R_1^a, R_2^a, \ldots, R_n^a) \in A$ that satisfies

$$\begin{aligned} & R_{i_0}^a(S): x, y, z \\ & R_i^a(S) \quad \text{for} \quad i \in V_0 \setminus \{i_0\}: y, z, x \\ & R_i^a(S) \quad \text{for} \quad i \in N \setminus V_0: z, x, y \end{aligned} \tag{3.17}$$

V_0 being globally decisive, $(y, z) \in \bigcap_{i \in V_0} P(R_i^a)$ in (3.17) implies that $\{y\} = C^a(\{y, z\})$. If we had $\{y\} = C^a(\{x, y\})$, $V_0 \setminus \{i_0\}$ would become almost decisive for F on $\{x, y\}$, and hence globally decisive by virtue of Lemma 3.1, in contradiction of the smallestness of $V_0 \in \mathscr{D}_F$. Therefore, $x \in C^a(\{x, y\})$ must be the case. Taking $\{y\} = C^a(\{y, z\})$ into consideration, we then have $\{x\} = C^a(\{x, z\})$, where use is made of full rationality of C^a. It then follows that $\{i_0\}$ is almost decisive for F on (x, z), and hence is globally decisive, so that we must conclude that $V_0 = \{i_0\}$ in view of the smallestness of $V_0 \in \mathscr{D}_F$. ▮

3 Refinements on Arrow's impossibility theorem

3.1 *Collective acyclic rationality*

Given the unrestricted domain (U), binary independence (BI), and the binary Pareto principle (BP), the requirement of collective rationality brings about an extremely "undemocratic" distribution of the decisive power among individuals: The requirement of collective full rationality can be accommodated only by admitting the existence of a dictator (Theorem 3.4), and the requirement of collective quasi-transitive rationality implies the existence of an oligarchy (Theorem 3.3). Confronted with these devastating and somewhat paradoxical results, one naturally feels that the requirement of collective rationality is far more insidious than it seems at first sight. In Section 4 we shall study extensively the raison d'être thereof and the effect of weakening it on the possibility of "democratic" collective decisions. Before coming to that, we should like to see the robustness of the foregoing results by considering several refinements on the Arrovian theorems.

In the first place, following Mas–Colell and Sonnenschein (1972), we consider the effect of still further weakening the requirement of collective rationality into collective acyclic rationality on the otherwise Arrovian collective choice rules. The importance of this investigation lies mainly in the fact that acyclic rationality is in fact the bare bone of the concept of rationality in our present context, where we assume $\mathcal{S} = \mathcal{S}_F$ (see Theorem 2.9).

With this purpose in mind, let us introduce several additional concepts. First, we say that an individual $i_0 \in N$ is a *vetoer* for a rule F if and only if the singleton set $\{i_0\}$ is globally blocking for F; that is,

$$(x, y) \in P(R^a_{i_0}) \to x \in C^a(\{x, y\}) \tag{3.18}$$

holds true for every $x, y \in X$ and every $a = (R^a_1, R^a_2, \ldots, R^a_n) \in A$. Second, we say, following Bordes and Salles (1978), that a vetoer $i_0 \in N$ for F is a *quasi dictator* for F if, in addition,

$$(x, y) \in P(R^a_{i_0}) \cap \left[\bigcup_{j \in N \setminus \{i_0\}} R^a_j \right] \to \{x\} = C^a(\{x, y\}) \tag{3.19}$$

holds true for every $x, y \in X$ and every $a = (R^a_1, R^a_2, \ldots, R^a_n) \in A$. In words, a quasi dictator can ensure nonrejection of x in the binary choice situation $\{x, y\}$ by his strictly preferring x to y, and he can ensure the unique choice of x over y if, additionally, he is at least weakly supported by at least one other individual. Finally, we require the following condition, an intuitive interpretation of which goes as follows. If an individual changes his preference by moving from strictly preferring y to x into indifference between them, or from indifference between x and y into strictly preferring x to y, then in the case where initially x was not rejected in the binary choice situation $\{x, y\}$, x will subsequently become the unique choice in rejection of y.

Condition PR (positive responsiveness)
Let $a = (R^a_1, R^a_2, \ldots, R^a_n) \in A$ and $i \in N$ be given and $x, y \in X$ be arbitrary. If $b = (R^b_1, R^b_2, \ldots, R^b_n) \in A$ results in $C^b = F(b)$, such that $x \in C^b(\{x, y\})$, $R^a_j = R^b_j$ for all $j \in N \setminus \{i\}$, and

$$\begin{cases} (y, x) \in P(R^b_i) \ \& \ (x, y) \in I(R^a_i) \\ \vee \\ (x, y) \in I(R^b_i) \ \& \ (x, y) \in P(R^a_i) \end{cases}$$

then $\{x\} = C^a(\{x, y\})$, where $C^a = F(a)$.[8]

Theorem 3.5
Assume that $\#X \geq 3$ and $n = \#N \geq 4$. If a collective choice rule F satisfies the unrestricted domain (U), acyclic rationality (AR), binary independence (BI), the binary Pareto principle (BP), and positive responsiveness (PR), then F admits the existence of a vetoer (Mas-Colell and Sonnenschein, 1972, Theorem 3).

Proof: Let F be a rule that satisfies all the mentioned conditions.

Step 1: We show that there exists an individual $i_0 \in N$ such that for some $(x^*, y^*) \in X \times X$,

$$(x^*, y^*) \in P(R^a_{i_0}) \;\&\; (y^*, x^*) \in \bigcap_{j \in N \setminus \{i_0\}} P(R^a_j) \rightarrow x^* \in C^a(\{x^*, y^*\}) \tag{3.20}$$

holds true for every $a = (R^a_1, R^a_2, \ldots, R^a_n) \in A$.

Let $V_0 \in \mathscr{V}_N$ be a *smallest* set that is decisive for F on some pair of states $(x, y) \in X \times X$. Note that the existence of such a set is guaranteed by condition BP. Note also that the decisive power of V_0 is merely local, namely, only on (x, y), our present set of conditions on F being insufficient to support an analogue of Lemma 3.1 to go through. If $\# V_0 = 1$, then there remains nothing more to prove; so let us assume that $\# V_0 \geq 2$. Without losing generality, assume that V_0 contains 1 and 2, and partition V_0 as $V_0 = \{1,2\} \cup V_1$. Take a $z \in X \setminus \{x, y\}$, and consider a profile $b = (R^b_1, R^b_2, \ldots, R^b_n) \in A$ that satisfies

$$R^b_1(S)\text{: } x, y, z$$

$$R^b_i(S) \quad \text{for} \quad i \in \{2\} \cup V_1\text{: } z, x, y$$

$$R^b_i(S) \quad \text{for} \quad i \in N \setminus V_0\text{: } y, z, x$$

where $S = \{x, y, z\} \in \mathscr{S}$. V_0 being decisive for F on (x, y), we have $\{x\} = C^b(\{x, y\})$. If $x \in C^b(\{x, z\})$ is the case, we have (3.20) for $i_0 = 1$, $x^* = x$, and $y^* = z$, by virtue of BI. Assume, therefore, that $\{z\} = C^b(\{x, z\})$. C^b being acyclic rational, we then have $z \in C^b(\{y, z\})$.

Consider next a profile $c = (R^c_1, R^c_2, \ldots, R^c_n) \in A$ such that

$$R^c_1(\{x, y\})\text{: } x, y$$

$$R^c_2(\{x, y\})\text{: } y, x$$

$$R^c_i(\{x, y\}) \quad \text{for} \quad i \in V_1\text{: } x, y$$

$$R^c_i(\{x, y\}) \quad \text{for} \quad i \in N \setminus V_0\text{: } y, x$$

V_0 being a smallest decisive set, we have $y \in C^c(\{x, y\})$. Let a profile $d = (R_1^d, R_2^d, \ldots, R_n^d) \in A$ be such that

$$R_1^d(S)\colon [x, y, z]$$

$$R_2^d(S)\colon z, y, x$$

$$R_i^d(S) \quad \text{for} \quad i \in V_1\colon x, z, y$$

$$R_i^d(S) \quad \text{for} \quad i \in N \setminus V_0\colon y, x, z$$

Comparing c and d on $\{x, y\}$ and noting that $y \in C^c(\{x, y\})$, we obtain $\{y\} = C^d(\{x, y\})$, thanks to BI and PR. Similarly, comparing b and d on $\{y, z\}$, we obtain $\{z\} = C^d(\{y, z\})$. Acyclic rationality of C^d then yields $z \in C^d(\{x, z\})$.

Examine now a profile $e = (R_1^e, R_2^e, \ldots, R_n^e) \in A$ that satisfies

$$R_1^e(\{x, z\})\colon z, x$$

$$R_2^e(\{x, z\})\colon z, x$$

$$R_i^e(\{x, z\}) \quad \text{for} \quad i \in V_1\colon x, z$$

$$R_i^e(\{x, z\}) \quad \text{for} \quad i \in N \setminus V_0\colon x, z$$

Comparing d and e on $\{x, z\}$ and invoking BI and PR, we obtain $\{z\} = C^e(\{x, z\})$. Note, then, that $\{1, 2\}$ turns out to be decisive for F on (z, x), so that $V_0 = \{1, 2\}$ by smallestness.

Finally, examine a profile $f = (R_1^f, R_2^f, \ldots, R_n^f) \in A$ that satisfies

$$R_1^f(S)\colon x, y, z$$

$$R_2^f(S)\colon z, x, y$$

$$R_i^f(S) \quad \text{for} \quad i \in N \setminus V_0\colon y, z, x$$

V_0 being decisive for F on (x, y), we have $\{x\} = C^f(\{x, y\})$. If $z \in C^f(\{y, z\})$ is the case, (3.20) is true with $i_0 = 2$, $x^* = z$, and $y^* = y$, and we are home. Assume, therefore, that $\{y\} = C^f(\{x, z\})$. By virtue of acyclic rationality of C^f, we obtain $x \in C^f(\{x, z\})$. Therefore, (3.20) holds true with $i_0 = 1$, $x^* = x$, and $y^* = z$. This finally establishes (3.20). Without losing generality, let us put $i_0 = 1$ in the following.

Step 2: We now show that $V_0 = \{1\}$ is in fact globally blocking for F, qualifying individual 1 as a vetoer. In the presence of PR, this can be established by proving that for all $s, t \in X$,

$$(s, t) \in P(R_i^a) \;\&\; (t, s) \in \bigcap_{j \in N \setminus \{1\}} P(R_j^a) \rightarrow s \in C^a(\{s, t\}) \tag{3.21}$$

holds true for every $a = (R_1^a, R_2^a, \ldots, R_n^a) \in A$.

Let us show, in the first place, that for all $t \in X \setminus \{x^*, y^*\}$,

$$(x^*, t) \in P(R_1^a) \;\&\; (t, x^*) \in \bigcap_{j \in N \setminus \{1\}} P(R_j^a) \rightarrow x^* \in C^a(\{x^*, t\}) \qquad (3.22)$$

holds true for every $a = (R_1^a, R_2^a, \ldots, R_n^a) \in A$.

Consider a profile $b = (R_1^b, R_2^b, \ldots, R_n^b) \in A$ satisfying

$$R_1^b(S^*)\colon x^*, y^*, t$$
$$R_2^b(S^*)\colon [x^*, y^*], t$$
$$R_3^b(S^*)\colon y^*, t, x^*$$
$$R_4^b(S^*)\colon y^*, t, x^*$$
$$R_i^b(S^*) \quad \text{for} \quad i \in N \setminus \{1, 2, 3, 4\}\colon y^*, t, x^*$$

where $S^* = \{x^*, y^*, t\} \in \mathscr{S}$. By virtue of (3.20) and PR, we have $\{x^*\} = C^b(\{x^*, y^*\})$, and BP entails $C^b(\{y^*, t\}) = \{y^*\}$. It then follows that $x^* \in C^b(\{x^*, t\})$ by virtue of acyclic rationality of C^b.

Next we consider a profile $c = (R_1^c, R_2^c, \ldots, R_n^c) \in A$ that satisfies

$$R_1^c(S^*)\colon y^*, x^*, t$$
$$R_2^c(S^*)\colon y^*, x^*, t$$
$$R_3^c(S^*)\colon t, y^*, x^*$$
$$R_4^c(S^*)\colon y^*, [x^*, t]$$
$$R_i^c(S^*) \quad \text{for} \quad i \in N \setminus \{1, 2, 3, 4\}\colon t, y^*, x^*$$

Comparing b and c on $\{x^*, t)$, and noting BI and PR on F, we get $C^c(\{x^*, t\}) = \{x^*\}$. By BP, we obtain $C^c(\{x^*, y^*\}) = \{y^*\}$. Acyclic rationality of C^c then implies that $y^* \in C^c(\{y^*, t\})$.

Consider now a profile $d = (R_1^d, R_2^d, \ldots, R_n^d) \in A$ such that

$$R_1^d(S^*)\colon x^*, y^*, t$$
$$R_2^d(S^*)\colon y^*, t, x^*$$
$$R_3^d(S^*)\colon [x^*, y^*, t]$$
$$R_4^d(S^*)\colon y^*, t, x^*$$
$$R_i^d(S^*) \quad \text{for} \quad i \in N \setminus \{1, 2, 3, 4\}\colon t, y^*, x^*$$

By virtue of (3.20) and PR, $C^d(\{x^*, y^*\}) = \{x^*\}$ holds true. Comparing c and d on $\{y^*, t\}$, and noting BI and PR, we obtain $C^d(\{y^*, t\}) = \{y^*\}$. Acyclic rationality of C^d then yields $x^* \in C^d(\{x^*, t\})$.

Examine now a profile $e = (R_1^e, R_2^e, \ldots, R_n^e) \in A$ such that

$$R_1^e(S^*)\colon y^*, x^*, t$$

$$R_2^e(S^*)\colon t, y^*, x^*$$

$$R_3^e(S^*)\colon y^*, x^*, t$$

$$R_4^e(S^*)\colon t, y^*, x^*$$

$$R_i^e(S^*) \quad \text{for} \quad i \in N \setminus \{1,2,3,4\}\colon t, y^*, x^*$$

Comparing d and e on $\{x^*, t\}$, and noting BI and PR, we obtain $C^e(\{x^*, t\}) = \{x^*\}$, and $\{y^*\} = C^e(\{x^*, y^*\})$ follows from BP. Acyclic rationality of C^e then yields $y^* \in C^e(\{y^*, t\})$.

Finally, consider a profile $f = (R_1^f, R_2^f, \ldots, R_n^f) \in A$ such that

$$R_1^f(S^*)\colon x^*, y^*, t$$

$$R_2^f(S^*)\colon t, [x^*, y^*]$$

$$R_3^f(S^*)\colon y^*, t, x^*$$

$$R_4^f(S^*)\colon [y^*, t], x^*$$

$$R_i^f(S^*) \quad \text{for} \quad i \in N \setminus \{1,2,3,4\}\colon t, y^*, x^*$$

Comparing e and f on $\{y^*, t\}$, BI and PR once again require $\{y^*\} = C^f(\{y^*, t\})$. By (3.20) and PR, we also obtain $C^f(\{x^*, y^*\}) = \{x^*\}$. Acyclic rationality of C^f yields $x^* \in C^f(\{x^*, t\})$. In view of BI, this establishes (3.22).

We have proved that (3.22) follows from (3.20). By similar argument we can prove that (3.21) follows from (3.22), concluding our proof. ∎

As a matter of fact, the assertion of Theorem 3.5 can be strengthened as follows: Not only does there exist a vetoer, there also exists a unique quasi dictator. To substantiate this claim, we have only to invoke the following result.

Theorem 3.6
Assume that $\#X \geq 3$ and $n = \#N \geq 3$. If a collective choice rule F satisfying the unrestricted domain (U), binary independence (BI), and positive responsiveness (PR) admits the existence of a vetoer, then there exists a unique quasi dictator (Bordes and Salles, 1978, Theorem 4).

Proof: Suppose that there are two vetoers for F, say 1 and 2. Consider a profile $a = (R_1^a, R_2^a, \ldots, R_n^a) \in A$ and $x, y \in X$ $(x \neq y)$ such that

$$(x, y) \in P(R_1^a) \;\&\; (y, x) \in P(R_i^a) \qquad (i = 2, 3) \tag{3.23}$$

Because 1 and 2 are vetoers, we obtain $\{x, y\} = C^a(\{x, y\})$, where $C^a = F(a)$. Consider a profile $b = (R_1^b, R_2^b, \ldots, R_n^b) \in A$ such that

$$\forall i \in N \setminus \{3\}: R_i^a(\{x, y\}) = R_i^b(\{x, y\}) \;\&\; (x, y) \in I(R_3^b) \tag{3.24}$$

By virtue of PR we then obtain $\{x\} = C^b(\{x, y\})$, which negates that individual 2 is a vetoer. Therefore, there can exist at most one vetoer for F that satisfies U, BI, and PR.

Suppose that the unique vetoer, say 1, is not a quasi dictator. Then there exist $x, y \in X$ $(x \neq y)$, $a = (R_1^a, R_2^a, \ldots, R_n^a) \in A$, and $i \in N \setminus \{1\}$ such that $(x, y) \in P(R_1^a) \cap R_i^a$ and $\{x, y\} = C^a(\{x, y\})$, where $C^a = F(a)$. Consider now another profile $b = (R_1^b, R_2^b, \ldots, R_n^b) \in A$ such that

$$\forall j \in N \setminus \{i\}: R_j^a(\{x, y\}) = R_j^b(\{x, y\})$$

$$[(x, y) \in P(R_i^a) \rightarrow (x, y) \in I(R_i^b)] \;\&\; [(x, y) \in I(R_i^a) \rightarrow (y, x) \in P(R_i^b)]$$

hold true. By virtue of PR we then have $\{y\} = C^b(\{x, y\})$, which negates 1's vetoer power. This contradiction shows us that 1 must be a quasi dictator after all. ∎

3.2 *Collective choice rules without the Pareto principle*

The second refinement on the Arrovian theorems concerns the effect of throwing away the general validity of the Pareto principle, keeping all other Arrovian axioms intact. The importance of this refinement lies basically in the fact that for all its almost unfailing endorsement in the literature on welfare economics, there are doubts concerning the unexceptional supremacy of the Paretian value judgments, and it is interesting to see how much extra mileage we can obtain if we do without the Paretian values altogether. Unfortunately, we must endorse a sad verdict: not very much.

Several modifications, together with some additions, to our previous terminology are in order. Take any $S \in \mathscr{S}$ and any $V \in \mathscr{V}_N$. We say that V is *decisive* [resp. *inversely decisive*] for a rule F on S if and only if, for every $x, y \in S$ and every $a = (R_1^a, R_2^a, \ldots, R_n^a) \in A$,

$$(x, y) \in \bigcap_{i \in V} P(R_i^a) \rightarrow \{x\} = C^a(\{x, y\}) \qquad [\text{resp. } \{y\} = C^a(\{x, y\})]$$

holds true, whereas we say that V is *blocking* [resp. *inversely blocking*] for F on S if and only if, for every $x, y \in S$ and every $a = (R_1^a, R_2^a, \ldots, R_n^a) \in A$,

$$(x, y) \in \bigcap_{i \in V} P(R_i^a) \rightarrow x \in C^a(\{x, y\}) \qquad [\text{resp. } y \in C^a(\{x, y\})]$$

holds true, where $C^a = F(a)$. Furthermore, we say that V is an *oligarchy* [resp. *inverse oligarchy*] for F on S if (a) V is decisive [resp. inversely decisive] for F on S and (b) each member of V is blocking [resp. inversely blocking] for F on S. If a singleton set $\{i_0\} \in \mathscr{V}_N$ is decisive [resp. inversely decisive] for F on S, we say that i_0 is a *dictator* [resp. *inverse dictator*] for F on S. In like manner, if a singleton set $\{i_0\} \in \mathscr{V}_N$ is blocking [resp. inversely blocking] for F on S, we say that i_0 is a *vetoer* [resp. *inverse vetoer*] for F on S.

Take any $x, y \in X$. We say that x is *imposed* [resp. *strongly imposed*] over y by F if and only if, for every $a = (R_1^a, R_2^a, \ldots, R_n^a) \in A$, $x \in C^a(\{x, y\})$ [resp. $\{x\} = C^a(\{x, y\})$] holds true, where $C^a = F(a)$.

Let us remember in passing that a *partition* of X is nothing but a family $\mathscr{E} = \{E(\lambda) \mid \lambda \in \Lambda\}$ of nonempty subsets of X such that

$$X = \bigcup_{\lambda \in \Lambda} E(\lambda) \quad \text{and} \quad E(\lambda_1) \cap E(\lambda_2) = \varnothing \quad \text{for every } \lambda_1, \lambda_2 \in \Lambda$$
$$\text{satisfying } \lambda_1 \neq \lambda_2 \tag{3.25}$$

holds true.

We are now ready to introduce a basic result due to Wilson (1972*b*) in an elaborated form by Binmore (1976).

Theorem 3.7
Suppose that a collective choice rule F satisfies the unrestricted domain (U), full rationality (FR), and binary independence (BI). Then there exists a partition $\mathscr{E} = \{E(\lambda) | \lambda \in \Lambda\}$ of X such that

(a) for every $E(\lambda_1), E(\lambda_2) \in \mathscr{E}$ $(\lambda_1 \neq \lambda_2)$, if $x \in E(\lambda_1)$ and $y \in E(\lambda_2)$, then either x is strongly imposed over y by F or y is strongly imposed over x by F,
(b) if $E(\lambda) \in \mathscr{E}$ is such that $\#E(\lambda) \geq 3$, then
(b1) there exists a dictator for F on $E(\lambda)$, or
(b2) there exists an inverse dictator for F on $E(\lambda)$, or
(b3) there exist two nonempty subsets $V_1(\lambda)$ and $V_2(\lambda)$ of N such that each member of $V_1(\lambda)$ [resp. $V_2(\lambda)$] is blocking [resp. inversely blocking] for F on $E(\lambda)$.[9]

Proof: Let a binary relation Ξ on X be defined by

$$(x, y) \in \Xi \leftrightarrow \begin{cases} x = y \\ \vee \\ \exists\, a, b \in A\colon x \in C^a(\{x, y\})\ \&\ y \in C^b(\{x, y\}) \end{cases} \tag{3.26}$$

Ξ is clearly reflexive and symmetric. To show transitivity thereof, let $(x, y) \in \Xi$ and $(y, z) \in \Xi$ be the case. If it so happens that

$x = y$ or $y = z$, $(x, z) \in \Xi$ follows immediately. Otherwise, we have

$$\exists\, a, b \in A: x \in C^a(\{x, y\})\ \&\ y \in C^b(\{y, z\}) \tag{3.27}$$

$$\exists\, a^*, b^* \in A: y \in C^{a^*}(\{x, y\})\ \&\ z \in C^{b^*}(\{y, z\}) \tag{3.28}$$

Let a profile $c \in A$ be such that

$$\forall i \in N: R_i^c(\{x, y\}) = R_i^a(\{x, y\})\ \&\ R_i^c(\{y, z\}) = R_i^b(\{y, z\})$$

It follows from (3.27) and BI that $x \in C^c(\{x, y\})$ and $y \in C^c(\{y, z\})$, so that we obtain $x \in C^c(\{x, z\})$ by virtue of full rationality of C^c. We can similarly make use of (3.28) to assert the existence of a profile $d \in A$ such that $z \in C^d(\{x, z\})$. Therefore, $(x, z) \in \Xi$ is true, as was to be verified.

Being an equivalence, Ξ induces a partition $\mathscr{E} = \{E(\lambda) | \lambda \in \Lambda\}$ of X that satisfies (a) by construction.

We now pick any $E(\lambda) \in \mathscr{E}$ such that $\# E(\lambda) \geq 3$. We prove that one and only one of the following is true for this $E(\lambda)$:

$$P_\lambda(1): \forall x, y \in E(\lambda), \forall a \in A: (x, y) \in \bigcap_{i \in N} P(R_i^a) \rightarrow \{x\} = C^a(\{x, y\})$$

$$P_\lambda(2): \forall x, y \in E(\lambda), \forall a \in A: (x, y) \in \bigcap_{i \in N} P(R_i^a) \rightarrow \{y\} = C^a(\{x, y\})$$

$$P_\lambda(3): \forall x, y \in E(\lambda), \forall a \in A: (x, y) \in \bigcap_{i \in N} P(R_i^a) \rightarrow \{x, y\} = C^a(\{x, y\})$$

Suppose that there exist $x, y, z, w \in E(\lambda)$ and $a, b \in A$ such that

$$(x, y) \in \bigcap_{i \in N} P(R_i^a)\ \&\ \{x\} = C^a(\{x, y\}) \tag{3.29}$$

and

$$(z, w) \in \bigcap_{i \in N} P(R_i^b)\ \&\ w \in C^b(\{z, w\}) \tag{3.30}$$

There are three cases to be treated separately.

Case 1: $x \neq w$

Consider a profile $c \in A$ satisfying $(x, w) \in \bigcap_{i \in N} P(R_i^c)$. Then either

$$\{x\} = C^c(\{x, w\}) \tag{3.31}$$

or

$$w \in C^c(\{x, w\}) \tag{3.32}$$

holds true. If (3.31) is the case, we consider a profile $d \in A$ such that $R_i^d(\{z, w\}) = R_i^b(\{z, w\})$ and $R_i^d(\{x, w\}) = R_i^c(\{x, w\})$ for all $i \in N$. By virtue of (3.30), (3.31), and BI, we then have $\{x\} = C^d(\{x, w\})$

and $w \in C^d(\{z, w\})$, which imply $\{x\} = C^d(\{x, z\})$ in view of full rationality of C^d. Because the profile d places no restriction on individual preferences on $\{x, z\}$, x is strongly imposed over z by F, contrary to the way $E(\lambda)$ is defined. If, on the other hand, (3.32) is the case, we consider a profile $e \in A$ that satisfies $R_i^e(\{x, y\}) = R_i^a(\{x, y\})$ and $R_i^e(\{x, w\}) = R_i^c(\{x, w\})$ for all $i \in N$. Thanks to (3.29), (3.32), and BI, we then obtain $\{x\} = C^e(\{x, y\})$ and $w \in C^e(\{x, w\})$, which yield $\{w\} = C^e(\{w, y\})$ by virtue of full rationality of C^e. Because e leaves individual preferences completely unrestricted on $\{w, y\}$, w is strongly imposed over y by F, a contradiction. Therefore, (3.29) and (3.30) cannot hold true simultaneously in this case.

Case 2: $x = w$ & $y \neq z$

Consider a profile $f \in A$ such that $(z, y) \in \bigcap_{i \in N} P(R_i^f)$. Then either

$$\{z\} = C^f(\{y, z\}) \tag{3.33}$$

or

$$y \in C^f(\{y, z\}) \tag{3.34}$$

holds true. If (3.33) [resp. (3.34)] is in fact the case, we consider a profile $g \in A$ [resp. $h \in A$] such that $R_i^g(\{z, w\}) = R_i^b(\{z, w\})$ and $R_i^g(\{y, z\}) = R_i^f(\{y, z\})$ [resp. $R_i^h(\{x, y\}) = R_i^a(\{x, y\})$ and $R_i^h(\{y, z\}) = R_i^f(\{y, z\})$] for all $i \in N$. In either case we can derive a contradiction just as in case 1.

Case 3: $x = w$ & $y = z$

Because $\# E(\lambda) \geq 3$ is true by assumption, we can take a $t \in E(\lambda) \setminus \{x, y\}$. Consider a profile $k \in A$ such that $(t, y) \in \bigcap_{i \in N} P(R_i^k)$ for which either

$$\{t\} = C^k(\{y, t\}) \tag{3.35}$$

or

$$y \in C^k(\{y, t\}) \tag{3.36}$$

is true. If (3.36) is the case, we can invoke a profile $l \in A$ such that $R_i^l(\{x, y\}) = R_i^a(\{x, y\})$ and $R_i^l(\{t, y\}) = R_i^k(\{t, y\})$ for all $i \in N$ to derive a contradiction as before. If, on the other hand, (3.35) is true, the situation is as follows:

$$(t, y) \in \bigcap_{i \in N} P(R_i^k) \ \& \ \{t\} = C^k(\{y, t\}) \tag{3.37}$$

$$(y, x) \in \bigcap_{i \in N} P(R_i^b) \ \& \ x \in C^b(\{x, y\}) \tag{3.38}$$

and $t \neq x$, where (3.30) is made use of in combination with $x = w$ and $y = z$. But this is essentially the same as case 1, and the same contradiction follows.

We have thus shown that if there exist $x, y \in E(\lambda)$ and $a \in A$ such that (3.29) is true, then $P_\lambda(1)$ must be the case. We can similarly prove that if there exist $x, y \in E(\lambda)$ and $a \in A$ such that

$$(x, y) \in \bigcap_{i \in N} P(R_i^a) \ \&\ \{y\} = C^a(\{x, y\}) \tag{3.39}$$

then $P_\lambda(2)$ must be the case. If there exist no $x, y \in E(\lambda)$ and $a \in A$ for which either (3.29) or (3.39) holds true, then clearly $P_\lambda(3)$ holds true.

Pick now any $E(\lambda) \in \mathscr{E}$ with $\# E(\lambda) \geq 3$. We are assured that one and only one of $P_\lambda(1)$, $P_\lambda(2)$, and $P_\lambda(3)$ is true.

If $P_\lambda(1)$ is the case on $E(\lambda)$, then we can invoke Theorem 3.4 to conclude the existence of a dictator on $E(\lambda)$.

Suppose now that $P_\lambda(2)$ is the case on $E(\lambda)$. Define a collective choice rule (CCR) F_λ on $E(\lambda)$ by

$$\forall a \in A, \forall x, y \in E(\lambda): x \in C_\lambda^a(\{x, y\}) \leftrightarrow y \in C^a(\{x, y\}) \tag{3.40}$$

where $C^a = F(a)$ and $C_\lambda^a = F_\lambda(a)$. Then F_λ satisfies FR, BI, and, by virtue of $P_\lambda(2)$ and (3.40), $P_\lambda(1)$ as well, so that there exists a dictator for F_λ on $E(\lambda)$. By virtue of (3.40), a dictator for F_λ is nothing other than an inverse dictator for F on $E(\lambda)$.

Finally, let $P_\lambda(3)$ be the case on $E(\lambda)$. Take any $x, y \in E(\lambda)$, and let $V_1(\lambda)$ be the smallest subset of N such that

$$\forall a \in A: (x, y) \in \bigcap_{i \in V_1(\lambda)} P(R_i^a) \rightarrow x \in C^a(\{x, y\}) \tag{3.41}$$

where $C^a = F(a)$. Such a $V_1(\lambda)$ always exists by virtue of $P_\lambda(3)$. We now prove that each member of $V_1(\lambda)$ is blocking for F on $E(\lambda)$. Take any $z \in E(\lambda) \setminus \{x, y\}$, and let a profile $b \in A$ such that $(z, y) \in \bigcup_{i \in V_1(\lambda)} P(R_i^b)$. In view of the definition of Ξ, there exists a profile $c \in A$ that yields $z \in C^c(\{x, z\})$. Let a profile $d \in A$ be such that

$$\forall i \in N: R_i^d(\{z, x\}) = R_i^c(\{z, x\}) \tag{3.42}$$

$$\begin{cases} \forall i \in V_1(\lambda): (x, y) \in P(R_i^d) \\ \& \\ \forall i \in N: R_i^d(\{y, z\}) = R_i^b(\{y, z\}) \end{cases} \tag{3.43}$$

Thanks to (3.41) and (3.43), we obtain $x \in C^d(\{x, y\})$. It follows from $z \in C^c(\{x, z\})$, (3.42), and BI that $z \in C^d(\{x, z\})$, which yields $z \in C^d(\{y, z\})$ in combination with $x \in C^d(\{x, y\})$, where use is made of full rationality of C^d. We now invoke (3.43) and BI to conclude that $z \in C^b(\{y, z\})$. We have thus shown that

$$\forall z \in E(\lambda) \setminus \{y\}, \forall a \in A: (z, y) \in \bigcup_{i \in V_1(\lambda)} P(R_i^a) \rightarrow z \in C^a(\{y, z\}) \tag{3.44}$$

By similar reasoning, we can prove that

$$\forall w \in E(\lambda) \setminus \{x\}, \forall a \in A: (x, w) \in \bigcup_{i \in V_1(\lambda)} P(R_i^a) \rightarrow x \in C^a(\{x, w\}) \tag{3.45}$$

Repeated use of (3.44) and (3.45) establishes that each member of $V_1(\lambda)$ is blocking for F on $E(\lambda)$. We can similarly prove the existence of $V_2(\lambda)$, each member of which is inversely blocking for F on $E(\lambda)$. This completes the proof. ▮

Theorem 3.8
Suppose that a collective choice rule F satisfies the unrestricted domain (U), quasi-transitive rationality (QTR), and binary independence (BI). Then there exists a partition $\mathscr{E}^* = \{E^*(\lambda) | \lambda \in \Lambda\}$ of X such that

(a) for every $E^*(\lambda_1), E^*(\lambda_2) \in \mathscr{E}^*$ $(\lambda_1 \neq \lambda_2)$, if $x \in E^*(\lambda_1)$ and $y \in E^*(\lambda_2)$, then either x is imposed over y by F or y is imposed over x by F,
(b) if $E^*(\lambda) \in \mathscr{E}^*$ is such that $\# E^*(\lambda) \geq 3$, then
(b1) there exists an oligarchy $V_+(\lambda)$ on $E^*(\lambda)$, or
(b2) there exists an inverse oligarchy $V_-(\lambda)$ on $E^*(\lambda)$, or
(b3) there exist two nonempty subsets $V_1(\lambda)$ and $V_2(\lambda)$ of N such that each member of $V_1(\lambda)$ [resp. $V_2(\lambda)$] is blocking [resp. inversely blocking] for F on $E^*(\lambda)$ (Fountain and Suzumura, 1982, Theorem 1).

Proof: Let a binary relation Ξ^* on X be defined by

$$(x, y) \in \Xi^* \leftrightarrow \begin{cases} x = y \\ \vee \\ \exists a, b \in A: \{x\} = C^a(\{x, y\}) \ \& \ \{y\} = C^b(\{x, y\}) \end{cases} \tag{3.46}$$

Ξ^* is clearly reflexive and symmetric. To prove transitivity thereof, let $x, y, z \in X$ be such that $(x, y) \in \Xi^*$ and $(y, z) \in \Xi^*$. If either $x = y$ or $y = z$ is the case, it follows immediately that $(x, z) \in \Xi^*$. Otherwise,

$$\exists a, b \in A: \{x\} = C^a(\{x, y\}) \ \& \ \{y\} = C^b(\{y, z\}) \tag{3.47}$$

$$\exists a^*, b^* \in A: \{y\} = C^{a^*}(\{x, y\}) \ \& \ \{z\} = C^{b^*}(\{y, z\}) \tag{3.48}$$

hold true. Let a profile $c \in A$ be such that $R_i^c(\{x, y\}) = R_i^a(\{x, y\})$ and $R_i^c(\{y, z\}) = R_i^b(\{y, z\})$ for all $i \in N$. It then follows from (3.47) and BI that $\{x\} = C^c(\{x, y\})$ and $\{y\} = C^c(\{y, z\})$, so that we have $\{x\} = C^c(\{x, z\})$ by virtue of quasi-transitive rationality of C^c. We can similarly make use of (3.48) to assert the existence of a profile $d \in A$ such that $\{z\} = C^d(\{x, z\})$. Therefore, $(x, z) \in \Xi^*$ is implied.

Ξ^* being an equivalence on X, we can represent X as a union of the Ξ^*-equivalence classes $\mathscr{E}^* = \{E^*(\lambda) | \lambda \in \Lambda\}$. By construction, (a) holds true.

We now pick any $E^*(\lambda) \in \mathscr{E}^*$ such that $\# E(\lambda) \geq 3$. Let us prove that one and only one of the following is true for this $E^*(\lambda)$:

$$P_\lambda(1)\colon \forall x, y \in E^*(\lambda), \forall a \in A\colon (x, y) \in \bigcap_{i \in N} P(R_i^a) \rightarrow \{x\} = C^a(\{x, y\})$$

$$P_\lambda(2)\colon \forall x, y \in E^*(\lambda), \forall a \in A\colon (x, y) \in \bigcap_{i \in N} P(R_i^a) \rightarrow \{y\} = C^a(\{x, y\})$$

$$P_\lambda(3)\colon \forall x, y \in E^*(\lambda), \forall a \in A\colon (x, y) \in \bigcap_{i \in N} P(R_i^a) \rightarrow \{x, y\} = C^a(\{x, y\})$$

Assume that there exist $x, y, z, w \in E^*(\lambda)$ and $a, b \in A$ such that

$$(x, y) \in \bigcap_{i \in N} P(R_i^a) \ \&\ \{x\} = C^a(\{x, y\}) \tag{3.49}$$

and

$$(z, w) \in \bigcap_{i \in N} P(R_i^b) \ \&\ w \in C^b(\{w, z\}) \tag{3.50}$$

There are three cases to be considered:

Case 1: $x \neq w$

Case 2: $x = w \ \&\ y \neq z$

Case 3: $x = w \ \&\ y = z$

In each case we can prove that $P_\lambda(1)$ must be true. The methods being very similar in all cases, we provide the proof in case 1 only.

Consider a profile $c \in A$ satisfying $(x, w) \in \bigcap_{i \in N} P(R_i^c)$. Then, either

$$\{x\} = C^c(\{x, w\}) \tag{3.51}$$

or

$$w \in C^c(\{x, w\}) \tag{3.52}$$

is true. If (3.51) is the case, then we consider a profile $d \in A$ such that $R_i^d(\{z, w\}) = R_i^b(\{z, w\})$ and $R_i^d(\{x, w\}) = R_i^c(\{x, w\})$ for all $i \in N$. Thanks to (3.50), (3.51), and BI, we then have $\{x\} = C^d(\{x, w\})$ and $w \in C^d(\{w, z\})$, which imply $x \in C^d(\{x, z\})$ by virtue of quasi-transitive rationality of C^d. Because d places no restriction whatsoever on the individual preferences on $\{x, z\}$, x is imposed over z by F, contrary to the definition of $E^*(\lambda)$. If (3.52) is the case, then we consider a profile $e \in A$ such that $R_i^e(\{x, y\}) = R_i^a(\{x, y\})$ and $R_i^e(\{x, w\}) = R_i^c(\{x, w\})$ for all $i \in N$. Thanks to (3.49), (3.52), and BI, we then have $\{x\} = C^e(\{x, y\})$ and $w \in C^e(\{x, w\})$, which imply $w \in C^e(\{y, w\})$ by virtue of quasi-transitive rationality of C^e. Because e leaves individual preferences completely free on $\{w, y\}$, w is imposed over y by F, a contradiction again.

We can similarly prove that if there exist $x, y \in E^*(\lambda)$ and $a \in A$ such that

$$(x, y) \in \bigcap_{i \in N} P(R_i^a) \;\&\; \{y\} = C^a(\{x, y\}) \tag{3.53}$$

then $P_\lambda(2)$ must be the case. If there exist no $x, y \in E^*(\lambda)$ and $a \in A$ for which either (3.49) or (3.53) holds true, then clearly $P_\lambda(3)$ follows.

Pick any $E^*(\lambda) \in \mathscr{E}^*$ with $\#E^*(\lambda) \geq 3$. We are assured that one and only one of $P_\lambda(1)$, $P_\lambda(2)$, and $P_\lambda(3)$ is true.

If $P_\lambda(1)$ is the case on $E^*(\lambda)$, then we can invoke Theorem 3.3 to conclude the existence of an oligarchy $V_+(\lambda)$ for F on $E^*(\lambda)$.

Suppose now that $P_\lambda(2)$ is the case on $E^*(\lambda)$. Define a collective choice rule F_λ on $E^*(\lambda)$ by

$$\forall a \in A, \forall x, y \in E^*(\lambda): x \in C_\lambda^a(\{x, y\}) \leftrightarrow y \in C^a(\{x, y\}) \tag{3.54}$$

where $C^a = F(a)$ and $C_\lambda^a = F_\lambda(a)$. Then F_λ satisfies QTR, BI, and, by virtue of $P_\lambda(2)$ and (3.54), $P_\lambda(1)$ as well, so that there exists an oligarchy $V_-(\lambda)$ for F_λ on $E^*(\lambda)$. By virtue of (3.54), $V_-(\lambda)$ is nothing other than an inverse oligarchy for F on $E^*(\lambda)$.

Finally, let $P_\lambda(3)$ be the case on $E^*(\lambda)$. Take any $x, y \in E^*(\lambda)$, and let $V_1(\lambda)$ be the smallest subset of N satisfying

$$\forall a \in A: (x, y) \in \bigcap_{i \in V_1(\lambda)} P(R_i^a) \rightarrow x \in C^a(\{x, y\}) \tag{3.55}$$

Such a $V_1(\lambda)$ always exists by virtue of $P_\lambda(3)$. We now prove that each member of $V_1(\lambda)$ is blocking for F on $E^*(\lambda)$. Take any $z \in E^*(\lambda) \setminus \{x, y\}$, and let a profile $b \in A$ be such that $(z, y) \in \bigcup_{i \in V_1(\lambda)} P(R_i^b)$. In view of the definition of Ξ^*, there exists a profile $c \in A$ that yields $\{z\} = C^c(\{x, z\})$. Let a profile $d \in A$ be such that

$$\forall i \in N: R_i^d(\{z, x\}) = R_i^c(\{z, x\}) \tag{3.56}$$

$$\begin{cases} \forall i \in V_1(\lambda): (x, y) \in P(R_i^d) \\ \& \\ \forall i \in N: R_i^d(\{y, z\}) = R_i^b(\{y, z\}) \end{cases} \tag{3.57}$$

Thanks to (3.55) and (3.57), we obtain $x \in C^d(\{x, y\})$. It follows from $\{z\} = C^c(\{x, z\})$, (3.56), and BI that $\{z\} = C^d(\{x, z\})$, which yields $z \in C^d(\{y, z\})$ in combination with $x \in C^d(\{x, y\})$, where use is made of QTR. We now invoke (3.57) and BI to conclude that $z \in C^b(\{y, z\})$. We have thus shown that

$$\forall z \in E^*(\lambda) \setminus \{y\}, \forall a \in A: (z, y) \in \bigcup_{i \in V_1(\lambda)} P(R_i^a) \rightarrow z \in C^a(\{y, z\}) \tag{3.58}$$

By similar reasoning, we can prove that

$$\forall w \in E^*(\lambda) \setminus \{x\}, \forall a \in A: (x, w) \in \bigcup_{i \in V_1(\lambda)} P(R_i^a) \rightarrow x \in C^a(\{x, w\}) \tag{3.59}$$

Repeated use of (3.58) and (3.59) establishes that each member of $V_1(\lambda)$ is blocking for F on $E^*(\lambda)$. We can similarly prove the existence of $V_2(\lambda)$, each member of which is inversely blocking for F on $E^*(\lambda)$, completing the proof of (b). ∎

At this juncture of our argument we need an additional condition on F that reads as follows.[10]

Condition PD (Pareto decisiveness)
For every profile $a = (R_1^a, R_2^a, \ldots, R_n^a) \in A$ and every $x, y \in X$,

$$(x, y) \in \bigcap_{i \in N} P(R_i^a) \rightarrow [\{x\} = C^a(\{x, y\}) \vee \{y\} = C^a(\{x, y\})] \tag{3.60}$$

holds true, where $C^a = F(a)$.

Theorem 3.9
Suppose that $n = \# N \geq 4$ and a collective choice rule F satisfies the unrestricted domain (U), acyclic rationality (AR), Pareto decisiveness (PD), binary independence (BI), and positive responsiveness (PR). Then there exists a partition $\mathscr{E}^* = \{E^*(\lambda) | \lambda \in \Lambda\}$ of X such that

(a) for every $E^*(\lambda_1), E^*(\lambda_2) \in \mathscr{E}^*$ $(\lambda_1 \neq \lambda_2)$, if $x \in E^*(\lambda_1)$ and $y \in E^*(\lambda_2)$, then either x is imposed over y by F or y is imposed over x by F,
(b) if $E^*(\lambda) \in \mathscr{E}^*$ is such that $\# E^*(\lambda) \geq 3$, then there exists a unique quasi dictator for F on $E^*(\lambda)$ (Fountain and Suzumura, 1982, Theorem 2 and Remark).

Proof: Define a binary relation Ξ^* on X as in the proof of Theorem 3.8, which is clearly reflexive and symmetric. To show transitivity thereof, let $x, y, z \in X$ be such that $(x, y) \in \Xi^*$ and $(y, z) \in \Xi^*$. We have only to consider the case where (3.47) and (3.48) hold true. Defining a profile $c \in A$ as in the proof of Theorem 3.8, we can assert that $\{x\} = C^c(\{x, y\})$ and $\{y\} = C^c(\{y, z\})$ hold true, yielding $x \in C^c(\{x, z\})$ by virtue of acyclic rationality of C^c. If it is the case that $(x, z) \in \bigcap_{i \in N} P(R_i^c)$, then PD and $x \in C^c(\{x, z\})$ jointly imply that $\{x\} = C^c(\{x, z\})$. Otherwise, we have $(z, x) \in R_i^c$ for some $i \in N$. In this case, we define a profile $d \in A$ by $R_j^d = R_j^c$ for all $j \in N \setminus \{i\}$ and $(x, z) \in P(R_i^d)$. By virtue of PR we obtain $\{x\} = C^d(\{x, z\})$. By similar reasoning we can assert the existence of a profile $e \in A$ such that $\{z\} = C^e(\{x, z\})$, completing the proof that $(x, z) \in \Xi^*$.

Ξ^* being an equivalence on X, there exists a family $\mathscr{E}^*$ of the Ξ^*-equivalence classes that satisfies (a) by construction.

Take any $E^*(\lambda) \in \mathscr{E}^*$ such that $\# E^*(\lambda) \geq 3$. We prove that either $P_\lambda(1)$ or $P_\lambda(2)$ must be true for this $E^*(\lambda)$. Take any $x, y \in E^*(\lambda)$ and $a \in A$ such that $(x, y) \in \bigcap_{i \in N} P(R_i^a)$. By virtue of PD, either

$$(x, y) \in \bigcap_{i \in N} P(R_i^a) \;\&\; \{x\} = C^a(\{x, y\}) \tag{3.61}$$

or

$$(x, y) \in \bigcap_{i \in N} P(R_i^a) \;\&\; \{y\} = C^a(\{x, y\}) \tag{3.62}$$

holds true. Consider first the case where (3.61) holds true. We show that

$$\exists\, z, w \in E^*(\lambda), \exists\, b \in A\colon (z, w) \in \bigcap_{i \in N} P(R_i^b) \;\&\; \{w\} = C^b(\{z,w\}) \tag{3.63}$$

brings about a contradiction. Assume that (3.63) is true. Assume further that $x \neq w$. (The case where $x = w$ can be treated similarly.)

Consider a profile $c \in A$ such that $(x, w) \in \bigcap_{i \in N} P(R_i^c)$. If $\{x\} = C^c(\{x, w\})$ holds true, then we consider a profile $d \in A$ such that $R_i^d(\{z, w\}) = R_i^b(\{z, w\})$ and $R_i^d(\{x, w\}) = R_i^c(\{x, w\})$ for all $i \in N$. By virtue of BI we then have $\{x\} = C^d(\{x, w\})$ and $\{w\} = C^d(\{z, w\})$, which yield $x \in C^d(\{x, z\})$, where use is made of acyclic rationality of C^d. Because d leaves individual preferences completely unrestricted on $\{x, z\}$, this contradicts the definition of $E^*(\lambda)$. If, on the other hand, $\{w\} = C^c(\{x, w\})$ is the case, we consider a profile $e \in A$ such that $R_i^e(\{x, y\}) = R_i^a(\{x, y\})$ and $R_i^e(\{x, w\}) = R_i^c(\{x, w\})$ for all $i \in N$. It follows that $\{x\} = C^e(\{x, y\})$ and $\{w\} = C^e(\{x, w\})$, which imply $w \in C^e(\{y, w\})$.

This also means a contradiction, as e places no restriction on individual preferences on $\{w, y\}$.

Now that (3.63) cannot be sustained in the presence of (3.61), we can conclude that $P_\lambda(1)$ holds true if (3.61) is the case. We can similarly prove that if (3.62) holds true, then $P_\lambda(2)$ must apply.

Take any $E^*(\lambda) \in \mathscr{E}^*$ such that $\#E^*(\lambda) \geq 3$. If $P_\lambda(1)$ applies, we can invoke Theorem 3.5 to conclude that there exists a vetoer on $E^*(\lambda)$. But, then, by virtue of Theorem 3.6, there exists a unique quasi dictator. Consider now the case where $P_\lambda(2)$ applies. Take any $x, y \in E^*(\lambda)$ such that $x \neq y$. By construction, there exists a profile $a \in A$ such that $\{x\} = C^a(\{x, y\})$. If it is the case that $(x, y) \in \bigcap_{i \in N} P(R_i^a)$, then $P_\lambda(2)$ entails $\{y\} = C^a(\{x, y\})$, in contradiction with $\{x\} = C^a(\{x, y\})$. Therefore, there exists a nonempty subset $J = \{j_1, j_2, \ldots, j_s\}$ of N such that $(y, x) \in R_j^a$ for all $j \in J$. Define a sequence of profiles $\{a(\tau)\}_{\tau=0}^s$ such that $a(0) = a$ and

$$\forall \tau \in \{1, 2, \ldots, s\}: \begin{cases} \forall j \in N \setminus \{j_\tau\}: R_j^{a(\tau)} = R_j^{a(\tau-1)} \\ \& \\ (x, y) \in P(R_{j_\tau}^{a(\tau)}) \end{cases} \tag{3.64}$$

Thanks to PR, we then have $\{x\} = C^{a(s)}(\{x, y\})$, and by construction we obtain $(x, y) \in \bigcap_{i \in N} P(R_i^{a(s)})$. But $P_\lambda(2)$ then entails $\{y\} = C^{a(s)}(\{x, y\})$, a contradiction. Therefore, this case cannot in fact happen, and the proof of the theorem is now complete. ∎

In concluding this section, several remarks are in order concerning the reason we have deleted or weakened the Pareto principle, which has previously been left almost unchallenged in the welfare economics literature. First, doing so represents a useful exercise of Ockham's razor, which enables us to highlight the critical role played by the collective rationality and independence axioms in the spectra of the Arrovian impossibility theorems. Furthermore, there are instances, where considerations such as equity and right matter, that might cast doubt on the supremacy of the traditional Paretian values. We shall discuss such instances in Chapter 7.

4 Impossibility theorems without collective rationality

4.1 *Rationale of collective rationality*

We must make a brief stop at this juncture in our argument and reflect critically on the role of the collective rationality requirement in the Arrovian impossibility theorems. The original Arrow theorem (Theorem 3.4) required full rationality – the strongest in the spectrum of rationality requirements we examined in Chapter 2 – of the social choice functions along with the requirements of unrestricted applicability of a rule, informational efficiency thereof, and the endorsement of the Paretian value judgments, only to encounter the universal existence of a dictator. One might then be tempted to weaken Arrow's arguably too stringent, collective full rationality requirement. Indeed, the weakening of full rationality into quasi-transitive rationality does change the picture a bit, but not very much: Oligarchy rather than dictatorship emerges from this weakened collective rationality requirement, given other Arrovian conditions on a rule, which is not democratic either (Theorem 3.3). Going one step further, one might try to settle with still weaker collective acyclic rationality, keeping all other Arrovian conditions intact. Unfortunately, one might still be unable to eradicate the Arrovian phantom if one wanted only a rule to respond to the individual's preferences positively, as Theorem 3.5 establishes: A vetoer always exists.

Some may have reservations, presumably with good reason, about the unexceptional sanctification of the Paretian value judgments, but to exclude the condition BP altogether may not broaden the class of eligible rules very much, as one is forced to realize in view of Theorems 3.7, 3.8, and 3.9. There is no escape route from the Arrovian dilemma here.

In view of the strenuous survival of the Arrovian phantom even under weakened versions of collective rationality requirements, it is all too natural to find attacks focusing directly on the very concept of collective rationality.

As an auxiliary step, note that the Arrovian full rationality requirement can be decomposed into two parts:

(a) *Rationality:* To each profile of individual preference orderings there corresponds a social preference relation that rationalizes social choices; that is,

$$\forall a \in A, \exists R^a = f(a), \forall S \in \mathcal{S}: C^a(S) = G(S, R^a)$$

where $C^a = F(a)$.[11]

(b) *Fullness:* The rationalization R^a for each $a \in A$ satisfies the axioms for an ordering (i.e., reflexivity, completeness, and transitivity).

Thus far, we have referred to the effect of successive weakening of part (b), keeping part (a) intact. It might well be asked, however, why we legitimately require part (a) in the first place.[12]

In this context, it is worthwhile to pay due attention to Buchanan's emphatic accusation against the very concept of *collective* rationality:

The mere introduction of the idea of social rationality suggests the fundamental philosophical issues involved. Rationality or irrationality as an attribute of the social group implies the imputation to the group of an organic existence apart from that of its individual components.... We may adopt the philosophical bases of individualism in which the individual is the only entity possessing ends or values. In this case no question of social or collective rationality may be raised. A social value scale simply does not exist. Alternatively, we may adopt some variant of the organic philosophical assumption in which the collectivity is an independent entity possessing its own value ordering. It is legitimate to test the rationality or irrationality of this entity only against this value ordering. [Buchanan, 1954*a*, p. 116]

To make a long story short, it is claimed that use of the concept of collective rationality in the individualistic conceptual framework is an illegitimate transplantation of a property of individuals only.

It was against this background that Arrow presented his first serious argument in support of the requirement of collective rationality. According to Arrow (1963, p. 120), who means by collective rationality the *full* rationality of social choice functions, "collective rationality in the social choice mechanism is not ... merely an illegitimate transfer from the individual to society, but an important attribute of a genuinely democratic system capable of full adaptation to varying environments," because it avoids the "democratic paralysis" – failure to act, not because of desire for inaction but because of inability to agree on the proper action – by guaranteeing "the independence of the final choice from the path to it."

Is this argument by Arrow strong enough to support the weight of full rationality in toto? In order to answer this question, we refer back to our argument in Chapter 2 on the Arrow–Plott path-independent choice functions, where we asserted that (a) full rationality (and, indeed, quasi-transitive rationality) implies path independence, but not vice versa, and (b) path independence per se cannot guarantee rationality of a choice function, to say nothing of transitivity of the rationalization. We cannot but conclude, therefore, that Arrow's ingenious argument invoking path independence does not establish the necessity of the requirement of collective rationality. Nevertheless, Arrow–Plott path-independence concepts yield rich harvest.

First of all, "if path independence, rather than rationality, is desired as a property of social choice, the stronger rationality conditions need not be imposed. One result of this relaxation is that the immediate impossibility result discovered by Arrow is avoided" (Plott, 1973, p. 1075). The question of the width of this suggested escape route from the Arrovian calamity constitutes an interesting agenda for logical scrutiny.

More generally, it is the Arrow–Plott path-independence argument that motivates us to focus directly on the choice-consistency properties rather than collective rationality requirements in the analysis of collective *choice*. A further question can be raised: Why collective choice consistency? But it is easier to answer that question than to answer the original question: Why collective rationality? Suppose that a rule F is proposed that violates the choice-consistency requirement of path independence. Then there exist a profile $a \in A$ and an opportunity set $S \in \mathscr{S}$ such that

$$C^a(C^a(S_1) \cup C^a(S_2)) \neq C^a(C^a(S_1^*) \cup C^a(S_2^*)) \tag{3.65}$$

holds true, where $C^a = F(a)$ and $S = S_1 \cup S_2 = S_1^* \cup S_2^*$. Citing a situation where (3.65) is the case, an argument against F may be constructed as follows: We may occasionally want to decompose a large problem S into smaller parts S_1 and S_2 thereof in order to lighten the computational burden, but we surely do not want the final choice to be affected by this computational device. But the proposed rule violates this, so that the social choice may well be biased by the way we apply the rule successively. This is highly undesirable, and I cannot but reject the proposal. There is a similar argument in favor of a rule satisfying various choice-consistency properties, as discussed in Chapter 2.[13] Does this change in emphasis (i.e., a change from rationality to choice consistency) qualify as a deus ex machina?

4.2 *Impossibility theorems for choice-consistent collective choice rules*

In order to answer this question properly, we need several additional concepts. Consider a choice function C on a choice space $(X, \mathscr{S})$, and let the base relation R^C for C be defined by (2.17). Let us say that C is

(a) base-transitive (BT) if and only if R^C is transitive[14]
(b) base-quasi-transitive (BQT) if and only if R^C is quasi-transitive
(c) base-acyclic (BA) if and only if R^C is acyclic
(d) base-triple-acyclic (BTA) if and only if R^C is triple-acyclic

For mnemonic convenience, let us summarize the logical implications that hold true among these properties vis-à-vis some of our already familiar concepts in the following simple theorem.

Theorem 3.10

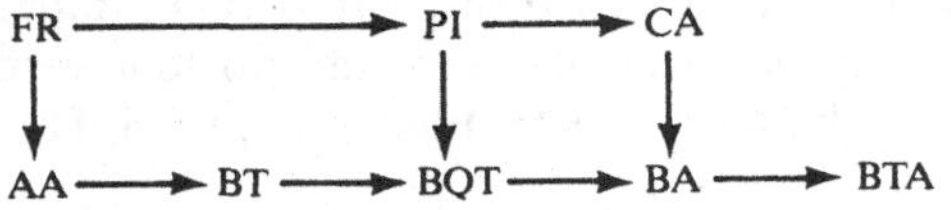

Proof: Among the properties enumerated in the theorem, we have only to provide justification for the following:

(a) AA (Arrow's axiom) implies BT.
(b) PI (path independence) implies BQT.
(c) CA (Chernoff's axiom) implies BA.

All the other properties either are trivially true by definition or have already been established in Chapter 2.

As a matter of fact, (a) is contained in Lemma 2.2(b), and (b) was established en route in proving Theorem 2.7. To prove (c), suppose that $x^1, x^2, \ldots, x^t \in X$ are such that $\{x^{\tau-1}\} = C(\{x^{\tau-1}, x^\tau\})$, and hence $(x^{\tau-1}, x^\tau) \in P(R^C)$, for $\tau = 2, 3, \ldots, t$. By virtue of CA, we then have $x^\tau \notin C(\{x^1, x^2, \ldots, x^t\})$ for all $\tau = 2, 3, \ldots, t$. Because $C(\{x^1, x^2, \ldots, x^t\})$ must be nonempty, $C(\{x^1, x^2, \ldots, x^t\}) = \{x^1\}$ holds true. By another application of CA, $x^1 \in \{x^1, x^t\} \cap C(\{x^1, x^2, \ldots, x^t\}) \subset C(\{x^1, x^t\})$, which implies that $(x^t, x^1) \notin P(R^C)$. Therefore, R^C is acyclic, as was to be established. ∎

Back, then, to our main argument. Scrutinizing the proofs of the Arrovian impossibility theorems, we recognize an important fact: *Nowhere did we in fact use the full implication of the collective rationality requirement in the proofs of these theorems.* Indeed, all the arguments proceeded in terms of some properties of social choice functions in the binary choice context only, so that the essential steps can be phrased in terms of and only of the base relation. For example, we can rephrase Theorem 3.3 in terms of a property of the base relation, throwing away an invidious requirement of collective rationality.

Theorem 3.11
Assume that $\#X \geq 3$. If a collective choice rule F satisfies the unrestricted domain (U), base quasi transitivity (BQT), binary independence (BI), and the binary Pareto principle (BP), then there exists an oligarchy for F.

If we require positive responsiveness of a rule additionally, the unequal distribution of decisive powers becomes much sharper. Indeed, we have the following theorem.

Theorem 3.12
Assume that $\#X \geq 3$ and $n = \#N \geq 3$. If a collective choice rule F satisfies the unrestricted domain (U), base quasi transitivity (BQT), binary independence (BI), the binary Pareto principle (BP), and positive responsiveness (PR), then there exists a dictator for F[15] (Blair et al., 1976, Theorem 5).

Proof: Suppose that there exists a rule F satisfying all the conditions. By virtue of Theorem 3.11 there exists an oligarchy V_0 for F. If $\#V_0 = 1$, there remains nothing further to be proved.

Suppose, therefore, that $\#V_0 \geq 2$. Without loss of generality, let us assume that $1, 2 \in V_0$. Suppose that a profile $a = (R_1^a, R_2^a, \ldots, R_n^a) \in A$ is such that $(x, y) \in P(R_1^a)$ and $(y, x) \in P(R_2^a)$ for some $x, y \in X$, and consider $C^a = F(a)$. Because $\{1\}$ as well as $\{2\}$ is blocking, by assumption, we have $\{x, y\} = C^a(\{x, y\})$, regardless of the preferences of other individuals, of whom there exists at least one by virtue of $n \equiv \#N \geq 3$. This is a clear violation of condition PR. Therefore, there cannot possibly exist a non-dictatorial rule satisfying all the nominated conditions. ∎

Coupled with Theorem 3.10, Theorems 3.11 and 3.12 yield the following negative results on the path-independent collective choice rules, dashing the hope of finding an escape route here.

Theorem 3.13
Assume that $\#X \geq 3$. If a collective choice rule F satisfies the unrestricted domain (U), path independence (PI), binary independence (BI), and the binary Pareto principle (BP), then there exists an oligarchy for F (Blair et al., 1976, Theorem 3).

Theorem 3.14
Assume that $\#X \geq 3$ and $n = \#N \geq 3$. If a collective choice rule F satisfies the unrestricted domain (U), path independence (PI), binary independence (BI), the binary Pareto principle (BP), and positive responsiveness (PR), then there exists a dictator for F.

So much for the path-independent collective choice rules. In view of the negative theorems hitherto proved, one might be tempted to retreat one step further and settle with the satisfaction of only Chernoff's axiom of choice consistency, which is strictly weaker than both rationality and path independence. On reflection, this condition is an appealing one to impose on collective choice rules. It is clearly desirable in piecemeal choice mechanisms where choices are made from unions of choices over subsets. If an alternative fails to be chosen in some subset, it need not be considered again at a later stage, for the contrapositive of Chernoff's axiom ensures that the alternative will not be among the final choices.[16] To the extent that Chernoff's axiom has strong intuitive appeal in the context of collective choice, our disappointment is that much greater, because, as the following theorem demonstrates, Chernoff's axiom cannot be satisfied by any, otherwise Arrovian, collective choice rule.

Theorem 3.15
Assume that $\#X \geq 3$ and $n = \#N \geq 4$. If a collective choice rule F satisfies the unrestricted domain (U), Chernoff's axiom of choice consistency (CA), binary independence (BI), the binary Pareto principle (BP), and positive responsiveness (PR), then there exists a vetoer for F (Blair et al., 1976, Theorem 6).

In view of Theorem 3.10, which asserts inter alia that Chernoff's axiom implies base triple acyclicity, the assertion of Theorem 3.15 follows from the following stronger proposition.

Theorem 3.16
Assume that $\#X \geq 3$ and $n = \#N \geq 4$. If a collective choice rule F satisfies the unrestricted domain (U), base triple acyclicity (BTA), binary independence (BI), the binary Pareto principle (BP), and positive responsiveness (PR), then there exists a vetoer for F (Blair et al., 1976, Theorem7).

To prove Theorem 3.16, we have only to notice that the proof of Theorem 3.5 does not require the full power of acyclic rationality, and base triple acyclicity in fact suffices.

These results show that the shift from collective rationality to choice consistency does not salvage us from the gloom of the Arrovian negative verdict on the possibility of a "satisfactory" collective choice rule.

Two further remarks are due. First, we can strengthen Theorem 3.15 and Theorem 3.16 by asserting the existence of a unique quasi dictator, rather than simply a vetoer, for F. The necessary step can be modeled after Theorem 3.6, and we need not linger here further. Second, we can dispose of the binary Pareto principle altogether and obtain the analogues of the theorems in Section 3.2. It is unnecessary to detail how this can by done.

In concluding this section, it is useful to look at two examples due to Fishburn (1970*d*, 1971*a*) that are designed to go against the requirement of collective full rationality.

Example 4.1
Consider a society (Fishburn, 1970*d*, p. 121) in which $N = \{1, 2, \ldots, 100\}$ and $X = S = \{x_0, x_1, \ldots, x_{100}\}$. Let a rule F be such that at least 99 of the 100 individuals preferring x to y ensures the win of x over y in the binary choice contest, so that if a profile $a = (R_1^a, R_2^a, \ldots, R_{100}^a) \in A$ is such that $\#\{i \in N \mid (x, y) \in P(R_i^a)\} \geq 99$, then $\{x\} = C^a(\{x, y\})$, where $C^a = F(a)$. Then collective full rationality must be rejected.

To substantiate this claim, consider the profile $a = (R_1^a, R_2^a, \ldots, R_n^a) \in A$ satisfying

$$R_1^a\colon x_0, x_{100}, x_{99}, \ldots, x_1$$

$$R_2^a\colon x_1, x_0, x_{100}, \ldots, x_2$$

$$\vdots$$

$$R_i^a\colon x_{i-1}, x_{i-2}, x_{i-3}, \ldots, x_i$$

$$\vdots$$

$$R_{100}^a\colon x_{99}, x_{98}, x_{97}, \ldots, x_{100}$$

Let $C^a = F(a)$, and consider $C^a(\{x_{i-1}, x_i\})$ for $i = 1, 2, \ldots, 100$. By virtue of the support by 99 of 100 individuals, we obtain $C^a(\{x_0, x_1\}) = \{x_1\}$, $C^a(\{x_1, x_2\}) = \{x_2\}, \ldots, C^a(\{x_{99}, x_{100}\}) = \{x_{100}\}$. If C^a is a full rational choice function, there exists an ordering R^a such that $(x_{100}, x_{99}) \in P(R^a)$, $(x_{99}, x_{98}) \in P(R^a), \ldots, (x_1, x_0) \in P(R^a)$, implying $(x_{100}, x_0) \in P(R^a)$. But by unanimous support, $C^a(\{x_0, x_{100}\}) = \{x_0\}$, and hence $(x_0, x_{100}) \in P(R^a)$, a contradiction. ▮

Example 4.2
Consider a society (Fishburn, 1971*a*, p. 137) in which $N = \{1, 2, \ldots, 101\}$ and $X = S = \{x_1, x_2, \ldots, x_{10}\}$. Let a rule F be such that the majority of individuals preferring x to y ensures the unique choice of x over y in the binary choice contest. Consider a profile $a = (R_1^a, R_2^a, \ldots, R_{101}^a)$ such that

$$R_i^a\,(i = 1, \ldots, 50)\colon x_1, x_2, x_3, \ldots, x_{10}$$

$$R_i^a\,(i = 51, \ldots, 100)\colon x_2, x_3, \ldots, x_{10}, x_1$$

$$R_{101}^a\colon x_1, x_3, \ldots, x_{10}, x_2$$

which yields $\{x_1\} = C^a(\{x_1, x_\tau\})$ $(\tau = 2, \ldots, 10)$. If F is rational, the rationalization R^a of C^a satisfies $(x_1, x_\tau) \in P(R^a)$ $(\tau = 2, \ldots, 10)$, so that we obtain $C^a(\{x_1, x_2, \ldots, x_{10}\}) = \{x_1\}$.

Note, however, that examination of this profile seems to suggest a strong reason to favor x_2 vis-à-vis x_1, because x_1 is ranked first [resp. last] by 51 [resp. 50] individuals, and x_2 is ranked first and second by 50 individuals each. If this observation catches your fancy, then you must reject collective rationality. ▮

One can obviate the bite of Example 4.2, which goes against rationality per se, by arguing: So much the worse is the majority principle.[17] But the thrust of Example 4.1, which goes against transitivity (and, indeed, much weaker acyclicity), is difficult to soften, and it becomes still more difficult if we enlarge the example by increasing the numbers of states and of individuals. Note, however, that this class of examples does not provide us with any reason to reject base triple acyclicity.[18] Nevertheless, Theorem 3.16 shows that this vestige of the Arrovian collective rationality requirement still retains its power to annihilate "democratic" collective choice rules and, as such, is quite disturbing.

5 Concluding remarks

A central theorem in social choice established by Arrow asserted that a collective choice rule that is unrestricted in applicability, is informationally efficient, and is compatible with the Paretian value judgments cannot but be extraordinarily unfair in its assignment of decisive power among individuals. In this chapter we have verified that this result is really robust and cannot be readily exorcised even if we dispose of fidelity to the Paretian values altogether. In our judgment, the weakest link in Arrow's framework is his requirement of collective rationality, but the more easily justifiable choice-consistency conditions essentially retain Arrow's negative conclusion.

Facing up to this strenuous survival of the negative conclusions on the "satisfactory" rule of collective decisions, there seem to be three alternative routes one can try:

1. One can settle with a rule that satisfies a less demanding domain condition than the absolutely unrestricted domain.
2. One can be ready to accept the potential usefulness of irrelevant (i.e., nonfeasible) alternatives in deciding socially over relevant (i.e., feasible) alternatives.
3. One can try to reformulate the conceptual framework of social choice theory with special reference to its informational basis.

All three directions are worthwhile to explore, and extensive work has been done in each. In the rest of this book, however, we shall confine ourselves to route (3), the reasons being, first, that this is a less cultivated but highly enticing avenue and, second, that the practical appeal of U (unrestricted domain) and I (independence of irrelevant alternatives) in the context of rule design in the primordial stage of ignorance is difficult to resist.[19] Before setting out on this route, however, it is necessary to become acquainted with the performance of the simple majority decision rule. The next chapter is devoted to that task.

CHAPTER 4

Simple majority rule and extensions

> The principle of majority rule must be taken ethically as a means of ascertaining a real "general will," not as a mechanism by which one set of interests is made subservient to another set. Political discussion must be assumed to represent a quest for an objectively ideal or "best" policy, not a contest between interests.
>
> Frank H. Knight*

0 Introduction

Traditionally, the concept "democracy" often has been construed to mean neither more nor less than rule by the majority of individuals. Suffice it to quote a passage from Bryce:

> The word Democracy has been used ever since the time of Herodotus to denote that form of government in which the ruling power of a State is legally vested, not in any particular class or classes, but in the members of the community as a whole. This means, in communities which act by voting, that rule belongs to the majority, as no other method has been found for determining peaceably and legally what is to be deemed the will of a community which is not unanimous. Usage has made this the accepted sense of the term, and usage is the safest guide in the employment of words. [Bryce, 1924, Vol. I, p. 20]

In view of this strong doctrinal association between democracy and majority rule, which we cannot simply neglect, it is important to have in hand an analysis of majority rule as a collective choice mechanism. Leaving the history and the doctrinal development of majority rule to Bryce (1924), Heinberg (1926, 1932), Riemer (1951–2), and others, our analysis in this chapter will be concerned exclusively with the formal aspects of majority rule. In so doing, our purpose is twofold. First, we want to see how majoritarian collective choice rules fare in the context of the Arrovian impossibility theorems, thereby motivating our analysis, which departs from the mechanical use of majority rule. Second, we want to prepare several relevant concepts and properties that are useful in Chapter 6 on the constrained majoritarian collective choice rules.

* F. H. Knight, "Economic Theory and Nationalism," in *The Ethics of Competition and Other Essays*. New York: Harper & Bros., 1931, p. 296, footnote.

The plan of this chapter is as follows. In Section 1 we define formally the simple majority decision rule (the SMD rule) and put forward an axiomatization thereof due to May (1952). In Section 2 we examine several methods of extending the SMD rule to non-binary-choice situations with a view toward examining the performance of majoritarian collective choice rules in terms of the Arrovian criteria. In Section 3 we introduce a particular extension of the SMD rule called the transitive closure of the SMD rule (the TCM rule). Section 4 concludes with two defects of the TCM rule with a view toward motivating our exploration in Chapter 5 and Chapter 6. Finally, the Appendix presents a self-contained exposition of the transitive closure choice functions and related concepts.

1 Simple majority decision rule: May's axiomatization

To begin with, let us present a formal definition of the simple majority decision rule (the SMD rule, for short).

For any profile $a = (R_1^a, R_2^a, \ldots, R_n^a) \in A$ and any social states $x, y \in X$, let $N^a(x, y)$ be defined by

$$N^a(x, y) = \#\{i \in N \mid (x, y) \in R_i^a\} \tag{4.1}$$

that is, the number of individuals who (at least weakly) prefer x to y at the profile a. Then let a subset $C_M^a(\{x, y\})$ of $\{x, y\} \in \mathscr{S}$ be defined by

$$C_M^a(\{x, y\}) = \begin{cases} \{x\} \leftrightarrow N^a(x, y) > N^a(y, x) \\ \{x, y\} \leftrightarrow N^a(x, y) = N^a(y, x) \\ \{y\} \leftrightarrow N^a(x, y) < N^a(y, x) \end{cases} \tag{4.2}$$

which is clearly nonempty. Therefore, C_M^a defines a choice function on a choice space $(X, \mathscr{S}_B)$, where $\mathscr{S}_B$ denotes the family of all binary choice environments that is defined by

$$\mathscr{S}_B = \{(x, y) \in X \times X \mid x \neq y\} \tag{4.3}$$

The SMD rule is nothing other than a function that maps each and every profile $a \in A$ into a choice function C_M^a on $\mathscr{S}_B$. It is intuitively clear that the SMD rule works for every profile (hence is unrestricted in applicability), is informationally very modest (in the sense that, in deciding social choice in the binary choice contest $\{x, y\} \in \mathscr{S}_B$, it need be fed only with $\{R_i^a(\{x, y\}) \mid i \in N\}$ as its informational material), and responds positively to changes in individuals' preferences.

Making our story a bit formal, a function F_B that maps each profile $a \in A$ into a choice function on a choice space $(X, \mathscr{S}_B)$ will be called a *binary collective choice rule* (BCCR). Then the foregoing properties of the SMD rule F_M can be stated formally as the following requirements on a BCCR F_B.

Condition U(B)
The domain of a binary collective choice rule F_B consists of all logically possible profiles of individual preference orderings.

Condition BI(B)
If $a = (R_1^a, R_2^a, \ldots, R_n^a) \in A$, $b = (R_1^b, R_2^b, \ldots, R_n^b) \in A$, and $x, y \in X$ are such that $R_i^a(\{x, y\}) = R_i^b(\{x, y\})$ for all $i \in N$, then $C_B^a(\{x, y\}) = C_B^b(\{x, y\})$ holds true, where $C_B^a = F_B(a)$ and $C_B^b = F_B(b)$.

Condition BP(B)
If $a = (R_1^a, R_2^a, \ldots, R_n^a) \in A$ and $x, y \in X$ are such that $(x, y) \in \bigcap_{i \in N} P(R_i^a)$, then $\{x\} = C_B^a(\{x, y\})$ holds true, where $C_B^a = F_B(a)$.

Condition PR(B)
If $a = (R_1^a, R_2^a, \ldots, R_n^a) \in A$, $b = (R_1^b, R_2^b, \ldots, R_n^b) \in A$, $i \in N$, and $x, y \in X$ are such that $R_j^b = R_j^a$ for all $j \in N \setminus \{i\}$, and either

$$(y, x) \in P(R_i^b) \;\&\; (x, y) \in I(R_i^a)$$

or

$$(x, y) \in I(R_i^b) \;\&\; (x, y) \in P(R_i^a)$$

holds true, then $x \in C_B^b(\{x, y\})$ implies $\{x\} = C_B^a(\{x, y\})$, where $C_B^a = F_B(a)$ and $C_B^b = F_B(b)$.

Furthermore, the SMD rule also satisfies the following two important properties.

Condition BAN (binary anonymity)
If $a = (R_1^a, R_2^a, \ldots, R_n^a) \in A$ is a reordering of $b = (R_1^b, R_2^b, \ldots, R_n^b) \in A$, then $C_B^a(\{x, y\}) = C_B^b(\{x, y\})$ holds true for every $\{x, y\} \in \mathcal{S}_B$, where $C_B^a = F_B(a)$ and $C_B^b = F_B(b)$.[1]

Condition BNE (binary neutrality)
If $a = (R_1^a, R_2^a, \ldots, R_n^a) \in A$ is obtained from $b = (R_1^b, R_2^b, \ldots, R_n^b) \in A$ by interchanging x and y in every R_i^b, then we have $x \in C_B^a(\{x, y\})$ if and only if $y \in C_B^b(\{x, y\})$, and $y \in C_B^a(\{x, y\})$ if and only if $x \in C_B^b(\{x, y\})$, for every $\{x, y\} \in \mathcal{S}_B$, where $C_B^a = F_B(a)$ and $C_B^b = F_B(b)$.

Intuitively speaking, BAN and BNE require that a rule not invidiously discriminate between individuals (in the case of BAN) or between alternatives (in the case of BNE) and, as such, are fairly reasonable.[2]

Not only does the SMD rule F_M satisfy conditions U(B), BI(B), BP(B), PR(B), BAN, and BNE, but also it is the *unique* BCCR that can qualify in this arena. Indeed, we have the following remarkable result due to May (1952).

Theorem 4.1
A BCCR F_B satisfies all of U(B), BI(B), BAN (binary anonymity), and BNE (binary neutrality) if and only if F_B coincides with the SMD rule F_M.

Proof: Clearly we have only to prove the necessity part. Assume that a BCCR F_B satisfies all of U(B), BI(B), PR(B), BAN, and BNE. Take any profile $a = (R_1^a, R_2^a, \ldots, R_n^a) \in A$ and any $\{x, y\} \in \mathscr{S}_B$. By virtue of BI(B) and BAN, the choice set $C_B^a(\{x, y\})$, where $C_B^a = F_B(a)$, depends only on $N^a(x, y)$ and $N^a(y, x)$. Let us verify that

$$N^a(x, y) = N^a(y, x) \rightarrow C_B^a(\{x, y\}) = \{x, y\} \tag{4.4}$$

holds true. Assume, to the contrary, that $C_B^a(\{x, y\}) = \{x\}$. Let $b = (R_1^b, R_2^b, \ldots, R_n^b) \in A$ be generated from $a \in A$ by everywhere interchanging the positions of x and y. By virtue of BNE, we then obtain $C_B^b(\{x, y\}) = \{y\}$. Because $N^b(x, y) = N^b(y, x) = N^a(x, y) = N^a(y, x)$, BAN implies that $C_B^a(\{x, y\}) = C_B^b(\{x, y\})$, a contradiction. By similar argument we can ascertain that $C_B^a(\{x, y\}) = \{y\}$ cannot be sustained either, so that (4.4) must be true. We can now invoke PR to conclude that $N^a(x, y) > N^a(y, x)$ [resp. $N^a(x, y) < N^a(y, x)$] implies $\{x\} = C_B^a(\{x, y\})$ [resp. $\{y\} = C_B^a(\{x, y\})$], which establishes that $F_B = F_M$, as desired. ∎

This, then, is the theoretical foundation of the simple majority decision rule.[3] The next order of business is to see how the SMD rule fares in the context of Arrow's problem discussed in Chapter 3. To this task we now turn.

2 Extensions of the SMD rule

2.1 Condorcet criterion

By definition, any BCCR F_B generates a choice function $C_B^a = F_B(a)$ on a choice space $(X, \mathscr{S}_B)$ for any profile $a \in A$, but C_B^a per se tells us nothing about what we should choose when we are confronted with a non-binary-choice environment $S \in \mathscr{S} \setminus \mathscr{S}_B$. Noting this fact, we say that a collective choice rule F is an *extension* of a binary collective choice rule F_B if and only if

$$\forall a \in A, \forall S \in \mathscr{S}_B: C^a(S) = C_B^a(S) \tag{4.5}$$

holds true, where $C^a = F(a)$ and $C_B^a = F_B(a)$.

Because the SMD rule F_M yields choice functions that can cope with only binary choice situations, it is of no direct relevance in the context of Arrow's problem. But it is relevant to ask how extensions of the SMD rule fare with respect to the Arrovian performance criteria.

In this analysis, an important role is played by what we call the *Condorcet function.* As an auxiliary step, let the *simple majority relation* (the SMD relation) be defined by

$$(x, y) \in M^a \leftrightarrow \# \{i \in N | (x, y) \in R_i^a\} \geq \# \{i \in N | (y, x) \in R_i^a\} \tag{4.6}$$

that is, $(x, y) \in M^a$ holds true if and only if the number of individuals who (at least weakly) prefer x to y at the profile $a \in A$ is no less than the number of individuals who (at least weakly) prefer y to x at $a \in A$. It is clear that M^a coincides with the base relation for $C_M^a = F_M(a)$ for every $a \in A$. We can now define the Condorcet function C_*^a by

$$\forall S \in \mathscr{S}: C_*^a(S) = \{x \in S | \forall y \in S \setminus \{x\}: (x, y) \in P(M^a)\} \tag{4.7}$$

We say that a state $x^* \in S$ is the *Condorcet winner* in S when the profile $a \in A$ prevails if and only if $x^* \in C_*^a(S)$ holds true. In words, the Condorcet winner in S is a state in S that defeats every other state in S by simple majority contest. Clearly, $\# C_*^a(S) = 0$ or 1 for every $a \in A$ and every $S \in \mathscr{S}$.[4]

Making use of the Condorcet function just introduced, we now define the *Condorcet criterion,* which serves as the watershed in the classification of various extensions of the SMD rule. We say that an extension F of the SMD rule satisfies the Condorcet criterion, or is a *Condorcet extension* of the SMD rule, if and only if

$$\forall a \in A, \forall S \in \mathscr{S}: C_*^a(S) \neq \varnothing \rightarrow C^a(S) = C_*^a(S) \tag{4.8}$$

holds true, where $C^a = F(a)$. Otherwise, an extension F of the SMD rule will be called a *non-Condorcet extension* of the SMD rule.[5]

It may well be asked: Why is the Condorcet criterion of interest in the first place? According to Black (1958, p. 57), "the criterion of standing highest on the average in the electors' preferences which, in the main, we would accept, is one which was first proposed by Condorcet; the majority candidate who, in a direct vote against them, would defeat each of the others, can be taken as standing higher than the others on the voters' schedules of preferences. There would be the corollary that where he exists, such a candidate ought to be elected." This may sound natural and easy, but careful inspection reveals that the way the Condorcet criterion defines which alternative stands highest on the average on individuals' preference schedules is rather insidious. According to this criterion, what matters in the comparison between x and y is which alternative is supported by the majority, and such numerical information as the size of the majority, the number of other feasible alternatives that are ranked between x and y, and so forth, are made totally irrelevant. It is arguable, however, that it is clearly relevant to take into account the sizes of majorities and the rank positions of the alternatives. By neglecting this information, it can be argued, the Condorcet criterion wastes potentially important knowledge about individual preferences. To highlight these pros and cons about the Condorcet criterion by contrast, we shall now discuss two concrete rules that extend the SMD rule, one Condorcet and another non-Condorcet.

2.2 *Borda and Condorcet*

To begin with, we formulate the Borda method of collective choice as an example of non-Condorcet extension of the SMD rule. The original Borda method, as translated and annotated by Grazia (1953), assumes that the profile of individual preference orderings does not contain any instance of individual indifference. Let us assume initially, for the sake of convenience, that this is indeed the case.

Let a profile $a = (R_1^a, R_2^a, \ldots, R_n^a) \in A$ and an opportunity set $S \in \mathscr{S}$ be given. To each $x \in S$ and $i \in N$ we assign the mark, to be called the *Borda count*, defined by $\beta_i^a(x|S) = \#\{y \in S | (x, y) \in P(R_i^a)\}$; that is, the number of alternatives above which x stands on the preference scale of individual i. The *Borda choice function* C_β^a on a choice space $(X, \mathscr{S})$ is then defined in terms of the total of Borda counts by

$$C_\beta^a(S) = \left\{ x \in S | \forall\, y \in S\colon \sum_{i \in N} \beta_i^a(x|S) \geq \sum_{i \in N} \beta_i^a(y|S) \right\} \tag{4.9}$$

for every $S \in \mathscr{S}$.

A clear merit of this method of choice is that it takes into account the positions of all alternatives on the preference scales of all individuals, in contradistinction to the essentially binary nature of the Condorcet criterion. So strong is this contrast that it is no surprise that the Borda choice function sometimes violates the Condorcet criterion.

Example 4.1
Suppose that $N = \{1, 2, \ldots, 35\}$, $S = \{x^1, x^2, x^3, x^4, x^5\}$, and consider the following profile $a \in A$ (Black, 1958, p. 61):

$$R_i^a(S) \quad \text{for} \quad i \in \{1, 2\}\colon x^1, x^2, x^3, x^4, x^5$$

$$R_i^a(S) \quad \text{for} \quad i \in \{3, \ldots, 17\}\colon x^2, x^1, x^3, x^4, x^5$$

$$R_{18}^a(S)\colon x^3, x^2, x^1, x^4, x^5$$

$$R_i^a(S) \quad \text{for} \quad i \in \{19, \ldots, 26\}\colon x^4, x^5, x^3, x^2, x^1$$

$$R_i^a(S) \quad \text{for} \quad i \in \{27, \ldots, 35\}\colon x^5, x^4, x^3, x^2, x^1$$

It is easy to verify that in this case $C^a_*(S) = \{x^3\}$, but x^3 defeats every other alternative by a slim margin of 18 pros versus 17 cons. The total Borda counts of these alternatives are $\beta^a(x^1|S) = 55$, $\beta^a(x^2|S) = 86$, $\beta^a(x^3|S) = 72$, $\beta^a(x^4|S) = 77$, and $\beta^a(x^5|S) = 60$, where $\beta^a(x|S) = \sum_{i=1}^{35} \beta^a_i(x|S)$ for all $x \in S$, so that $C^a_\beta(S) = \{x^2\}$ holds true, which is a clear violation of the Condorcet criterion. ∎

Let us now generalize the original Borda method in such a way as to cover the case in which individual indifferences intervene.[6] There are two possible methods for performing this, both of which are quite natural. In the event in which several alternatives are placed at the indifference level in an individual's preference scale, method 1 awards each alternative the mean of the counts it would receive if it appeared separately on the preference scale. Method 2 gives a credit of 1 mark to an alternative x for each alternative above which x stands on the preference scale of any individual, a discredit of -1 mark for each alternative below which x is placed, and 0 credit for each alternative with which x is bracketed indifferent.

Formally, let a profile $a = (R^a_1, R^a_2, \ldots, R^a_n) \in A$ and an opportunity set $S \in \mathscr{S}$ be given. For each individual $i \in N$ and each alternative $x \in S$, let $\beta^a_{1,i}(x|S)$ and $\beta^a_{2,i}(x|S)$ denote, respectively, the Borda count of x recorded by i according to method 1 and method 2. Notice that if R^a_i does not in fact contain any instance of indifference, then $\beta^a_{1,i}(x|S) = \beta^a_i(x|S)$ holds true. To relate $\beta^a_{1,i}(x|S)$ and $\beta^a_{2,i}(x|S)$, suppose that R^a_i and S are such that there are r_i alternatives in S that are less preferred to x, s_i alternatives in S that are indifferent to x, and $\#S - r_i - s_i$ alternatives in S that are more preferred to x. We then obtain

$$\beta^a_{1,i}(x|S) = \frac{1}{s_i}\{r_i + (r_i + 1) + \cdots + (r_i + s_i - 1)\}$$

$$= r_i + \frac{1}{2}(s_i - 1) \tag{4.10}$$

and

$$\beta^a_{2,i}(x|S) = \#\{y \in S | (x, y) \in P(R^a_i)\} - \#\{y \in S | (y, x) \in P(R^a_i)\}$$

$$= r_i - (\#S - r_i - s_i)$$

$$= 2\{r_i + \tfrac{1}{2}(s_i - 1)\} - (\#S - 1) \tag{4.11}$$

It follows from (4.10) and (4.11) that

$$\sum_{i \in N} \beta^a_{2,i}(x|S) = 2 \sum_{i \in N} \beta^a_{1,i}(x|S) - n(\#S - 1) \tag{4.12}$$

so that the choice in accordance with the greatest total Borda score given by method 1 coincides with that given by method 2. In view of this fact, we can now formally define the general Borda method as follows.

Take any profile $a = (R_1^a, R_2^a, \ldots, R_n^a) \in A$. Define the *Borda choice function* C_β^a by

$$C_\beta^a(S) = \{x \in S | \forall y \in S: \sum_{i \in N} \beta_{2,i}^a(x|S) \geq \sum_{i \in N} \beta_{2,i}^a(y|S)\} \tag{4.13}$$

for every $S \in \mathscr{S}$. The *Borda rule* F_β is finally defined by associating C_β^a with the profile $a \in A$.[7]

Let us now turn to an example of Condorcet extension of the SMD rule, which reportedly is due to A. H. Copeland.[8] Choose any profile $a = (R_1^a, R_2^a, \ldots, R_n^a) \in A$ and an opportunity set $S \in \mathscr{S}$, and define the *Copeland score* $\gamma^a(x|S)$ of each $x \in S$ by

$$\gamma^a(x|S) = \#\{y \in S | (x, y) \in P(M^a)\} - \#\{y \in S | (y, x) \in P(M^a)\} \tag{4.14}$$

In words, the Copeland score of x in S is the number of alternatives in S over which x has a strict simple majority minus the number of alternatives in S that have strict simple majority over x. We now define the *Copeland choice function* C_γ^a on a choice space $(X, \mathscr{S})$ by

$$C_\gamma^a(S) = \{x \in S | \forall y \in S: \gamma^a(x|S) \geq \gamma^a(y|S)\} \tag{4.15}$$

for every $S \in \mathscr{S}$. The *Copeland rule* F_γ is then defined by associating C_γ^a with the profile $a \in A$. Clearly, F_γ is a Condorcet extension of the SMD rule.

We have thus obtained two concrete extensions of the SMD rule, one of which (the Copeland rule) is Condorcet, whereas the other (the Borda rule) is non-Condorcet. By construction, they coincide with the SMD rule as far as the choices over pair-sets are concerned. Let us examine how these rules fare in relation to the Arrovian requirements on "satisfactory" rules. Needless to say, F_β and F_γ cannot possibly satisfy all of them, else we would have counterexample(s) to the Arrovian general impossibility theorems. Indeed, just where F_β and/or F_γ fail to pass the Arrovian test is the focus of our concern in this inquiry.

It is clearly the case that F_β and F_γ satisfy U (unrestricted domain), BI (binary independence), BP (binary Pareto principle), PR (positive responsiveness), BAN (binary anonymity), and BNE (binary neutrality). That leaves only rationality and/or choice-consistency conditions, and it is indeed here that F_β and F_γ fail, badly at that.

Example 4.2

Suppose that $N = \{1, 2, 3\}$, $X = \{x, y, z, w\}$, $S_1 = \{z, w\}$, and $S_2 = X$, and consider the following profile $a \in A$ (Suzumura, 1981*a*):

R_1^a: w, y, x, z

R_2^a: z, w, y, x

R_3^a: x, z, y, w

The Borda and Copeland scores for each and every alternative can then be calculated as follows:

$$\sum_{i=1}^{3} \beta_{2,i}^{a}(z|S_1) = 1, \quad \sum_{i=1}^{3} \beta_{2,i}^{a}(w|S_1) = -1, \quad \sum_{i=1}^{3} \beta_{2,i}^{a}(x|S_2) = -1,$$

$$\sum_{i=1}^{3} \beta_{2,i}^{a}(y|S_2) = -1, \quad \sum_{i=1}^{3} \beta_{2,i}^{a}(z|S_2) = 1, \quad \sum_{i=1}^{3} \beta_{2,i}^{a}(w|S_2) = 1$$

$$\gamma^a(z|S_1) = 1, \quad \gamma^a(w|S_1) = -1, \quad \gamma^a(x|S_2) = -1,$$

$$\gamma^a(y|S_2) = -1, \quad \gamma^a(z|S_2) = 1, \quad \gamma^a(w|S_2) = 1$$

We then have $C_\beta^a(S_1) = C_\gamma^a(S_1) = \{z\}$ and $C_\beta^a(S_2) = C_\gamma^a(S_2) = S_1$, which imply that $C_\alpha^a(C_\alpha^a(S_2)) \neq C_\alpha^a(S_2)$ for $\alpha = \beta$ and γ, so that the Borda rule, as well as the Copeland rule, fails to satisfy the stability axiom. A fortiori, C_β^a and C_γ^a are neither path-independent nor rational. ∎

2.3 *Impossibility theorems on extensions of the SMD rule*

Example 4.2 shows that the Borda rule and the Copeland rule, which are representative non-Condorcet and Condorcet extensions of the SMD rule, perform very badly on the requirement of choice consistency. A quite natural question suggests itself: Is there any collective choice rule that extends the SMD rule and performs better than the Borda and Copeland rules in this arena? Several impossibility theorems that follow suffice to suggest that not much can be hoped for.

Theorem 4.2
Assume that $\#X \geq 3$ and $n = \#N \geq 3$. Then there exists no collective choice rule that extends the SMD rule and satisfies the unrestricted domain (U) and Chernoff's axiom of choice consistency (CA).

Proof: Assume that F is an eligible rule. Let $S = \{x, y, z\} \subset X$, and consider a profile $a = (R_1^a, R_2^a, \ldots, R_n^a) \in A$, the restriction of which on S satisfies the following condition:

$R_1^a(S)$: x, y, z

$R_2^a(S)$: y, z, x

$R_3^a(S)$: z, x, y

$R_i^a(S)$ for all $i \in N \setminus \{1, 2, 3\}$: $[x, y, z]$

Let $C^a = F(a)$, and consider $C^a(\{x, y\})$, $C^a(\{y, z\})$, and $C^a(\{x, z\})$. Because F is an extension of the SMD rule and C^a satisfies CA, we obtain the following:

$$\{x, y\} \cap C^a(S) \subset C^a(\{x, y\}) = \{x\}$$
$$\{y, z\} \cap C^a(S) \subset C^a(\{y, z\}) = \{y\}$$
$$\{x, z\} \cap C^a(S) \subset C^a(\{x, z\}) = \{z\}$$

which inevitably implies that $C^a(S) = \varnothing$, a contradiction. ∎

Theorem 4.3
Assume that $\#X \geq 3$. Then there exists no collective choice rule that extends the SMD rule and satisfies the unrestricted domain (U), the dual Chernoff axiom (DCA), and the strong Pareto principle (SP) (Richelson, 1978, Theorem 1).[9]

Proof: Let F be an eligible rule, assuming that one exists, and let $S = \{x, y, z\}$. Consider a profile $a = (R_1^a, R_2^a, \ldots, R_n^a) \in A$ such that

$$R_1^a(S): x, z, y$$
$$R_2^a(S): z, y, x$$
$$R_i^a(S) \quad \text{for all} \quad i \in N \setminus \{1, 2\}: [x, y, z]$$

Let $C^a = F(a)$. F being an extension of the SMD rule, we obtain $C^a(\{x, y\}) = \{x, y\}$, $C^a(\{x, z\}) = \{x, z\}$, and $C^a(\{y, z\}) = \{z\}$. By virtue of SP, we also obtain $y \notin C^a(S)$, which implies that

$$C^a(S) = \{x\} \vee \{z\} \vee \{x, z\} \tag{4.16}$$

By virtue of DCA on C^a, we obtain

$$\{x, y\} \cap C^a(S) = \varnothing \vee \{x, y\} \subset \{x, y\} \cap C^a(S) \tag{4.17}$$
$$\{x, z\} \cap C^a(S) = \varnothing \vee \{x, z\} \subset \{x, z\} \cap C^a(S) \tag{4.18}$$

where use is made of $C^a(\{x, y\}) = \{x, y\}$ and $C^a(\{x, z\}) = \{x, z\}$. There are three cases to consider, in view of (4.16):

Case 1: $C^a(S) = \{x\}$

It follows from (4.17) that $\{x, y\} \subset \{x, y\} \cap \{x\} = \{x\}$, a contradiction.

Case 2: $C^a(S) = \{z\}$

It follows from (4.18) that $\{x, z\} \subset \{z\}$, a contradiction.

Case 3: $C^a(S) = \{x, z\}$

A similar contradiction follows from (4.17) as well as from (4.18). ∎

Recollect that Chernoff's axiom and the dual Chernoff axiom decompose Arrow's axiom, which is necessary and sufficient for full rationality. Theorems 4.2 and 4.3 tell us that retaining only one-half of Arrow's axiom is still disallowed if we are interested in an extension of the SMD rule with unrestricted domain. How about path independence? The sad verdict of the following theorem is that there is not much hope in that direction either.

Theorem 4.4
Assume that $\#X \geq 4$ and $n = \#N \geq 5$. Then there exists no collective choice rule that extends the SMD rule and satisfies the unrestricted domain (U), weak path independence $\alpha 1$ [WPI($\alpha 1$)], and the Pareto principle (P) (Ferejohn and Grether, 1977*a*, Theorem 5).

Proof: Let F be a rule that satisfies all the specified conditions. Because n is an integer, there exists a unique pair of integers (m, p) such that $n = 3m + p, 0 \leq p < 3$. We now divide N into, at most, 5 nonoverlapping groups $N_1, N_2, \ldots, N_5$ in such a way that $\#N_1 = \#N_2 = \#N_3 = m$, $\#N_4 = 1$ if and only if $p = 1$ or 2, and $\#N_5 = 1$ if and only if $p = 2$. Let $S = \{x, y, z\}$, and assume that a profile $a = (R_1^a, R_2^a, \ldots, R_n^a) \in A$ satisfies the following condition:

$R_i^a(S)$ for $i \in N_1$: x, y, z, w

$R_i^a(S)$ for $i \in N_2$: y, z, w, x

$R_i^a(S)$ for $i \in N_3$: z, w, x, y

$R_i^a(S)$ for $i \in N_4$: x, y, z, w

$R_i^a(S)$ for $i \in N_5$: y, z, w, x

Let $C^a = F(a)$. F being an extension of the SMD rule, we obtain $C^a(\{x, y\}) = \{x\}$ and $C^a(\{x, w\}) = \{w\}$, so that

$$\{w\} = C^a(C^a(\{x, y\}) \cup C^a(\{w\})) \subset C^a(\{x, y, w\}) \tag{4.19}$$

holds true by virtue of WPI($\alpha 1$). Similarly, we obtain

$$\{x\} = C^a(C^a(\{y, w\}) \cup C^a(\{x\})) \subset C^a(\{x, y, w\}) \tag{4.20}$$

and

$$\{y\} = C^a(C^a(\{x, y\}) \cup C^a(\{y\})) \subset C^a(\{x, y, w\}) \tag{4.21}$$

It follows from (4.19), (4.20), and (4.21) that $C^a(\{x, y, w\}) = \{x, y, w\}$, which implies that

$$\{w\} \subset C^a(C^a(\{x, y, w\}) \cup C^a(\{y, z\})) \subset C^a(S) \tag{4.22}$$

Because $(z, w) \in P(R_i^a)$ for all $i \in N$, (4.22) contradicts the claim of the Pareto principle P. ∎

In classifying various extensions of the SMD rule, the role of watershed was played by the Condorcet criterion. As we have briefly discussed, there are pros and cons on the reasonableness of this criterion. To those individuals who regard this criterion to be reasonable, the following condition (which requires that a feasible alternative that beats a chosen alternative by the simple majority contest should itself be among the chosen alternatives) may also be considered to be appealing.

Condition CT (Condorcet transitivity)[10]
If $a = (R_1^a, R_2^a, \ldots, R_n^a) \in A$, $x, y \in X$, and $S \in \mathscr{S}$ are such that $x \in S$, $y \in C^a(S)$, and $(x, y) \in P(M^a)$, then $x \in C^a(S)$ holds true, where $C^a = F(a)$.

Appealing though this condition may seem to be, we cannot hope to design a Paretian collective choice rule that satisfies this majoritarian condition, *even though we do not require any other choice-consistency condition.*

Theorem 4.5
Assume that $\#X \geq 4$ and $n = \#N \geq 5$. Then there exists no collective choice rule that satisfies the unrestricted domain (U), Condorcet transitivity (CT), and the Pareto principle (P).

Proof: Let F be a rule that satisfies all of the specified conditions. We divide N into $N_1, N_2, \ldots, N_5$ as in the proof of Theorem 4.4. Let $S = \{x, y, z, w\}$, and consider the following profile $a = (R_1^a, R_2^a, \ldots, R_n^a) \in A$:

$R_i^a(S)$ for $i \in N_1$: x, y, z, w

$R_i^a(S)$ for $i \in N_2$: w, x, y, z

$R_i^a(S)$ for $i \in N_3$: z, w, x, y

$R_i^a(S)$ for $i \in N_4$: w, x, y, z

$R_i^a(S)$ for $i \in N_5$: x, z, w, y

Let $C^a = F(a)$, and consider $C^a(S)$:

Case 1: $x \in C^a(S)$
Because $(x, y) \in P(M^a)$, Condorcet transitivity implies that $w \in C^a(S)$.

Case 2: $y \in C^a(S)$
Because $(x, y) \in P(M^a)$, we have $x \in C^a(S)$, thanks to Condorcet transitivity.

Case 3: $z \in C^a(S)$
Because $(y, z) \in P(M^a)$, it follows from Condorcet transitivity that $y \in C^a(S)$.

Case 4: $w \in C^a(S)$
Condorcet transitivity assures us that $z \in C^a(S)$, where use is made of $(z, w) \in P(M^a)$.

It follows that $C^a(S) = S$, which contradicts the Pareto principle P in view of the fact that x Pareto dominates y. ▮

So much for the negative results on the majoritarian collective choice rules. Let us now turn to another extension of the SMD rule that, according to Arrow (1977*b*, p. 620), "does provide an interesting resolution of the social choice paradox which appears to be a relatively slight weakening of the condition of rationality of social preference."

3 Transitive closure of the SMD rule

3.1 Motivation behind the rule

To motivate a particular majoritarian rule on which we shall focus our attention in this section, let us consider a situation[11] where $N = \{1, 2, 3\}$, $X = \{x, y, z\}$, and

$$R_1^a: x, y, z, \quad R_2^a: y, z, x, \quad R_3^a: z, x, y$$

The SMD relation corresponding to this profile is given by

$$M^a = \{(x, x), (y, y), (z, z), (x, y), (y, z), (z, x)\} \tag{4.23}$$

so that we obtain a strict majority cycle: $(x, y) \in P(M^a)$, $(y, z) \in P(M^a)$, and $(z, x) \in P(M^a)$.

Because of the full symmetry that prevails among x, y, and z in (4.23), the problem of majoritarian social choice from the opportunity set $S = \{x, y, z\}$ generates a particular problem. Unless we are allowed to gather some additional information about individual preferences that will enable us to detect some relevant discriminatory features of x, y, and z, we seem to be left with only two options: Either to choose nothing (as is done by the Condorcet function C^a_* as well as by the quasi-Condorcet function C^a_{**}) or to choose all (as in the case of the Borda function C^a_β and the Copeland function C^a_γ). As a matter of fact, the first option is no real contender, because our task is to design a rule that unfailingly enables us to choose. On the other hand, the second option can be embodied by many rules (other than C^a_β and C^a_γ), one particular method being to regard the alternatives in a preference cycle as socially indifferent. Technically speaking, we take the transitive closure of the SMD relation on the set of available states. This brings us to the transitive closure of the SMD rule (the TCM rule).

3.2 *Transitive closure of the SMD rule: formal definition and properties*

It is now time for us to define the TCM rule formally. Consider any profile $a = (R^a_1, R^a_2, \ldots, R^a_n) \in A$ and define the SMD relation M^a by (4.6). Take any $S \in \mathscr{S}$ and define a subset $C^a_{TM}(S)$ thereof by

$$C^a_{TM}(S) = G[S, T(M^a(S))] \qquad (4.24)$$

where $T(M^a(S))$ denotes the transitive closure of M^a on S. M^a being reflexive and complete, $T(M^a(S))$ is an ordering on S. Therefore, C^a_{TM} qualifies as a well-defined choice function on a choice space $(X, \mathscr{S})$. Associating C^a_{TM} thus constructed with the profile $a \in A$ from which we started, we obtain a complete description of the TCM rule.[12] It is easy to ascertain that the TCM rule is a Condorcet extension of the SMD rule.[13]

The reader is referred to Theorem A(1) in the Appendix at the end of this chapter for a characterization of the transitive closure choice function. Coupled with the associated remark, this theorem provides a reason why this special method of extending the SMD rule deserves our particular scrutiny.

Generalizing a simple idea of regarding the alternatives in a SMD cycle as socially indifferent, we have arrived at the TCM rule. An obvious question to be asked is this: How does the TCM rule fare with respect to the Arrovian performance criteria? It is easy to ascertain that the TCM rule satisfies the unrestricted domain (U), independence (I), the binary strong Pareto principle (BSP), and positive responsiveness (PR) and that it does not allow the existence of a vetoer. Furthermore, invoking Theorem A(2) in the Appendix at the end of this chapter, we may assert that C^a_{TM} satisfies the dual Chernoff axiom of choice consistency for all $a \in A$. In addition, it can easily be verified that the TCM rule satisfies the following nonbinary extension of binary anonymity (BAN) and that of binary neutrality (BNE).

Condition AN (anonymity)
If $a = (R_1^a, R_2^a, \ldots, R_n^a) \in A$ is a reordering of $b = (R_1^b, R_2^b, \ldots, R_n^b) \in A$, then $C^a(S) = C^b(S)$ holds true for every $S \in \mathscr{S}$, where $C^a = F(a)$ and $C^b = F(b)$.

Condition NE (neutrality)
If $a = (R_1^a, R_2^a, \ldots, R_n^a) \in A$ is obtained from $b = (R_1^b, R_2^b, \ldots, R_n^b) \in A$ by interchanging x and y in every R_i^b, then we have $x \in C^a(S)$ if and only if $y \in C^b(S)$, and $y \in C^a(S)$ if and only if $x \in C^b(S)$, for every $S \in \mathscr{S}$ such that $\{x, y\} \subset S$, where $C^a = F(a)$ and $C^b = F(b)$.

It is instructive to compare these positive performance characteristics of the TCM rule with the negative assertion of Theorem 3.15. On the face of it, it seems to be the case that the possibility of a collective choice rule that satisfies the unrestricted domain, binary independence, the binary Pareto principle, and positive responsiveness without admitting the existence of a vetoer hinges squarely on whether we want to retain the Chernoff-axiom half of Arrow's axiom (which is equivalent to full rationality of social choice functions) or settle with only the dual-Chernoff-axiom half of Arrow's axiom. If we are modest enough not to require the Chernoff-axiom half, some of the nominated conditions can be strengthened and a few conditions added without upsetting the possibility result. This is certainly an interesting and telling way to locate the gulf between the possibility and impossibility results along the spectrum of choice-consistency axioms.[14] Can we be pleased that we have thereby succeeded in tracking down the critical factor that is responsible for Arrovian impossibility theorems?

Unfortunately, we do not think we can do so open-handedly, for at least two reasons that we shall explain in what follows. As Arrow (1963, p. 109) once remarked in another context: "the paradox of social choice cannot be so easily exorcised."

4 Concluding observations: two defects of the TCM rule

The careful reader must have noticed that all the enumerated conditions that the TCM rule demonstrably satisfies are *nonbinary*, save for the binary strong Pareto principle. This cannot be otherwise, because the TCM rule is a Condorcet extension of the SMD rule, and Theorem 4.3 generally asserts the nonexistence of an extension of the SMD rule satisfying U (unrestricted domain), DCA (dual Chernoff axiom), and SP (strong Pareto principle). Indeed, even a weaker condition P (Pareto principle) may not necessarily be satisfied by the TCM rule, as the following example clearly shows.

Example 4.3
Consider a society where $N = \{1,2,3\}$ and $X = S = \{x, y, z, w\}$ (Fishburn, 1973, p. 87; see also Ferejohn and Grether, 1977*a*; Kalai et al., 1976). Consider, then, the following profile $a \in A$:

$$R_1^a: x, y, z, w$$

$$R_2^a: y, z, w, x$$

$$R_3^a: z, w, x, y$$

and examine the choice function C_{TM}^a generated by the TCM rule. Because $M^a = \{(x,x), (y,y), (z,z), (w,w), (x,y), (y,z), (z,w), (w,x)\}$, we obtain $C_{TM}^a(S) = S$, even though $(z, w) \in \bigcap_{i=1}^3 P(R_i^a)$, which clearly violates condition *P*. ∎

This, then, is the first difficulty with the TCM rule we referred to earlier. It is, of course, possible to design a few extensions of the SMD rule that do satisfy condition P, but only at the cost of throwing away the nice choice-consistency property. To exemplify this point, we have only to refer back to the Borda rule F_β and the Copeland rule F_γ. Example 4.2 clearly shows the difficulty. Although F_β (as well as F_γ) satisfies the strong Pareto principle, the stability axiom (hence such stronger axioms as Nash's and Chernoff's) fails to be satisfied by them. The following example strengthens this negative verdict.[15]

Example 4.4
Consider a society where $N = \{1,2\}$, $X = \{x, y, z\}$, $S_1 = \{x, y\}$, and $S_2 = X$. Consider the following profile $a \in A$:

$$R_1^a: x, y, z$$

$$R_2^a: y, z, x$$

It is easy to calculate the total Borda and Copeland scores to obtain

$$\beta^a(x|S_1) = 0, \quad \beta^a(y|S_1) = 0;$$

$$\beta^a(x|S_2) = 0, \quad \beta^a(y|S_2) = 2, \quad \beta^a(z|S_2) = -2$$

$$\gamma^a(x|S_1) = 0, \quad \gamma^a(y|S_1) = 0;$$

$$\gamma^a(x|S_2) = 0, \quad \gamma^a(y|S_2) = 1, \quad \gamma^a(z|S_2) = -1$$

It then follows that

$$C_\beta^a(S_1) = S_1, \quad C_\beta^a(S_2) = \{y\};$$

$$C_\gamma^a(S_1) = S_1, \quad C_\gamma^a(S_2) = \{y\}$$

so that we have

$$S_1 \subset S_2, \quad C_\alpha^a(S_2) = \{y\} \subset \subset S_1 = C_\alpha^a(S_1) = \{x, y\} \tag{4.25}$$

where $\alpha = \beta$ and γ. Clearly, then, F_β (as well as F_γ) fails to satisfy the superset axiom of choice consistency. ∎

The second difficulty with the TCM rule is deeply rooted in its essential use of the simple majority decision rule in the binary choice situation. As we noted in the introduction to this chapter, there is a strong historical and doctrinal association between democracy and rule by majority that our search for a "democratic" collective choice rule cannot simply neglect. Searching for an essentially majoritarian collective choice rule seems therefore to be a legitimate attempt to substantiate the traditional ideal of democracy. At the same time, however, we should guard ourselves against a danger underlying this route to the effect that blind reliance on simple majority decision rule is susceptible to oppression of the (intense) minority by the (apathetic) majority. A rule that unexceptionally allows the majority to rule the roost at the sacrifice of the minority in the conflict situation is likely to be suspect in the primordial game of rule selection, where nobody knows his fate in the future, and everybody understands that the rule chosen now will be binding indefinitely. It was naturally with good reason that Thomas Jefferson, who drafted the Declaration of Independence and a constitution for the state of Virginia, deliberately stipulated the following proviso in the realm of rule by majority: "All too will bear in mind this sacred principle that though the will of the majority is in all cases to prevail, that will, to be rightful, must be reasonable: that the minority possess equal rights, which equal laws must protect, and to violate would be oppression" (Jefferson, 1801, Vol. VIII, p. 2).

To bring our point home, let us consider the following simple problem of cake division.

Example 4.5

There is a piece of cake that we want to divide among three individuals. Let us consider the following four feasible divisions:

$$x = (\tfrac{1}{2}, \tfrac{1}{2}, 0), \quad y = (\tfrac{1}{2}, 0, \tfrac{1}{2}), \quad z = (0, \tfrac{1}{2}, \tfrac{1}{2}), \quad w = (\tfrac{1}{3}, \tfrac{1}{3}, \tfrac{1}{3})$$

where the component i of each vector denotes the proportion of the cake to be given to individual i ($i = 1, 2, 3$). The subjective preferences over these divisions by each and every individual, which represent each one's preference ranking of the alternatives from one's personal point of view, are likely to be

R_1: $[x, y], w, z$

R_2: $[x, z], w, y$

R_3: $[y, z], w, x$

where R_i denotes the preference ordering over the set $S = \{x, y, z, w\}$ by individual i ($i = 1, 2, 3$). Equipped only with this intrapersonally ordinal and interpersonally noncomparable profile (R_1, R_2, R_3), which alternative out of S should this society of three choose? This is probably the simplest possible, yet nontrivial, distributional problem, and any sensible collective choice rule should be able to help us resolve this conflict situation.

What does the simple majority decision rule recommend in this situation? We can easily verify that x and y, y and z, and z and x all tie with each other in the pairwise SMD contest, and each element of $\{x, y, z\}$ beats w by a two-to-one majority. There seems to be no unambiguous choice recommended by the rule, because there does not exist a Condorcet winner.

One possible way to proceed is to declare that each one of x, y, and z is equally eligible from S in the exclusion of w. This verdict is commonly endorsed by the extensions of the SMD rule discussed in this chapter (i.e., the Borda method, the Copeland method, and the TCM rule). Recollect, however, that eventually a single alternative should be picked from among the alternatives in $\{x, y, z\}$, and whatever tie-breaking mechanism we may use for this purpose, the fact remains that it is "best," according to these collective choice rules, to sacrifice an unlucky individual for the benefit of the privileged majority group. We cannot but believe that a collective choice rule that always empowers a majority in the resolution of distributional conflict exemplified here, *even though there is a perfectly egalitarian alternative among feasible ones,* is most likely to be rejected in the primordial game of rule selection, in which individuals choose a rule of conflict resolution once and for all without knowing the actual realization of the social and personal contingencies.[16] ▮

In view of these defects of the extensions of the SMD rule in general and the TCM rule in particular, one may be tempted to avoid altogether reliance on the SMD rule in the binary choice context. If one adopts this route, one can easily get rid of the difficulty revealed by Example 4.5 in several ways.

One natural way is to endow each and every individual with a right of vetoing an alternative that he wants to avoid. In the case of Example 4.5, x will be vetoed by individual 3, y by individual 2, and z by individual 1, leaving w for a unique nonvetoed alternative.

The second way of resolving the situation in Example 4.5 requires that information be available about individuals' extended preferences of the following form: It is better (or worse) for me to be in individual i's position in one social state than to be in individual j's position in another social state. People in fact seem to be prepared to make comparisons of this type, and in the context of our specified example, it makes good sense to assume that the following extended preference *ordering* is commonly held by all individuals: $[(x,1),(x,2),(y,1),(y,2),(z,2),(z,3)]$, $[(w,1),(w,2),(w,3)]$, $[(x,3)$ $(y,2),(z,1)]$, where $(x,1)$ signifies being put in the position of individual 1 when the social state x prevails, and so on. According to this extended preference, $(x,1)$ is better than $(x,3)$, $(y,3)$ is better than $(y,2)$, and $(z,2)$ is better than $(z,1)$. It then follows that individual 3 envies individual 1's position if the state x prevails, individual 2 envies individual 3's position if the state y prevails, and individual 1 envies individual 2's position if the state z prevails. If we say, following Foley (1967) and Varian (1974, 1975, 1976), that a social state is *equitable* if and only if no individual envies the position of another individual when the chosen state prevails, there is only one state in S that is equitable in this sense (i.e., w). Because w is Pareto-efficient in S as well, it is the unique *fair* state in S in the Foley–Varian sense. Why not choose w for this good reason?

Both ways seem to be worth exploring and, indeed, have been vigorously explored in various contexts.[17] In the next chapter we shall be engaged in exploring some social choice implications of the fairness-as-no-envy approach.

Appendix: Transitive closure choice functions

1. In the main text of Chapter 4, as well as in Chapter 6, we make frequent reference to a particular class of choice functions called the *transitive closure choice functions.* To facilitate our argument, this appendix presents a self-contained analysis of this and closely related concepts, capitalizing mainly on the work by Bordes (1976, 1979). The interested reader should consult such related works as Campbell (1976, 1978*a*, 1978*b*, 1980), Deb (1977), Kalai et al. (1976), Kalai and Schmeidler (1977), and Schwartz (1972) for further clarifications.

2. Let R be an arbitrary reflexive and complete binary relation on X. Take any $S \in \mathscr{S}$, and let a subset $C_t(S|R)$ of S be defined by

$$C_t(S|R) = G[S, T(R(S))] \tag{A.1}$$

where $R(S) = R \cap (S \times S)$ is the restriction of R on S and $T(R(S))$ is the transitive closure of $R(S)$. R being reflexive and complete by assumption, $T(R(S))$ is an ordering on S, so that $C_t(\cdot|R)$ qualifies as a well-defined choice function on a choice space $(X, \mathscr{S})$. This is the transitive closure choice function determined by R.

3. Two simple preliminary remarks are in order. First, the base relation for $C_t(\cdot|R)$ coincides with R. We have only to note that

$$x \in C_t(\{x, y\}|R) \leftrightarrow (x, y) \in T(R(\{x, y\}))$$

$$\leftrightarrow (x, y) \in R$$

holds true for every $\{x, y\} \in \mathscr{S}_B$. Second, the transitive closure choice function determined by R is full rational if R happens to be transitive, but it is an "irrational" choice function in general. To bring this point home, let us present the following:

Example A(1)
Suppose that $X = \{x, y, z\}$ and

$$R = \Delta_X \cup \{(x, y), (y, z), (x, z), (z, x)\}$$

where $\Delta_X = \{(x, x), (y, y), (z, z)\}$. It can easily be verified that

$$C_t(\{x, y, z\}|R) = \{x, y, z\}, \qquad C_t(\{x, y\}|R) = \{x\}$$

hold true. Suppose that this $C_t(\cdot|R)$ has a rationalization R_0. It then follows from $C_t(\{x, y, z\} | R) = \{x, y, z\}$ that $(x, y) \in I(R_0), (y, z) \in I(R_0)$, and $(x, z) \in I(R_0)$, which imply that

$$G(\{x, y\}, R_0) = \{x, y\} \neq C_t(\{x, y\}|R)$$

Therefore, $C_t(\cdot|R)$ cannot have a rationalization. ∎

4. A characterization of the transitive closure choice function can be given in terms of the concept of an R-cut, which played a vital role in our rationalizability theory presented in Chapter 2. Recollect that a choice function C on a choice space $(X, \mathscr{S})$ is an R-cut if and only if

$$\forall S \in \mathscr{S}: x \in C(S) \leftrightarrow [x \in S \;\&\; \exists y \in C(S): (x, y) \in R] \tag{A.2}$$

holds true. It is easy to verify that the trivial choice function C such that $C(S) = S$ for all $S \in \mathscr{S}$ does satisfy (A.2), which, however, is not selective at all. A natural and interesting question is this: What is the *most selective* R-cut?

To prepare for our answer to this question, let $\mathscr{C}_R^{cu}$ denote the set of all R-cuts on $\mathscr{S}$. Because the trivial choice function belongs to $\mathscr{C}_R^{cu}$, it is clear that $\mathscr{C}_R^{cu}$ is nonempty. For every $S \in \mathscr{S}$, let us define

$$\mathscr{C}_R^{cu}(S) = \{C(S) | C \in \mathscr{C}_R^{cu}\}$$

We now prove that $\mathscr{C}_R^{cu}(S)$ is a nest; that is, $\subset$ is complete on $\mathscr{C}_R^{cu}(S)$. With this purpose in mind, take any $C^1(S), C^2(S) \in \mathscr{C}_R^{cu}(S)$. If there exist $x, y \in X$ such that $x \in C^1(S) \setminus C^2(S)$ and $y \in C^2(S) \setminus C^1(S)$, then we obtain

$$x \in C^1(S) \tag{A.3}$$

$$x \notin S \vee [\forall z \in C^2(S): (z, x) \in P(R)] \tag{A.4}$$

$$y \in C^2(S) \tag{A.5}$$

and

$$y \notin S \vee [\forall z \in C^1(S): (z, y) \in P(R)] \tag{A.6}$$

where use is made of (A.2) and the completeness of R. Combined use of (A.3) and (A.6) yields $(x, y) \in P(R)$, whereas (A.4) and (A.5) yield $(y, x) \in P(R)$, a contradiction. Therefore, either $C^1(S) \subset C^2(S)$ or $C^1(S) \supset C^2(S)$ must be true, as desired.

Note that for every $S \in \mathscr{S}$, $\mathscr{C}_R^{cu}(S)$ is a finite set, over which the set-theoretic inclusion $\subset$ is an ordering, so that there exists the smallest set $C_{st}(S) \in \mathscr{C}_R^{cu}(S)$.[18] We have thus obtained a choice function $C_{st} \in \mathscr{C}_R^{cu}$ on a choice space $(X, \mathscr{S})$ that, by construction, is the most selective R-cut.

We are now ready to put forward the following characterization theorem for the transitive closure choice function.

Theorem A(1)
The transitive closure choice function determined by R is the most selective R-cut, namely, $C_t(\cdot|R) = C_{st}$.

Proof: To begin with, let us show that $C_t(\cdot|R) \in \mathscr{C}_R^{cu}$ holds true. R being reflexive, it is clear that

$$x \in C_t(S|R) \rightarrow [x \in S \;\&\; \exists y \in C_t(S|R): (x, y) \in R] \tag{A.7}$$

holds true for every $S \in \mathscr{S}$. To show that the converse of (A.7) also holds true, take any $S \in \mathscr{S}$, and suppose that $x \in S$ and $(x, y) \in R$ hold true for some $y \in C_t(S|R)$. By definition of $C_t(\cdot|R)$ we then have $(y, z) \in T(R(S))$ for all $z \in S$, which, coupled with $(x, y) \in R(S)$, yields $(x, z) \in T(R(S))$ for all $z \in S$. It then follows that $x \in C_t(S|R)$ is true, as desired.

Second, we show that $C_t(S|R)$ is the smallest set in $\mathscr{C}_R^{cu}(S)$, namely $C_t(S|R) = C_{st}(S)$, for every $S \in \mathscr{S}$. Suppose, to the contrary, that

$$\exists S \in \mathscr{S}: C_{st}(S) \subset\subset C_t(S|R) \tag{A.8}$$

holds true. Because $C_{st}(S) \in \mathscr{C}_R^{cu}(S)$ by definition, we have

$$x \notin C_{st}(S) \rightarrow [x \notin S \vee \forall y \in C_{st}(S): (y, x) \in P(R)]$$

namely,

$$\forall x \in S \setminus C_{st}(S), \forall y \in C_{st}(S): (y, x) \in P(R) \tag{A.9}$$

In view of (A.8), there exists a $u \in C_t(S|R) \setminus C_{st}(S)$. Take any $v \in C_{st}(S)$. We then have $(u, v) \in T(R(S))$, so that

$$\exists z^1, z^2, \ldots, z^m \in S:$$
$$z^1 = u, \quad (z^t, z^{t+1}) \in R \; (\forall t \in \{1, 2, \ldots, m-1\}) \quad \text{and} \quad z^m = v \tag{A.10}$$

If we have $z^t \in S \setminus C_{st}(S)$ and $z^{t+1} \in C_{st}(S)$ for some $t \in \{1, 2, \ldots, m-1\}$, we obtain from (A.9) that $(z^{t+1}, z^t) \in P(R)$, in contradiction of (A.10). Therefore, it is true that

$$\forall t \in \{1, 2, \ldots, m-1\}: z^{t+1} \in C_{st}(S) \to z^t \in C_{st}(S) \quad \text{(A.11)}$$

Starting from $z^m = v \in C_{st}(S)$, successive applications of (A.11) yield in the end that $z^1 = u \in C_{st}(S)$, in contradiction to $u \in C_t(S|R) \setminus C_{st}(S)$. Because $\subset$ is complete on $\mathscr{C}_R^{cu}(S)$ and $C_{st}(S)$ is defined to be the smallest set in $\mathscr{C}_R^{cu}(S)$, we must conclude that $C_{st}(S) = C_t(S|R)$ for every $S \in \mathscr{S}$. ∎

With the purpose of crystallizing a salient feature of the transitive closure choice function, take *any* choice function C on a choice space $(X, \mathscr{S})$ such that the base relation for C defined by (2.17) coincides with R. Let R_C be a revealed preference relation induced by C, which is defined by (2.4). Clearly, we obtain $R \subset R_C$. Therefore, C being an R-cut is a necessary condition for C being an R_C-cut. We now invoke Theorem 2.10, according to which C being an R_C-cut is necessary and sufficient for C being full rational. Now, $C_t(\cdot|R)$ need not be full rational, but it does satisfy this necessary condition, most selectively at that. Hence the interest of this class of choice functions.

5. The transitive closure choice function determined by R has rather nice choice-consistency properties that will frequently be referred to later. That is to say, the following assertion is true.

Theorem A(2)
The transitive closure choice function $C_t(\cdot\,|\,R)$ determined by a reflexive and complete binary relation R satisfies the dual Chernoff axiom (DCA) as well as Nash's axiom (NA) (Bordes, 1976, 1979).

Proof: To prove that $C_t(\cdot|R)$ satisfies DCA, let $S_1, S_2 \in \mathscr{S}$ be such that $S_1 \subset S_2$ and $S_1 \cap C_t(S_2|R) \neq \varnothing$. Suppose that there exists an $x \in X$ such that $x \in C_t(S_1|R)$ and $x \notin S_1 \cap C_t(S_2|R)$. Noting that $S_1 \cap C_t(S_2|R) \neq \varnothing$, take any $y \in S_1 \cap C_t(S_2|R)$. Because $x \in C_t(S_1|R)$ and $y \in S_1$ are true, we have $(x, y) \in T(R(S_1)) \subset T(R(S_2))$. Coupled with $y \in C_t(S_2|R)$, which yields $(y, z) \in T(R(S_2))$ for every $z \in S_2$, this entails $x \in C_t(S_2|R)$, a contradiction. It then follows that $C_t(S_1|R) \subset S_1 \cap C_t(S_2|R)$, which implies that $C_t(\cdot|R)$ satisfies DCA.

To prove that $C_t(\cdot|R)$ satisfies NA, suppose that $S_1, S_2 \in \mathscr{S}$ are such that $S_1 \subset S_2$, $C_t(S_2|R) \subset S_1$, and $C_t(S_1|R) \neq C_t(S_2|R)$. Because $C_t(\cdot|R)$ satisfies DCA, as we showed earlier, it follows that

$$C_t(S_2|R) = S_1 \cap C_t(S_2|R) \supset C_t(S_1|R)$$

which implies, in view of $C_t(S_1|R) \neq C_t(S_2|R)$, that

$$C_t(S_1|R) \subset \subset C_t(S_2|R) \tag{A.12}$$

We now establish that

$$x \in C_t(S_1|R) \leftrightarrow [x \in S_2 \ \& \ \exists\, y \in C_t(S_1|R): (x, y) \in R] \tag{A.13}$$

holds true. R being reflexive and $C_t(S_1|R) \subset S_1 \subset S_2$, it is clear that the rightward implication in (A.13) is valid. On the other hand, the leftward implication in (A.13) is easily seen to be valid if $x \in S_1$. Assume, therefore, that $x \notin S_1$; hence $x \notin C_t(S_2|R)$. By virtue of $C_t(\cdot|R) \in \mathscr{C}_R^{cu}$, $x \notin C_t(S_2|R)$ is the case if and only if

$$x \notin S_2 \vee \forall z \in C_t(S_2|R): (z, x) \in P(R) \tag{A.14}$$

holds true. But both alternatives in (A.14) bring us into contradiction. To verify this fact, we have only to notice that $x \in S_2$ and that $y \in C_t(S_1|R) \subset C_t(S_2|R)$ and $(x, y) \in R$. The assertion (A.13) being now established, it is true that

$$C_t(S_1|R) \in \mathscr{C}_R^{cu}(S_2)$$

Thanks to Theorem A(1), we then obtain $C_t(S_2|R) \subset C_t(S_1|R)$, in contradiction of (A.12). Therefore, we can conclude that $C_t(\cdot|R)$ does satisfy NA. ∎

6. Instead of applying the transitive closure choice mechanism directly to an opportunity set $S \in \mathscr{S}$, we may occasionally want to apply it to some specified subset of S. We shall encounter several examples of this hybrid procedure in Chapter 6, where the following auxiliary theorem will play an important role.

Theorem A(3)

Suppose that two binary relations R^1 and R^2 are such that

(a) R^1 is complete and reflexive and $P(R^2)$ is transitive,
(b) $P(R^2) \subset P(R^1)$, and
(c) $P(R^1)P(R^2) \cup P(R^2)P(R^1) \subset P(R^1)$.

Then a choice function C defined on a choice space $(X, \mathscr{S})$ by

$$\forall S \in \mathscr{S}: C(S) = G[V_S, T(R^1(V_S))]$$

where $V_S = G(S, R^2)$, satisfies Nash's axiom of choice consistency (Bordes, 1979).

Proof: Let us define a family of sets $\mathscr{V}$ by

$$\mathscr{V} = \{V_S | S \in \mathscr{S}\}$$

Let $S_1, S_2 \in \mathscr{S}$ be such that $S_1 \subset S_2$ and $C(S_2) \subset S_1$. Let V_τ be an abbreviation of V_{S_τ} for $\tau = 1, 2$. $G(\cdot|R^2)$ being a rational choice function, it satisfies Chernoff's axiom of choice consistency, so that we have $S_1 \cap G(S_2, R^2) \subset G(S_1, R^2)$; that is,

$$S_1 \cap V_2 \subset V_1 \tag{A.15}$$

We now define a choice function C^+ on a choice space $(X, \mathscr{S})$ by

$$\forall S \in \mathscr{S}: C^+(S) = G[S, T(R^1(S))] \tag{A.16}$$

so that we have $C^+(V_\tau) = C(S_\tau)$ for $\tau = 1, 2$. Because C^+ satisfies Nash's axiom of choice consistency, as is asserted by Theorem A(2), and because $C(S_2) \subset S_1 \cap V_2$ is implied by $C(S_2) \subset S_1$ and $C(S_2) \subset V_2$, it follows from $C^+(V_2) = C(S_2) \subset S_1 \cap V_2 \subset V_2$ that

$$C^+(S_1 \cap V_2) = C^+(V_2) \tag{A.17}$$

holds true. Coupled with (A.15), (A.17) yields

$$C^+(V_2) \subset S_1 \cap V_2 \subset V_1 \subset S_1 \tag{A.18}$$

Let us now take any $x \in V_1 \setminus C^+(V_2)$. In view of (A.15), we then have two cases to be treated separately.

Case 1: $x \in S_1 \cap V_2$

By virtue of (A.18) and $x \notin C^+(V_2)$, we obtain $x \notin C^+(S_1 \cap V_2)$. Therefore,

$$\forall y \in C^+(V_2): (y, x) \in P(R_1) \tag{A.19}$$

must be the case, where use is made of the characterization of the choice function C^+ as the smallest R^1-cut. See Theorem A(1).

Case 2: $x \in V_1 \setminus (S_1 \cap V_2)$

In this case, $x \notin V_2$ should be the case, so that

$$\exists z \in V_2: (z, x) \in P(R^2) \tag{A.20}$$

holds true. If it so happens that $z \in C^+(V_2)$, then (A.18) entails $z \in S_1$, in contradiction of $x \in V_1$ in view of (A.20) and (b). Therefore, we must have $z \in V_2 \setminus C^+(V_2)$, which yields

$$\forall y \in C^+(V_2): (y, z) \in P(R^1) \tag{A.21}$$

Coupled with (A.20), (A.21) implies that (A.19) is valid in this case as well, where use is made of (c).

We have thus verified that

$$x \in V_1 \setminus C^+(V_2) \rightarrow \forall y \in C^+(V_2): (y, x) \in P(R^1) \tag{A.22}$$

holds true. It then follows that $V_1 \setminus C^+(V_2) \in \mathscr{C}^{cu}_{R^1}(V_1)$, where

$$\mathscr{C}^{cu}_{R^1}(V_1) = \{C(V_1) | C \text{ is an } R^1\text{-cut}\} \tag{A.23}$$

Therefore, we obtain

$$C^+(V_1) \subset C^+(V_2) \tag{A.24}$$

in view of the smallestness of $C^+(V_1)$ in $\mathscr{C}^{cu}_{R^1}(V_1)$.

We are now almost home. Thanks to (A.18), we have $C^+(V_2) \subset V_1$. Taking (A.24) into consideration, we obtain $C^+(V_1) = C^+(C^+(V_2)) = C^+(V_2)$, where use is made of the stability property of C^+ (which follows from the Nash property thereof). This implies $C(S_1) = C(S_2)$, as was to be verified. ∎

CHAPTER 5

The fairness-as-no-envy approach in social choice theory

> There is something extraordinary, and seemingly unaccountable in the operation of our passions, when we consider the fortune and situation of others. Very often another's advancement and prosperity produces envy, which has a strong mixture of hatred, and arises chiefly from the comparison of ourselves with the person. At the very same time, or at least in very short intervals, we may feel the passion of respect, which is a species of affection or good-will, with a mixture of humility. On the other hand, the misfortunes of our fellows often causes pity, which has in it a strong mixture of good-will. This sentiment of pity is nearly allied to contempt, which is a species of dislike, with a mixture of pride. I only point out these phenomena, as a subject of speculation to such as are curious with regard to moral enquiries.
>
> David Hume*

0 Introduction

Consider the problem of dividing a cake among three individuals once again. Reliance on the Pareto efficiency criterion in finding an appropriate division will be of no help, because all divisions that leave nothing to be wasted will be Pareto-efficient. If we take recourse to the simple majority decision rule, our choice will be narrowed down, but the outcome thereby arrived at may well be strongly unappealing, as we have illustrated by Example 4.5. Invoking the no-envy concept of equity, we can also narrow down the range of eligible divisions. But joint use of the Pareto efficiency criterion and that of no-envy equity encounters difficulty when the amount to be divided depends on the contributions made by individuals among whom ability differential prevails, because there may then be no eligible division at all.[1]

Confronted with this dilemma, one may simply observe that from the viewpoint of moral philosophy it is not altogether clear if a concept of equity based on such a "mean" feeling as envy can be ethically relevant in the first place, and then wash one's hands of the business. Tempting though

* D. Hume, *Enquiries Concerning the Human Understanding and Concerning the Principles of Morals* (reprinted from the posthumous edition of 1777), edited by L. A. Silby–Bigge. Oxford at the Clarendon Press, 1902, p. 248, footnote.

this attitude toward a no-envy concept of equity might be, we believe we should at least try to determine just where the proposed concept of equity and several variants thereof[2] bring us in this relatively less cultivated area in welfare economics and social choice theory, particularly because it is much easier to cite concrete instances of indisputably inequitable situations than to crystallize an abstract concept of equity.[3] In this chapter we embed the concept of fairness as no-envy-equity-cum-efficiency in the conceptual framework of social choice theory, with a view toward evaluating how the identified dilemma would be located in the perennial enigma of designing "satisfactory" collective choice rules.

The plan of the chapter is as follows. In Section 1 we introduce an extended conceptual framework that enables us to perform our social-choice-theoretic analysis of a no-envy equity concept. In Section 2 we present several impossibility theorems on the compatibility between the no-envy equity and Pareto-efficiency. Section 3 is devoted to examining a particular collective choice rule based on the proposed fairness concept, which is due essentially to Goldman and Sussangkarn (1978), whereas Section 4 proposes what we call the leximin envy collective choice rule. These two sections are meant to illustrate the potentiality of the no-envy approach in social choice theory. Finally, Section 5 concludes with several qualifying remarks.

1 Framework of analysis

1.1 Extended preference orderings

As Varian (1975, pp. 240–1) has aptly observed, "the theory of fairness ... is founded in the notion of 'extended sympathy' and in the idea of 'symmetry' in the treatment of agents.... In effect, we are asking each agent to put himself in the position of each of the other agents to determine if that is a better or a worse position than the one he is now in."

To formalize this foundation of the theory of fairness, let X and $N = \{1, 2, \ldots, n\}$ $(2 \leq n < +\infty)$ stand, respectively, for the set of all conceivable social states and the set of individuals, a social state being a complete description of the relevant aspects of the world. For each individual $i \in N$, we describe his views on the society by extended preference ordering $\tilde{R}_i$ on the Cartesian product $X \times N$,

$$((x, j), (y, k)) \in \tilde{R}_i$$

denoting the fact that being in the position of individual j in the social state x is at least as good as being in the position of individual k in the social state y according to i's view.

A list of extended preference orderings, one ordering for each individual, will be called an *extended profile*, and alternative extended profiles will be indexed by α, $\beta, \ldots,$ like $\alpha = (\tilde{R}_1^\alpha, \tilde{R}_2^\alpha, \ldots, \tilde{R}_n^\alpha)$, $\beta = (\tilde{R}_1^\beta, \tilde{R}_2^\beta, \ldots, \tilde{R}_n^\beta)$, and so on. We denote the set of all logically possible extended profiles by $\mathscr{A}$. As before, the set of all nonempty finite subsets of X will be denoted by $\mathscr{S}$, each and every $S \in \mathscr{S}$ being construed to represent a set of available states under the specified environmental conditions.

Our problem is to design a rule or function Ψ that maps each extended profile $\alpha \in \mathscr{A}$ into a choice function $C^\alpha = \Psi(\alpha)$ on a choice space $(X, \mathscr{S})$. Such a rule will be referred to as an *extended collective choice rule.*

1.2 *Subjective preferences, Pareto efficiency, and no-envy equity*

Take any extended profile $\alpha = (\tilde{R}_1^\alpha, \tilde{R}_2^\alpha, \ldots, \tilde{R}_n^\alpha) \in \mathscr{A}$ and an opportunity set $S \in \mathscr{S}$, and fix them for the time being. For each individual $i \in N$, let i's *subjective preference ordering* R_i^α be defined by

$$R_i^\alpha = \{(x, y) \in X \times X \mid ((x, i), (y, i)) \in \tilde{R}_i^\alpha\} \tag{5.1}$$

It is clear that R_i^α is an ordering on X for each $\alpha \in \mathscr{A}$ and $i \in N$. We can then define the *Pareto quasi ordering* R_f^α by

$$R_f^\alpha = \bigcap_{i \in N} R_i^\alpha \tag{5.2}$$

which can be used to define the set of Pareto efficient states in S by

$$E_f^\alpha(S) = \{x \in S \mid \forall\, y \in S: (y, x) \notin P(R_f^\alpha)\} \tag{5.3}$$

It is now time we define formally the no-envy concept of equity and that of fairness. Following Foley's classic definition (1967), we say that individual $i \in N$ envies individual $j \in N$ at $x \in X$ when the profile $\alpha \in \mathscr{A}$ prevails if and only if $((x, j), (x, i)) \in P(\tilde{R}_i^\alpha)$ holds true. We say that x is *no-envy-equitable* if and only if nobody envies other individual at x when the profile $\alpha \in \mathscr{A}$ prevails. We denote the set of all no-envy-equitable states in $S \in \mathscr{S}$ by

$$E_q^\alpha(S) = \{x \in S \mid \forall\, i, j \in N: ((x, i), (x, j)) \in \tilde{R}_i^\alpha\} \tag{5.4}$$

If a state x in S is simultaneously Pareto-efficient and no-envy-equitable, we say that x is *no-envy-fair* in S. The set of all no-envy-fair states in S, to be called the no-envy-fair set in S, will be defined by

$$F^\alpha(S) = E_f^\alpha(S) \cap E_q^\alpha(S) \tag{5.5}$$

2 Fairness-as-no-envy and Pareto efficiency: I. Some impossibility theorems

2.1 Fairness criteria for extended collective choice rules

The first observation to be made on the concept of the no-envy-fair set in S is that it may turn out to be empty. Indeed, it may even be the case that $E_q^\alpha(X) = \varnothing$ for some $\alpha \in \mathscr{A}$; that is, there may exist no no-envy-equitable state anywhere. Even if Pareto efficiency and no-envy equity are *individually* self-consistent (in the sense that they can respectively be satisfied), they may well be *jointly* incompatible, as can easily be exemplified as follows.

Example 5.1
Let $X = \{x, y\}$ and $N = \{1, 2\}$. Let an extended profile $\alpha \in \mathscr{A}$ be specified by

$$\tilde{R}_1^\alpha: (y, 2), (y, 1), (x, 1), (x, 2)$$

$$\tilde{R}_2^\alpha: (y, 2), (y, 1), (x, 2), (x, 1)$$

Clearly, then, $E_q^\alpha(\{x, y\}) = \{x\}$ and $P(R_f^\alpha) = \{(y, x)\}$ hold true, so that we have $F^\alpha(\{x, y\}) = \varnothing$. ∎

In view of this possible nonexistence of a no-envy-fair state for some extended profile $\alpha \in \mathscr{A}$, care should be taken with the sense in which we talk about an extended collective choice rule as being fair or unfair. As an auxiliary step in introducing our fairness criteria, let us define the no-less-equitable relation R_q^α on X by

$$R_q^\alpha = \{(x, y) \in X \times X \mid \sim [y \in E_q^\alpha(X) \;\&\; x \notin E_q^\alpha(X)]\} \tag{5.6}$$

that is, $(x, y) \in R_q^\alpha$ is the case if and only if either $x \in E_q^\alpha(X)$ or $y \notin E_q^\alpha(X)$ holds true. We can now assert the following:

Lemma 5.1
For every extended profile $\alpha = (\tilde{R}_1^\alpha, \tilde{R}_2^\alpha, \ldots, \tilde{R}_n^\alpha) \in \mathscr{A}$, R_q^α is an ordering on X. Furthermore,

$$\forall S \in \mathscr{S}: E_q^\alpha(S) = G(S, R_q^\alpha)$$

holds true unless $E_q^\alpha(S) = \varnothing$.

Proof: Reflexivity of R_q^α is obvious by definition. To show completeness thereof, let x and y be such that $(x, y) \notin R_q^\alpha$ and $(y, x) \notin R_q^\alpha$. We then have $[y \in E_q^\alpha(X) \;\&\; x \notin E_q^\alpha(X)]$ and $[x \in E_q^\alpha(X) \;\&\; y \notin E_q^\alpha(X)]$, a contradiction. To show transitivity of R_q^α, let

$x, y, z \in X$ be such that $(x, y) \in R^\alpha_q$ and $(y, z) \in R^\alpha_q$. We then have $[x \in E^\alpha_q(X) \vee y \notin E^\alpha_q(X)]$ and $[y \in E^\alpha_q(X) \vee z \notin E^\alpha_q(X)]$, which imply that $[x \in E^\alpha_q(X) \vee z \notin E^\alpha_q(X)]$, that is, $(x, z) \in R^\alpha_q$, as desired. Assume now that $E^\alpha_q(S)$ is nonempty. Assume further that $x \in S$ and $(x, y) \in R^\alpha_q$ for all $y \in S$. If we take $y \in E^\alpha_q(S) \subset S$, we obtain $x \in E^\alpha_q(S)$, as desired. If, conversely, we have $x \in E^\alpha_q(S)$, we obtain $(x, y) \in R^\alpha_q$ for all $y \in S$, in view of definition (5.6). ∎

Let us now define a binary relation Q^α on X by $Q^\alpha = P(R^\alpha_f) \cup P(R^\alpha_q)$. Clearly, we have $(x, y) \in Q^\alpha$ if and only if x is either "more efficient" or "more equitable" than y when the extended profile $\alpha \in \mathscr{A}$ prevails.

We are now ready to define our fairness criteria for the extended collective choice rule, which read as follows.

Condition FE (fairness extension)
For every extended profile $\alpha \in \mathscr{A}$, $C^\alpha = \Psi(\alpha)$ satisfies

$$\forall S \in \mathscr{S}: C^\alpha(S) = F^\alpha(S)$$

unless $F^\alpha(S) = \emptyset$.

Condition FI (fairness inclusion)
If $\alpha \in \mathscr{A}$ and $S \in \mathscr{S}$ are such that $F^\alpha(S) = \emptyset$, then

$$[x \in S, (x, y) \in Q^\alpha \;\&\; y \in C^\alpha(S)] \rightarrow x \in C^\alpha(S)$$

holds true, where $C^\alpha = \Psi(\alpha)$.

In words, an extended collective choice rule Ψ satisfies condition FE if it always generates a choice function that chooses the set of all no-envy-fair states as far as the latter set is nonempty. On the other hand, Ψ is said to satisfy condition FI if, in a case where there exists no no-envy-fair state, it unfailingly generates a choice function that includes among the chosen states a state that is either "more equitable" or "more efficient" than a state that is chosen. As far as we accept the no-envy-fairness concept, condition FE, as well as condition FI, seems to be rather persuasive.

2.2 *Impossibility theorems*

Let us examine the possibility of constructing an extended collective choice rule that is "fair" in the sense specified earlier. Unless otherwise circumscribed, it is clearly desirable to have a rule that is robust enough.

Condition EU (unrestricted domain)
The domain of an extended collective choice rule consists of all logically possible extended profiles.

Unfortunately, there exists a clear limit to the hope for having an extended collective choice rule with unrestricted domain that is "fair," as we are informed by the following:

Theorem 5.1
Assume that $\# X \geq 3$. Then there exists no extended collective choice rule that satisfies the unrestricted domain (EU), fairness extension (FE), and the superset axiom of choice consistency (SUA) (Suzumura, 1981*b*, Theorem 2).

Proof: Assume that Ψ satisfies EU as well as FE. Take three distinct social states x, y, and $z \in X$, and let $S_1 = \{x, y\}$ and $S_2 = \{x, y, z\}$. Let an extended profile $\alpha = (\tilde{R}_1^\alpha, \tilde{R}_2^\alpha, \ldots, \tilde{R}_n^\alpha) \in \mathscr{A}$ be defined by

$$\tilde{R}_1^\alpha: (x, 1), (z, 2), (z, 1), (y, 1), (y, 2), (x, 2), [(X \setminus S_2) \times (N \setminus \{1, 2\})]$$

$$\tilde{R}_2^\alpha: (z, 2), (y, 2), (x, 2), (x, 1), (z, 1), (y, 1), [(X \setminus S_2) \times (N \setminus \{1, 2\})]$$

and

$$\tilde{R}_i^\alpha: [(X \setminus S_2) \times (N \setminus \{1, 2\})], \tilde{R}_1^\alpha(S_2 \times \{1, 2\})$$

for all $i \in N \setminus \{1, 2\}$, where $[(X \setminus S_2) \times (N \setminus \{1, 2\})]$ denotes the universal binary relation on $(X \setminus S_2) \times (N \setminus \{1, 2\})$; that is,

$$[(X \setminus S_2) \times (N \setminus \{1, 2\})] = \{(X \setminus S_2) \times (N \setminus \{1, 2\})\} \times \{(X \setminus S_2) \times (N \setminus \{1, 2\})\}$$

Note that $E_q^\alpha(S_2) = \{x, y\}$ and $P(R_J^\alpha) \cap (S_2 \times S_2) = \{(z, y)\}$. Therefore, $C^\alpha(S_1) = F^\alpha(S_1) = S_1$ and $C^\alpha(S_2) = F^\alpha(S_2) = \{x\}$ hold true, where $C^\alpha = \Psi(\alpha)$ and use is made of FE. We then obtain $S_1 \subset S_2$, $C^\alpha(S_2) \subset C^\alpha(S_1)$, and $C^\alpha(S_1) \neq C^\alpha(S_2)$. Therefore, a Ψ that satisfies EU and FE cannot possibly satisfy SUA. ∎

Note that Theorem 5.1 does not refer to condition FI; neither does it make any reference to the Pareto principle. As an auxiliary step in examining the possibility of an extended collective choice rule that is fairness-inclusive, we should like to introduce now a variant of the Pareto principle. But we need a careful step forward in this slippery area. To require the exclusion of a state y from a choice set for a binary choice environment $\{x, y\}$ just because x happens to be Pareto-superior to y would be grossly inappropriate in the context in which we care about equity and the like, because doing so would mean to empower the Pareto-dominance relation to outweigh the equity consideration in the binary choice situation.

But this lopsided sanctification of Pareto dominance quite simply contradicts the emphasis put on the equity consideration in the fairness approach. This argument, if accepted, would lead us to the following conditional variant of the Pareto principle.

Condition CBEP (conditional binary exclusion Pareto)
If $\alpha \in \mathscr{A}$ and $x, y \in X$ are such that $E_q^\alpha(\{x, y\}) = \varnothing$ and $(x, y) \in P(R_f^\alpha)$, then $\{x\} = C^\alpha(\{x, y\})$ holds true, where $C^\alpha = \Psi(\alpha)$.

What emerges from this mild-looking Paretian condition in combination with other conditions on an extended collective choice rule is another impossibility theorem to the following effect.

Theorem 5.2
Assume that $\# X \geq 3$. Then there exists no extended collective choice rule that satisfies the unrestricted domain (EU), fairness inclusion (FI), conditional binary exclusion Pareto (CBEP), and Chernoff's axiom of choice consistency (CA) (Suzumura, 1981*b*, Theorem 3).

Proof: Assume that Ψ satisfies EU, FI, and CBEP. Take three distinct social states x, y, and $z \in X$, and let $S_1 = \{x, y\}$ and $S_2 = \{x, y, z\}$. Let an extended profile $\alpha = (\tilde{R}_1^\alpha, \tilde{R}_2^\alpha, \ldots, \tilde{R}_n^\alpha) \in \mathscr{A}$ be defined by

$\tilde{R}_1^\alpha$: $(x,2), (x,1), (y,2), (y,1), (z,1),$
$(z,2), [(X \setminus S_2) \times (N \setminus \{1,2\})]$

$\tilde{R}_2^\alpha$: $(x,1), (x,2), (y,1), (y,2), (z,2),$
$(z,1), [(X \setminus S_2) \times (N \setminus \{1,2\})]$

and

$\tilde{R}_i^\alpha[(X \setminus S_2) \times (N \setminus \{1,2\})], \tilde{R}_1^\alpha(S_2 \times \{1,2\})$

for all $i \in N \setminus \{1,2\}$. Noticing that $E_q^\alpha(S_2) = \{z\}$ and $P(R_f^\alpha) \cap (S_2 \times S_2) = \{(x, y), (y, z), (x, z)\}$ hold true, we obtain $C^\alpha(S_1) = \{x\}$ by virtue of CBEP, where $C^\alpha = \Psi(\alpha)$. Consider now $C^\alpha(S_2)$. If $x \in C^\alpha(S_2)$ is the case, then $z \in C^\alpha(S_2)$ holds true by virtue of FI. If $z \in C^\alpha(S_2)$ is true, then $x, y \in C^\alpha(S_2)$ must be the case, thanks again to FI. As $C^\alpha(S_2)$ is nonempty, we should conclude that $C^\alpha(S_2) = S_2$. Now we have $S_1 \subset S_2$, $S_1 \cap C^\alpha(S_2) \not\subset C^\alpha(S_1)$, which implies that an extended collective choice rule satisfying EU, FI, and CBEP cannot possibly satisfy CA. ∎

Simple corollaries of Theorems 5.1 and 5.2 are worth mentioning. Referring back to the logical relationship that holds true among choice-consistency axioms, as summarized in Figure 2.2, we obtain the following results. In view of the strong intuitive appeal of the path-independence argument, these corollaries may better crystallize the logical difficulty identified by Theorems 5.1 and 5.2.

Corollary 5.1
Assume that $\# X \geq 3$. Then there exists no extended collective choice rule that satisfies the unrestricted domain (EU), fairness extension (FE),and weak path independence ($\beta 2$) [WPI($\beta 2$)].

Corollary 5.2
Assume that $\# X \geq 3$. Then there exists no extended collective choice rule that satisfies the unrestricted domain (EU), fairness inclusion (FI), conditional binary exclusion Pareto (CBEP), and weak path independence ($\beta 1$) [WPI($\beta 1$)].

Simple though these impossibility results are, they serve to show unambiguously that there exists a clear limit to the possibility of constructing an extended collective choice rule that is "fair."

2.3 *Axiom of identity and axiom of complete identity*

Before going any further, a reflection on our current conceptual framework seems to be in order. In talking about extended preference orderings, which are based on imaginary interpersonal exchange of circumstances, an important role is played by what Sen (1970*b*, p. 156) called the axiom of identity and the axiom of complete identity. To introduce these concepts formally, let a binary relation R_{ij}^{α} be defined by

$$R_{ij}^{\alpha} = \{(x, y) \in X \times X \mid ((x, j), (y, j)) \in \tilde{R}_i^{\alpha}\} \tag{5.7}$$

for every $\alpha \in \mathscr{A}$ and every $i, j \in N$. Clearly, it is true that $R_i^{\alpha} = R_{ii}^{\alpha}$ for all $\alpha \in \mathscr{A}$ and all $i \in N$. Note that $(x, y) \in R_i^{\alpha}$ means that individual i thinks that x is no worse for him than y, and $(x, y) \in R_{ij}^{\alpha}$ means that i thinks that it is no worse for j to be in x rather than in y. With this interpretation of R_i^{α} and R_{ij}^{α}, it seems fairly natural in the context in which we talk about welfare judgments based on extended preference orderings that we require fulfillment of the following axiom, which requires in essence nonpaternalistic acceptance of one another's subjective preferences.

Condition ID (axiom of identity)
For every extended profile $\alpha \in \mathscr{A}$ and every $i, j \in N$, $R_{ij}^{\alpha} = R_j^{\alpha}$ holds true.

It is important to recognize that condition ID differs substantially from, and is much weaker than, the following requirement.

Condition CID (axiom of complete identity)
For every extended profile $\alpha \in \mathscr{A}$ and every $i, j \in N$, $\tilde{R}_i^\alpha = \tilde{R}_j^\alpha$ holds true.

Note that condition CID and, a fortiori, condition ID place no restriction whatsoever on the profile of subjective preferences; neither do they imply any implicit commensurability of individuals' extended welfare judgments.

In view of their critical importance in many subsequent contexts, it is worthwhile to make a little detour and examine carefully the nature of these axioms.

There are two possible formulations we can use in talking about these concepts, the first one being essentially due to Arrow (1977*a*), Harsanyi (1955, 1977), and Pattanaik (1968), whereas the second can be attributed to Sen (1970*b*) and Suppes (1966). *Throughout this side argument, we shall use slightly different notation to make our argument unambiguous.*

Let X and Θ denote, respectively, the set of all conceivable social states and the set of all conceivable personal characteristics. We can suppose that every objectively relevant description of the world and every subjectively relevant description of the individual that in one way or the other affect the individual's welfare are completely specified by $x \in X$ and $\theta \in \Theta$, respectively. The complete description of the society's situation can then be given by specifying a social state $x \in X$ and a profile of characteristics $(\theta^1, \theta^2, \ldots, \theta^n) \in \Theta^N \equiv \Theta \times \Theta \times \cdots \times \Theta$ (n times).

Let us now consider a grand conceptual experiment of ordering each and every triplet $(x, i, \theta^j) \in X \times N \times \Theta$ vis-à-vis others, where (x, i, θ^j) denotes a circumstance in which the evaluating individual occupies individual i's objective position in the social state x, (x, i), with the personal characteristics θ^j of individual j.

Conceptually, there is nothing anomalous about this experiment. As Arrow (1963, p. 115) observed, "the possession of tools would ordinarily be regarded as part of the social state; why not the possession of the skills to use the tools and the intelligence which lies behind those skills? Individuals, in appraising each other's states of well-being, consider not only material possessions but also find themselves 'desiring this man's scope and that man's art'."

Note that everyone shares the *same* ordering on $X \times N \times \Theta$, which we represent by a grand welfare function W, *if indeed the descriptions of the state and the personal characteristics are relevantly complete.* To justify this claim, suppose that two individuals i and j, for example, differ on the welfare they will obtain from entertaining (x, k, θ^l). This could happen only if the description of either x or θ^l were so incomplete that something was left out of the description in the first place, something that would induce i and j to feel differently even though they occupy the same objective position (x, k) and identify themselves, by imaginary transformation of personality, with the individual l characterized by θ^l. Needless to say, this does not mean that individuals i and j, for example, agree on the personal welfare from a state x, the latter being given by $w^{\theta^i}(x) \equiv W(x, i, \theta^i)$ and $w^{\theta^j}(x) \equiv W(x, j, \theta^j)$, respectively, when a characteristics profile $(\theta^1, \ldots, \theta^i, \ldots, \theta^j, \ldots, \theta^n) \in \Theta^N$ prevails.

With this commonly held grand welfare function in hand, let us now define the extended preference orderings for each and every individual, when a characteristics profile $(\theta^1, \theta^2, \ldots, \theta^n) \in \Theta^N$ prevails, by

$$((x, j), (y, k)) \in R(\theta^i) \leftrightarrow W(x, j, \theta^j) \geq W(y, k, \theta^k) \tag{5.8}$$

for all $x, y \in X$ and all $i, j, k \in N$. Note that the extended profile $(R(\theta^1), R(\theta^2), \ldots, R(\theta^n))$ thus defined always satisfies the complete identity axiom for all characteristics profiles: $R(\theta^i) = R(\theta^j)$ for all $i, j \in N$ and all $(\theta^1, \theta^2, \ldots, \theta^n) \in \Theta^N$. A fortiori, the identity axiom, which requires that $((x, j), (y, j)) \in R(\theta^i)$ if and only if $w^{\theta^j}(x) \geq w^{\theta^j}(y)$ for all $x, y \in X$ and all $i, j \in N$, is always satisfied for all $(\theta^1, \theta^2, \ldots, \theta^n) \in \Theta^N$.[4]

A natural question now suggests itself: Why should we assume the axiom of identity (as we often shall later) when the validity of an even stronger axiom of complete identity is always guaranteed by the foregoing logically impeccable construction?

Our plea is that the finest imaginable descriptions of the objective states and the personal characteristics are difficult to come by, and even if we accept the possibility thereof, for the sake of argument, an individual has no operational means to ascertain which personal characteristics, so finely demarcated, in fact apply to the other individuals. Therefore, "unanimity [on the extended preferences] is not absurd to assume ... since everyone orders the positions, bearing in mind that being person i in state x means not merely to have the social positions of i but also his precise subjective features" (Sen, 1970*b*, p. 138), if only we are prepared to assume such extraordinarily fine ability of classification and identification on the part of individuals. Certainly we do not want to assume generally such excessive capabilities of individuals, because doing so would inevitably impose quite strong limitations on the applicability of our construction. Furthermore, "reducing an individual to a specified list of qualities is denying his individuality in a deep sense.... [The] autonomy of individuals, an element of mutual incommensurability among people seems denied by the possibility of interpersonal comparisons [in the form rationalized earlier]" (Arrow, 1977*a*, p. 225).

Let us therefore turn to the second possibility and define the extended preference ordering corresponding to each characteristics profile $(\theta^1, \theta^2, \ldots, \theta^n) \in \Theta^N$ by

$$((x, j), (y, k)) \in \tilde{R}^*(\theta^i) \leftrightarrow W(x, j, \theta^i) \geq W(y, k, \theta^i) \tag{5.9}$$

for all $x, y \in X$ and all $i, j, k \in N$. Note that the extended profile $(\tilde{R}^*(\theta^1), \tilde{R}^*(\theta^2), \ldots, \tilde{R}^*(\theta^n))$ thus defined has no intrinsic reason to satisfy the axiom of identity, which, in our present notation, reads as follows:

$$\forall x, y \in X, \forall i, j \in X: ((x, j), (y, j)) \in \tilde{R}^*(\theta^i) \leftrightarrow w^{\theta^j}(x) \geq w^{\theta^j}(y)$$

An important feature of this second approach is that in evaluating the objective position (x, j) via the extended preference ordering $\tilde{R}^*(\theta^i)$, individual i does not identify himself subjectively with individual j by imaginary transformation of his personality θ^i into θ^j, as indeed he cannot do for lack of detailed knowledge about the finely circumscribed characteristics θ^j, with the result that the welfare ranking embodied in $\tilde{R}^*(\theta^i)$ is in general not an interpersonal welfare comparison but is what Alchian (1953) called the intrapersonal, intersituational comparison. With the imposition of the axiom of identity, which is now a genuine restriction on the class of admissible profiles of characteristics, we are requiring that θ^i be such that $R^*(\theta^i)$ accepts j's subjective preferences over pairs like $(x, j) \in X \times \{j\}$, which is because the axiom of identity is sometimes called the *principle of acceptance* (Harsanyi, 1977, p. 52).

Note that the informational requirement of this second approach is much lighter than that in the first. In order to comply with the requirement of the axiom, an individual need not know others' personality characteristics in detail. It is sufficient if one knows others' preferences over their objective personal positions, which can be recognized by observing their choices, their verbal and facial expressions, and the like. It is this second approach that we adopt in what follows.[5] Having established this point, let us come back to the main stream of our argument.

With the axiom of identity at our disposal, we can now make two further observations on what has already been said.

First, the extended profile assumed in Example 5.1 and that in the proof of Theorems 5.1 and 5.2 do satisfy the axiom of identity, so that the pathology thereby identified cannot be attributed to lack of sympathetic acceptance of one another's subjective preferences.

Second, we shall briefly examine several alternative no-envy-fairness concepts proposed by Feldman and Kirman (1974), Daniel (1975, 1978), and Pazner (1977), with a view toward testing the robustness of our preceding negative verdicts on the possibility of Foley-fair extended collective choice rule.

To start with, note that the original Foley fairness concept is an essentially all-or-nothing concept that decomposes the set of available states into the fair states and the unfair states without allowing any finer relative fairness judgments. A suggestion due to Feldman and Kirman (1974, p. 995) is meant to rectify this extreme nature of the Foley concept, according to which "[a] completely fair social state is one in which no citizen would prefer what another has to what he himself has; a relatively fair social state is one in which few citizens would prefer what others have to what they themselves have; a totally unfair state is one in which every citizen finds his position to be inferior to that of everyone else." Clearly, what Feldman and Kirman call a "completely fair social state" corresponds to the no-envy equitable state.

In order to crystallize this contrast in a formal way, let us formulate the Feldman–Kirman relative fairness concept. Take any extended profile $\alpha \in \mathscr{A}$, and let $\varepsilon_i^\alpha(x)$ denote the number of individuals whom individual $i \in N$ envies at $x \in X$ when α prevails; that is,

$$\varepsilon_i^\alpha(x) = \#\{j \in N | ((x, j), (x, i)) \in P(\tilde{R}_i^\alpha)\} \tag{5.10}$$

and let

$$\varepsilon^\alpha(x) = (\varepsilon_1^\alpha(x), \varepsilon_2^\alpha(x), \ldots, \varepsilon_n^\alpha(x)) \tag{5.11}$$

We can now define the Feldman–Kirman relative equity ordering $R_{q,fk}^\alpha$ and the set $F_{fk}^\alpha(S)$ of the Feldman–Kirman fair states in $S \in \mathscr{S}$ as follows:

$$R_{q,fk}^\alpha = \left\{(x, y) \in X \times X \,\middle|\, \sum_{i \in N} \varepsilon_i^\alpha(x) \leq \sum_{i \in N} \varepsilon_i^\alpha(y)\right\} \tag{5.12}$$

and

$$F_{fk}^\alpha(S) = E_f^\alpha(S) \cap G(S, R_{q,fk}^\alpha) \tag{5.13}$$

An alternative rectification of the Foley concept with a different motivation behind it, which is occasionally in sharp contrast with the Feldman–Kirman proposal, is due to Daniel (1975, 1978), according to whom "in the absence of points of no envy, points of mutual envy should be chosen" (Daniel, 1975, p. 99). Formally speaking, "if the number of people who envy a person is equal to the number of people that he envies, then he will be said to be *balanced* with respect to envy at that allocation. An allocation will be called *balanced* if everyone is balanced at it" (Daniel, 1975, p. 102). It goes without saying that "balancedness" differs substantially from "relative fairness." The clearest contrast between them comes to the fore when we consider a social state where everyone envies everyone else. Feldman and Kirman call this a "totally unfair" state, whereas Daniel calls it "balanced" and (if it happens to be Pareto-efficient as well) "just."

To formalize Daniel's proposed concept, take any extended profile $\alpha \in \mathscr{A}$ and any state $x \in X$, and define, for each $i \in N$,

$$\mu_i^\alpha(x) = \#\{j \in N | ((x, i), (x, j)) \in P(\tilde{R}_j^\alpha)\} \tag{5.14}$$

Then the Daniel balanced set in $S \in \mathscr{S}$ can be formalized as

$$B^\alpha(S) = \{x \in S | \forall i \in N: \varepsilon_i^\alpha(x) = \mu_i^\alpha(x)\} \tag{5.15}$$

Because $x \in E_q^\alpha(S)$ holds true if and only if $\varepsilon_i^\alpha(x) = \mu_i^\alpha(x) = 0$ holds true for all $i \in N$, $E_q^\alpha(S) \subset B^\alpha(S)$ is true for every $(\alpha, S) \in \mathscr{A} \times \mathscr{S}$. If we define

$$R_{q,d}^\alpha = \{(x, y) \in X \times X | \sim [y \in B^\alpha(S) \; \& \; x \notin B^\alpha(S)]\} \tag{5.16}$$

and

$$F_d^\alpha(S) = E_f^\alpha(S) \cap G(S, R_{q,d}^\alpha) \tag{5.17}$$

it can easily be verified that $B^\alpha(S) = G(S, R_{q,d}^\alpha)$ holds true for every $(\alpha, S) \in \mathscr{A} \times \mathscr{S}$, so that $F_d^\alpha(S)$ is nothing other than the Daniel just set.

The third alternative concept of fairness that we shall examine is due to Pazner, according to whom (1977, p. 463), "an allocation will be said to be *fair-equivalent* if there exists a fair allocation in some hypothetical economy in which each person enjoys the same welfare level as that enjoyed by him at the allocation under consideration." As Daniel (1978) pointed out acutely, the ethical relevance of the Pazner fairness concept is highly dubious, because it implies that the inequity in the status quo may well be left unrectified even though there exists a more equitable and more efficient state that is feasible in the *existing* environment if only there is a fair state under the *hypothetical* environment giving each individual the same welfare as he has in the status quo. This rather obvious defect notwithstanding, we pursue the logical consequence of the proposal by Pazner with a view toward showing that the Pazner fairness concept does not dissipate the gloomy verdict we arrived at by using Foley's original no-envy-fairness concept.

To start with, let us take care of an incongruence in terminology. For Pazner, "an allocation is said to be fair if no person in the economy prefers anyone else's consumption bundle over his own" (Pazner, 1977, p. 458), which corresponds to the concept of equity (rather than to that of fairness) in the Foley–Varian terminology. In view of this, we must somehow incorporate the Pareto-efficiency consideration into the Pazner fairness criterion so as to make it comparable with the Foley concept.

Two possibilities naturally suggest themselves. The first is to christen a state x in $S \in \mathscr{S}$ to be (modified) fair-equivalent if there exists a Foley-fair state y in some environment $S^* \in \mathscr{S}$ such that every individual is indifferent between being in x and being in y. This leads us to the following first formulation of the Pazner-fair set in $S \in \mathscr{S}$:

$$F^{\alpha}_{p(1)}(S) = \left\{ x \in X \,\middle|\, \exists\, y \in \bigcup_{S^* \in \mathscr{S}} F^{\alpha}(S^*) \colon (x, y) \in \bigcap_{i \in N} I(R^{\alpha}_{i}) \right\} \tag{5.18}$$

which, however, has a serious defect: A state $x \in F^{\alpha}_{p(1)}(S)$ may well be Pareto-inefficient in S even if the reference state $y \in F^{\alpha}(S^*)$ is Pareto-efficient as well as no-envy equitable in S^*. As far as we are concerned with a fairness concept that is Paretian in spirit, the definition (5.18) does not seem to warrant any further pursuit. The second possibility is to modify the definition of the no-envy-fair set in S as follows:

$$F^{\alpha}_{p(2)}(S) = E^{\alpha}_{f}(S) \cap E^{\alpha}_{q,p(2)}(S) \tag{5.19}$$

where

$$E^{\alpha}_{q,p(2)}(S) = \left\{ x \in S \mid \exists\, y \in X, \forall\, i, j \in N \colon \begin{Bmatrix} ((x, i), (y, i)) \in I(\tilde{R}^{\alpha}_{i}) \\ \& \\ ((y, i), (y, j)) \in \tilde{R}^{\alpha}_{i} \end{Bmatrix} \right\}$$

It is clearly the case that $F^{\alpha}(S) \subset F^{\alpha}_{p(2)}(S)$ holds true for all $(\alpha, S) \in \mathscr{A} \times \mathscr{S}$, but $F^{\alpha}_{p(2)}(S)$ may still be empty. We now define the Pazner equity relation $R^{\alpha}_{q,p(2)}$ on X by

$$R^{\alpha}_{q,p(2)} = \{(x, y) \in X \times X \mid \sim [y \in E^{\alpha}_{q,p(2)}(S) \;\&\; x \notin E^{\alpha}_{q,p(2)}(S)]\} \tag{5.20}$$

We are now ready to complete our examination of the effects that various alternative fairness concepts have on our preceding negative results. Let a series of conditions FE(τ), FI(τ), and CBEP(τ) on an extended collective choice rule Ψ be defined by replacing $F^{\alpha}(S)$ by $F^{\alpha}_{\tau}(S)$, R^{α}_{q} by $R^{\alpha}_{q,\tau}$, and $E^{\alpha}_{q}(\{x, y\})$ by $E^{\alpha}_{q,\tau}(\{x, y\})$ in FE, FI, and CBEP, respectively, where $\tau = fk, d$, and $p(2)$. We can then claim that the various variants of the Foley fairness concept formulated earlier do not change the negative verdict on the possibility of a "fair" extended collective choice rule at all by establishing the following propositions.

Theorem 5.3
Assume that $\# X \geq 3$. Then there exists no extended collective choice rule that satisfies the unrestricted domain (EU), the fairness extension of type τ [FE(τ)], and the superset axiom of choice consistency (SUA) for each $\tau \in \{fk, d, p(2)\}$.

Theorem 5.4
Assume that $\# X \geq 3$. Then there exists no extended collective choice rule that satisfies the unrestricted domain (EU), the fairness inclusion of type τ [FI(τ)], the conditional binary exclusion Pareto of type τ [CBEP(τ)], and Chernoff's axiom of choice consistency (CA) for each $\tau \in \{fk, d, p(2)\}$.

For $\tau = fk$ and d, these theorems are very easy to prove. We have only to notice that the extended profiles that we used in establishing Theorem 5.1 and Theorem 5.2 are so constructed that $F^{\alpha}(S) = F^{\alpha}_{\tau}(S)$, $R^{\alpha}_{q} = R^{\alpha}_{q,\tau}$, and $E^{\alpha}_{q}(\{x, y\}) = E^{\alpha}_{q,\tau}(\{x, y\})$ for $\tau = fk$ and d.

To prove these theorems for $\tau = p(2)$ by one stroke, it clearly suffices if we show that $E^{\alpha}_{q}(X) = E^{\alpha}_{q,p(2)}(X)$ holds true for every extended profile $\alpha \in \mathscr{A}$ that satisfies the axiom of identity, because if this is in fact the case, the assertion of Theorem 5.3 as well as that of Theorem 5.4 for $\tau = p(2)$ follow from that of Theorem 5.1 and that of Theorem 5.2, respectively. By definition, it is always true that $E^{\alpha}_{q}(X) \subset E^{\alpha}_{q,p(2)}(X)$ for every $\alpha \in \mathscr{A}$, so that we have only to prove that $E^{\alpha}_{q}(X) \supset E^{\alpha}_{q,p(2)}(X)$ is true for every $\alpha \in \mathscr{A}$ satisfying the axiom of identity. Suppose, to the contrary, that there exists an $\alpha \in \mathscr{A}$ and an $x \in X$ such that $x \in E^{\alpha}_{q,p(2)}(X)$ and $x \notin E^{\alpha}_{q}(X)$. Then there exists an individual who envies somebody else at x when the extended profile α prevails. Without loss of generality, suppose that individual 1 envies individual 2 at x, so that $((x, 2), (x, 1)) \in P(\tilde{R}^{\alpha}_{1})$ holds true. Because it is the case that $x \in E^{\alpha}_{q,p(2)}(X)$ holds true by assumption, there exists a rectifying state, say y, that satisfies

$$\forall i, j \in N: ((x, i), (y, i)) \in I(\tilde{R}^{\alpha}_{i}) \;\&\; ((y, i), (y, j)) \in \tilde{R}^{\alpha}_{i} \tag{5.21}$$

$\tilde{R}^{\alpha}_{i}$ being transitive, we then obtain

$$((x, 2), (y, 2)) \in P(\tilde{R}^{\alpha}_{1}) \;\&\; ((x, 2), (y, 2)) \in I(\tilde{R}^{\alpha}_{2}) \tag{5.22}$$

which is a clear violation of the axiom of identity by this α. Therefore, we are home.[6]

Note in passing that Theorems 5.1, 5.2, 5.3, and 5.4 nowhere invoke any interprofile independence condition. Indeed, only a single extended profile is made effective use of in establishing these theorems individually, so that the unrestricted domain condition EU is in fact much stronger than is needed. Instead of requiring the condition EU, we can do throughout with the following *states richness condition* suggested by Kemp and Ng (1976), Parks (1976*a*), and Pollak (1979) in a different context, which is a single-profile analogue of the multiple-profile condition EU. To phrase this condition, let $\alpha \in \mathscr{A}$ be a given fixed profile.

Condition SRC (states richness condition)
Let $\beta(S_0)$ denote any logically possible subprofile over the hypothetical triple set $S_0 \subset X$. Then there exists a one-to-one correspondence γ_{β} from S_0 into X such that

$$((\gamma_{\beta}(x), i), (\gamma_{\beta}(y), j)) \in \tilde{R}^{\alpha}_{k} \leftrightarrow ((x, i), (y, j)) \in \tilde{R}^{\beta}_{k}$$

holds true for all $x, y \in S_0$ and all $i, j, k \in N$.[7]

It should be clear that the condition SRC, which requires in essence that the set of states X be rich enough, can replace the condition EU, which is a requirement to the effect that the set of extended profiles $\mathscr{A}$ be rich enough, to yield single-profile analogues of the preceding impossibility theorems.

3 Fairness-as-no-envy and Pareto efficiency: II. Goldman-Sussangkarn extended collective choice rule

3.1 Construction of the rule

Our impossibility theorems help demarcate the area where it is in vain to sow the seeds of a "fair" extended collective choice rule. There still remains hope for designing an extended collective choice rule that is "fair," however, if we settle on a weaker choice-consistency requirement on a rule. In this and the following sections, we put forward two concrete rules with a view toward shedding light on the extent to which the present approach gains score with respect to the essentially Arrovian performance criteria. For the sake of brevity of our exposition, we shall be concerned in the rest of this chapter solely with the original Foley concept of no-envy fairness.

The first rule we construct was originally suggested by Goldman and Sussangkarn (1978) in a slightly different context. Because this rule is founded on a juxtaposition of the no-envy equity relation and the Pareto quasi ordering, the intrinsic attractiveness of this rule (which we shall call the GS rule for short) might well be in doubt, but it does serve to exemplify the potentiality of this approach.

Let $\alpha \in \mathscr{A}$ be taken arbitrarily, and define, as before, a binary relation Q^α on X by $Q^\alpha = P(R_f^\alpha) \cup P(R_q^\alpha)$, where R_f^α and R_q^α are defined by (5.2) and (5.6), respectively. We then define a choice function C_{GS}^α on a choice space $(X, \mathscr{S})$ by

$$C_{GS}^\alpha(S) = \left\{ x \in S \mid \forall\, y \in S\colon \begin{Bmatrix} (x, y) \in T(Q^\alpha(S)) \\ \vee \\ (y, x) \notin T(Q^\alpha(S)) \end{Bmatrix} \right\} \tag{5.23}$$

for all $S \in \mathscr{S}$, where $T(Q^\alpha(S))$ denotes the transitive closure of Q^α on S.[8] $T(Q^\alpha(S))$ being transitive and S being a finite set, $C_{GS}^\alpha(S)$ is a nonempty subset of S for every $(\alpha, S) \in \mathscr{A} \times \mathscr{S}$. Associating this well-defined choice function C_{GS}^α on a choice space $(X, \mathscr{S})$ with each extended profile $\alpha \in \mathscr{A}$, we complete our description of the GS rule Ψ_{GS}.

3.2 Some relevant properties of the rule

The first order of business is to verify that Ψ_{GS} is indeed a "fair" extended collective choice rule.

Theorem 5.5
The GS rule Ψ_{GS} satisfies fairness extension (FE) as well as fairness inclusion (FI) (Suzumura, 1981*a*, Theorem 1).

Proof: Step 1: To show that Ψ_{GS} satisfies condition FE, let $\alpha \in \mathscr{A}$ and $S \in \mathscr{S}$ be such that $F^\alpha(S) \neq \varnothing$. In order to prove that $F^\alpha(S) \subset C^\alpha_{GS}(S)$, take any $x \in F^\alpha(S)$ and suppose that $(y, x) \in T(Q^\alpha(S))$ holds true for some $y \in S$. Then there exist an integer $t > 0$ and a sequence $z^1, z^2, \ldots, z^t$ in X such that $y = z^1, (z^1, z^2) \in Q^\alpha(S), \ldots, (z^{t-1}, z^t) \in Q^\alpha(S)$ and $z^t = x$. It follows that either $(z^{t-1}, x) \in P(R^\alpha_f)$ or $[z^{t-1} \in E^\alpha_q(X)\ \&\ x \notin E^\alpha_q(X)]$ is true, both of which contradict $x \in F^\alpha(S)$. Therefore, $(y, x) \notin T(Q^\alpha(S))$ must be true for all $y \in S$, so that we have $x \in C^\alpha_{GS}(S)$, as desired.

Let us now prove that $C^\alpha_{GS}(S) \subset F^\alpha(S)$. Let $x \in S \setminus F^\alpha(S)$. Then either $x \notin E^\alpha_q(X)$ or $x \notin E^\alpha_f(S)$ should be true.

(a) If $x \notin E^\alpha_q(X)$ is the case, we obtain $(y, x) \in P(R^\alpha_q(S)) \subset T(Q^\alpha(S))$ for any $y \in F^\alpha(S)$. We also have $(x, y) \notin T(Q^\alpha(S))$ by virtue of the argument used earlier. Therefore, we have

$$\exists\, y \in S: (x, y) \notin T(Q^\alpha(S))\ \&\ (y, x) \in T(Q^\alpha(S)) \tag{5.24}$$

so that $x \notin C^\alpha_{GS}(S)$ holds true.

(b) Consider now the case where $x \in E^\alpha_q(X)$ and $x \notin E^\alpha_f(S)$. Then there exists a $z \in S$ such that $(z, x) \in P(R^\alpha_f) \subset T(Q^\alpha(S))$. S being finite and $P(R^\alpha_f)$ being transitive, we can assume without losing generality that $z \in E^\alpha_f(S)$. If $z \in F^\alpha(S)$, we obtain (5.24) with $y = z$, which allows us to conclude that $x \notin C^\alpha_{GS}(S)$. Otherwise, we choose a $y \in F^\alpha(S)$ and obtain from $y \in E^\alpha_q(X)$ and $z \notin E^\alpha_q(X)$ that $(y, z) \in P(R^\alpha_q) \subset Q^\alpha$. Coupled with $(z, x) \in T(Q^\alpha(S))$, this yields $(y, x) \in T(Q^\alpha(S))$. As before, $y \in F^\alpha(S)$ and $x \in S$ yield $(x, y) \notin T(Q^\alpha(S))$. Therefore, we have $x \notin C^\alpha_{GS}(S)$ in this case as well, completing the proof that Ψ_{GS} satisfies FE.

Step 2: To prove that Ψ_{GS} satisfies condition FI, let $\alpha \in \mathscr{A}$, $x \in X$, and $S \in \mathscr{S}$ be such that $x \in S$ and $(x, y) \in Q^\alpha$ for some $y \in C^\alpha_{GS}(S)$. Suppose that $x \notin C^\alpha_{GS}(S)$ holds true. It then follows that

$$\exists\, w \in S: (x, w) \notin T(Q^\alpha(S))\ \&\ (w, x) \in T(Q^\alpha(S)) \tag{5.25}$$

In view of (5.23) and $y \in C^\alpha_{GS}(S)$, we have for this $w \in S$ that

$$(y, w) \in T(Q^\alpha(S)) \vee (w, y) \notin T(Q^\alpha(S)) \tag{5.26}$$

Coupled with (5.25), $(x, y) \in Q^\alpha$ yields $(w, y) \in T(Q^\alpha(S))$, so that we have $(y, w) \in T(Q^\alpha(S))$, thanks to (5.26). If $(x, y) \in Q^\alpha$ is added to this, we obtain $(x, w) \in T(Q^\alpha(S))$, in contradiction of (5.25). This completes the proof. ∎

Let us now examine the performance of the GS rule with respect to the Arrovian criteria for satisfactoriness.

Note first that we imposed no restriction whatsoever on the class of extended profiles for which Ψ_{GS} can generate a choice function, so that the rule Ψ_{GS} is indeed maximally versatile as a preference aggregator in the sense that it satisfies the unrestricted domain condition (EU).

Second, we can easily verify that Ψ_{GS} satisfies the following condition of informational efficiency to the effect that, in order to decide the social choice from a set S, the rule requires only the informational gathering and processing of the individuals' views on the set of available states.

Condition EI (independence)
If two extended profiles $\alpha = (\tilde{R}_1^\alpha, \tilde{R}_2^\alpha, \ldots, \tilde{R}_n^\alpha)$, $\beta = (\tilde{R}_1^\beta, \tilde{R}_2^\beta, \ldots, \tilde{R}_n^\beta) \in \mathscr{A}$ and an opportunity set $S \in \mathscr{S}$ are such that $\tilde{R}_i^\alpha(S \times N) = \tilde{R}_i^\beta(S \times N)$ for all $i \in N$, then $C^\alpha(S) = C^\beta(S)$ holds true, where $C^\alpha = \Psi(\alpha)$ and $C^\beta = \Psi(\beta)$.

Third, we enquire if Ψ_{GS} treats individuals without prejudice, that is, whether or not Ψ_{GS} passes the test of anonymity. To define this criterion in a way appropriate in the present context, let Π_N denote the set of all permutations on N. For any $\pi \in \Pi_N$ and any extended ordering $\tilde{R}$, let $\pi(\tilde{R})$ be defined by

$$((x, j), (y, k)) \in \pi(\tilde{R}) \leftrightarrow [(x, \pi(j)), (y, \pi(k))] \in \tilde{R}$$

for all $x, y \in X$ and all $j, k \in N$. We can then define the permuted profile $\pi(\alpha)$ for any $\pi \in \Pi_N$ and any $\alpha \in \mathscr{A}$ by

$$\pi(\alpha) = \left(\pi(\tilde{R}_{\pi(1)}^\alpha), \pi(\tilde{R}_{\pi(2)}^\alpha), \ldots, \pi(\tilde{R}_{\pi(n)}^\alpha)\right)$$

in terms of which the condition of anonymity can be phrased as follows.

Condition EAN (anonymity)
For every $\alpha \in \mathscr{A}$ and $\pi \in \Pi_N$, $C^\alpha = C^{\pi(\alpha)}$ holds true, where $C^\alpha = \Psi(\alpha)$ and $C^{\pi(\alpha)} = \Psi(\pi(\alpha))$.

To show that Ψ_{GS} indeed satisfies the condition EAN, we have only to show that $Q^\alpha = Q^{\pi(\alpha)}$, which in turn can be established by showing that $R_f^\alpha = R_f^{\pi(\alpha)}$ and $R_q^\alpha = R_q^{\pi(\alpha)}$ for all $\alpha \in \mathscr{A}$ and $\pi \in \Pi_N$. Note that

$$\begin{aligned} (x, y) \in R_f^{\pi(\alpha)} &\leftrightarrow ((x, i), (y, i)) \in \pi(\tilde{R}_{\pi(i)}^\alpha) \quad \text{for all} \quad i \in N \\ &\leftrightarrow [(x, \pi(i)), (y, \pi(i))] \in \tilde{R}_{\pi(i)}^\alpha \quad \text{for all} \quad i \in N \\ &\leftrightarrow (x, y) \in \tilde{R}_f^\alpha \end{aligned}$$

so that we have $R_f^\alpha = R_f^{\pi(\alpha)}$. Note also that

$$\begin{aligned} x \in E_q^{\pi(\alpha)}(X) &\leftrightarrow ((x,i),(x,j)) \in \tilde{R}_i^{\pi(\alpha)} \quad \text{for all} \quad i,j \in N \\ &\leftrightarrow ((x,i),(x,j)) \in \pi(\tilde{R}_{\pi(i)}^\alpha) \quad \text{for all} \quad i,j \in N \\ &\leftrightarrow [(x,\pi(i)),(x,\pi(j))] \in \tilde{R}_{\pi(i)}^\alpha \quad \text{for all} \quad i,j \in N \\ &\leftrightarrow x \in E_q^\alpha(X) \end{aligned}$$

which establishes, in effect, that $R_q^\alpha = R_q^{\pi(\alpha)}$. Therefore, Ψ_{GS} treats similar individuals similarly, as desired.

So far, so good. A seemingly uncomfortable fact about the working of Ψ_{GS} comes to the fore when we realize that the rule does not necessarily satisfy the condition of the binary Pareto principle, which has been left almost unchallenged in the social choice literature. To bring this point home, let us have a second look at Example 5.1. Note that $C_{GS}^\alpha(\{x, y\}) = \{x, y\}$ in this case, even though $(y, x) \in P(R_f^\alpha)$, contrary to the requirement of the binary Pareto principle. We can show, however, that Ψ_{GS} satisfies a doctored version of the binary Pareto unanimity requirement in the form of the condition CBEP. To substantiate this claim, let $\alpha \in \mathscr{A}$ and $x, y \in X$ be such that $E_q^\alpha(\{x, y\}) = \emptyset$ and $(x, y) \in \bigcap_{i \in N} P(R_i^\alpha)$. Suppose that $y \in C_{GS}^\alpha(\{x, y\})$ happens to be the case. By virtue of (5.23) we must then have

$$(y, x) \in T(Q^\alpha(\{x, y\})) \vee (x, y) \notin T(Q^\alpha(\{x, y\})) \tag{5.27}$$

However, because $(x, y) \in \bigcap_{i \in N} P(R_i^\alpha) \subset P(R_f^\alpha) \subset Q^\alpha$ and $y \notin E_q^\alpha(\{x, y\})$ are the case, (5.27) cannot possibly be true. Therefore, Ψ_{GS} in fact satisfies CBEP.[9]

How does Ψ_{GS} fare with respect to the choice-consistency conditions that have been found useful in social and individual choice contexts? We can show by examples that choice functions generated by Ψ_{GS} need not necessarily satisfy Chernoff's axiom of choice consistency; neither do they necessarily satisfy the superset axiom of choice consistency.

Example 5.2
Let $X = \{x, y, z\}$, $N = \{1,2\}$, $S_1 = \{x,z\}$, and $S_2 = \{x, y, z\}$, and let an extended profile $\alpha \in \mathscr{A}$ be defined as follows:

$$\tilde{R}_1^\alpha\colon (x, 1), (y, 2), (y, 1), (z, 1), (z, 2), (x, 2)$$

$$\tilde{R}_2^\alpha\colon (y, 2), (z, 2), (x, 2), (x, 1), (y, 1), (z, 1)$$

It can easily be verified that $E_q^\alpha(\{x, y, z\}) = \{x,z\}$ and $P(R_f^\alpha) = \{(y,z)\}$, so that we have $C_{GS}^\alpha(S_1) = \{x,z\}$ and $C_{GS}^\alpha(S_2) = \{x\}$. Because $S_1 \subset S_2$ and $C_{GS}^\alpha(S_2) \subset \subset C_{GS}^\alpha(S_1)$ hold true, this is a clear violation of the superset axiom of choice consistency. ∎

Example 5.3
Let $X = \{x, y, z\}$, $N = \{1,2\}$, $S_1 = \{x, y\}$, and $S_2 = X$, and let an extended profile $\alpha \in \mathscr{A}$ be defined by

$$\tilde{R}_1^\alpha: (x,2), (x,1), (y,2), (y,1), (z,1), (z,2)$$

$$\tilde{R}_2^\alpha: (x,1), (x,2), (y,1), (y,2), (z,2), (z,1)$$

It follows that $R_q^\alpha = \{(z,x), (z,y)\}$ and $P(R_f^\alpha) = \{(x,y), (y,z), (x,z)\}$, so that we have $C_{GS}^\alpha(S_1) = \{x\}$ and $C_{GS}^\alpha(S_2) = \{x, y, z\}$. Therefore, $S_1 \subset S_2$, $S_1 \cap C_{GS}^\alpha(S_2) = \{x, y\} \not\subset C_{GS}^\alpha(S_1) = \{x\}$ hold true, so that C_{GS}^α fails to satisfy Chernoff's axiom of choice consistency. ▮

A question still remains: What kind of choice-consistency axiom, if any, does Ψ_{GS} generally satisfy? In reply to this question, we can prove the following proposition.

Theorem 5.6
For every extended profile $\alpha \in \mathscr{A}$, $C_{GS}^\alpha = \Psi_{GS}(\alpha)$ satisfies the stability axiom of choice consistency (Suzumura, 1981*a*, Theorem 2).

Proof: Suppose, to the contrary, that there exist an $\alpha \in \mathscr{A}$ and an $S \in \mathscr{S}$ such that $C_{GS}^\alpha(C_{GS}^\alpha(S)) \subset\subset C_{GS}^\alpha(S)$ holds true. Then there exists an $x \in C_{GS}^\alpha(S)$ such that $x \notin C_{GS}^\alpha(C_{GS}^\alpha(S))$. It then follows that

$$\exists y \in C_{GS}^\alpha(S): (x,y) \notin T[Q^\alpha(C_{GS}^\alpha(S))] \ \& \ (y,x) \in T[Q^\alpha(C_{GS}^\alpha(S))] \tag{5.28}$$

Because $(y,x) \in T[Q^\alpha(C_{GS}^\alpha(S))]$ holds true, there exists an integer $t > 0$ such that

$$\exists z^1, z^2, \ldots, z^t \in C_{GS}^\alpha(S): \quad z^1 = y, \quad (z^\tau, z^{\tau+1}) \in Q^\alpha \quad (\tau = 1, 2, \ldots, t-1) \quad \text{and} \quad z^t = x \tag{5.29}$$

We now prove that

$$\forall \tau \in \{1, 2, \ldots, t-1\}: (z^{\tau+1}, z^\tau) \in T[Q^\alpha(C_{GS}^\alpha(S))] \tag{5.30}$$

If (5.30) is established, we obtain therefrom that $(z^t, z^1) = (x, y)$ belongs to $T[Q^\alpha(C_{GS}^\alpha(S))]$ by virtue of transitivity of $T[Q^\alpha(C_{GS}^\alpha(S))]$, in contradiction of (5.28). To prove (5.30), take any $\tau \in \{1, 2, \ldots, t-1\}$. Because $z^{\tau+1} \in C_{GS}^\alpha(S)$ and $z^\tau \in C_{GS}^\alpha(S) \subset S$, we obtain either $(z^{\tau+1}, z^\tau) \in T(Q^\alpha(S))$ or $(z^\tau, z^{\tau+1}) \notin T(Q^\alpha(S))$. The latter possibility is out, because it contradicts $(z^\tau, z^{\tau+1}) \in Q^\alpha$. Therefore, the former must be the case, so that

$$\exists\, w^1, w^2, \ldots, w^m \in S:$$
$$z^{\tau+1} = w^1, \quad (w^\mu, w^{\mu+1}) \in Q^\alpha \quad (\mu = 1, 2, \ldots, m-1)$$
$$\text{and} \quad w^m = z \tag{5.31}$$

for some integer $m > 0$. We are home if we can show that

$$\forall\, \mu \in \{1, 2, \ldots, m-1\}: w^\mu \in C^\alpha_{GS}(S) \tag{5.32}$$

Consider w^{m-1} first. Because $(w^{m-1}, w^m) \in Q^\alpha(S)$ and $w^m = z^\tau \in C^\alpha_{GS}(S)$, we know that $w^{m-1} \in S$, $(w^{m-1}, w^m) \in Q^\alpha$, and

$$\forall\, v \in S: (w^m, v) \in T(Q^\alpha(S)) \vee (v, w^m) \notin T(Q^\alpha(S)) \tag{5.33}$$

holds true. If it is the case that $w^{m-1} \notin C^\alpha_{GS}(S)$, then we obtain

$$\exists\, u \in S: (w^{m-1}, u) \notin T(Q^\alpha(S)) \;\&\; (u, w^{m-1}) \in T(Q^\alpha(S)) \tag{5.34}$$

Coupled with $(w^{m-1}, w^m) \in Q^\alpha$, $(u, w^{m-1}) \in T(Q^\alpha(S))$ yields $(u, w^m) \in T(Q^\alpha(S))$. Thanks to (5.33), we then obtain $(w^m, u) \in T(Q^\alpha(S))$. By the second use of $(w^{m-1}, w^m) \in Q^\alpha$ we can get $(w^{m-1}, u) \in T(Q^\alpha(S))$. But this contradicts (5.34). Therefore, $w^{m-1} \in C^\alpha_{GS}(S)$ must be the case. Repeating this procedure using w^{m-2} in place of w^{m-1} and w^{m-1} in place of w^m, we obtain $w^{m-2} \in C^\alpha_{GS}(S)$, and the process continues. It is now clear that (5.32) should hold true, and with it we are home. ∎

Putting all the pieces together, we can now assert that the GS rule Ψ_{GS} exemplifies the existence of a "fair" extended collective choice rule that has unrestricted domain, that satisfies the independence-of-irrelevant-alternatives axiom, that treats similar individuals similarly, that satisfies the equity-constrained binary exclusion Pareto condition, and that satisfies the stability axiom of choice consistency.

3.3 *A characterization of the GS rule*

There are many extended collective choice rules other than Ψ_{GS} that are "fair" in the sense of satisfying condition FE and condition FI. A trivial example can be easily constructed as follows. For any extended profile $\alpha \in \mathscr{A}$, let a choice function C^α_* on a choice space $(X, \mathscr{S})$ be defined by

$$\forall\, S \in \mathscr{S}: C^\alpha_*(S) = \begin{cases} F^\alpha(S) & \text{if} \quad F^\alpha(S) \neq \varnothing \\ \& & \\ S & \text{otherwise} \end{cases} \tag{5.35}$$

Associating C^α_* with the $\alpha \in \mathscr{A}$ we started from, we obtain an extended collective choice rule Ψ_*, which clearly satisfies condition FE and condition FI.[10] It seems rather obvious that Ψ_* is unattractive even if it passes the test of being "fair." A natural question suggests itself: What is the characterizing property of Ψ_{GS} among all "fair" extended collective choice rules? Fortunately, an adaptation of the work of Deb (1977), Kalai and Schmeidler (1977), and Schwartz (1972) enables us to settle this question completely by establishing a full characterization theorem for Ψ_{GS}.

To start with, take any $(\alpha, S) \in \mathscr{A} \times \mathscr{S}$. We say that a nonempty subset V of S is *Q^α-closed* if it satisfies

$$\begin{cases} V = F^\alpha(S) \quad \text{if} \quad F^\alpha(S) \neq \varnothing \\ \& \\ [x \in S, (x, y) \in Q^\alpha \ \& \ y \in V] \rightarrow x \in V \quad \text{otherwise} \end{cases} \tag{5.36}$$

Let $\mathscr{V}_S^\alpha$ denote the family of *minimal* Q^α-closed subsets of S; that is, $V \in \mathscr{V}_S^\alpha$ holds true if and only if (i) V satisfies (5.36) and (ii) no nonempty *proper* subset of V satisfies (5.36).

We are now at the stage of providing the following:

Theorem 5.7
For every $(\alpha, S) \in \mathscr{A} \times \mathscr{S}$, $C_{GS}^\alpha(S)$ coincides with the union of all minimal Q^α-closed subsets of S, that is

$$C_{GS}^\alpha(S) = \bigcup_{V \in \mathscr{V}_S^\alpha} V$$

holds true (Suzumura, 1981*a*, Theorem 3).

Proof: Take any $\alpha \in \mathscr{A}$ and define

$$\mathscr{S}_0^\alpha = \{S \in \mathscr{S} \mid F^\alpha(S) \neq \varnothing\} \tag{5.37}$$

There are two cases to be treated separately.

Case 1: $S \in \mathscr{S}_0^\alpha$

In view of (5.36), we then obtain

$$V^\alpha(S) \equiv \bigcup_{V \in \mathscr{V}_S^\alpha} V = F^\alpha(S) = C_{GS}^\alpha(S) \tag{5.38}$$

Case 2: $S \in \mathscr{S} \setminus \mathscr{S}_0$

Step 1: To prove that $V^\alpha(S) \subset C_{GS}^\alpha(S)$, suppose that there exists an x such that $x \in V^\alpha(S) \setminus C_{GS}^\alpha(S)$. Then there exists a $V_x \in \mathscr{V}_S^\alpha$ such that

$$x \in V_x \ \& \ [y \in S, (y, z) \in Q^\alpha \ \& \ z \in V_x \rightarrow y \in V_x] \tag{5.39}$$

holds true. By virtue of (5.23) and $x \notin C_{GS}^\alpha(S)$ we obtain

$$\exists x^* \in S: (x, x^*) \notin T(Q^\alpha(S)) \ \& \ (x^*, x) \in T(Q^\alpha(S)) \tag{5.40}$$

Then there exist $z^1, z^2, \ldots, z^t \in S$ for some integer $t > 0$ satisfying $x^* = z^1, (z^\tau, z^{\tau+1}) \in Q^\alpha(S)$ $(\tau = 1, 2, \ldots, t-1)$ and $z^t = x$. In view of (5.39), we know from $z^{t-1} \in S$, $(z^{t-1}, x) \in Q^\alpha$, and $x \in V_x$ that $z^{t-1} \in V_x$ is the case. It then follows from inductive argument that $z^\tau \in V_x$ holds true for all $\tau = 1, 2, \ldots, t-1$. In particular, it is true that $x^* = z^1 \in V_x$. In view of this fact, the set

$$A^\alpha(x^*) = \{x^*\} \cup \{z \in V_x | (z, x^*) \in T(Q^\alpha(S))\} \tag{5.41}$$

is contained in V_x. Thanks to (5.40), we have $x \notin A^\alpha(x^*)$, so that $A^\alpha(x^*)$ is in fact a *proper* subset of V_x. We now show that

$$w \in S, (w, z) \in Q^\alpha \ \& \ z \in A^\alpha(x^*) \rightarrow w \in A^\alpha(x^*) \tag{5.42}$$

is true. Assume that the LHS of (5.42) holds true and that $w \notin A^\alpha(x^*)$ is the case, so that we have

$$w \neq x^* \ \& \ (w, x^*) \notin T(Q^\alpha(S)) \tag{5.43}$$

and we have either $z = x^*$ or $(z, x^*) \in T(Q^\alpha(S))$, in view of $z \in A^\alpha(x^*)$. If the former is the case, we have $(w, x^*) \in Q^\alpha(S) \subset T(Q^\alpha(S))$, by virtue of (5.42), in contradiction of (5.43). On the other hand, it follows from $(w, z) \in Q^\alpha(S)$ and $(z, x^*) \in T(Q^\alpha(S))$ that $(w, x^*) \in T(Q^\alpha(S))$, in contradiction of (5.43) once again. Now that (5.42) is true, $A^\alpha(x^*)$ turns out to be a Q^α-closed *proper* subset of V_x, in contradiction of the minimality of $V_x \in \mathscr{V}^\alpha_S$. Therefore, $V^\alpha(S) \subset C^\alpha_{GS}(S)$ must be true.

Step 2: To prove that $C^\alpha_{GS}(S) \subset V^\alpha(S)$, assume that there exists an $x \in C^\alpha_{GS}(S) \setminus V^\alpha(S)$, and define a subset $B^\alpha(x)$ of S by

$$B^\alpha(x) = \{x\} \cup \{z \in S | (z, x) \in T(Q^\alpha(S))\} \tag{5.44}$$

It can easily be verified that $B^\alpha(x)$ is Q^α-closed, so that we are home if the minimality of $B^\alpha(x)$ is established. Therefore, take any non-empty subset B of $B^\alpha(x)$ satisfying

$$w \in S, (w, z) \in Q^\alpha \ \& \ z \in B \rightarrow w \in B \tag{5.45}$$

Suppose that there exists a y in $B^\alpha(x) \setminus B$. We arrive at a desired contradiction if we show that $x \in B$ by virtue of (5.44) and (5.45), because $x \in B$ and $y \in B^\alpha(x)$ necessarily imply $y \in B$. Assume, to the contrary, that $x \notin B$, so that $(x, z) \notin Q^\alpha$ holds true for all $z \in B$, thanks to (5.45). Because $x \in C^\alpha_{GS}(S)$ is the case, we have

$$\forall v \in S: (v, x) \notin T(Q^\alpha(S)) \vee (x, v) \in T(Q^\alpha(S)) \tag{5.46}$$

Applying (5.46) to a $z \in B \subset B^\alpha(x) \subset S$, and noting that either $z = x$ or $(z, x) \in T(Q^\alpha(S))$ holds true by virtue of $z \in B^\alpha(x)$, we obtain

$(x, z) \in T(Q^\alpha(S))$. Using (5.45) inductively, we obtain $x \in B$, which is enough to conclude the proof, as we observed earlier. ▮

4 Fairness-as-no-envy and Pareto efficiency: III. Leximin envy rule

4.1 Construction of the rule

As an auxiliary step in defining our second concrete extended collective choice rule based on the no-envy equity concept, let us introduce the *lexicographic ordering* $\geq_L$ on the Euclidean n-space $E^{(n)}$. For every $v \in E^{(n)}$, let $i(v)$ denote the index of the ith *largest* component thereof, ties being broken arbitrarily, so that we have

$$\forall v \in E^{(n)}: v_{1(v)} \geq v_{2(v)} \geq \cdots \geq v_{n(v)} \tag{5.47}$$

We may then define three binary relations $>_L$, $=_L$, and $\geq_L$ on $E^{(n)}$ by

$$v^1 >_L v^2 \leftrightarrow \exists r \in N: \begin{cases} \forall i \in \{1, 2, \ldots, r-1\}: v^1_{i(v^1)} = v^2_{i(v^2)} \\ \& \\ v^1_{r(v^1)} > v^2_{r(v^2)} \end{cases} \tag{5.48}$$

$$v^1 =_L v^2 \leftrightarrow \forall i \in N: v^1_{i(v^1)} = v^2_{i(v^2)} \tag{5.49}$$

and

$$v^1 \geq_L v^2 \leftrightarrow v^1 >_L v^2 \vee v^1 =_L v^2 \tag{5.50}$$

for all $v^1, v^2 \in E^{(n)}$.

We are now at the stage of constructing an extended collective choice rule that we call the *lexicographic envy rule* – *leximin envy rule*, for short. To start with, let the lexicographic envy ordering R^α_ε on X be defined in terms of $\varepsilon^\alpha(x)$, which we defined by (5.10) and (5.11), as follows:

$$R^\alpha_\varepsilon = \{(x, y) \in X \times X \mid \varepsilon^\alpha(y) \geq_L \varepsilon^\alpha(x)\} \tag{5.51}$$

Note that R^α_ε enables us to judge unambiguously whether any state x is more or less equitable than any other state y when $\alpha \in \mathscr{A}$ prevails. It is of interest to contrast the relative equity judgments afforded by R^α_ε with those afforded by the Feldman–Kirman relative equity ordering $R^\alpha_{q,fk}$ defined by (5.12). With this purpose in mind, consider the following situation.

Example 5.4

Consider an extended profile $\alpha \in \mathscr{A}$ that yields

$$\varepsilon^\alpha(x) = (\overbrace{1, 1, \ldots, 1}^{n}), \qquad \varepsilon^\alpha(y) = (\overbrace{n-1, 0, \ldots, 0}^{n}) \tag{5.52}$$

for $x, y \in X$, where $n \geq 3$. It is clearly the case that

$$\varepsilon^\alpha(y) >_L \varepsilon^\alpha(x), \qquad \sum_{i \in N} \varepsilon_i^\alpha(y) = n - 1 < n = \sum_{i \in N} \varepsilon_i^\alpha(x)$$

so that we obtain

$$(y, x) \in P(R_{q,fk}^\alpha), \qquad (x, y) \in P(R_\varepsilon^\alpha) \tag{5.53}$$

a sharp contrast indeed.

If we scrutinize (5.52), we cannot fail to observe that each individual feels envious toward just one other individual at x, whereas individuals $2, \dots, n$ feel no envy at all, leaving individual 1 alone to envy all other individuals at y. It seems to be intuitively appealing to say that x is more equitable in this case than y, which is to support the judgment afforded by R_ε^α in (5.53) in rejection of that afforded by $R_{q,fk}^\alpha$. ∎

Using R_ε^α thus constructed, we define a subset $C_\varepsilon^\alpha(S)$ of $S \in \mathscr{S}$ by

$$C_\varepsilon^\alpha(S) = G(E_f^\alpha(S), R_\varepsilon^\alpha) \tag{5.54}$$

which is clearly a nonempty subset of $E_f^\alpha(S)$. The leximin envy rule Ψ_ε is nothing other than a rule that associates a choice function C_ε^α on a choice space $(X, \mathscr{S})$ with each extended profile $\alpha \in \mathscr{A}$.

4.2 *Some relevant properties of the rule*

We can now prove a theorem that summarizes the performance of the leximin envy rule.

Theorem 5.8

The leximin envy rule Ψ_ε satisfies the unrestricted domain (EU), independence (EI), anonymity (EAN), the conditional binary exclusion Pareto (CBEP), fairness extension (FE), and the stability axiom of choice consistency (ST).

Proof: To show that Ψ_ε satisfies condition FE, take any $(\alpha, S) \in \mathscr{A} \times \mathscr{S}$ such that $F^\alpha(S) \neq \varnothing$. By definition (5.54), $x \in C_\varepsilon(S)$ yields $x \in E_f^\alpha(S)$, and

$$\forall y \in E_f^\alpha(S): \varepsilon^\alpha(y) \geq_L \varepsilon^\alpha(x) \tag{5.55}$$

Because (5.55) applies to $z \in F^\alpha(S) = E_f^\alpha(S) \cap E_q^\alpha(S)$ as well, which satisfies $\varepsilon^\alpha(z) = 0$, we must have $\varepsilon^\alpha(x) = 0$; that is, $x \in E_q^\alpha(S)$. Therefore, $C_\varepsilon^\alpha(S) \subset F^\alpha(S)$ holds true.

Conversely, if $x \in F^\alpha(S)$ is the case, we obtain $x \in E_f^\alpha(S)$ and $\varepsilon^\alpha(x) = 0$, so that we can assert that $x \in C_\varepsilon^\alpha(S)$, as desired for $F^\alpha(S) \subset C_\varepsilon^\alpha(S)$.

To show next that C_ε^α satisfies the stability axiom of choice consistency, it suffices if we can prove that

$$\forall(\alpha, S) \in \mathscr{A} \times \mathscr{S}: C_\varepsilon^\alpha(S) \subset C_\varepsilon^\alpha(C_\varepsilon^\alpha(S)) \tag{5.56}$$

holds true. Suppose, to the contrary, that there exist $(\alpha, S) \in \mathscr{A} \times \mathscr{S}$ and $x \in S$ such that $x \in C_\varepsilon^\alpha(S)$ and $x \notin C_\varepsilon^\alpha(C_\varepsilon^\alpha(S))$. We then obtain either

$$x \notin E_f^\alpha(C_\varepsilon^\alpha(S)) \tag{5.57}$$

or

$$\exists\, y \in E_f^\alpha(C_\varepsilon^\alpha(S)): \varepsilon^\alpha(x) >_L \varepsilon^\alpha(y) \tag{5.58}$$

On the other hand, $x \in C_\varepsilon^\alpha(S)$ entails

$$x \in E_f^\alpha(S) \tag{5.59}$$

and

$$\forall z \in E_f^\alpha(S): \varepsilon^\alpha(z) \geq_L \varepsilon^\alpha(x) \tag{5.60}$$

Suppose that (5.57) is true. Then there exists a $w \in C_\varepsilon^\alpha(S) \subset S$ such that $(w, x) \in P(R_f^\alpha)$, in contradiction of (5.59). The other alternative (5.58) cannot be sustained either, in view of $E_f^\alpha(C_\varepsilon^\alpha(S)) \subset C_\varepsilon^\alpha(S) \subset E_f^\alpha(S)$. Therefore, (5.56) must be true.

The other assertions in the theorem are obviously true. ∎

The essential idea embodied by the leximin envy rule is quite intuitive: Within the boundary circumscribed by the efficiency consideration, it tries to improve the position of the least favored individual (in the sense of suffering from the most instances of envy toward others) in the society as much as possible. The formal properties of Ψ_ε are much like those of Ψ_{GS}, and it again exemplifies the potentiality of the present approach in social choice theory.[11]

5 *Concluding remarks*

In this chapter we have explored the social choice implications of the fairness-as-no-envy approach in welfare economics. We have shown that there exists no rule that can choose Foley-fair social states unless we are rather modest in our requirement of choice consistency. Such a negative verdict has been proved to be the case for alternative criteria of fairness that are based on the no-envy concept as well. These impossibility theorems circumscribe the arena in which the fairness-as-no-envy approach cannot hope to record victory. To gauge just how rich the remaining area will be, we have constructed two concrete extended collective choice rules, the GS rule and the leximin envy rule, which perform fairly well in terms of the essentially Arrovian criteria.

Two concluding observations on this approach seem to be in order.

1. According to Varian (1974, p. 65), "social decision theory asks for too much out of the [preference aggregation] process in that it asks for an entire *ordering* of the various social states.... The original question asked only for a good allocation; there was no requirement to rank all allocations. The fairness criterion in fact limits itself to answering the original question. It is limited in that it gives no indication of the merits of two nonfair allocations, but by restricting itself in this way it allows for a reasonable solution to the original problem." This contrast between "social decision theory" and "fairness criterion" is no doubt a useful one, but it seems to us that the two approaches can be subsumed in a more general choice-functional social choice framework. In so doing, it is hoped that we can enrich our understanding of one theory in light of the implications of the other theory on the same ground, and vice versa. This is precisely the kind of exercise we have tried to perform in this chapter.

2. It is often suggested that the prime virtue of the theory of fairness is that it requires no such things as *externally imposed* interpersonal welfare comparisons, hypothetical welfare functions, and the like. Notice that our analysis of the concept of no-envy fairness in the framework of social choice theory fully retains this alleged prime virtue of the theory of fairness.

Recollect that our investigation was motivated by the "failure" of the extensions of the simple majority decision rule in the distributional context. The voting-by-veto approach of Mueller (1979*a*; 1979*b*, Chapter 4) and Moulin (1981), on the one hand, and the fairness-as-no-envy approach, on the other, are two explicitly *nonmajoritarian* methods of coping with this difficulty. However, this is not the only route one can follow, and there are ways of restricting the mechanical applications of the simple majority decision rule with a view toward defining several *constrained majoritarian* collective choice rules. To these alternative constructions we now turn.

CHAPTER 6

Impartiality and extended sympathy

> It is ... certain that pity is a natural sentiment, which, by moderating in every individual the activity of self-love, contributes to the mutual preservation of the whole species. It is this pity which hurries us without reflection to the assistance of those we see in distress; it is this pity which, in a state of nature, takes the place of laws, manners, virtue, with this advantage, that no one is tempted to disobey her gentle voice:... it is this pity which, instead of that sublime maxim of rational justice, *Do to others as you would have others do to you,* inspires all men with that other maxim of natural goodness a great deal less perfect, but perhaps more useful, *Do good to yourself with as little prejudice as you can to others.*
>
> Jean-Jacques Rousseau*

0 Introduction

According to Dahl (1956, p. 36), "no one has ever advocated, and no one except its enemies has ever defined democracy to mean, that a majority would or should do anything it felt an impulse to do. Every advocate of democracy of whom I am aware, and every friendly definition of it, includes the idea of restraints on majorities." Therefore, it may well be claimed that a difficulty identified by Example 4.5, which comes to the fore only when we apply the simple majority decision rule mechanically, can hardly be attributable to this rule as its intrinsic defect. "But one central issue is whether these restraints are, or should be, (1) primarily internalized restraints in the individual behavior system, such as the conscience and other products of social indoctrination, (2) primarily social checks and balances of several kinds, or (3) primarily prescribed constitutional checks" (Dahl, 1956, p. 36). In this chapter we shall explore several ways of implementing "prescribed constitutional checks" in the essentially majoritarian rules with a view toward establishing a balanced evaluation of the performance of majoritarian collective choice rules.

The plan of the chapter is as follows. In Section 1 we explain our conceptual framework, which differs slightly from that of Chapter 5. In

* J.-J. Rousseau, *Discourse on the Origin and Foundation of Inequality among Mankind* (English translation by L. G. Crocker). New York: Washington Square Press, 1964, p. 204.

Section 2 we introduce the concept of an impartial principle of justice. There are two main rival principles of justice that appeal to many; they have been discussed by a long series of moral philosophers, and there is considerable contrast between them – the Benthamite principle of utilitarianism and the Rawlsian lexicographic maximin principle. Capitalizing on the works of Arrow (1973, 1977*a*), d'Aspremont and Gevers (1977), Deschamps and Gevers (1978), Gevers (1979), Hammond (1976, 1979), Maskin (1978), Sen (1970*b*, Chapter 9*; 1977*c*; 1983), and Strasnick (1976*a*, 1976*b*, 1977, 1979*a*, 1979*b*), these two impartial principles of justice will be axiomatically characterized and their contrasts highlighted. We shall also make some remarks on the ethical relevance of the no-envy equity concept that played a central role in Chapter 5. In Section 3 we set about constructing constrained majoritarian rules. Some concluding observations will be made in Section 4.

1 Framework of analysis

1.1 *Generalized utility function and generalized collective choice rule*

In this chapter we shall be concerned with a *generalized collective choice rule* (GCCR) that maps each list of the individuals' *generalized utility functions* over $X \times N$ into a social choice function on a choice space $(X, \mathscr{S})$. This is a slight modification of our framework in the previous chapter.

For each $i \in N$, u_i denotes individual i's generalized utility function over $X \times N$,

$$u_i(x, j) \geq u_i(y, k)$$

denoting that being in the position of individual j at social state x is at least as good as being in the position of individual k at social state y according to individual i's view. An n-list of generalized utility functions, one function for each individual, will be called a *generalized profile,* and alternative generalized profiles will be indexed by v, like $v = (u_1^v, u_2^v, \ldots, u_n^v)$. The set of all generalized profiles will be denoted by $\mathscr{U}$. Therefore, a GCCR is a function Φ that maps each $v \in \mathscr{U}$ into a choice function C^v on a choice space $(X, \mathscr{S})$.

1.2 *Subjective preferences and Pareto principles*

For any generalized profile $v = (u_1^v, u_2^v, \ldots, u_n^v) \in \mathscr{U}$, individual i's *subjective preference ordering* R_i^v is defined by

$$R_i^v = \{(x, y) \in X \times X \mid u_i^v(x, i) \geq u_i^v(y, i)\} \tag{6.1}$$

for each and every $i \in N$. We can then introduce two versions of the Pareto principle that we invoke in this chapter.

Condition P (Pareto principle)
For every generalized profile $v = (u_1^v, u_2^v, \ldots, u_n^v) \in \mathcal{U}$ and every $x, y \in X$, if $(x, y) \in \bigcap_{i \in N} P(R_i^v)$, then $[x \in S \rightarrow y \notin C^v(S)]$ for all $S \in \mathcal{S}$, where $C^v = \Phi(v)$.

Condition SP (strong Pareto principle)
For every generalized profile $v = (u_1^v, u_2^v, \ldots, u_n^v) \in \mathcal{U}$ and every $x, y \in X$, if $(x, y) \in P(\bigcap_{i \in N} R_i^v)$, then $[x \in S \rightarrow y \notin C^v(S)]$ for all $S \in \mathcal{S}$, where $C^v = \Phi(v)$.

2 Impartiality and principle of justice

2.1 Reflection on the equity principle

In order to crystallize our concept of an impartial principle of justice, to be introduced later, let us have a brief reflection on the Foley equity concept. Let us take any generalized profile $v = (u_1^v, u_2^v, \ldots, u_n^v) \in \mathcal{U}$ and define, for each $i \in N$ and each $S \in \mathcal{S}$, a set

$$E_{qi}^v(S) = \{x \in S \mid \forall j \in N: u_i^v(x, i) \geq u_i^v(x, j)\} \tag{6.2}$$

If $x \in E_{qi}^v(S)$ is the case, individual i feels no envy of anybody else at x, so that x is no-envy-equitable *as far as individual i is concerned*. It is clear that $E_q^v(S) = \bigcap_{i \in N} E_{qi}^v(S)$ corresponds precisely to the set of all no-envy-equitable states defined by (5.4). Making use of $E_{qi}^v(X)$, we can define individual i's no-less-equitable relation R_{qi}^v by

$$R_{qi}^v = \{(x, y) \in X \times X \mid \sim [y \in E_{qi}^v(X) \;\&\; x \notin E_{qi}^v(X)]\} \tag{6.3}$$

after the manner of (5.6).

Note that any generalized profile $v \in \mathcal{U}$ generates two profiles of individual preference orderings, $(R_1^v, R_2^v, \ldots, R_n^v)$ and $(R_{q1}^v, R_{q2}^v, \ldots, R_{qn}^v)$, both of which represent individuals' genuine preferences. If $(x, y) \in P(R_i^v)$ [resp. $(x, y) \in P(R_{qi}^v)$] holds true, individual i feels that he is personally better off with x than with y [resp. x is more equitable than y according to his judgment]. It is worth mentioning, however, that the "ethical" judgment embodied in R_{qi}^v is exclusively self-oriented, without paying any attention whatsoever to the fate of others. To bring this feature into relief, let us consider a two-person society in which individual 1 has the following generalized utility function over $\{x, y\} \times \{1, 2\}$:

$$u_1^v(x, 2) > u_1^v(x, 1) > u_1^v(y, 1) \geq u_1^v(y, 2) \tag{6.4}$$

According to this preference, individual 1 judges that x is strictly better than y whichever position (1 or 2) he happens to be in, so that it is appealing to say that x is a better state than y from the *impartial* and *ethical* viewpoint. Yet this is not endorsed by R^v_{q1}, because $E^v_{q1}(\{x, y\}) = \{y\}$ entails $(y, x) \in P(R^v_{q1})$, so that the ethical relevance of the no-envy equity concept is indeed rather doubtful.

2.2 *Impartial principle of justice*

What we call an impartial principle of justice is meant to crystallize the impartiality of the ethical judgments suggested earlier. Let a *principle of justice* be defined as a process or rule ω that maps a generalized utility function u on $X \times N$ into a quasi ordering $\omega(u)$ on X such that x is judged to be at least as just as y if and only if $(x, y) \in \omega(u)$. In particular, ω is said to be a *complete principle of justice* if $\omega(u)$ is an ordering on X for each and every u.

An example of the incomplete principle of justice is the *Suppesian principle of justice* ω_S, which is defined by

$$(x, y) \in \omega_S(u) \leftrightarrow \exists \pi \in \Pi_N, \forall i \in N: u(x, i) \geq u(y, \pi(i)) \tag{6.5}$$

for all $x, y \in X$. It was shown by Sen (1970*b*, Lemma 9*c) that $\omega_S(u)$ is a quasi ordering on X for every u. In words, $(x, y) \in \omega_S(u)$ holds true if and only if we can start from the utility distribution under y to arrive at that under x by first making an interpersonal permutation of utility levels at y and then making a Pareto-wise improvement. It should be emphasized that by making an interpersonal permutation of utility levels an integral part thereof, $\omega_S(u)$ crystallizes an intuitive idea of impartiality in an operational way.[1] In terms of the Suppesian principle of justice, we may now formalize the following:

Condition IM_ω *(impartiality)*
For every generalized utility function u, $\omega(u)$ is an extension of $\omega_S(u)$, namely, $\omega_S(u) \subset \omega(u)$ and $P(\omega_S(u)) \subset P(\omega(u))$ hold true.

Let us stress that the condition IM_ω is indeed a fairly weak and intuitive requirement of impartiality of an ethical value judgment.

2.3 *Two rival impartial principles of justice*

There are two major rival principles of justice that deserve careful scrutiny: The *Benthamite principle of utilitarian justice* ω_B and the *Rawlsian principle of lexicographic maximin justice* ω_R. These principles of justice provide us with important examples of the complete and impartial principles of justice. As we observed earlier in Section 2.1, the no-less-equitable relation R^{v}_{qi} is a complete principle of justice that does not satisfy condition IM_{ω}.

The Benthamite principle of justice ω_B is easy to define. Given any generalized utility function u, let an ordering $\omega_B(u)$ on X be defined by

$$(x, y) \in \omega_B(u) \leftrightarrow \sum_{i=1}^{n} u(x, i) \geq \sum_{i=1}^{n} u(y, i) \tag{6.6}$$

for all $x, y \in X$. In words, a state x is more just than another state y according to ω_B if and only if the aggregate welfare under x is larger than that under y, the evaluation of both aggregates being performed in terms of the generalized utility function held by the evaluating individual.

The Rawlsian principle of justice ω_R can be defined as follows. For every $v \in E^{(n)}$, let $i^*(v)$ denote the index of the ith *smallest* component thereof, ties being broken arbitrarily. We then define two binary relations $>^*_L$ and $=^*_L$ by

$$v^1 >^*_L v^2 \leftrightarrow \exists r \in N: \begin{cases} \forall i \in \{1, 2, \ldots, r-1\}: v^1_{i^*(v^1)} = v^2_{i^*(v^2)} \\ v^1_{r^*(v^1)} > v^2_{r^*(v^2)} \end{cases}$$

and

$$v^1 =^*_L v^2 \leftrightarrow \forall i \in N: v^1_{i^*(v^1)} = v^2_{i^*(v^2)}$$

for all $v^1, v^2 \in E^{(n)}$.[2] For any generalized utility function u, we let $u^N(x)$ be the shorthand for $(u(x,1), u(x,2), \ldots, u(x,n))$. For any $x, y \in X$, let $(x, y) \in \omega_R(u)$ be the case if and only if $u^N(x) >^*_L u^N(y)$ or $u^N(x) =^*_L u^N(y)$ holds true. In the former case we have $(x, y) \in P(\omega_R(u))$, and in the latter case we have $(x, y) \in I(\omega_R(u))$.

In words, a state x is more just than another state y according to ω_R if and only if there exists a position, say $k \in N$, such that the welfare level of the kth worst-off individual under x is higher than that of the kth worst-off individual under y and such that for all $i \in \{1, 2, \ldots, k-1\}$ the welfare level of the ith worst-off individual under x is the same as that of the ith worst-off individual under y, all welfare level comparisons being performed in terms of the generalized utility function held by the evaluating individual.

2.4 *Rawlsian principle of justice: an axiomatization*[3]

Capitalizing mainly on the work by d'Aspremont and Gevers (1977), Hammond (1976, 1979), Sen (1970*b*, Chapter 9*; 1977*c*), and Strasnick (1976*a*, 1976*b*, 1977, 1979*a*), let us present now an axiomatization of the Rawlsian principle of justice with a view toward crystallizing the contrast thereof with the Benthamite principle later on.

Consider the following series of requirements on a principle of justice.

Condition U_ω (unrestricted applicability)
ω should be able to determine the justice relation $\omega(u)$ for every generalized utility function u.

Condition I_ω (independence)
If u^1, u^2 and $S \in \mathscr{S}$ are such that

$$\forall x \in S, \forall i \in N: u^1(x, i) = u^2(x, i)$$

then $R^1(S) = R^2(S)$ holds true, where $R^1 = \omega(u^1)$ and $R^2 = \omega(u^2)$.

Condition P^0_ω (Pareto indifference)
If u and $x, y \in X$ are such that $u(x, i) = u(y, i)$ for all $i \in N$ [i.e., $u^N(x) = u^N(y)$], then $(x, y) \in I(\omega(u))$ holds true.

Other things being equal, each one of these requirements seems to be reasonable enough. Condition U_ω requires that ω be robust enough, and condition I_ω requires ω to work with a modest informational input. If the evaluator feels indifferent between x and y whichever position he may happen to be in, then ω should dictate that x and y are ethically indifferent (condition P^0_ω). The following lemma highlights the joint effect of these individually innocuous conditions.

Lemma 6.1
Suppose that a complete principle of justice ω satisfies unrestricted applicability (U_ω), independence (I_ω), and Pareto indifference (P^0_ω). Then there exists an ordering ω_* on $E^{(n)}$ such that

$$(x, y) \in \omega(u) \leftrightarrow (u^N(x), u^N(y)) \in \omega_* \tag{6.7}$$

holds true for all $x, y \in X$ (d'Aspremont and Gevers, 1977, Lemma 3; Hammond, 1979, Theorem 1).

Proof: Let a binary relation ω_* on $E^{(n)}$ be defined by

$$(v, w) \in \omega_* \leftrightarrow \exists x, y \in X, \exists u: v = u^N(x), \quad w = u^N(y), \quad (x, y) \in \omega(u) \tag{6.8}$$

Clearly, then, $(x, y) \in \omega(u)$ implies that $(u^N(x), u^N(y)) \in \omega_*$. To show the converse implication in (6.7), let u and $x, y \in X$ be such that $v = u^N(x)$, $w = u^N(y)$, and $(v, w) \in \omega_*$. By (6.8), there exist $a, b \in X$ and u^1 such that

$$v = u^{1N}(a), \quad w = u^{1N}(b), \quad (a, b) \in \omega(u^1) \tag{6.9}$$

Thanks to condition U_ω, there exists a u^2 such that

$$v = u^{2N}(x) = u^{2N}(a), \quad w = u^{2N}(y) = u^{2N}(b) \tag{6.10}$$

Because u^1 and u^2 coincide on $\{a, b\} \times N$, it follows from $(a, b) \in \omega(u^1)$ that $(a, b) \in \omega(u^2)$, where use is made of condition I_ω. On the other hand, condition P^0_ω ensures that $(a, x) \in I(\omega(u^2))$ and $(b, y) \in I(\omega(u^2))$, so that $(x, y) \in \omega(u^2)$ obtains, thanks to transitivity of $\omega(u^2)$. Because u and u^2 coincide on $\{x, y\} \times N$, we then obtain $(x, y) \in \omega(u)$, as desired.

Next, let us show that ω_* is an ordering on $E^{(n)}$. Take any v, $w \in E^{(n)}$ and any $x, y \in X$. By virtue of condition U_ω, there exists a u that satisfies $u^N(x) = v$ and $u^N(y) = w$. Because $\omega(u)$ is complete, either $(x, y) \in \omega(u)$ or $(y, x) \in \omega(u)$ holds true, so that we have either $(v, w) \in \omega_*$ or $(w, v) \in \omega_*$. Therefore, ω_* is complete as well as reflexive on $E^{(n)}$. To show transitivity of ω_*, let $v^1, v^2, v^3 \in E^{(n)}$ be such that (v^1, v^2), $(v^2, v^3) \in \omega_*$. By definition, there exist a, b, x, $y \in X$ and u^1, u^2 such that

$$v^1 = u^{1N}(a), \quad v^2 = u^{1N}(b) = u^{2N}(x), \quad v^3 = u^{2N}(y),$$
$$(a, b) \in \omega(u^1), \quad \text{and} \quad (x, y) \in \omega(u^2)$$

By virtue of condition U_ω, there exists a u_* such that

$$v^1 = u^N_*(a), \quad v^2 = u^N_*(b) = u^N_*(x), \quad v^3 = u^N_*(y)$$

Because $u^1 = u_*$ on $\{a, b\} \times N$, $(a, b) \in \omega(u^1)$ entails $(a, b) \in \omega(u_*)$. Similarly, $(x, y) \in \omega(u_*)$ follows from $u^2 = u_*$ on $\{x, y\} \times N$ and $(x, y) \in \omega(u^2)$. On the other hand, $(b, x) \in I(\omega(u_*))$ holds true, thanks to condition P^0_ω. Therefore, $(a, y) \in \omega(u_*)$ follows from $(a, b) \in \omega(u_*)$, $(b, x) \in I(\omega(u_*))$, $(x, y) \in \omega(u_*)$, and transitivity of $\omega(u_*)$, which implies in its turn that $(u^N_*(a), u^N_*(y)) \in \omega_*$; that is, $(v^1, v^3) \in \omega_*$, as desired. ∎

The importance of this lemma lies in the fact that the justice judgment concerning x vis-à-vis y can be reduced to the comparison of welfare distribution under x and that under y in full negligence of all other nonwelfare characteristics of these states. In Sen's terminology (1979*c*), the conditions U_ω, I_ω, and P^0_ω guarantee that ω is a welfaristic principle of justice.

It is worthwhile to note that condition IM_ω implies the following requirement of the strong Pareto inclusiveness of ω.

Condition SP_ω (strong Pareto inclusiveness)
If u and $x, y \in X$ are such that $u^N(x) \geq u^N(y)$ [resp. $u^N(x) > u^N(y)$], then $(x, y) \in \omega(u)$ [resp. $(x, y) \in P(\omega(u))$].

Because condition SP_ω implies condition P^0_ω, it then follows from Lemma 6.1 that any complete principle of justice ω satisfying U_ω, I_ω, and IM_ω admits the existence of an ordering ω_* with the property (6.7).

The final characterizing axiom for ω_R is now to be introduced. Suppose that there exists a pair $\{j, k\}$ of individuals such that, in the evaluator's judgment, the position of individual k is less favored than that of individual j whichever state between x and y may prevail, and all other individuals are construed to be indifferent between x and y. Other things being equal, it seems to be intuitively appealing to judge that, in this situation, a state in $\{x, y\}$ that is more preferred to the other by the less favored individual k is no less just than the other.

Condition SHE_ω (Sen–Hammond equity)
If u and $x, y \in X$ are such that there exist j and k in N satisfying

$$u(y, j) > u(x, j) > u(x, k) > u(y, k) \ \&$$
$$\forall i \in N \setminus \{j, k\}: u(x, i) = u(y, i)$$

then $(x, y) \in \omega(u)$.[4]

Now the following characterization theorem for ω_R holds true.

Theorem 6.1
The Rawlsian principle of justice ω_R is the unique complete principle of justice that satisfies unrestricted applicability (U_ω), independence (I_ω), impartiality (IM_ω), and Sen–Hammond equity (SHE_ω) (Hammond, 1979, Theorem 7.2).

Proof: It is clear that ω_R satisfies all of U_ω, I_ω, IM_ω, and SHE_ω, so that we have only to show the converse. Suppose that a complete principle of justice ω satisfies these nominated axioms. We should prove that

$$u^N(x) >^*_L u^N(y) \leftrightarrow (x, y) \in P(\omega(u)) \tag{6.11}$$

and

$$u^N(x) =^*_L u^N(y) \leftrightarrow (x, y) \in I(\omega(u)) \tag{6.12}$$

hold true for any u and any $x, y \in X$. As we noted earlier, ω admits the existence of an ordering ω_* on $E^{(n)}$ satisfying (6.7).

Step 1: Consider first a special case where $x, y \in X$, u, and $j, k \in N$ satisfy

$$\forall i \in N \setminus \{j, k\}: u(x, i) = u(y, i) \tag{6.13}$$

Let $v = u^N(x)$ and $w = u^N(y)$, and define

$$v_{\max} = \max\{v_j, v_k\}, \qquad v_{\min} = \min\{v_j, v_k\}$$

$$w_{\max} = \max\{w_j, w_k\}, \qquad w_{\min} = \min\{w_j, w_k\}$$

If $v_{\max} = w_{\max}$ and $v_{\min} = w_{\min}$, then there exists a $\pi \in \Pi_N$ such that $v = (w_{\pi(1)}, w_{\pi(2)}, \ldots, w_{\pi(n)})$. Therefore, IM_ω implies that $(v, w) \in I(\omega_*)$, so that we obtain $(x, y) \in I(\omega(u))$ by virtue of (6.7). Suppose now that $v >_L^* w$. There are three cases to consider.

Case 1: $v_{\min} = w_{\min}$ and $v_{\max} > w_{\max}$

In this case, IM_ω implies that $(x, y) \in P(\omega(u))$.

Case 2: $v_{\min} > w_{\min}$ and $v_{\max} \geq w_{\max}$

We can again invoke IM_ω to conclude that $(x, y) \in P(\omega(u))$.

Case 3: $v_{\min} > w_{\min}$ and $v_{\max} < w_{\max}$

Without loss of generality, we can assume that $w_j \leq w_k$. We then obtain

$$w_k > v_{\max} \geq v_{\min} > w_j$$

Let $v^* \in E^{(n)}$ be such that

$$\forall i \in N \setminus \{j, k\}: v_i^* = v_i = w_i$$

$$w_k > v_{\max} \geq v_{\min} > v_k^* > v_j^* > w_j$$

It follows from IM_ω that $(v, v^*) \in P(\omega_*)$, and SHE_ω implies that $(v^*, w) \in \omega_*$, so that we obtain $(v, w) \in P(\omega_*)$ by virtue of transitivity of ω_*. Therefore, $(x, y) \in P(\omega(u))$ holds true, as desired.

Step 2: We now proceed to the general case. If $v = u^N(x)$ and $w = u^N(y)$ are such that $v =_L^* w$, then there exists a $\pi \in \Pi_N$ such that $v = (w_{\pi(1)}, w_{\pi(2)}, \ldots, w_{\pi(n)})$. By virtue of IM_ω we then obtain $(v, w) \in I(\omega_*)$, so that we get $(x, y) \in I(\omega(u))$. Suppose next that $v >_L^* w$. Then there exists an $r \in N$ such that $v_{i*(v)} = w_{i*(w)}$ for all $i = 1, 2, \ldots, r - 1$ and $v_{r*(v)} > w_{r*(w)}$. If $r = n$, then IM_ω can be invoked to conclude that $(v, w) \in P(\omega_*)$, namely, $(x, y) \in P(\omega(u))$. Consider now the case where $r < n$. Let a vector $s^\mu \in E^{(n)}$ be defined, for each $\mu \in \{0, 1, \ldots, n - r\}$, by

$$s_i^\mu = \begin{cases} v_{i*(v)} & (i = 1, \ldots, r - 1) \\ \dfrac{1}{n-1}[\mu v_{r*(v)} + (n - r - \mu) w_{r*(w)}] & (i = r) \\ v_{i*(v)} & (i = r + 1, \ldots, r + \mu) \\ w_{i*(w)} & (i = r + \mu + 1, \ldots, n) \end{cases}$$

Notice that $s_i^0 = w_{i*(w)}$ and $s_i^{n-r} = v_{i*(v)}$ for all $i \in N$. It then follows from IM_ω that $(s^0, w) \in I(\omega_*)$ and $(s^{n-r}, v) \in I(\omega_*)$. We are home if we can prove that $(s^{n-r}, s^0) \in P(\omega_*)$, because then we have $(v, w) \in P(\omega_*)$; that is, $(x, y) \in P(\omega(u))$, as desired. Notice that, for each $\mu \in \{1, 2, \ldots, n-r\}$, we have

$$\forall i \in N \setminus \{r, r+\mu\}: s_i^{\mu-1} = s_i^{\mu}$$

$$v_{r*(v)} \geq s_r^{\mu} > s_r^{\mu-1} \geq w_{r*(w)}$$

and

$$v_{(r+\mu)*(v)} \geq v_{r*(v)}$$

Therefore, $s_{r+\mu}^{\mu} \geq s_r^{\mu}$ holds true, which implies that

$$\min\{s_r^{\mu}, s_{r+\mu}^{\mu}\} > \min\{s_r^{\mu-1}, s_{r+\mu}^{\mu-1}\}$$

By virtue of Step 1, we then obtain $(s^{\mu}, s^{\mu-1}) \in P(\omega_*)$ for all $\mu \in \{1, 2, \ldots, n-r\}$, so that we can conclude that $(s^{n-r}, s^0) \in P(\omega_*)$, in view of transitivity of $P(\omega_*)$, as desired.

Step 3: To complete the proof, let $x, y \in X$ and u be such that $(x, y) \in P(\omega(u))$. Because $\omega_R(u)$ is complete, we have either $(x, y) \in P(\omega_R(u))$ or $(y, x) \in \omega_R(u)$. In the latter case, it follows from Step 2 that $(y, x) \in \omega(u)$, which is a contradiction. Therefore, (6.11) holds true. By similar argument we can assert the validity of (6.12). This completes the proof. ▮

2.5 *Benthamite principle of justice: an axiomatization*

Let us now turn our attention to the axiomatic characterization of the utilitarianism ω_B. As a matter of fact, most of the characterizing axioms for ω_B are in common with those for ω_R, and we can focus our attention on the informational contrast between ω_B and ω_R. Note that the Rawlsian principle of justice ω_R is compatible with the following ordinal level comparability of welfare, which says basically that only the ordinal ranking of $(x, i) \in X \times N$ accorded by u is made effective use of by the principle of justice ω in forming ethical value judgment over X.

Condition OL_ω (ordinal level comparability)
If u^1 and u^2 are such that there exists a monotone-increasing real-valued function ϕ on E satisfying $u^1(x, i) = \phi(u^2(x, i))$ for all $(x, i) \in X \times N$, then $\omega(u^1) = \omega(u^2)$ holds true.

It is true that condition OL_ω does not appear explicitly in the characterization of ω_R, but it is there all the same. The following cardinal unit comparability condition plays a more explicit role in the axiomatization of ω_B.

Condition CU_ω (cardinal unit comparability)
If u^1 and u^2 are such that there exist real numbers a_i $(i \in N)$ and $b > 0$ satisfying $u^1(x,i) = a_i + bu^2(x,i)$ for all $(x,i) \in X \times N$, then $\omega(u^1) = \omega(u^2)$ holds true.

Note that a principle of justice ω satisfying CU_ω responds to the utility *difference* between $(x,i) \in X \times N$ and $(y,j) \in X \times N$, but not to the utility *level* attained respectively by (x,i) and (y,j), in judging the relative ethical worth of x vis-à-vis y.

We are now at the stage of presenting the following axiomatization of ω_B.

Theorem 6.2
The Benthamite principle of justice ω_B is the unique complete principle of justice that satisfies unrestricted applicability (U_ω), independence (I_ω), impartiality (IM_ω), and cardinal unit comparability (CU_ω).

To facilitate the proof of this assertion, let us begin with two simple lemmas.

Lemma 6.2
Assume that a principle of justice ω satisfies cardinal unit comparability (CU_ω). If u^1 and u^2 are such that $u^1(x,i) - u^1(y,i) = u^2(x,i) - u^2(y,i)$ for all $x, y \in X$ and all $i \in N$, then $\omega(u^1) = \omega(u^2)$ holds true.

Proof: Let $u^1(x,i) - u^2(x,i) = \alpha_i(x)$ and $u^1(y,i) - u^2(y,i) = \alpha_i(y)$. We then have

$$\alpha_i(x) - \alpha_i(y) = \{u^1(x,i) - u^1(y,i)\} - \{u^2(x,i) - u^2(y,i)\} = 0$$

so that we have $\alpha_i(x) = \alpha_i$, which is independent of x, for all $i \in N$. It then follows that

$$\forall (x,i) \in X \times N: u^1(x,i) = \alpha_i + u^2(x,i)$$

so that we obtain $\omega(u^1) = \omega(u^2)$ by virtue of CU_ω. ∎

Lemma 6.3
If a principle of justice ω satisfies unrestricted applicability (U_ω), independence (I_ω), and impartiality (IM_ω), then ω also satisfies the following requirement (Sen, 1977*c*, Theorem 7).

Condition SAN_ω (strong anonymity)
For any u^1 and u^2, if there exists a permutation $\pi \in \Pi_N$ such that, for some $x \in X$ and all $y \in X \setminus \{x\}$,

$$\forall i \in N: \begin{cases} u^1(x,i) = u^2(x,\pi(i)) \\ \& \\ u^1(y,i) = u^2(y,i) \end{cases} \tag{6.14}$$

then $\omega(u^1) = \omega(u^2)$ holds true.

Proof: Suppose that u^1 and u^2, $\pi \in \Pi_N$, and $x \in X$ are as stipulated in condition SAN_ω. Because ω satisfies condition I_ω, we then obtain

$$\omega(u^1) \cap [(X \setminus \{x\}) \times (X \setminus \{x\})] = \omega(u^2) \cap [(X \setminus \{x\}) \times (X \setminus \{x\})]$$

so that we have only to prove that

$$\forall y \in X \setminus \{x\}: \begin{cases} (x,y) \in \omega(u^1) \leftrightarrow (x,y) \in \omega(u^2) \\ \& \\ (y,x) \in \omega(u^1) \leftrightarrow (y,x) \in \omega(u^2) \end{cases}$$

holds true. Therefore, take any $y \in X \setminus \{x\}$ and take any $z \in X \setminus \{x, y\}$. By virtue of condition U_ω, there exist u^1_* and u^2_* such that

$$u^1(x,i) = u^1_*(x,i) = u^1_*(z,i) = u^2_*(z,i) \tag{6.15}$$

$$u^2(x,i) = u^2_*(x,i) \tag{6.16}$$

$$u^1(y,i) = u^1_*(y,i) = u^2(y,i) = u^2_*(y,i) \tag{6.17}$$

Suppose that $(x,y) \in \omega(u^1)$ is true. By virtue of (6.15), (6.17), and condition I_ω, we then obtain $(x,y) \in \omega(u^1_*)$. We also have $(x,z) \in I(\omega(u^1_*))$, in view of (6.15) and condition IM_ω. It then follows from transitivity of $\omega(u^1_*)$ that $(z,y) \in \omega(u^1_*)$, which, in turn, yields $(z,y) \in \omega(u^1_*)$, in view of (6.15), (6.17), and condition I_ω. Because we have

$$u^1(x,i) = u^2(x,\pi(i)) = u^2_*(x,\pi(i)) = u^2_*(z,i)$$

we obtain $(x,z) \in I(\omega(u^2_*))$ by virtue of condition IM_ω. It then follows that $(x,y) \in \omega(u^2_*)$, establishing that $(x,y) \in \omega(u^2)$, in view of (6.15), (6.17), and condition I_ω. The other case can be treated similarly. ∎

Proof of Theorem 6.2: It is clear that ω_B satisfies all of the conditions U_ω, I_ω, IM_ω, and CU_ω, so that we have only to prove the converse. Take any u, and let u^1 be such that

$$\forall i \in N: \begin{cases} u^1(x,i) = u(x,1) + \sum_{k=1}^{i-1} \{u(y,k) - u(x,k)\} \\ \& \\ u^1(y,i) = u(x,1) + \sum_{k=1}^{i} \{u(y,k) - u(x,k)\} \end{cases}$$

for all $x, y \in X$. We then have

$$\forall i \in N, \forall x, y \in X: u^1(x,i) - u^1(y,i) = u(x,i) - u(y,i)$$

so that we have $\omega(u) = \omega(u^1)$, thanks to Lemma 6.2. Let π be a cyclic permutation on N such that $\pi(i) = i + 1$ $(i = 1, 2, \ldots, n-1)$ and $\pi(n) = 1$. Define u^2 by

$$\forall i \in N, \forall x, y \in X: \begin{cases} u^2(x,i) = u^1(x,\pi(i)) \\ \& \\ u^2(y,i) = u^1(y,i) \end{cases}$$

Thanks to Lemma 6.3, we then have $\omega(u^1) = \omega(u^2)$. Because it is true that

$$\forall i \in N \setminus \{n\}: u^2(x,i) = u^1(x,i+1) = u^2(y,i)$$

for all $x, y \in X$, we obtain from condition IM_ω that

$$(x,y) \in P(\omega(u^2)) \leftrightarrow u^2(x,n) > u^2(y,n)$$

$$(x,y) \in I(\omega(u^2)) \leftrightarrow u^2(x,n) = u^2(y,n)$$

and

$$(y,x) \in P(\omega(u^2)) \leftrightarrow u^2(x,n) < u^2(y,n)$$

Note, however, that

$$u^2(x,n) = u^1(x,1) = u(x,1)$$

$$u^2(y,n) = u(x,1) + \sum_{k=1}^{n} \{u(y,k) - u(x,k)\}$$

Because $\omega(u^2) = \omega(u)$, we have established that

$$\forall x, y \in X: (x,y) \in \omega(u) \leftrightarrow \sum_{k=1}^{n} u(x,k) \geq \sum_{k=1}^{n} u(y,k)$$

namely, that $\omega = \omega_B$. ∎

2.6 Rawlsian and Benthamite principles of justice: a comparison

We are now in a position to put forward a summary comparison between the Rawlsian principle and the Benthamite principle. First of all, the Rawlsian lexicographic maximin principle (leximin principle, for short) requires *ordinal* comparability of welfare *levels,* whereas classical utilitarianism requires *cardinal* comparability of welfare *units.* This is an important contrast between these principles from the informational point of view.

Second, the focus of our comparison is on the trade-off, or the lack thereof, between equity and aggregate welfare. Suppose a change from y to x diminishes the welfare of the worst-off individual by a marginal amount but increases the welfare of all others by a great deal, assuming for the sake of argument that both welfare levels and welfare gains and losses are interpersonally comparable. It may seem fairly reasonable to claim that if the loss to the worst-off individual is small enough, while the gains to everybody else are large enough, the large aggregate welfare gains should not be sacrificed for the purpose of preventing a tiny loss to the worst-off individual. But this claim is not endorsed by Rawls. If, in contrast, there were no loss to the worst-off individual, the Rawlsian principle would declare that x is more just than y if all other individuals gain therefrom. This fact shows clearly that the justice judgments rendered by ω_R lack *continuity*. Presumably, this exclusive concern of ω_R with the welfare of the worst-off individual, in disregard of the aggregate welfare, appears to be too extreme to many, although there are, no doubt, some persons who enthusiastically support Rawls when he writes: "To respect persons is to recognize that they possess an inviolability founded on justice that even the welfare of society as a whole cannot override" (Rawls, 1971, p. 586).

The Benthamite principle of utilitarianism does admit the trade-off between equity and aggregate welfare.[5] As a matter of fact, it goes to the other extreme and pays no attention to the equity of the distribution of aggregate welfare among individuals. Indeed, it fails to satisfy the Sen–Hammond equity axiom SHE_ω, which is a key axiom in the characterization of ω_R.

The contrasting claims of ω_B and ω_R are so sharp that it is impossible to define a complete principle of justice that is compatible with cardinal full comparability of welfare and satisfies both the continuity requirement, on which the Benthamite principle gains a score, and the equity requirement which is the franchise of the leximin principle, together with other axioms U_ω, I_ω, and IM_ω, over which no confrontation exists between ω_B and ω_R. In view of this incompatibility, it is important to recognize that "[although the Suppesian principle of justice ω_S] does not yield a complete social ordering, it does squeeze out as much juice as possible out of the use of dominance (or vector inequality), which is the common element in the maximum criterion, utilitarianism, and a number of other collective choice procedures involving interpersonal comparability" (Sen, 1970*b*, p. 151).

In what follows, we assume that any admissible principle of justice satisfies condition U_ω (unrestricted applicability), condition I_ω (independence), and condition IM_ω (impartiality). Therefore, ω_B, ω_R, and ω_S are representative admissible principles of justice, whereas the no-less-equitable relation based on the no-envy equity concept is inadmissible because it fails to satisfy the requirement of impartiality, as we exemplified earlier.

3 Constrained majoritarian rules

3.1 Construction of the rule

Let us assume that an n-list of admissible principles of justice, one principle ω_i for each individual $i \in N$, is specified as a summary description of each and every individual's impartial moral sense of justice. Given a generalized profile $v = (u_1^v, u_2^v, \ldots, u_n^v) \in \mathscr{U}$, we then obtain, for each individual $i \in N$, his subjective preference R_i^v, which is defined by (6.1), and his *ethical preference* $\omega_i(u_i^v)$, in the sense of Harsanyi (1955). Corresponding to any generalized profile $v \in \mathscr{U}$, we thus obtain a *subjective profile*

$$\Sigma(v) = (R_1^v, R_2^v, \ldots, R_n^v)$$

and an *ethical profile*, given $\omega = (\omega_1, \omega_2, \ldots, \omega_n)$,

$$\Omega(v|\omega) = (\omega_1(u_1^v), \omega_2(u_2^v), \ldots, \omega_n(u_n^v))$$

It is worthwhile to emphasize that in our present framework,

> each individual is supposed to have a social welfare function of his own, expressing his own individual value – in the same way as each individual has a utility function of his own, expressing his own individual taste.... Even if both an individual's social welfare function and his utility function in a sense express his own individual preferences, they must express preferences of different sorts: the former must express what this individual prefers (or, rather, would prefer) on the basis of impersonal social considerations alone, and the latter must express what he actually prefers, whether on the basis of his personal interests or on any other basis. The former may be called his "ethical" preferences, the latter his "subjective" preferences. [Harsanyi, 1955, p. 315]

Our problem is to design a generalized collective choice rule that aggregates this double heterogeneity, as it were, of the authentic individual preferences into a "just" social choice function.

3.2 Nonpaternalism and the lexical combination of preferences

Unless otherwise circumscribed, it is clearly desirable to have a GCCR with the widest possible domain. Hence our first requirement:

Condition U (unrestricted domain)
The domain of a generalized collective choice rule consists of all logically possible generalized profiles.

A simple impossibility theorem that is due essentially to Sen (1970*b*, pp. 149–50) negates the possibility of designing such a robust GCCR. Consider the following unanimity conditions on the ethical profile.

Condition JU (justice unanimity principle)
For every generalized profile $v = (u_1^v, u_2^v, \ldots, u_n^v) \in \mathscr{U}$ and every $x, y \in X$, if $(x, y) \in \bigcap_{i \in N} P(\omega_i(u_i^v))$, then $[x \in S \rightarrow y \notin C^v(S)]$ for all $S \in \mathscr{S}$, where $C^v = \Phi(v)$.

Condition SJU (strong justice unanimity principle)
For every generalized profile $v = (u_1^v, u_2^v, \ldots, u_n^v) \in \mathscr{U}$ and every $x, y \in X$, if $(x, y) \in P(\bigcap_{i \in N} \omega_i(u_i^v))$, then $[x \in S \rightarrow y \notin C^v(S)]$ for all $S \in \mathscr{S}$, where $C^v = \Phi(v)$.

We then have the following theorem, which shows that two unanimity principles – Pareto unanimity and justice unanimity – conflict squarely.

Theorem 6.3
There exists no generalized collective choice rule that satisfies the unrestricted domain (U), the strong Pareto principle (SP), and the justice unanimity principle (JU).[6]

> *Proof:* Suppose that there exists an eligible GCCR Φ. Take any distinct $x, y \in X$, and let a generalized profile $v = (u_1^v, u_2^v, \ldots, u_n^v) \in \mathscr{U}$ be such that
>
> $$u_1^v(x, 2) > u_1^v(y, 1) > u_1^v(x, 1) > u_1^v(y, 2)$$
> $$u_2^v(x, 1) > u_2^v(y, 2) > u_2^v(x, 2) > u_2^v(y, 1)$$
> $$\forall i \in N \setminus \{1, 2\}, \forall (z, k) \in \{x, y\} \times \{1, 2\}: u_i^v(z, k) = u_2^v(z, k)$$
> $$\forall i \in N, \forall k \in N \setminus \{1, 2\}: u_i^v(x, k) = u_i^v(y, k)$$
>
> Because we have
>
> $$(y, x) \in P(R_1^v) \cap P(R_2^v) \cap \left[\bigcap_{k \in N \setminus \{1, 2\}} I(R_k^v) \right]$$

condition SP yields $\{y\} = C^{v}(\{x, y\})$. On the other hand, we can easily verify that $(x, y) \in \omega_S(u_i^v)$ holds true for all $i \in N$, so that we have $(x, y) \in \bigcap_{i \in N} P(\omega_i(u_i^v))$ by virtue of the impartiality condition. It then follows from condition JU that $\{x\} = C^{v}(\{x, y\})$, a contradiction. ∎

The culprit of this impossibility result is very easy to track down. If we examine the generalized profile v that we used in proving Theorem 6.3, we can easily recognize that $(y, x) \in P(R_1^v)$, $(x, y) \in P(R_{21}^v)$, $(y, x) \in P(R_2^v)$, and $(x, y) \in P(R_{12}^v)$ hold true. There is a clear pattern here. Although individual 1 feels better to be in y rather than in x, individual 2 maintains that it is better for individual 1 to be in x rather than in y, and vice versa. No wonder we cannot arbitrate such mutually meddlesome claims.

The source of trouble crystallized in Theorem 6.3 being the lack of nonpaternalistic acceptance of each other's subjective preferences, it makes sense to introduce a doctored version of condition U as follows. Let $\mathscr{U}_{ID}$ be the set of all generalized profiles that satisfy the axiom of identity:

$$\mathscr{U}_{ID} = \{v = (u_1^v, u_2^v, \ldots, u_n^v) \in \mathscr{U} \mid \forall\, i, j \in N: R_{ij}^v = R_j^v\} \tag{6.18}$$

Condition UID (unrestricted domain under identity axiom)
The domain of a generalized collective choice rule is $\mathscr{U}_{ID}$.

We now set about constructing several concrete majoritarian rules that satisfy condition UID of nonpaternalism. For any $v = (u_1^v, u_2^v, \ldots, u_n^v) \in \mathscr{U}_{ID}$, let two majority binary relations M_ε^v and M_σ^v be defined by

$$(x, y) \in M_\varepsilon^v \leftrightarrow \#\{i \in N \mid (x, y) \in \omega_i(u_i^v)\} \geq \#\{i \in N \mid (y, x) \in \omega_i(u_i^v)\} \tag{6.19}$$

and

$$(x, y) \in M_\sigma^v \leftrightarrow \#\{i \in N \mid (x, y) \in R_i^v\} \geq \#\{i \in N \mid (y, x) \in R_i^v\} \tag{6.20}$$

respectively. In words, $(x, y) \in M_\varepsilon^v$ [resp. $(x, y) \in M_\sigma^v$] holds true if and only if the number of individuals who at least weakly prefer x to y with respect to the ethical profile $\Omega(v|\omega)$ [resp. the subjective profile $\Sigma(v)$] is not less than the number of individuals who at least weakly prefer y to x.

Take any $S \in \mathscr{S}$ and let $C_\varepsilon^v(S)$ and $C_\sigma^v(S)$ be defined, respectively, by

$$C_\varepsilon^v(S) = \{x \in S \mid \forall\, y \in S: (y, x) \notin P(\omega_N(v))\} \tag{6.21}$$

and

$$C_\sigma^v(S) = \{x \in S \mid \forall\, y \in S: (y, x) \notin P(R_N^v)\} \tag{6.22}$$

where $\omega_N(v) = \bigcap_{i \in N} \omega_i(u_i^v)$ and $R_N^v = \bigcap_{i \in N} R_i^v$. The idea behind these sets is very simple. $C_\varepsilon^v(S)$ [resp. $C_\sigma^v(S)$] is nothing other than the Pareto-efficient subset of S with respect to the ethical profile $\Omega(v|\omega)$ [resp. the subjective profile $\Sigma(v)$], both of which are nonempty in view of transitivity of $\omega_N(v)$ and R_N^v.

We can assert that

$$\forall S \in \mathscr{S}: C_\varepsilon^v(S) \subset C_\sigma^v(S) \tag{6.23}$$

holds true for any $v \in \mathscr{U}$. To prove (6.23), we have only to note that

$$\forall v \in \mathscr{U}_{ID}: P(R_N^v) \subset \bigcap_{i \in N} P(\omega_S(u_i^v)) \tag{6.24}$$

holds true as far as each ω_i $(i \in N)$ satisfies condition IM_ω (Sen, 1970*b*, p. 138).

Going one step further, we now construct two choice functions $C_{\varepsilon\tau}^v$ and $C_{\sigma\tau}^v$ on a choice space $(X, \mathscr{S})$ by

$$\forall S \in \mathscr{S}: \begin{cases} C_{\varepsilon\tau}^v(S) = \{x \in S | \forall y \in S: (x, y) \in T(M_\varepsilon^v(S))\} \\ \& \\ C_{\sigma\tau}^v(S) = \{x \in S | \forall y \in S: (x, y) \in T(M_\sigma^v(S))\} \end{cases} \tag{6.25}$$

where $T(M_\varepsilon^v(S))$ [resp. $T(M_\sigma^v(S))$] denotes the transitive closure of $M_\varepsilon^v(S) = M_\varepsilon^v \cap (S \times S)$ [resp. $M_\sigma^v(S) = M_\sigma^v \cap (S \times S)$]. Clearly, $C_{\sigma\tau}^v$ is essentially what we called in Chapter 4 the TCM choice function.

Finally, we introduce four choice functions $C_{\varepsilon\varepsilon}^v$, $C_{\varepsilon\sigma}^v$, $C_{\sigma\varepsilon}^v$, and $C_{\sigma\sigma}^v$ on a choice space $(X, \mathscr{S})$ by

$$\begin{aligned} C_{\varepsilon\varepsilon}^v(S) &= C_{\varepsilon\tau}^v(C_\varepsilon^v(S)), \quad & C_{\varepsilon\sigma}^v(S) &= C_{\varepsilon\tau}^v(C_\sigma^v(S)) \\ C_{\sigma\varepsilon}^v(S) &= C_{\sigma\tau}^v(C_\varepsilon^v(S)), \quad & C_{\sigma\sigma}^v(S) &= C_{\sigma\tau}^v(C_\sigma^v(S)) \end{aligned} \tag{6.26}$$

for all $S \in \mathscr{S}$. Associating each one of these well-defined choice functions with the generalized profile $v \in \mathscr{U}$ we started from, we obtain a series of generalized collective choice rules on $\mathscr{U}_{ID}$ that we denote by $\Phi_{\varepsilon\varepsilon}$, $\Phi_{\varepsilon\sigma}$, $\Phi_{\sigma\varepsilon}$, and $\Phi_{\sigma\sigma}$, respectively.

Complicated though our construction of these rules might seem to be, they are formalizations of a quite intuitive idea in each case. They use in common the transitive closure of the simple majority relation restricted on the efficiency frontier. The use of the transitive closure is motivated by the need to circumvent the difficulty arising from the majority cycle, whereas the restriction thereof on the efficiency frontier is motivated by the need to avoid the choice of an inefficient state that may arise from unadulterated application of transitive closure. The reader is referred back to Chapter 4 if he is in need of further motivational explanation on these devices.

The rule $\Phi_{\varepsilon\varepsilon}$ uses only the ethical profile in defining the simple majority relation as well as in defining the efficiency frontier, and the rule $\Phi_{\sigma\sigma}$ uses only the subjective profile for both purposes. In contrast, the two rules $\Phi_{\varepsilon\sigma}$ and $\Phi_{\sigma\varepsilon}$ combine both subjective and ethical profiles hierarchically. $\Phi_{\varepsilon\sigma}$ uses the subjective profile $\Sigma(v)$ in defining the efficiency frontier $C^v_\sigma(S)$, to which the transitive closure of the simple majority relation with respect to the ethical profile $\Omega(v|\omega)$ is applied, whereas $\Phi_{\sigma\varepsilon}$ reverses the order of application of the subjective and ethical profiles. In what follows, we shall focus on $\Phi_{\varepsilon\sigma}$ (the *Pareto-constrained ethical majoritarianism*) and $\Phi_{\sigma\varepsilon}$ (the *justice-constrained subjective majoritarianism*), referring to $\Phi_{\varepsilon\varepsilon}$ and $\Phi_{\sigma\sigma}$ only when doing so will clarify the nature of $\Phi_{\varepsilon\sigma}$ and $\Phi_{\sigma\varepsilon}$ by contrast. The reason for our lopsided treatment is that $\Phi_{\varepsilon\sigma}$ and $\Phi_{\sigma\varepsilon}$ represent precisely our attempted ways of incorporating ethical constraints on mechanical application of the majoritarian collective choice rules.

3.3 *Some properties of the constrained majoritarianism*

To begin with, let us clarify how the choice sets generated by the rules constructed thus far are related to each other.

Theorem 6.4
For any generalized profile $v = (u^v_1, u^v_2, \ldots, u^v_n) \in \mathscr{U}_{ID}$ and any $S \in \mathscr{S}$, we have the following set-theoretic inclusions:

(a) $C^v_{\sigma\sigma}(S) \subset C^v_{\sigma\tau}(S) \cap C^v_\sigma(S)$,
(b) $C^v_{\varepsilon\varepsilon}(S) \subset C^v_{\varepsilon\tau}(S) \cap C^v_\varepsilon(S)$,
(c) $C^v_{\varepsilon\sigma}(S) \subset C^v_{\varepsilon\tau}(S) \cap C^v_\sigma(S)$,
(d) $C^v_{\sigma\varepsilon}(S) \subset C^v_{\sigma\sigma}(S)$ if and only if $C^v_\varepsilon(S) \cap C^v_{\sigma\sigma}(S) \neq \varnothing$, and
(e) $C^v_{\varepsilon\varepsilon}(S) \subset C^v_{\varepsilon\sigma}(S)$ if and only if $C^v_\varepsilon(S) \cap C^v_{\varepsilon\sigma}(S) \neq \varnothing$ (Suzumura, 1983, Theorem 2).

Proof of (a): Take any $S \in \mathscr{S}$, any $x \in C^v_{\sigma\sigma}(S)$, and any $z \in S$. If it so happens that $z \in C^v_\sigma(S)$, we obtain $(x, z) \in T[M^v_\sigma(C^v_\sigma(S))]$. Because it is true that $T[M^v_\sigma(C^v_\sigma(S))] \subset T(M^v_\sigma(S))$ for all $S \in \mathscr{S}$, we then obtain

$$\forall z \in C^v_\sigma(S): (x, z) \in T(M^v_\sigma(S)) \tag{6.27}$$

If, on the other hand, $z \in S \setminus C^v_\sigma(S)$ is the case, the definition of $C^v_\sigma(S)$ yields $(y^1, z) \in P(R^v_N)$ for some $y^1 \in S$. This y^1, in turn, either belongs to $C^v_\sigma(S)$ or satisfies $(y^2, y^1) \in P(R^v_N)$ for some $y^2 \in S$. Repeating this procedure and taking the transitivity of R^v_N and the finiteness of S into consideration, we obtain

$$\forall z \in S \setminus C^v_\sigma(S), \exists y_z \in C^v_\sigma(S): (y_z, z) \in P(R^v_N) \tag{6.28}$$

Because $x \in C^v_{\sigma\sigma}(S)$ and $y_z \in C^v_\sigma(S)$ are true, we then have

$$(x, y_z) \in T[M^v_\sigma(C^v_\sigma(S))] \subset T(M^v_\sigma(S)) \tag{6.29}$$

It is clearly the case that $P(R^v_N) \cap (S \times S) \subset T(M^v_\sigma(S))$ for all $S \in \mathscr{S}$, so that (6.28) and (6.29) imply that

$$\forall z \in S \setminus C^v_\sigma(S): (x, z) \in T(M^v_\sigma(S)) \tag{6.30}$$

Coupled with (6.27), (6.30) yields $(x, z) \in T(M^v_\sigma(S))$ for all $z \in S$; that is, $x \in C^v_{\sigma\tau}(S)$. Taking $C^v_{\sigma\sigma}(S) \subset C^v_\sigma(S)$ into consideration, we arrive at (a), as desired. ∎

Proof of (b): Replacing all occurrences of σ in the foregoing proof of (a) by ε, we obtain a valid proof of (b), thanks to the symmetry of the definitions. ∎

Proof of (c): Once again, the method of proof of (a) essentially applies here. We have only to invoke en route that

$$P(R^v_N) \cap (S \times S) \subset P(\omega_N(v)) \cap (S \times S) \subset M^v_\varepsilon(S)$$

holds true, the left-hand inclusion being implied by $v \in \mathscr{U}_{ID}$ and the condition IM_ω on ω_i $(i \in N)$. ∎

Proof of (d): Because $S^1 \subset S^2$ implies $T(M^v_\sigma(S^1)) \subset T(M^v_\sigma(S^2))$, we have

$$\forall S^1, S^2 \in \mathscr{S}: S^1 \subset S^2 \rightarrow G[S^1, T(M^v_\sigma(S^1))] \subset G[S^1, T(M^v_\sigma(S^2))] \tag{6.31}$$

$T(M^v_\sigma(S))$ being an ordering on S for every $S \in \mathscr{S}$, $C^*(\cdot) = G[\cdot, T(M^v_\sigma(S))]$ defines a full rational choice function on a choice space $(S, \mathscr{S}(S))$, where $\mathscr{S}(S)$ denotes the family of all nonempty subsets of S. It then follows from Theorem 2.3 that

$$\forall S^1, S^2 \in \mathscr{S}: S^1 \subset S^2 \ \&\ S^1 \cap G[S^2, T(M^v_\sigma(S^2))] \neq \varnothing \rightarrow S^1 \cap G[S^2, T(M^v_\sigma(S^2))] = G[S^1, T(M^v_\sigma(S^2))] \tag{6.32}$$

In view of (6.31), (6.32) implies that

$$\forall S^1, S^2 \in \mathscr{S}: S^1 \subset S^2 \ \&\ S^1 \cap G[S^2, T(M^v_\sigma(S^2))] \neq \varnothing \rightarrow G[S^1, T(M^v_\sigma(S^1))] \subset G[S^2, T(M^v_\sigma(S^2))] \tag{6.33}$$

We now make use of (6.33) to establish (d). If we let $S^1 = C^v_\varepsilon(S)$ and $S^2 = C^v_\sigma(S)$, we obtain, from (6.33),

$$\forall S \in \mathscr{S}: C^v_\varepsilon(S) \cap C^v_{\sigma\sigma}(S) \neq \varnothing \rightarrow C^v_{\sigma\varepsilon}(S) \subset C^v_{\sigma\sigma}(S) \tag{6.34}$$

where use is made of (6.23). To complete the proof of (d), assume that $C^v_{\sigma\varepsilon}(S) \subset C^v_{\sigma\sigma}(S)$ holds true. Then we obtain

$$C^v_\varepsilon(S) \cap C^v_{\sigma\sigma}(S) \supset C^v_\varepsilon(S) \cap C^v_{\sigma\varepsilon}(S) = C^v_{\sigma\varepsilon}(S)$$

which is nonempty by construction. The proof of (d) is thereby complete. ▮

Proof of (e): By similar reasoning, we can prove that a statement that is the same as (6.33) save for the replacement of σ by ε holds true, which we call (6.33:ε). Take any $S \in \mathscr{S}$, and let $S^1 = C_\varepsilon^v(S)$ and $S^2 = C_\sigma^v(S)$ be substituted into (6.33:ε) to obtain

$$\forall S \in \mathscr{S}: C_\varepsilon^v(S) \cap C_{\varepsilon\sigma}^v(S) \neq \varnothing \rightarrow C_{\varepsilon\varepsilon}^v(S) \subset C_{\varepsilon\sigma}^v(S) \tag{6.35}$$

Just as we could reverse the arrow in (6.34), we can reverse the arrow in (6.35) to complete the proof of (e). ▮

Although $\Phi_{\varepsilon\sigma}$ and $\Phi_{\sigma\varepsilon}$ are quite symmetrically constructed by exchanging the roles assigned to the ethical and the subjective profiles, the counterpart of Theorem 6.4(c) does not hold true for $\Phi_{\sigma\varepsilon}$, as we can exemplify in the following:

Example 6.1

Let $N = \{1, 2, 3\}$, $X = \{x, y, z\}$, and $\omega = (\omega_R, \omega_R, \omega_R)$, and consider a generalized profile $v = (u_*^v, u_*^v, u_*^v)$ such that

$$u_*^v(z,1) > u_*^v(y,1) > u_*^v(x,1) > u_*^v(z,3) > u_*^v(x,3)$$
$$> u_*^v(y,2) > u_*^v(x,2) > u_*^v(z,2) > u_*^v(y,3)$$

It then follows that

$$\omega_R(u_*^v): x, z, y$$

$$R_1^v: z, y, x, \qquad R_2^v: y, x, z, \qquad R_3^v: z, x, y$$

which yield $C_\varepsilon^v(S) = \{x\}$, $C_{\sigma\varepsilon}^v(S) = \{x\}$, $C_{\sigma\tau}^v(S) = \{z\}$, where $S = X$. It is clear that

$$C_{\sigma\varepsilon}^v(S) \subset C_{\sigma\tau}^v(S) \cap C_\varepsilon^v(S)$$

does not hold true for this (v, S). ▮

How do $\Phi_{\varepsilon\sigma}$ and $\Phi_{\sigma\varepsilon}$ fare in terms of the choice-consistency properties? We may assert the following:

Theorem 6.5

For any generalized profile $v \in \mathscr{U}_{ID}$,

(a) $C_{\varepsilon\sigma}^v$ satisfies Nash's axiom of choice consistency (NA), and

(b) $C_{\sigma\varepsilon}^v$ satisfies the stability axiom of choice consistency (ST).

Proof of (a): Take any $v \in \mathscr{U}_{ID}$ and define a binary relation O^v on X by

$$O^v = \{(x, y) \in X \times X \mid (x, y) \in P(R_N^v) \vee (y, x) \notin P(R_N^v)\} \tag{6.36}$$

It is easy to verify that O^v is reflexive and complete. We can also verify that $P(O^v) = P(R_N^v)$ holds true, which implies that $P(O^v)$ is transitive. Furthermore,

$$\forall S \in \mathscr{S}: G(S, O^v) = M(S, R_N^v) \tag{6.37}$$

is true.

In order to prove that

$$P(O^v)P(M_\varepsilon^v) \cup P(M_\varepsilon^v)P(O^v) \subset P(M_\varepsilon^v) \tag{6.38}$$

holds true, let $x, y \in X$ be such that $(x, y) \in P(O^v)P(M_\varepsilon^v)$. Then there exists $z \in X$ such that $(x, z) \in P(O^v) = P(R_N^v)$ and $(z, y) \in P(M_\varepsilon^v)$. Because ω_i satisfies condition IM_ω for all $i \in N$, we are assured that $P(R_N^v) \subset \bigcap_{i \in N} P(\omega_i(u_i^v))$ holds true. By virtue of transitivity of $\omega_i(u_i^v)$ for all $i \in N$, we then obtain $(x, y) \in P(M_\varepsilon^v)$, establishing $P(O^v)P(M_\varepsilon^v) \subset P(M_\varepsilon^v)$. Similarly, we can prove that $P(M_\varepsilon^v)P(O^v) \subset P(M_\varepsilon^v)$ is valid, to complete the proof of (6.38).

We can now invoke Theorem A(3) in the Appendix to Chapter 4 for $R^1 = M_\varepsilon^v$ and $R^2 = O^v$ to conclude that

$$\begin{aligned} G[G(S, O^v), T(M_\varepsilon^v(G(S, O^v)))] &= G[M(S, R_N^v), T(M_\varepsilon^v(M(S, R_N^v)))] \\ &= G[C_\sigma^v(S), T(M_\varepsilon^v(C_\sigma^v(S)))] \\ &= C_{\varepsilon\sigma}^v(S) \end{aligned}$$

satisfies Nash's axiom of choice consistency, where use is made of (6.37). ∎

Proof of (b): To begin with, let us verify that

$$\forall S_1, S_2 \in \mathscr{S}: S_1 \subset C_\varepsilon^v(S_2) \rightarrow S_1 = C_\varepsilon^v(S_1) \tag{6.39}$$

holds true for any $v \in \mathscr{U}_{ID}$. Because $C_\varepsilon^v(S_1) \subset S_1$ is always true, (6.39) can be false only when there exists an $x \in X$ such that $x \in S_1 \setminus C_\varepsilon^v(S_1)$; that is,

$$\exists x \in S_1, \exists y \in S_1: (y, x) \in P(\omega_N(v))$$

even if $S_1 \subset C_\varepsilon^v(S_2)$ is true. It then follows that

$$\exists (x, y) \in C_\varepsilon^v(S_2) \times S_2: (y, x) \in P(\omega_N(v))$$

which is an apparent contradiction.

To prove that $C_{\sigma\varepsilon}^v$ satisfies the stability axiom, let $v \in \mathscr{U}_{ID}$ and $S \in \mathscr{S}$ be taken arbitrarily, and define $S_0 = C_{\sigma\varepsilon}^v(S)$. We then have

$$S_0 = C_{\sigma\tau}^v(C_\varepsilon^v(S)) \subset C_\varepsilon^v(S) \tag{6.40}$$

so that (6.39) implies that $S_0 = C^{\nu}_{\varepsilon}(S_0)$; that is,

$$C^{\nu}_{\varepsilon}(C^{\nu}_{\sigma\varepsilon}(S)) = C^{\nu}_{\sigma\varepsilon}(S) \tag{6.41}$$

is valid. If we put $S_1 = C^{\nu}_{\varepsilon}(C^{\nu}_{\sigma\varepsilon}(S))$ and $S_2 = C^{\nu}_{\varepsilon}(S)$, we obtain

$$S_1 \subset S_2, \qquad C^{\nu}_{\sigma\tau}(S_2) = C^{\nu}_{\sigma\varepsilon}(S) = S_1 \tag{6.42}$$

where use is made of (6.40) and (6.41). We now apply Theorem A(3) in the Appendix to Chapter 4 to $R^1 = M^{\nu}_{\sigma}$ and $R^2 = X \times X$ to assert that $C^{\nu}_{\sigma\tau}$ satisfies Nash's axiom. It then follows that $C^{\nu}_{\sigma\tau}(S_1) = C^{\nu}_{\sigma\tau}(S_2)$ holds true. Because

$$C^{\nu}_{\sigma\tau}(S_1) = C^{\nu}_{\sigma\tau}[C^{\nu}_{\varepsilon}(C^{\nu}_{\sigma\varepsilon}(S))] = C^{\nu}_{\sigma\varepsilon}(C^{\nu}_{\sigma\varepsilon}(S))$$

and

$$C^{\nu}_{\sigma\tau}(S_2) = C^{\nu}_{\sigma\tau}(C^{\nu}_{\varepsilon}(S)) = C^{\nu}_{\sigma\varepsilon}(S)$$

are true, we are home. ∎

Note that Theorem 6.5(b) can only assure that $C^{\nu}_{\sigma\varepsilon}$ satisfies the stability axiom, which is much weaker than Nash's axiom that $C^{\nu}_{\varepsilon\sigma}$ satisfies, as Theorem 6.5(a) asserts. To show that this cannot be otherwise, we put forward the following:

Example 6.2
Let $N = \{1,2,3\}$, $X = \{x, y, z\}$, and $\omega = (\omega_R, \omega_R, \omega_R)$, and consider the following generalized profile $\nu \in \mathscr{U}_{ID}$:

$$u^{\nu}_1(x,3) = u^{\nu}_1(y,3) > u^{\nu}_1(z,3) > u^{\nu}_1(x,2) > u^{\nu}_1(z,2)$$
$$> u^{\nu}_1(y,2) > u^{\nu}_1(y,1) > u^{\nu}_1(z,1) > u^{\nu}_1(x,1)$$

$$u^{\nu}_2(x,3) = u^{\nu}_2(y,3) > u^{\nu}_2(z,3) > u^{\nu}_2(y,1) > u^{\nu}_2(z,1)$$
$$> u^{\nu}_2(x,2) > u^{\nu}_2(z,2) > u^{\nu}_2(x,1) > u^{\nu}_2(y,2)$$

$$u^{\nu}_3(x,3) = u^{\nu}_3(y,3) > u^{\nu}_3(x,2) > u^{\nu}_3(z,2) > u^{\nu}_3(y,1)$$
$$> u^{\nu}_3(z,1) > u^{\nu}_3(z,3) > u^{\nu}_3(y,2) > u^{\nu}_3(x,1)$$

We can easily verify that

$$\omega_R(u^{\nu}_1): y, z, x, \qquad \omega_R(u^{\nu}_2): z, x, y, \qquad \omega_R(u^{\nu}_3): z, y, x$$

$$R^{\nu}_1: y, z, x, \qquad R^{\nu}_2: x, z, y, \qquad R^{\nu}_3: [x, y], z$$

Let $S_1 = \{x, y\}$ and $S_2 = X$. Because $(x, y), (y, x) \in M^{\nu}_{\sigma}$, $(y, z) \in P(M^{\nu}_{\sigma})$, $(x, z) \in P(M^{\nu}_{\sigma})$, and $\bigcap_{i \in N} \omega_R(u^{\nu}_i) = \Delta_X \cup \{(z, x)\}$, where $\Delta_X = \{(x, x), (y, y), (z, z)\}$, we can obtain $C^{\nu}_{\sigma\varepsilon}(S_1) = S_1 \supset \supset C^{\nu}_{\sigma\varepsilon}(S_2) = \{y\}$, even if $S_1 \subset S_2$, which is a clear violation of Nash's axiom by this $C^{\nu}_{\sigma\varepsilon}$. ∎

Let us now examine $\Phi_{\sigma\varepsilon}$ and $\Phi_{\varepsilon\sigma}$ with respect to several other performance criteria that are now familiar to us.

In the first place, $\Phi_{\sigma\varepsilon}$ as well as $\Phi_{\varepsilon\sigma}$ is Paretian in the sense that the strong Pareto principle (SP) is thereby satisfied. Consider $\Phi_{\sigma\varepsilon}$ first. Let $v \in \mathscr{U}_{ID}$, $S \in \mathscr{S}$, and $x, y \in X$ be such that $(x, y) \in P(R_N^v)$, $x \in S$, and $y \in C_{\sigma\varepsilon}^v(S)$ hold true. This is an immediate contradiction, however, because $(x, y) \in P(R_N^v)$ and $x \in S$ imply $y \notin C_\sigma^v(S)$, and hence $y \notin C_\varepsilon^v(S)$, in view of (6.23), whereas $y \in C_{\sigma\varepsilon}^v(S)$ implies $y \in C_\varepsilon^v(S)$. Only a few trivial changes are required in the foregoing proof to establish that $\Phi_{\varepsilon\sigma}$ also satisfies condition SP.

As a matter of fact, the case for $\Phi_{\sigma\varepsilon}$ can be strengthened somewhat. The method of proof we used earlier essentially goes through to show that $\Phi_{\sigma\varepsilon}$ satisfies the strong justice unanimity principle (SJU) on $\mathscr{U}_{ID}$, which is stronger than condition SP. Similar generalization does not apply to $\Phi_{\varepsilon\sigma}$, as will be exemplified next.

Example 6.3
Let $N = \{1,2\}$, $X = \{x, y, z, w\}$, and $\omega = (\omega_R, \omega_R)$, and let a generalized profile $v = (u_1^v, u_2^v) \in \mathscr{U}_{ID}$ be such that

$$u_1^v(z,2) > u_1^v(w,2) > u_1^v(y,2) > u_1^v(x,2)$$
$$> u_1^v(x,1) > u_1^v(w,1) > u_1^v(y,1) > u_1^v(z,1)$$

$$u_2^v(z,2) > u_2^v(w,2) > u_2^v(y,2) > u_2^v(x,1)$$
$$> u_2^v(w,1) > u_2^v(y,1) > u_2^v(z,1) > u_2^v(x,2)$$

It can easily be seen that

$$\omega_R(u_1^v)\colon x, w, y, z, \qquad \omega_R(u_2^v)\colon w, y, z, x$$

$$R_1^v\colon x, w, y, z, \qquad R_2^v\colon z, w, y, x$$

Let $S = \{x, y, z, w\}$. We can verify that $C_\sigma^v(S) = C_{\varepsilon\sigma}^v(S) = \{x, w, z\}$, which means that $(y, z) \in P(\omega_N(v))$, $z \in C_{\varepsilon\sigma}^v(S)$, and $y \notin C_{\varepsilon\sigma}^v(S)$, which negate the validity of condition SJU for $\Phi_{\varepsilon\sigma}$. ∎

We now turn to the informational requirement of $\Phi_{\sigma\varepsilon}$ and $\Phi_{\varepsilon\sigma}$. Reflection on the construction of these rules convinces us that $\Phi_{\sigma\varepsilon}$ as well as $\Phi_{\varepsilon\sigma}$ satisfies the following condition of informational modesty.

Condition I (independence)
If $v^1 = (u_1^{v^1}, u_2^{v^1}, \ldots, u_n^{v^1})$, $v^2 = (u_1^{v^2}, u_2^{v^2}, \ldots, u_n^{v^2})$, and $S \in \mathscr{S}$ are such that

$$\forall\, i, j \in N, \forall\, x \in S\colon u_i^{v^1}(x, j) = u_i^{v^2}(x, j)$$

holds true, then we have $C^{v^1}(S) = C^{v^2}(S)$, where $C^{v^\tau} = \Phi(v^\tau)$ $(\tau = 1, 2)$.

The next property to be examined is whether $\Phi_{\sigma\varepsilon}$ and $\Phi_{\varepsilon\sigma}$ treat individuals without prejudice or favoritism. In other words, do $\Phi_{\sigma\varepsilon}$ and $\Phi_{\varepsilon\sigma}$ treat similar individuals similarly?

Care should be taken with the sense in which we mean individuals to be similar. Because an individual is characterized in our present framework not only by his generalized utility function but also by his impartial principle of justice, the requirement of similar treatment of similar individuals should read as follows: *If the generalized profile and the profile of the principles of justice are simultaneously and identically permuted among individuals, the social choice function should remain intact.*

To make our point explicit, let a GCCR be parametrized by the profile of the principles of justice $\omega = (\omega_1, \omega_2, \ldots, \omega_n)$ as Φ^{ω}. We then take any generalized profile $v = (u_1^v, u_2^v, \ldots, u_n^v)$ and any permutation $\pi \in \Pi_N$. Define the permuted generalized profile $\pi(v)$ and the permuted profile of the justice principle $\pi(\omega)$ by

$$\forall (x, j) \in X \times N\colon \pi(v)(x, j) = [u_{\pi(1)}^v(x, \pi(j)), u_{\pi(2)}^v(x, \pi(j)), \ldots, u_{\pi(n)}^v(x, \pi(j))]$$

and

$$\pi(\omega) = (\omega_{\pi(1)}, \omega_{\pi(2)}, \ldots, \omega_{\pi(n)})$$

respectively. Because $C_{\sigma\varepsilon}^v = \Phi_{\sigma\varepsilon}^{\omega}(v)$ depends only on $\omega_N(v)$ and M_{σ}^v, and $C_{\varepsilon\sigma}^v = \Phi_{\varepsilon\sigma}^{\omega}(v)$ depends only on R_N^v and M_{ε}^v, it is easy to see that $\Phi_{\sigma\varepsilon}^{\omega}$ as well as $\Phi_{\varepsilon\sigma}^{\omega}$ satisfies the following requirement.

Condition GAN (generalized anonymity)
For any $v = (u_1^v, u_2^v, \ldots, u_n^v)$ and any $\pi \in \Pi_N$, $C^{\pi(v)} = C^v$ holds true, where $C^{\pi(v)} = \Phi^{\pi(\omega)}(\pi(v))$ and $C^v = \Phi^{\omega}(v)$.

Putting all these pieces together, we can present the following summary evaluation of the performance of $\Phi_{\sigma\varepsilon}$ and $\Phi_{\varepsilon\sigma}$.

Theorem 6.6

(a) $\Phi_{\varepsilon\sigma}$ is a generalized collective choice rule that satisfies the unrestricted domain under the axiom of identity (UID), the strong Pareto principle (SP), independence (I), generalized anonymity (GAN), and Nash's axiom of choice consistency (NA).

(b) $\Phi_{\sigma\varepsilon}$ is a generalized collective choice rule that satisfies the unrestricted domain under the axiom of identity (UID), the strong justice unanimity principle (SJU), independence (I), generalized anonymity (GAN), and the stability axiom of choice consistency (ST).

4 Discussion and remarks on the literature

In this chapter we have formalized two constrained majoritarian collective choice rules, the formal properties of which are summarized in Theorem 6.6. What remains is to compare these rules with each other as well as with $\Phi_{\sigma\sigma}$ and $\Phi_{\varepsilon\varepsilon}$ with a view toward clarifying them further by contrast. We shall also make some remarks on the existing literature related to the central concern of this chapter.

Recollect that the justice-constrained subjective majoritarianism $\Phi_{\sigma\varepsilon}$ is based on a very simple idea to the effect that a proper restraint should be imposed on the reign by majorities. It is worthwhile to notice that $\Phi_{\varepsilon\varepsilon}$ satisfies all the formal properties that $\Phi_{\sigma\varepsilon}$ is asserted to satisfy, and goes one step further; that is, $\Phi_{\varepsilon\varepsilon}$ satisfies Nash's axiom of choice consistency, which is stronger than the stability axiom. Furthermore, in the concrete instance of a cake-division problem (Example 4.5) that propelled us to diverge from mechanical reliance on the majority principle, not only $\Phi_{\sigma\varepsilon}$ and $\Phi_{\varepsilon\sigma}$ but also $\Phi_{\varepsilon\varepsilon}$ chooses the egalitarian alternative $w = (\frac{1}{3}, \frac{1}{3}, \frac{1}{3})$. However, an appeal of $\Phi_{\sigma\varepsilon}$ and $\Phi_{\varepsilon\sigma}$ over $\Phi_{\varepsilon\varepsilon}$ does seem to exist: Whereas $\Phi_{\sigma\varepsilon}$ and $\Phi_{\varepsilon\sigma}$ combine the ethical and subjective profiles lexically, $\Phi_{\varepsilon\varepsilon}$ makes use only of an individual's ethical preferences that "express what can in only a qualified sense be called his 'preferences': They will, by definition, express what he prefers only in those possibly rare moments when he forces a special impartial and impersonal attitude upon himself" (Harsanyi, 1955, p. 315).

Let us now turn to $\Phi_{\sigma\sigma}$, which uses only the subjective profile. As Bordes (1979) has shown, $\Phi_{\sigma\sigma}$ scores fairly well in terms of the performance criteria we have made use of in this chapter. It might well be asked: How many *additional* niceties could we secure by introducing the lexical combination of the subjective and ethical profiles? Our plea is twofold. First, $\Phi_{\sigma\varepsilon}$ and $\Phi_{\varepsilon\sigma}$ are "just" generalized collective choice rules in the following sense: $\Phi_{\sigma\varepsilon}$ is just in that it satisfies the justice unanimity condition, and $\Phi_{\varepsilon\sigma}$ is just in that $C^{v}_{\varepsilon\sigma}(S) \subset C^{v}_{\varepsilon\tau}(S)$ holds true for all $v \in \mathscr{U}_{ID}$ and all $S \in \mathscr{S}$, which follows from Theorem 6.4(c). In consequence, in a cake-division problem (Example 4.5), we obtain

$$C_{\sigma\sigma}(S) = \{x, y, z\}, \qquad C_{\varepsilon\sigma}(S) = C_{\sigma\varepsilon}(S) = \{w\}$$

where $S = \{x, y, z, w\}$, a contrast that is worth noticing. Second, we should like to call the reader's attention to the relationship between the *selective power* of a rule and the *informational requirement* thereof. To make our point, let $(v, S) \in \mathscr{U}_{ID} \times \mathscr{S}$ be such that $C^{v}_{\varepsilon}(S) \cap C^{v}_{\sigma\sigma}(S) \neq \varnothing$. We then obtain

$$C^{v}_{\sigma\varepsilon}(S) \subset C^{v}_{\varepsilon}(S) \cap C^{v}_{\sigma\sigma}(S) \subset C^{v}_{\sigma\sigma}(S) \subset C^{v}_{\sigma\tau}(S) \cap C^{v}_{\sigma}(S) \subset C^{v}_{\sigma\tau}(S) \tag{6.43}$$

where use is made of Theorem 6.4 once again. Note that $\Phi_{\sigma\tau}$, which is nothing other than the transitive closure of the simple majority decision rule, which we examined in Chapter 4, uses only the simple majority relation M_σ^v with respect to the subjective profile $\Sigma(v)$. As such, $\Phi_{\sigma\tau}$ is informationally least demanding at the cost of being least selective among $\Phi_{\sigma\varepsilon}, \Phi_{\sigma\sigma}$, and $\Phi_{\sigma\tau}$. So low is the selective power of $\Phi_{\sigma\tau}$ that the choice set thereby generated may sometimes contain a Pareto-inefficient state, as noted. This apparent defect of $\Phi_{\sigma\tau}$ can be rectified if we use $P(R_N^v)$ along with M_σ^v and choose in accordance with the rule $\Phi_{\sigma\sigma}$, which, by construction, ensures that $C_{\sigma\sigma}^v(S)$ is contained in the Pareto-efficient subset $C_\sigma^v(S)$ of S. Further strengthening of the informational base to the extent of having not only the subjective profile $\Sigma(v)$ but also the ethical profile $\Omega(v|\omega)$ enables us to choose in accordance with the rule $\Phi_{\sigma\varepsilon}$. Not only is the choice dictated by $\Phi_{\sigma\varepsilon}$ "just," but also it is the most selective choice mechanism among $\Phi_{\sigma\varepsilon}, \Phi_{\sigma\sigma}$, and $\Phi_{\sigma\tau}$.[7]

A final observation on $\Phi_{\sigma\varepsilon}$ and $\Phi_{\varepsilon\sigma}$ might be in order. They show, in effect, that the lexical combination of the impartial concern about social justice and the pursuit of self-love fares rather well in terms of the social choice performance criteria. In this framework, it is not required that individuals share identical senses of justice in arriving at their ethical judgments. Some may be Rawlsian and judge the ethical worth of each social state, whatever social position they may happen to occupy personally, in accordance with the situation of the least favored individual. Some others may be Benthamite utilitarian and make impartial ethical judgments by placing themselves, through imaginary exchange of circumstances, in the position of others in turn and calculating the aggregate welfare. Still others may settle with the modest justice principle proposed by Suppes, making ethical judgments based solely on the dominance-cum-interpersonal permutation of welfare levels. Being based on the transitive closure device, $\Phi_{\varepsilon\sigma}$ as well as $\Phi_{\sigma\varepsilon}$ may tend to be rather "unselective" in the sense of generating "large" subsets of S for many $(v, S) \in \mathscr{U}_{ID} \times \mathscr{S}$. Our modest hope is that they will serve to suggest once more the potentiality of the extended sympathy approach in social choice theory, thereby enticing further exploration thereof in the future.

CHAPTER 7

Individual rights and libertarian claims

> What, then, is the rightful limit to the sovereignty of the individual over himself? Where does the authority of society begin? How much of human life should be assigned to individuality, and how much to society?
>
> Each will receive its proper share, if each has that which more particularly concerns it. To individuality should belong the part of life in which it is chiefly the individual that is interested; to society, the part which chiefly interests society.
>
> John Stuart Mill*

0 Introduction

Some libertarians in the tradition of Locke, Mill, and de Tocqueville would claim that there ought to exist in human life a certain minimum sphere of personal liberty that should not be interfered with by anybody other than the person in question. The question where exactly to draw the boundary between the sphere of personal liberty and that of collective authority is a matter of great dispute, and, indeed, what a libertarian might claim is not unequivocal in the first place.[1] Nevertheless, a claim for the inviolability of a minimum extent of individual libertarian rights seems to be deeply rooted in our social and political ideals.

Granting the existence of a minimum sphere of personal liberty, can we design an otherwise democratic collective choice rule in such a way that each person is empowered to decide what should be socially chosen, no matter what others may claim, in choices over states that specifically concern him? To put it differently, is it possible to construct a democratic collective choice rule that realizes the inviolability of a minimum amount of personal liberty? This question is nontrivial and of great interest, because "the connexion between democracy and individual liberty is a good deal more tenuous than it seemed to many advocates of both. The desire to be governed by myself, or at any rate to participate in the process by which my

* J. S. Mill, *On Liberty*. London: Parker, 1859; reprinted in *The Collected Works of John Stuart Mill, Vol. XVIII*, edited by J. M. Robson. Toronto: University of Toronto Press, 1977, p. 276.

life is to be controlled, may be as deep a wish as that of a free area for action, and perhaps historically older. But it is not a desire for the same thing. So different is it, indeed, as to have led in the end to the great clash of ideologies that dominates our world" (Berlin, 1958, pp. 15–16).

It was Sen (1970*a*; 1970*b*, Chapter 6*) who showed in a particularly illuminating way that the answer to our question is generally in the negative; that is, there exists no Pareto-inclusive collective choice rule (with unrestricted applicability) satisfying a mild libertarian claim. The purpose of this chapter is to dig into the logical structure of Sen's impossibility theorem and to examine some of the proposed resolutions thereof with a view toward shedding further light on the prerequisite for successful design of a collective choice rule.

The plan of the chapter is as follows. In Section 1, a concept of inviolable individual rights will be made precise in the collective choice framework and the conflict thereof with a mild democratic value – the Pareto principle – will be shown. Several proposed resolutions of this conflict will be critically examined with a view toward clarifying the nature of the Pareto libertarian paradox. The conflict in question may partly be due to the internal inconsistency of the rights assignment. In order to separate this possibility, Section 2 introduces the concept of a coherent rights system. Even if we assume that the rights system is coherent in the specified sense, however, there remains ample room for the impossibility of Pareto libertarianism. We then proceed to put forward our first resolution of Sen's paradox, which prevents the difficulty from surfacing by restricting mechanical use of the Pareto principle. Section 3 extends this result in order to cover the problem of democratic group autonomy. In Section 4 we shall examine the effect of making use of intersituational welfare comparisons in the form of extended sympathy in the present arena. It will be shown that if the rights-exercising is restricted by the impartial justice consideration in a proper way, the modified libertarian claim is made compatible with the Pareto principle. Although the possibility theorem we shall thereby establish is a fairly weak one, it well suffices to qualify Sen's assertion (1976, p. 228) to the effect that "for this class of impossibility results, introducing interpersonal comparisons is not much of a cure (in contrast with the impossibility result of the Arrow type)," which he has drawn from Kelly's *impossibility of a just liberal* (1976*a*; 1978, Chapter 8). In Section 5 we shall reconsider the structure of the libertarian rights system. Under one natural interpretation proposed by Gibbard (1974), it so happens that the libertarian rights system turns out to be *incoherent*. Several problems that crop up from this important observation will be discussed briefly. Finally, Section 6 summarizes the main implications of our analysis and puts forward several qualifications.

1 Inviolable rights, Pareto principle, and an impossibility theorem

1.1 Sen's example: the Lady Chatterley's Lover case

Because there are many different conceptions of what a libertarian might claim, it is worthwhile to start with some examples with a view toward clarifying an intuitive idea of the libertarian claim that we should like to formalize, thereby bringing out the nature of the conflict of values that we should like to resolve eventually. The first example is due to Sen (1970*a*; 1970*b*, Chapter 6).

Example 7.1
There is a single copy of *Lady Chatterley's Lover*. Everything else remaining the same, there are three social states: Mr. A (the prude) reading it (r_A), Mr. B (the lascivious) reading it (r_B), and no one reading it (r_0). The prude A prefers r_0 most, next r_A (wishing thereby to take the hurt upon himself), and lastly r_B (for fear of the possible misbehavior of the lascivious B). The lascivious B prefers r_A most (in order to educate the reactionary Mr. A), r_B next, and lastly r_0. On the grounds of individual right of reading, r_0 is *socially* better than r_A, because the sole difference between r_0 and r_A is whether or not A reads the book, and A does not want to read it. By the same token, r_B is *socially* better than r_0, in view of the fact that B wants to read the book rather than waste it and the fact that A does not read the book anyway in r_B as well as in r_0. But r_A is Pareto-superior to r_B, completing a social cycle: r_A is better than r_B, which is better than r_0, which in turn is better than r_A. ∎

1.2 Gibbard's example: the Angelina–Edwin marriage case

A second example in which individuals' libertarian claims of rights apparently conflict with the Pareto principle was constructed by Gibbard (1974), who made use of it as a model to construct his resolution scheme for the Pareto libertarian paradox.

Example 7.2
Angelina wants to marry Edwin, but she will settle for the judge, who wants whatever Angelina wants. Edwin wants to remain single, but he would rather wed Angelina than see her wed the judge. Denoting "Edwin weds Angelina" as w_E, "the judge weds Angelina and Edwin remains single" as w_J, and "both Edwin and Angelina remain single" as w_0, the pattern of their preferences over $S = \{w_E, w_J, w_0\}$ is such that Angelina prefers w_E to w_J to w_0, and Edwin prefers w_0 to w_E to w_J. Now, Angelina has a right to marry

the willing judge instead of remaining single, and she prefers w_J to w_0, so that w_0 should not be chosen from S. Edwin, in his turn, has his right to remain single rather than wed Angelina, and he prefers w_0 to w_E, so that w_E should be excluded from the choice set from S. Finally, all prefer w_E to w_J, so that w_J should not be chosen from S, by virtue of the Pareto principle. Therefore, naive exercise of individual rights, coupled with mechanical use of the Pareto principle, yields a social impasse. ∎

The careful reader must have noticed that Example 7.1 and Example 7.2 are in fact two alternative interpretations of the same conflict situation. We have deliberately chosen two interpretations thereof, because the reasonableness and/or persuasiveness of the resolutions of this conflict situation will depend rather delicately on the interpretation we associate with the abstract model.

1.3 An impossibility theorem: Pareto libertarian paradox

Let us now set about formulating the central concern of this chapter formally and put forward an impossibility theorem due to Sen (1970*a*; 1970*b*, Chapter 6*).

Let $(X, \mathscr{S})$ denote the choice space of a society consisting of n individuals who are numbered as $i = 1, 2, \ldots, n$. As before, X stands for the set of all conceivable social states and $\mathscr{S}$ the family of all nonempty finite subsets of X. Let F be a collective choice rule that aggregates each and every profile $a = (R_1^a, R_2^a, \ldots, R_n^a) \in A$ of individual preference orderings on X into a social choice function $C^a = F(a)$ on $(X, \mathscr{S})$.

What we call a *rights system* is an assignment of ordered pairs of states to each and every individual, that is, an n-tuple $D = (D_1, D_2, \ldots, D_n)$ of subsets of $X \times X$. When $(x, y) \in D_i$ holds true, we say that the rights system D assigns the pair of states (x, y) to individual $i \in N = \{1, 2, \ldots, n\}$. We say that D is *symmetric* if and only if $(x, y) \in D_i \leftrightarrow (y, x) \in D_i$ holds true for all $i \in N$ and all $x, y \in X$. We also say that D is *nondiagonal* if and only if $(x, y) \in D_i \rightarrow x \neq y$ holds true for all $i \in N$ and all $x, y \in X$.

A concept of central importance is the *realization of a rights system D by a collective choice rule F*, which reads as follows. We say that F realizes D if and only if

$$(x, y) \in D_i \cap P(R_i^a) \rightarrow \forall S \in \mathscr{S}: [x \in S \rightarrow y \notin C^a(S)] \tag{7.1}$$

holds true, where $C^a = F(a)$, for all $a \in A$, all $i \in N$, and all $x, y \in X$. To recognize the meaning of this definition, assume that F does not satisfy the stipulated condition. Then there exist $a \in A$, $i \in N$, $x, y \in X$, and $S \in \mathscr{S}$ such that y is chosen from S [i.e., $y \in C^a(S)$] even if $(x, y) \in D_i \cap P(R_i^a)$ and $x \in S$ hold true [so that individual i is assigned the pair (x, y) and he prefers x to

y], which is to say that F does not protect the assigned right for the pair (x, y) accorded to i. Such a situation will never surface if F realizes the rights system D. Note that each and every $i \in N$ can impose his will for x against y to the society if F realizes the rights system D and $(x, y) \in D_i$ holds true. In this sense, it would not be out of place to call D_i the *protected sphere* of individual $i \in N$.

We can now enumerate several conditions on a collective choice rule.

Condition U (unrestricted domain)
The domain of F consists of the set A of all logically possible profiles.

Condition P (Pareto principle)
For every profile $a = (R_1^a, R_2^a, \ldots, R_n^a) \in A$ and every $x, y \in X$, if we have $(x, y) \in \bigcap_{i \in N} P(R_i^a)$, then $[x \in S \rightarrow y \notin C^a(S)]$ holds true for every $S \in \mathcal{S}$, where $C^a = F(a)$.

Condition SL (Sen's libertarian claim)
There exists a symmetric and nondiagonal rights system D such that

(a) D_i is nonempty for at least two $i \in N$, and
(b) the collective choice rule F realizes D.

Theorem 7.1
There exists no collective choice rule that satisfies the unrestricted domain (U), the Pareto principle (P), and Sen's libertarian claim (SL) (Sen, 1970*b*, Theorem 6*1).

Proof: Let D be the rights system with the properties stipulated by SL. Without loss of generality, we can assume that $(x, y) \in D_1$ and $(z, w) \in D_2$ are true. There are three cases to be treated separately.

Case 1: $\{x, y\} = \{z, w\}$

D being nondiagonal, we have $x \neq y$ and $z \neq w$. Suppose that $x = z$ and $y = w$ hold true. Consider a profile $a = (R_1^a, R_2^a, \ldots, R_n^a) \in A$ such that $(x, y) \in P(R_1^a)$ and $(w, z) \in P(R_2^a)$ hold true, and examine $C^a(\{x, y\})$, where $C^a = F(a)$. By virtue of SL(b), we obtain $y \notin C^a(\{x, y\})$ and $z = x \notin C^a(\{x, y\})$, in view of $(x, y) \in D_1 \cap P(R_1^a)$ and $(w, z) \in D_2 \cap P(R_2^a)$, so that $C^a(\{x, y\}) = \varnothing$ is implied, which is a contradiction. The case where $x = w$ and $y = z$ can be treated similarly.

Case 2: $\{x, y\}$ and $\{z, w\}$ have one element in common, say $x = z$

Consider a profile $b = (R_1^b, R_2^b, \ldots, R_n^b) \in A$ such that

$R_1^b(\{x, y, w\})$: x, y, w

$R_2^b(\{x, y, w\})$: y, w, x

$\forall i \in N \setminus \{1,2\}: (y, w) \in P(R_i^b)$

Consider $C^b(\{x, y, w\})$, where $C^b = F(b)$. By virtue of P, $w \notin C^b(\{x, y, w\})$ holds true, and $y \notin C^b(\{x, y, w\})$ and $x \notin C^b(\{x, y, w\})$ follow from $(x, y) \in D_1 \cap P(R_1^b)$ and $(w, z) \in D_2 \cap P(R_2^b)$ by virtue of SL(b) and $x = z$. Therefore, $C^b(\{x, y, w\}) = \varnothing$ is implied, which is a contradiction.

Case 3: $\{x, y\} \cap \{z, w\} = \varnothing$

Let a profile $c = (R_1^c, R_2^c, \ldots, R_n^c) \in A$ be such that

$R_1^c(\{x, y, z, w\})$: z, x, y, w

$R_2^c(\{x, y, z, w\})$: y, w, z, x

$\forall i \in N \setminus \{1,2\}: (z, x) \in P(R_i^c)$ & $(y, w) \in P(R_i^c)$

Consider $C^c(\{x, y, z, w\})$, where $C^c = F(c)$. By virtue of P, $x \notin C^c(\{x, y, z, w\})$ and $w \notin C^c(\{x, y, z, w\})$. Because $(x, y) \in D_1 \cap P(R_1^c)$ and $(w, z) \in D_2 \cap P(R_2^c)$ hold true, it follows from SL(b) that $y \notin C^c(\{x, y, z, w\})$ and $z \notin C^c(\{x, y, z, w\})$, and a contradiction to the effect that $C^c(\{x, y, z, w\}) = \varnothing$ is implied.

Because we have exhausted all possible cases, there cannot possibly exist a collective choice rule satisfying all the nominated conditions. ∎

How disturbing is this simple impossibility theorem? In general, it is difficult to go against the Pareto principle, so that the skeptics puzzled by this Pareto libertarian paradox are likely to focus on the reasonableness or unreasonableness of condition SL. Osborne (1975) and Seidl (1975), for example, criticized the existential form in which condition SL is phrased. Osborne (1975, p. 1286) argued that "[SL] permits ... a person to govern on a pair belonging to another person's protected sphere. [SL] is as consistent with universal busybodyness as with liberalism." In a similar vein, Seidl (1975, p. 279) pointed out that "it is perfectly consistent with [SL], if individual j is socially decisive on individual k's sleeping on back or belly, whereas k is socially decisive on individual j's sleeping on back or belly." Although these criticisms are certainly correct, they do not seem to dissipate the gloom brought on by the Pareto libertarian paradox. The gist is that if condition SL is negated, not only the universal busybodyness but also *every* conceivable rights system will be prevented from being realized by a collective choice rule at one stroke, and that is why Theorem 7.1 seems to be so disturbing.

More explicitly, an argument in favor of condition SL goes as follows: "The appeal of [SL] would depend on the nature of the alternatives that are offered for choice. If the choices are all non-personal, e.g., to outlaw untouchability or not, to declare war against another country or not, [SL] should not have much appeal. However, in choices involving personal varieties [SL] would be appealing" (Sen, 1970*b*, p. 83).

How, then, can we resolve the Pareto libertarian paradox in the framework of social choice theory? Before we present our own proposals, let us briefly examine some of the proposed resolution schemes existing in the literature, partly because we can thereby obtain a better understanding of the paradox in question, and partly because we can thereby motivate our own approach by contrast.

1.4 Blau's proposal: suspension of meddler's libertarian rights

Blau (1975) has proposed an interesting resolution scheme for a two-person libertarian paradox that is based on the concept of *ordinal intensity of preferences,* which is of independent interest.

Consider three preference orderings R^1, R^2, and R^3 that exhibit the following properties if they are restricted on $S = \{x, y, z, w\}$:

$$R^1(S): x, y, z, w$$

$$R^2(S): [x, y], z, w$$

$$R^3(S): x, y, [z, w]$$

A salient common feature of these preference orderings is that

$$\forall R \in \{R^1, R^2, R^3\}: (x, y) \in R, \qquad (y, z) \in P(R), \qquad (z, w) \in R$$

holds true, with at least one of the two instances of R being in fact $P(R)$. In this case, a strict preference $(x, w) \in P(R)$ is said to be ordinally stronger than a strict preference $(y, z) \in P(R)$.

Making use of this concept, Blau (1975) calls an individual to be meddlesome if and only if his opposition to someone else's preference over a pair of states in that person's protected sphere is ordinally stronger than his preference over a pair of states in his own protected sphere. It is noted, then, that both individuals are meddlesome in this sense in the examples given earlier: "Each wishes to give up his supposedly cherished personal choice provided he can thereby cause the other to give up his. That one of them might exhibit such a preference is remarkable enough, but that both should do so seems to border on the socially pathological" (Blau, 1975, p. 396).

Blau proposes three modified versions of a libertarian claim that makes our collective choice rule respect one's libertarian right if and only if he is not meddlesome. It is shown that there exists a rule that has the unrestricted domain and satisfies both the Pareto principle and the modified libertarian claim if there are only two individuals (Blau, 1975, p. 398), whereas if there are three or more individuals the modified libertarian claim is still incompatible with the Pareto principle, given the unrestricted domain of the collective choice rule (Blau, 1975, pp. 398–9).

It is clear, then, that Blau's proposal is not a general resolution of a Pareto libertarian paradox. Furthermore, even in the special case of a two-person society where Blau's scheme does work, it does not seem to be a very liberal resolution, as Sen (1976) has persuasively argued: In the situation of mutual meddling, Blau's scheme declares that libertarian rights will be suspended for both. True enough, this will break the impasse, but on what grounds should we suspend libertarian rights in the presence of mutual meddling? The reason to protect libertarian rights is that much stronger (not weaker) in the case of mutual meddling, and we are not sure if we can duly call a person libertarian when he cries content with Blau's modified libertarian claim.

1.5 Farrell's proposal: amendment of illiberal preferences[2]

Farrell (1976) has proposed a two-stage resolution scheme for the Pareto libertarian paradox. The first stage of his scheme consists of systematic amendment of an individual's preferences so that (i) "he is deemed indifferent between any pair of states for which some other individual is to be decisive" (Farrell, 1976, p. 8) and so that (ii) each and every individual preference *after the amendment* satisfies the axiom of transitivity, whereas the second stage thereof is application to the amended preferences of the *strong Pareto principle:* For all $a = (R_1^a, R_2^a, \dots, R_n^a) \in A$ and all $x, y \in X$,

$$(x, y) \in P\left(\bigcap_{i \in N} \bar{R}_i^a\right) \rightarrow \forall S \in \mathscr{S}: [x \in S \rightarrow y \notin C^a(S)] \tag{7.2}$$

holds true, where $\bar{R}_i^a$ denotes the amended preference ordering of $i \in N$ corresponding to the original preference ordering R_i^a and $C^a = F(a)$. The critical stage (i) is meant to be "an analytic device" (Farrell, 1976, p. 4) for implementing formally the idea of ignoring an individual's meddling with strict preferences on choices that are none of his business. It is shown that if the rights system is *coherent* in the sense to be made precise later, the two-stage procedure systematically resolves the Pareto libertarian paradox.

With a view toward examining how this proposed scheme works, let us consider Example 7.1. Because $(r_0, r_A) \in D_A \cap P(R_A)$ is the case, Farrell amends B's preference $(r_A, r_0) \in P(R_B)$ into $(r_A, r_0) \in I(\bar{R}_B)$. Similarly, because $(r_B, r_0) \in D_B \cap P(R_B)$ holds true, $(r_0, r_B) \in P(R_A)$ is amended into $(r_0, r_B) \in I(\bar{R}_A)$. Farrell requires the amended preferences $\bar{R}_A$ and $\bar{R}_B$ to be orderings, which compels us either to amend $(r_0, r_A) \in P(R_A)$ into $(r_A, r_0) \in P(\bar{R}_A)$ or to amend $(r_A, r_B) \in P(R_A)$ into $(r_B, r_A) \in P(\bar{R}_A)$ for individual A, and also either to amend $(r_A, r_B) \in P(R_B)$ into $(r_B, r_A) \in P(\bar{R}_B)$ or to amend $(r_B, r_0) \in P(R_B)$ into $(r_0, r_B) \in P(\bar{R}_B)$ for individual B. Farrell chooses the latter option in each case,[3] so that the amended profile $(\bar{R}_A, \bar{R}_B)$ turns out to be as follows:

$$\bar{R}_A = \Delta_X \cup \{(r_0, r_B), (r_B, r_0), (r_0, r_A), (r_B, r_A)\}$$

and

$$\bar{R}_B = \Delta_X \cup \{(r_0, r_A), (r_A, r_0), (r_A, r_B), (r_0, r_B)\}$$

where $\Delta_X = \{(r_0, r_0), (r_A, r_A), (r_B, r_B)\}$. Applying the strong Pareto principle (7.2) to this $(\bar{R}_A, \bar{R}_B)$, we can easily verify that $C(\{r_0, r_A, r_B\}) = \{r_0\}$ holds true.

There are two objections that we should like to raise against Farrell's proposal. Our first objection can be phrased in terms of the application thereof to Example 7.1. Notice that B's original preference for r_B against r_0 is "amended" into the opposite preference even if (r_B, r_0) is B's protected pair. This amendment was necessitated by Farrell's desire to make the amended preference relation transitive. Now a natural question suggests itself: *Why should we give precedence to the logical requirement of transitivity over the individual's preference on his protected pair?* It is admittedly true that this difficulty is brought out by Farrell's rigid convention to "raise the less preferred to the indifference class of the more preferred" in amending preferences, according to which r_B is raised in the preference ladder to the indifference class of r_0 for Mr. A and r_0 to the indifference class of r_A for Mr. B. As Farrell himself noted, "there is, of course, a large class of amendment rules which will implement decisive pairs and still preserve orderings" (Farrell, 1976, p. 5). For example, if we lower r_A to the indifference class of r_0 in amending Mr. B's preferences, keeping the amendment method for Mr. A intact, the particular problem spotted earlier does not surface. Note, however, that in the original profile, r_A is unanimously preferred to r_B, whereas in the amended profile just constructed, it is r_B, not r_A, that is unanimously preferred. How could we justify application of the strong Pareto principle to the amended profile in this situation? In one way or another, Farrell's scheme seems to be in considerable trouble.

Our second objection focuses directly on the idea of amending individuals' preferences. It seems to us that the idea of amending individuals' preferences, of deeming a man indifferent between two states when he is not so, is deeply illiberal and paternalistic. Paternalism is the greatest despotism imaginable, as a sage once said, and Farrell's proposal can hardly be qualified as a satisfactory resolution of a *libertarian* paradox.[4]

1.6 Nozick's proposal: rights as constraints

A straightforward resolution scheme for the Pareto libertarian paradox has been proposed by Nozick (1974, p. 166), according to which the conflict between the claim of libertarian rights and that of the Pareto principle is to be resolved by assigning quite different roles to these requirements: "Individual rights are co-possible; each person may exercise his rights as he chooses. The exercise of these rights fixes some features of the world. Within the constraints of these fixed features, a choice may be made by a social choice mechanism based upon a social ordering; if there are any choices left to make! Rights do not determine a social ordering but instead set the constraints within which a social choice is to be made, by excluding certain alternatives, fixing others, and so on.... *How else can one cope with Sen's result?*"

If we apply Nozick's scheme to Example 7.2, we can easily verify that the Nozick's choice function C^N yields $C^N(\{w_E, w_J, w_0\}) = \{w_J\}$ by letting Angelina [resp. Edwin] exercise her [resp. his] right for w_J against w_0 [resp. for w_0 against w_E].

This is undoubtedly a clear-cut proposal, but we believe we are obliged to raise two objections to this scheme. First of all, note that this scheme is based on an extremely mechanical view of libertarian exercise of rights in that the *rights endowment* automatically implies *rights-exercising* without leaving any room for negotiation and bargaining based on the individual's rational calculus. In view of "a strong libertarian tradition of free contract," according to which "a person's rights are his to use or bargain away as he sees fit" (Gibbard, 1974, p. 397), the attractiveness of Nozick's scheme seems to be abated rather substantially. Our second objection comes to the fore if we examine the performance of this scheme in Example 7.2 in a bit more detail. It is easy to verify that $C^N(\{w_J, w_0\}) = \{w_J\}$, $C^N(\{w_E, w_J\}) = \{w_E\}$, and $C^N(\{w_E, w_0\}) = \{w_0\}$ hold true. It then follows that

$$C^N(C^N(\{w_J\}) \cup C^N(\{w_E, w_0\})) = C^N(\{w_J, w_0\}) = \{w_J\}$$

and

$$C^N(C^N(\{w_E\}) \cup C^N(\{w_J, w_0\})) = C^N(\{w_E, w_J\}) = \{w_E\}$$

are implied, which shows that C^N is not path-independent. Neither is C^N rational, because $C^N(\{w_J, w_0\}) = \{w_J\}$, $C^N(\{w_E, w_J\}) = \{w_E\}$, and

$C^N(\{w_E, w_O\}) = \{w_O\}$ must imply $C^N(\{w_J, w_E, w_O\}) = \varnothing$ if C^N is rational. Therefore, Nozick's resolution scheme performs rather poorly in terms of choice-consistency properties.

1.7 Gibbard's proposal: alienability of libertarian rights

Gibbard (1974) has presented a deep and penetrating analysis of inviolable individual rights and the Pareto libertarian paradox culminating in the edifice of the alienable rights system, which is in sharp contrast with Nozick's proposed scheme. The gist of his approach is to make libertarian rights alienable if they conflict with another person's libertarian rights or the Pareto principle or the combination of both.

In order to understand how his resolution scheme works, let us examine Example 7.2 once more. Recollect that the rights system $D = (D_A, D_E)$ and the profile (R_A, R_E), where A and E stand for Angelina and Edwin, respectively, are such that

$$(w_J, w_O) \in D_A \cap P(R_A) \tag{7.3}$$

$$(w_O, w_E) \in D_E \cap P(R_E) \tag{7.4}$$

and

$$(w_E, w_J) \in P(R_A) \cap P(R_E) \tag{7.5}$$

By virtue of (7.4), Edwin can exclude w_E from $C(\{w_J, w_E, w_O\})$ if he decides to exercise his right for w_O over w_E and the rule realizes D. But if Angelina counters by exercising her right $(w_J, w_O) \in D_A$, the outcome will be the choice of w_J, and Edwin strictly prefers w_E to w_J, according to (7.5). Therefore, by exercising his right $(w_O, w_E) \in D_E$, Edwin gets something he likes no better, so that it is wise for Edwin to alienate his endowed right in this situation. "Left freely to bargain away their rights, then, Edwin and Angelina would agree to the outcome w_E: Wedding each other. Hence, a libertarian may well hold that – deplorable though Edwin's motives be – w_E is a *just* outcome under the circumstances" (Gibbard, 1974, p. 398, italics added).

Generalizing the moral of this example, Gibbard proposes a libertarian claim that is contingent on an individual's voluntary and deliberate exercise of his endowed right, and he proves the existence of a rational collective choice rule with unrestricted domain, which satisfies the Pareto principle and realizes the alienable rights system he proposes. It deserves emphasis that a great merit of Gibbard's scheme is that it resolves the Pareto libertarian paradox by introducing voluntary waiving of individual rights induced by the selfish rational calculus of the relevant individual himself.

Great though the attractiveness of Gibbard's scheme, there are several objections that one can raise against it.

Our first objection stems from application of Gibbard's scheme to Example 7.1, which has the same abstract structure as Example 7.2. It is easy to verify that Gibbard's solution in Example 7.1 is r_A (i.e., delivering *Lady Chatterley's Lover* to Mr. *A*). One cannot but ask: In what sense is it "liberal" to give a book to an individual who wants to read it just to prevent another individual from being exposed to it? It seems to us that the reasonableness of Gibbard's solution in the Angelina–Edwin marriage case is due mainly to the particular interpretation associated with this example, and if we "generalize the moral of the example" (Gibbard, 1974, p. 398), the outcome may turn out to be inappropriate as a "liberal" or "just" resolution of the Pareto libertarian paradox.

Our second objection is nothing other than what Kelly (1976*b*; 1978, Chapter 9) called the *correctable miscalculation* that occasionally vitiates Gibbard's rights-waiving rule. Consider the following example.

Example 7.3[5]
Let there be two individuals, 1 and 2, and four social states, x, y, z, and w. Let the profile (R_1, R_2) and the rights system $D = (D_1, D_2)$ be specified by

$$R_1(\{x, y, z, w\}): w, x, y, z$$

$$R_2(\{x, y, z, w\}): y, z, w, x$$

and

$$D_1 = \{(x, y), (y, x)\}, \qquad D_2 = \{(z, w), (w, z)\}$$

Let C be the social choice function that a rule associates with the profile (R_1, R_2), and consider $C(\{x, y, z, w\})$. Suppose that the rights system D is realized and the Pareto principle endorsed. Then $(x, y) \in D_1 \cap P(R_1)$ and $(z, w) \in D_2 \cap P(R_2)$ yield $y \notin C(\{x, y, z, w\})$ and $w \notin C(\{x, y, z, w\})$, respectively, and $x \notin C(\{x, y, z, w\})$ and $z \notin C(\{x, y, z, w\})$ are implied by the Pareto principle. Therefore, we are brought to an impasse; that is, $C(\{x, y, z, w\}) = \varnothing$.

This impasse can be broken by Gibbard's scheme as follows. In view of the fact that

$$(w, x) \in P(R_1) \cap P(R_2), \quad (z, w) \in D_2 \cap P(R_2), \quad \text{and} \quad (y, z) \in P(R_1)$$

individual 1 will waive his right for $(x, y) \in D_1$, and

$$(y, z) \in P(R_1) \cap P(R_2), \quad (x, y) \in D_1 \cap P(R_1), \quad \text{and} \quad (w, x) \in P(R_2)$$

will induce individual 2 to waive his right for $(z, w) \in D_2$. Because both individuals will waive their rights, two Pareto-efficient states, y and w, will become eligible for social choice, thereby breaking the impasse.

Notice, however, that individual 1 [resp. individual 2] waives his right on the supposition that individual 2 [resp. individual 1] will exercise his right, so that the foregoing resolution works on the miscalculations that individuals commit on others' rights-exercising. ∎

It is quite true that people do commit mistakes and that a committed mistake may turn out to be good after all. But to count on this phenomenon as a pivotal part of the scheme for resolving the conflict of moral values does not seem to be an attractive feature of Gibbard's scheme.[6]

2 Coherent rights system and liberal individual: a possibility theorem

2.1 *Motivation behind a resolution scheme*

Our critical evaluations of some existing resolution schemes for the Pareto libertarian paradox have brought our desiderata on the satisfactory resolution scheme into relief:

1. We want our resolution scheme to protect an individual's libertarian rights in the situation of mutual meddling.
2. We want our resolution scheme not to impose "amended" preferences on individuals from outside.
3. We want our resolution scheme to be choice-consistent.
4. We want our resolution scheme not to hinge on mistakes or miscalculations by individuals.

It is now time we set about constructing resolution schemes that are satisfactory in terms of the foregoing desiderata. In this section we shall discuss our first resolution scheme, which works on an informational framework that does not require any interpersonal information.

The intuitive motivation of our first resolution scheme may be in order. Scrutinizing the Pareto libertarian paradox, which is exemplified by the *Lady Chatterley's Lover* case and the Angelina–Edwin marriage case, it turns out that mechanical use of the Pareto principle in situations like these (irrespective of the motivations behind individuals' preferences) appears rather insidious. In the *Lady Chatterley's Lover* case, for example, Mr. *A*, as well as Mr. *B*, prefers r_A to r_B, and by invoking the Pareto principle, r_A is given social precedence over r_B. Recollect, however, that Mr. *A* prefers r_A to r_B only to prevent the lascivious Mr. *B* from being exposed to a "dangerous" book, whereas Mr. *B* in his turn prefers r_A to r_B with a view toward giving a good shock to a naive Mr. *A*, and we cannot but believe that such busybody motivation behind individual preferences works to abate the reasonableness of the Pareto principle. Admittedly, it is difficult to go against a statement that a social state unanimously preferred to another state should be socially chosen over the latter, and it is indeed rare to find an attack on the Pareto principle. How, then, should we proceed?

To orient our approach, consider the following monologue: "I think that wearing red clothes is in extremely bad taste. Everything else being the same, I think therefore a state in which Mr. A wears green clothes, x, is socially better than a state in which Mr. A wears red clothes, y. But to choose green or red as a color of his clothes is Mr. A's personal matter and none of my business, so that my meddlesome concern – no matter how strong it may be – should not count in socially deciding whether he should choose red or green."

In what follows, it will be shown that if the rights system is coherent in the sense to be specified later and if there exists an individual having the foregoing attitude toward others' personal matters (Why not call him a liberal?), a universally applicable rational collective choice rule exists that realizes the given rights system and satisfies the Pareto principle with respect to the individual preferences that individuals wish to be counted in social choice. This resolution scheme for the Pareto libertarian paradox is essentially a reformulation of Sen's proposal (1976, Section XI).

2.2 *Coherent rights system and a property thereof*

The first step to be taken is to formulate the concept of a *coherent rights system*, which is due originally to Farrell (1976).

Let $D = (D_1, D_2, \ldots, D_n)$ be an n-tuple of subsets of $X \times X$. A *critical loop* in D is a sequence of the ordered pairs $\{(x^\mu, y^\mu)\}_{\mu=1}^t$ $(t \geq 2)$ such that

(a) $(x^\mu, y^\mu) \in \bigcup_{i=1}^n D_i$ for all $\mu \in \{1, 2, \ldots, t\}$,

(b) there exists no $i^* \in \{1, 2, \ldots, n\}$ such that $(x^\mu, y^\mu) \in D_{i^*}$ for all $\mu \in \{1, 2, \ldots, t\}$, and

(c) $x^1 = y^t$ and $x^\mu = y^{\mu-1}$ hold true for all $\mu \in \{2, 3, \ldots, t\}$.

We say that $D = (D_1, D_2, \ldots, D_n)$ is *coherent* if and only if there exists no critical loop in D.

In order to bring the critical importance of the concept of a coherent rights system into relief, let us suppose that the rights system $D = (D_1, D_2, \ldots, D_n)$ contains a critical loop $\{(x^\mu, y^\mu)\}_{\mu=1}^t$ $(t \geq 2)$ that, by definition, satisfies (a), (b), and (c). Then there exists a mapping $\kappa: \{1, 2, \ldots, t\} \to N$ such that

$$\forall \mu \in \{1, 2, \ldots, t\}: (x^\mu, y^\mu) \in D_{\kappa(\mu)} \tag{7.6}$$

and

$$\exists \mu^1, \mu^2 \in \{1, 2, \ldots, t\}: \kappa(\mu^1) \neq \kappa(\mu^2) \tag{7.7}$$

Consider a profile $a = (R_1^a, R_2^a, \ldots, R_n^a) \in A$ such that

$$(x^1, x^2) \in P(R_{\kappa(1)}^a), (x^2, x^3) \in P(R_{\kappa(2)}^a), \ldots, (x^t, x^1) \in P(R_{\kappa(t)}^a) \tag{7.8}$$

Thanks to (7.7), there is no contradiction in (7.8) with transitivity of R_i^a $(i \in N)$. If we require the collective choice rule F to be universally applicable and to realize the rights system D, then (7.6) and (7.8) yield

$$\forall \mu \in \{1, 2, \ldots, t-1\}: (x^\mu, x^{\mu+1}) \in D_{\kappa(\mu)} \cap P(R_{\kappa(\mu)}^a) \rightarrow x^{\mu+1} \notin C^a(S)$$

and

$$(x^t, x^1) \in D_{\kappa(t)} \cap P(R_{\kappa(t)}^a) \rightarrow x^1 \notin C^a(S)$$

where $C^a = F(a)$ and $S = \{x^1, x^2, \ldots, x^t\}$, so that we obtain $C^a(S) = \varnothing$.

We have thus shown that if D contains a critical loop, it is impossible to construct a universally applicable collective choice rule that realizes D without invoking the Pareto principle. It is in view of this result that we assume the coherence of the rights system in our first attempt to design a universally applicable and essentially Paretian collective choice rule that realizes D. We shall have more to say on the assumption of a coherent rights system in Section 5.

An apparently different concept of a coherent rights system has been proposed by Sen (1976, p. 243), according to which a rights system $D = (D_1, D_2, \ldots, D_n)$ is coherent if and only if, for every profile $a = (R_1^a, R_2^a, \ldots, R_n^a) \in A$, there exists an ordering extension R^a of each and every $D_i \cap R_i^a (i \in N)$. As a matter of fact, these two concepts are the same, as the following theorem establishes (Suzumura, 1978, Lemma 1).

Theorem 7.2

A rights system $D = (D_1, D_2, \ldots, D_n)$ is coherent if and only if it is coherent in the sense of Sen.

Proof: Let D be coherent, and take any profile $a = (R_1^a, R_2^a, \ldots, R_n^a) \in A$. Let Q^a be defined by

$$Q_i^a = D_i \cap R_i^a \quad (i \in N); \qquad Q^a = \bigcup_{i \in N} Q_i^a \tag{7.9}$$

Let us show that Q^a is consistent. Suppose, to the contrary, that there exists a set $\{x^1, x^2, \ldots, x^t\} \in \mathscr{S}$ such that $(x^1, x^2) \in P(Q^a)$, $(x^\mu, x^{\mu+1}) \in Q^a$ $(\mu = 2, 3, \ldots, t-1)$, and $(x^t, x^1) \in Q^a$ hold true. By definition, $(x^1, x^2) \in P(Q^a)$ holds true if and only if $(x^1, x^2) \in Q_i^a$ for some $i \in N$ and $(x^2, x^1) \notin Q_i^a$ for all $i \in N$ are the case, so that we have $(x^1, x^2) \in P(Q_i^a)$ for some $i \in N$. Therefore, there exists a mapping $\kappa: \{1, 2, \ldots, t\} \rightarrow N$ such that $(x^1, x^2) \in P(Q_{\kappa(1)}^a)$, $(x^\mu, x^{\mu+1}) \in Q_{\kappa(\mu)}^a$ for all $\mu \in \{2, 3, \ldots, t-1\}$, and $(x^t, x^1) \in Q_{\kappa(t)}^a$ hold true. It follows that

(a) $\{\kappa(1), \kappa(2), \ldots, \kappa(t)\}$ is not a singleton set, and
(b) $(x^\mu, x^{\mu+1}) \in D_{\kappa(\mu)}$ $(\mu = 1, 2, \ldots, t-1)$ and $(x^t, x^1) \in D_{\kappa(t)}$.

Therefore, D contains a critical loop, a contradiction. Now that Q^a turns out to be consistent, there exists an ordering extension R^a of Q^a by virtue of Theorem A(5) in the Appendix to Chapter 1.

By construction, we have $Q_i^a \subset Q^a \subset R^a$ $(i \in N)$ and $P(Q^a) \subset P(R^a)$. If we can show that

$$\forall i \in N: P(Q_i^a) \subset P(Q^a) \qquad (7.10)$$

is true, then we are home. Suppose, therefore, that there exist $i \in N$ and $x, y \in X$ such that $(x, y) \in P(Q_i^a)$ and $(y, x) \in Q_{i'}^a$ for some $i' \in N$. But D then contains a critical loop, a contradiction.

To prove the converse, suppose, to the contrary, that D is not coherent. Then we have a critical loop in D; that is, there exists a sequence $\{x^\mu\}_{\mu=1}^t$ such that $(x^1, x^2) \in D_{\kappa(1)}, (x^2, x^3) \in D_{\kappa(2)}, \ldots, (x^t, x^1) \in D_{\kappa(t)}$ for some mapping $\kappa: \{1, 2, \ldots, t\} \to N$. Let a profile $a = (R_1^a, R_2^a, \ldots, R_n^a) \in A$ be such that

$$(x^1, x^2) \in P(Q_{\kappa(1)}^a), (x^2, x^3) \in Q_{\kappa(2)}^a, \ldots, (x^t, x^1) \in Q_{\kappa(t)}^a \qquad (7.11)$$

where $Q_i^a = D_i \cap R_i^a$ $(i \in N)$. Because $\{\kappa(1), \kappa(2), \ldots, \kappa(t)\}$ is not a singleton set, there is no contradiction in (7.11) with transitivity of R_i^a $(i \in N)$.

Let R^a be an ordering extension of all Q_i^a $(i \in N)$ in common. Then (7.11) implies that

$$(x^1, x^2) \in P(R^a), (x^2, x^3) \in R^a, \ldots, (x^t, x^1) \in R^a$$

in contradiction with transitivity of R^a. This completes the proof. ∎

2.3 *Liberal individual and realization of a coherent rights system*

It is now time to formalize a concept of a "liberal" individual and a constrained version of the Pareto principle. Let $a = (R_1^a, R_2^a, \ldots, R_n^a) \in A$ be an arbitrarily specified profile, and let R_i^{0a} be a transitive subrelation of R_i^a that individual i wants to be counted in collective decisions. Therefore, $(x, y) \in P(R_i^a)$ holds true if individual i prefers x to y personally, whereas we have $(x, y) \in P(R_i^{0a})$ if individual i wants his preference for x against y to count in social choice. The motivating idea behind this distinction is that "the guarantee of a minimal amount of personal liberty may require that certain parts of individual rankings should not count in some specific social choices, and in some cases even the persons in question may agree with this" (Sen, 1976, pp. 237–8).

We can now introduce a version of the conditional strong Pareto principle.

Condition CP (conditional Pareto principle)
For every $a = (R_1^a, R_2^a, \ldots, R_n^a) \in A$ and every $x, y \in X$,

(a) $(x, y) \in R_N^{0a} \to \forall S \in \mathcal{S}: [x \in S \setminus C^a(S) \to y \notin C^a(S)]$, and

(b) $(x, y) \in P(R_N^{0a}) \to \forall S \in \mathcal{S}: [x \in S \to y \notin C^a(S)]$

hold true, where $C^a = F(a)$ and $R_N^{0a} = \bigcap_{i \in N} R_i^{0a}$.

It is clear that the effect on the Pareto libertarian paradox of replacing the Pareto principle by the conditional version thereof hinges squarely on how the conditional profile $(R_1^{0a}, R_2^{0a}, \ldots, R_n^{0a})$ is generated from the original profile $a = (R_1^a, R_2^a, \ldots, R_n^a) \in A$. If, for example, $R_i^{0a} = R_i^a$ holds true for all $i \in N$, then the paradox clearly remains intact. On the other hand, if $R_i^{0a} = \varnothing$ is the case for all $i \in N$, then condition CP becomes vacuous, and the paradox is "resolved" or, rather, evaporated. The real problem, then, is to formalize a "reasonable" and "liberal" way of restricting R_i^a into R_i^{0a} so that condition CP becomes compatible with realization of the coherent rights system by a universally applicable rule. Capitalizing on Sen's suggestion (1976, Section XI), let us now try out one possible method to this effect.

Let $D = (D_1, D_2, \ldots, D_n)$ be any coherent rights system, and let a profile $a = (R_1^a, R_2^a, \ldots, R_n^a) \in A$ be chosen arbitrarily. D being coherent, there exists an ordering R^a that subsumes each and every individual preference over their respective protected spheres. There may well be multiple ordering extensions; so we let $\mathcal{R}^a$ denote the set of all such orderings corresponding to the profile $a \in A$. Let individual $j \in N$ be called a *liberal* if and only if

$$R_j^{0a} = R_j^a \cap R \qquad \text{for some } R \in \mathcal{R}^a \tag{7.12}$$

That is, an individual is said to be liberal if and only if he claims only those parts of his preferences that are compatible with others' preferences over their respective protected spheres to count in social choice.

Some remarks on this basic concept may be in order. First, it should be emphasized that a liberal never drops his preferences over his own protected sphere, so that a liberal need not die a martyr for his faith in liberalism. Second, a liberal need not really care very much just how the ordering extension R is constructed from $Q^a = \bigcup_{i \in N}(R_i^a \cap D_i)$. An "active" liberal will hold a clear idea of that part of his preference ordering that he wants to count in social choice. Obviously he needs a lot of information about the structure of the rights system as well as about the preferences of other individuals. On the other hand, a "passive" liberal does not know his R_i^{0a}; instead, he knows only his R_i^a, and he knows that he wants to be liberal. A well-informed referee then constructs an ordering extension R of Q^a and thereby constrains the preference ordering of an individual who wishes to be liberal. Our concept of a liberal individual admits both species.[7]

We can now assert the following possibility theorem (Sen, 1976, Theorem 9; Suzumura, 1978, Theorem 1) on Pareto libertarianism.

Theorem 7.3
Let $D = (D_1, D_2, \ldots, D_n)$ be an arbitrarily given coherent rights system. If there exists at least one liberal individual in the society, there exists a rational collective choice rule that satisfies the unrestricted domain (U) and the conditional Pareto principle (CP) and realizes the rights system D.

Proof: Let N_1 stand for the set of all liberal individuals, which is a nonempty subset of N by assumption. Take any profile $a = (R_1^a, R_2^a, \ldots, R_n^a) \in A$, and let $\mathscr{R}^a$ denote the set of all ordering extensions of $Q^a = \bigcup_{i \in N}(R_i^a \cap D_i)$. Let R_i^{0a} be defined by

$$R_i^{0a} = \begin{cases} \exists R^i \in \mathscr{R}^a : R_i^a \cap R^i & \text{if } i \in N_1 \\ R_i^a \quad \text{otherwise} & \end{cases} \tag{7.13}$$

and let R_0^a be given by

$$R_0^a = \{(x, y) \in X \times X \mid (y, x) \notin P \cup P(R_N^{0a})\} \tag{7.14}$$

where $P = \bigcap_{i \in N_1} P(R^i)$ and $R_N^{0a} = \bigcap_{i \in N} R_i^{0a}$.

Let us prove that R_0^a is complete as well as reflexive. Assume, to the contrary, that there exist $x, y \in X$ such that $(x, y) \notin R_0^a$ and $(y, x) \notin R_0^a$. Then we obtain $(x, y) \in P \cup P(R_N^{0a})$ and $(y, x) \in P \cup P(R_N^{0a})$. There are four cases to be treated:

(a) $(x, y) \in P$ & $(y, x) \in P$,

(b) $(x, y) \in P(R_N^{0a})$ & $(y, x) \in P(R_N^{0a})$,

(c) $(x, y) \in P$ & $(y, x) \in P(R_N^{0a})$, and

(d) $(x, y) \in P(R_N^{0a})$ & $(y, x) \in P$.

Case (a) and case (b) contradict, respectively, the asymmetry of P and that of $P(R_N^{0a})$. To consider case (c) and case (d), take any $i_0 \in N_1$. We then obtain $P \subset P(R^{i_0})$ and $P(R_N^{0a}) \subset R_{i_0}^{0a} \subset R^{i_0}$, so that case (c) and case (d) contradict the fact that R^{i_0} is an ordering. We have thus shown that R_0^a is complete as well as reflexive.

The next order of business is to establish

$$P(R_0^a) = P \cup P(R_N^{0a}) \tag{7.15}$$

If $(x, y) \in P(R_0^a)$ holds true, then $(y, x) \notin R_0^a$ must be the case, which implies $(x, y) \in P \cup P(R_N^{0a})$ by definition. Therefore, $P(R_0^a) \subset P \cup P(R_N^{0a})$ is true. To show the converse, suppose that there exists an ordered pair $(x, y) \in X \times X$ such that $(x, y) \in P \cup P(R_N^{0a})$, but $(x, y) \notin P(R_0^a)$, so that $(y, x) \notin R_0^a$ and $(x, y) \notin P(R_0^a)$ hold true. But this contradicts the completeness and reflexivity of R_0^a established earlier. Therefore, (7.15) is valid.

We now prove that R_0^a is acyclic. If there exists a set $\{x^1, x^2, \ldots, x^t\} \in \mathcal{S}$ such that $(x^\mu, x^{\mu+1}) \in P(R_0^a)$ for all $\mu \in \{1, 2, \ldots, t-1\}$ and $(x^t, x^1) \in P(R_0^a)$, then we arrive at a contradiction with the transitivity of R^i $(i \in N_1)$ or that of R_N^{0a} by virtue of the fact that $P(R_N^{0a}) \subset R^i$ $(i \in N_1)$, which suffices to prove acyclicity of R_0^a.

Now that R_0^a has been shown to be complete, reflexive, and acyclic,

$$\forall S \in \mathcal{S}: C^a(S) = G(S, R_0^a) \tag{7.16}$$

defines a well-behaved rational choice function C^a on a choice space $(X, \mathcal{S})$. Associating this C^a with the profile $a \in A$ we started from, we obtain a well-defined rational collective choice rule.

In order to show that this rule satisfies condition CP(a), suppose that there exist $x, y \in X$ such that $(x, y) \in R_N^{0a}$, $x \in S \setminus C^a(S)$, and $y \in C^a(S)$ for some $S \in \mathcal{S}$. We shall bring out a contradiction from this supposition by proving that $(x, z) \in R_0^a$ holds true for all $z \in S$, so that $x \in C^a(S)$ should be the case in view of (7.16). Take, therefore, any $z \in S$. Because $y \in C^a(S)$ is the case by assumption, we obtain $(z, y) \notin P \cup P(R_N^{0a})$, so that $(z, y) \notin P$ and $[(z, y) \in R_N^{0a} \vee (y, z) \in R_N^{0a}]$ must be the case. By virtue of the definition of P, we have $(z, y) \notin P$ if and only if $(y, z) \in R^i$ for some $i \in N_1$. By assumption, $(x, y) \in R_N^{0a}$ is the case, so that we obtain $(x, y) \in R_i^{0a} \subset R^i$ for this $i \in N_1$. R^i being transitive, $(x, y) \in R^i$ and $(y, z) \in R^i$ imply that $(z, x) \notin P(R^i)$ is true, which implies that

$$(z, x) \notin P \tag{7.17}$$

must be the case. Suppose now that $(z, y) \notin R_N^{0a}$ holds true, which implies $(z, y) \notin R_i^{0a}$ for some $i \in N$. If $i \in N \setminus N_1$ is the case, we obtain $(y, z) \in P(R_i^a)$. Because $(x, y) \in R_i^a$ follows from $(x, y) \in R_N^{0a}$, we obtain $(x, z) \in P(R_i^a)$; that is, $(z, x) \notin R_i^a$. Therefore, $(z, x) \notin R_N^{0a}$ is implied. If $i \in N_1$ is the case, $[(z, y) \notin R_i^a \vee (z, y) \notin R^i]$, that is, $[(y, z) \in P(R_i^a) \vee (y, z) \in P(R^i)]$, holds true, which implies $(x, z) \in P(R_i^a) \cup P(R^i)$, in view of $(x, y) \in R_N^{0a}$. Coupled with $(x, y) \in R_N^{0a}$, this implies that $(x, z) \in R_N^{0a}$, hence $(z, x) \notin P(R_N^{0a})$. Therefore, in every conceivable case, we obtain

$$(z, x) \notin P(R_N^{0a}) \tag{7.18}$$

It follows from (7.17) and (7.18) that $(z, x) \notin P \cup P(R_N^{0a})$, so that we have $(x, z) \in R_0^a$, as desired. The proof of satisfaction of condition CP(a) is now complete.

To prove that the rule satisfies condition CP(b), suppose that there exist $x, y \in X$ and $S \in \mathscr{S}$ such that $(x, y) \in P(R_N^{0a})$, $x \in S$, and $y \in C^a(S)$. Then we obtain $(y, x) \in R_0^a$, so that $(x, y) \notin P \cup P(R_N^{0a})$ is implied. But this is a contradiction of $(x, y) \in P(R_N^{0a})$, as desired.

Finally, we must show that the rule realizes the given rights system D. Suppose, to the contrary, that there exist $i \in N$ and $S \in \mathscr{S}$ that satisfy $(x, y) \in D_i \cap P(R_i^a)$, $x \in S$, and $y \in C^a(S)$. Then we obtain $(y, x) \in R_0^a$, entailing $(x, y) \notin P \cup P(R_N^{0a})$. Thanks to the definition of $\mathscr{R}^a$, we have $P(Q^a) \subset \bigcap_{i \in N_1} P(R^i) = P$, so that if we can show that

$$D_i \cap P(R_i^a) \subset P(Q^a) \tag{7.19}$$

is true, we are home, because then we obtain $(x, y) \in D_i \cap P(R_i^a) \subset P$, in contradiction of $(x, y) \notin P \cup P(R_N^{0a})$. To show the validity of (7.19), let $(w, z) \in D_i \cap P(R_i^a)$. Clearly, then, $(w, z) \in Q^a$ is true, so that if $(w, z) \notin P(Q^a)$ is the case, $(z, w) \in Q^a = \bigcup_{i \in N} Q_i^a$ is true. Then there exists $j \in N$ $(j \neq i)$ such that $(z, w) \in D_j \cap R_j^a$ holds true. It follows that D contains a critical loop, a contradiction of the assumed coherence of D. ∎

The gist of this resolution scheme is very simple and intuitive. The Pareto principle is enforced only by unanimous agreement, so that its use can be vetoed by any one individual, and a liberal individual may well serve as a vetoer. Note that a liberal individual is, by definition, one who always (for every profile) exercises the veto in favor of every expressed protected right, and of every consequence of all these.

It might help if we exemplify how this resolution scheme works. Consider the *Lady Chatterley's Lover* case once more. Recollect that the profile (R_A, R_B) and the rights system $D = (D_A, D_B)$ in this example are such that

$$R_A: r_0, r_A, r_B, \qquad R_B: r_A, r_B, r_0$$

and

$$D_A = \{(r_0, r_A), (r_A, r_0)\}, \qquad D_B = \{(r_0, r_B), (r_B, r_0)\}$$

It is clear that D is a coherent rights system. In this case, we have $Q_A = R_A \cap D_A = \{(r_0, r_A)\}$ and $Q_B = R_B \cap D_B = \{(r_B, r_0)\}$, so that $Q = \{(r_0, r_A), (r_B, r_0)\}$ holds true. The ordering extension of this Q is unique and reads as follows:

$$R = \Delta_X \cup \{(r_B, r_0), (r_0, r_A), (r_B, r_A)\}$$

where $\Delta_X = \{(r_O, r_O), (r_A, r_A), (r_B, r_B)\}$. Suppose now that Mr. A is liberal and Mr. B is not, so that $R_A^0 = R \cap R_A = \Delta_X \cup \{(r_O, r_A)\}$ and $R_B^0 = R_B$ hold true. It then follows that $R^0 = R_A^0 \cap R_B^0 = \Delta_X$, and we obtain

$$R_0 = \Delta_X \cup \{(r_B, r_O), (r_O, r_A), (r_B, r_A)\}$$

so that $G(\{r_O, r_A, r_B\}, R_0) = \{r_B\}$ is implied. Hence, our suggested solution for the *Lady Chatterley's Lover* case: Give the copy to the lascivious Mr. B.

A few clarifying remarks may be in order here. First, in line with the statement of Sen's libertarian claim (SL), we supposed that D_A and D_B were symmetric in the *Lady Chatterley's Lover* case. Sen's paradox still holds, however, even if $D_A = \{(r_O, r_A)\}$ and $D_B = \{(r_B, r_O)\}$. It is easy to verify that our resolution given earlier still applies without any change. Second, our solution to the *Lady Chatterley's Lover* case does not hinge on our supposition that it is Mr. A who is liberal, because Mr. B being liberal instead of Mr. A brings us to the same solution. Is it generally the case that the solution by our resolution scheme is invariant with respect to the distribution of liberalism among individuals? To show that it is not, let us apply our resolution scheme to Example 7.3. It is easy to see that the rights system $D = (D_1, D_2)$ in this example is coherent and that $Q = \{(x, y), (z, w)\}$ is implied. There are multiple ordering extensions of this Q, thirteen altogether, from which we pick out

$$R^\alpha = \Delta_X \cup \{(x, y), (x, z), (x, w), (y, z), (y, w), (z, w)\}$$

$$R^\beta = \Delta_X \cup \{(z, w), (z, x), (z, y), (w, x), (w, y), (x, y)\}$$

and

$$R^\gamma = \Delta_X \cup \{(x, z), (z, x), (x, y), (x, w), (z, y), (z, w), (y, w)\}$$

where $\Delta_X = \{(x, x), (y, y), (z, z), (w, w)\}$. Depending on who is liberal and which ordering extension is used, there are different scenarios. Let a scenario where individual 1 is liberal and the ordering extension α is used be denoted by $(1, \alpha)$, and so on. It is easy, if tedious, to verify that the solution in scenario $(1, \alpha)$ is $\{x\}$, that in scenario $(2, \beta)$ is $\{z\}$, and that in scenario $(\{1, 2\}, \gamma)$ is $\{x, z\}$. Third, we should like to emphasize that (a) unlike Blau's scheme, our scheme does not suspend anyone's libertarian right in the presence of mutual meddling, (b) unlike Farrell's scheme, our scheme does not amend anybody's preferences from outside, (c) unlike Nozick's scheme, our scheme provides us with a rational choice rule, and (d) unlike Gibbard's scheme, our scheme does not count on people's errors or miscalculations as an integral part thereof.

3 On the consistency of group autonomy

3.1 A paradox of group autonomy

The focus of this chapter has been social realization of libertarian individual rights. However, it is important to pay due attention to the fact that the problem posed by the Pareto libertarian paradox has an important implication for the possibility of group autonomy. This observation is due originally to Batra and Pattanaik (1972). Let us examine this side of the coin in this section.

Some additional formalities should come first. Let an s-tuple of the subsets of N, $G = (G^1, G^2, \ldots, G^s)$ be called a *group structure* within a society if

(a) $\varnothing \neq G^\tau \subset N$ holds true for all $\tau \in \{1, 2, \ldots, s\}$,
(b) $\tau_1 \neq \tau_2$ implies $G^{\tau_1} \neq G^{\tau_2}$ for all $\tau_1, \tau_2 \in \{1, 2, \ldots, s\}$, and
(c) $\bigcup_{\tau=1}^{s} G^\tau = N$

hold true. Note that it is not assumed that $G^{\tau_1} \cap G^{\tau_2} = \varnothing$ whenever $\tau_1 \neq \tau_2$, so that an individual can belong to several groups simultaneously.

By the introduction of a group structure, the passage from a profile $a = (R_1^a, R_2^a, \ldots, R_n^a) \in A$ to a social choice function $C^a = F(a)$ can conceptually be decomposed into two stages: In the first stage, the preferences of the members of each group G^τ are aggregated into a group choice function C^a_τ, and in the second stage, the s-tuple of group choice functions is aggregated into a social choice function. Thus,

$$C^a = \eta(C_1^a, C_2^a, \ldots, C_s^a) = \eta(\{\zeta^\tau(\{R_i^a\}_{i \in G^\tau})\}_{\tau=1}^{s}) \tag{7.20}$$

where the function ζ^τ is nothing other than what we call a *group choice rule* for the group G^τ ($\tau \in \{1, 2, \ldots, s\}$).

Let us say that the rule $(\eta, \{\zeta^\tau\}_{\tau=1}^{s})$ allows the group G^τ *autonomy* over $D^\tau \subset X \times X$ if and only if

$$\forall a = (R_1^a, R_2^a, \ldots, R_n^a) \in A, \forall x, y \in X:$$
$$(x, y) \in D^\tau \cap R^*_{C^a_\tau} \to \forall S \in \mathscr{S}: [x \in S \to y \notin C^a(S)]$$

holds true, where $R^*_{C^a_\tau}$ denotes, as in Chapter 2, a revealed preference relation induced by C^a_τ that is defined by

$$R^*_{C^a_\tau} = \bigcup_{S \in \mathscr{S}} [C^a_\tau(S) \times \{S \setminus C^a_\tau(S)\}] \tag{7.21}$$

Let $D_G = (D^1, D^2, \ldots, D^s)$ be called a G rights system. Then we can assert the following impossibility theorem, which is a variant of what Batra and Pattanaik (1972) called the *impossibility of the Pareto federalism.*

Theorem 7.4
Let a group structure $G = (G^1, G^2, \ldots, G^s)$ and a G rights system $D_G = (D^1, D^2, \ldots, D^s)$ be such that there exist τ_1 and τ_2 ($\tau_1 \neq \tau_2$) satisfying

(a) $G^{\tau_1} \cap G^{\tau_2} = \varnothing$, and
(b) D^{τ_1} and D^{τ_2} are nonempty, symmetric, and nondiagonal.

Then there exists no universally applicable rule $(\eta, \{\zeta^\tau\}_{\tau=1}^s)$ that allows each group G^τ ($\tau \in \{1, 2, \ldots, s\}$) autonomy over D^τ without violating the following unanimity conditions.

Condition P(1)

$\forall \tau \in \{1, 2, \ldots, s\}, \forall a = (R_1^a, R_2^a, \ldots, R_n^a) \in A$:

$$(x, y) \in \bigcap_{i \in G^\tau} P(R_i^a) \rightarrow \forall S \in \mathscr{S}: [x \in S \rightarrow y \notin C_\tau^a(S)]$$

Condition P(2)

$\forall a = (R_1^a, R_2^a, \ldots, R_n^a) \in A$:

$$(x, y) \in \bigcap_{\tau=1}^{s} R_{C_\tau^a}^* \rightarrow \forall S \in \mathscr{S}: [x \in S \rightarrow y \notin C^a(S)]$$

Proof: Let us suppose that $(x, y) \in D^{\tau_1}$ ($x \neq y$) and $(z, w) \in D^{\tau_2}$ ($z \neq w$) are such that $\{x, y\} \cap \{z, w\} = \varnothing$. Consider a profile $a = (R_1^a, R_2^a, \ldots, R_n^a) \in A$ satisfying

$\forall i \in G^{\tau_1}$: x, w, z, y

$\forall i \in G^{\tau_2}$: z, y, x, w

$\forall i \in N \setminus (G^{\tau_1} \cup G^{\tau_2})$: x, w, z, y

Assume that there exists a rule $(\eta, \{\zeta^\tau\}_{\tau=1}^s)$ that satisfies all the stipulated conditions, and consider $C^a(\{x, y, z, w\})$, where C^a stands for $\eta(\{\zeta^\tau(\{R_i^a\}_{i \in G_\tau})\}_{\tau=1}^s)$. By virtue of condition P(1), we obtain $C_{\tau_1}^a(\{x, y\}) = \{x\}$ and $C_{\tau_2}^a(\{z, w\}) = \{z\}$, so that $(x, y) \in R_{C_{\tau_1}^a}^*$ and $(z, w) \in R_{C_{\tau_2}^a}^*$ are implied. Because the rule allows the group G^{τ_1} [resp. the group G^{τ_2}] autonomy over D^{τ_1} [resp. D^{τ_2}], we obtain

$$(x, y) \in D^{\tau_1} \cap R_{C_{\tau_1}^a}^* \rightarrow y \notin C^a(\{x, y, z, w\})$$

and

$$(z, w) \in D^{\tau_2} \cap R_{C_{\tau_2}^a}^* \rightarrow w \notin C^a(\{x, y, z, w\})$$

Another application of condition P(1) yields $C_\tau^a(\{x, w\}) = \{x\}$ and $C_\tau^a(\{y, z\}) = \{z\}$ for all $\tau \in \{1, 2, \ldots, s\}$, so that we obtain

$$(x, w) \in \bigcap_{\tau=1}^{s} R^*_{C^a_\tau} \rightarrow w \notin C^a(\{x, y, z, w\})$$

and

$$(z, y) \in \bigcap_{\tau=1}^{s} R^*_{C^a_\tau} \rightarrow y \notin C^a(\{x, y, z, w\})$$

which implies that $C^a(\{x, y, z, w\}) = \varnothing$, a contradiction.

The proof for the case where $\{x, y\}$ and $\{z, w\}$ have one or two elements in common is similar but simpler. ▮

How disturbing is this impossibility theorem? The answer clearly hinges on the desirability of having a rule that allows some degree of group autonomy. An argument in favor of the requirement of group autonomy can go as follows: "Even if one rejects [condition SL] one may still find [the requirement of group autonomy] acceptable in so far as the recognition of some amount of autonomy over at least some spheres of decision-making, for various social groups (which exist practically in every society) may constitute a basic precondition for these social groups to agree to be parts of the same society at all" (Batra and Pattanaik, 1972, p. 7). If one finds this argument persuasive, one must seek for a way out of the difficulty crystallized in Theorem 7.4.

3.2 *A resolution of the group autonomy paradox*

We should like to show that our resolution of the Pareto libertarian paradox can be easily modified to resolve the group autonomy paradox as well.

Given any group structure $G = (G^1, G^2, \ldots, G^s)$, a G rights system $D_G = (D^1, D^2, \ldots, D^s)$, and the group choice rules $\{\zeta^\tau\}_{\tau=1}^{s}$, we proceed as follows. Take any profile $a = (R^a_1, R^a_2, \ldots, R^a_n) \in A$, and let $R^*_{C^a_\tau}$ be defined by (7.21), where $C^a_\tau = \zeta^\tau(\{R^a_i\}_{i \in G^\tau})$. We then define Q^a_G by

$$Q^a_G = \bigcup_{\tau=1}^{s} (D^\tau \cap R^*_{C^a_\tau}) \tag{7.22}$$

and let $\mathscr{R}^a_G$ denote the set of all ordering extensions of Q^a_G. We say that G^τ is a *liberal group* if and only if, for any profile $a = (R^a_1, R^a_2, \ldots, R^a_n) \in A$, and the group preference relation R^{0a}_τ, which G^τ wants to be reflected in the global social choice, is such that

$$R^{0a}_\tau = R^*_{C^a_\tau} \cap R \quad \text{for some} \quad R \in \mathscr{R}^a_G \tag{7.23}$$

For a group G^τ that is not liberal, we let $R^{0a}_\tau = R^*_{C^a_\tau}$.

We can now assert the following possibility theorem, which is an extension of Theorem 7.3 to the problem of group autonomy.

Theorem 7.5
Let a group structure $G = (G^1, G^2, \ldots, G^s)$, a G rights system $D_G = (D^1, D^2, \ldots, D^s)$, and the group choice rules $\{\zeta^\tau\}_{\tau=1}^{s}$ be such that

(a) D_G is coherent, and
(b) ζ^τ generates choice functions that satisfy Arrow's axiom of choice consistency for all $\tau \in \{1, 2, \ldots, s\}$.

Assume that there exists at least one liberal group. Then there exists a rule η that entertains the following properties:

(i) for any profile $a = (R_1^a, R_2^a, \ldots, R_n^a) \in A$, $C^a = \eta(\{\zeta^\tau(\{R_i^a\}_{i \in G^\tau})\}_{\tau=1}^{s})$ is a rational choice function,
(ii) $(\eta, \{\zeta^\tau\}_{\tau=1}^{s})$ allows each and every G^τ autonomy over D^τ, and
(iii) for any profile $a = (R_1^a, R_2^a, \ldots, R_n^a) \in A$ and any $x, y \in X$,

$$(x, y) \in P\left(\bigcap_{\tau=1}^{s} R_\tau^{0a}\right) \rightarrow \forall S \in \mathscr{S}: [x \in S \rightarrow y \notin C^a(S)]$$

holds true.

Sketch of proof: Let L denote the set of all indices of a liberal group. Take any profile $a = (R_1^a, R_2^a, \ldots, R_n^a) \in A$, and let $\mathscr{R}_G^a$ denote the set of all ordering extensions of $\dot{Q}_G^a = \bigcup_{\tau=1}^{s} (D^\tau \cap R^*_{C_\tau^a})$. Since $\mathscr{S} = \mathscr{S}_F$ is finitely additive, we may invoke Theorem A(9) in Chapter 2 to assert that $R^*_{C_\tau^a}$ is transitive for all $\tau \in \{1, 2, \ldots, s\}$. Then $\mathscr{R}_G^a$ is nonempty in view of the coherence of D_G. Let R_τ^{0a} be defined by

$$R_\tau^{0a} = \begin{cases} \exists R^\tau \in \mathscr{R}_G^a: R^*_{C_\tau^a} \cap R^\tau & \text{if } \tau \in L \\ \& & \\ R^*_{C_\tau^a} & \text{otherwise} \end{cases}$$

and let

$$R_0^a = \left\{(x, y) \in X \times X \mid (y, x) \notin \left(\bigcap_{\tau \in L} P(R^\tau)\right) \cup P\left(\bigcap_{\tau=1}^{s} R_\tau^{0a}\right)\right\}$$

It can be verified that R_0^a is complete, reflexive, and acyclic, so that a function C^a on $\mathscr{S}$ that is defined by

$$\forall S \in \mathscr{S}: C^a(S) = G(S, R_0^a)$$

is a well-defined choice function on a choice space $(X, \mathscr{S})$. Associating this C^a with $\{\zeta^\tau(\{R_i^a\}_{i \in G^\tau})\}_{\tau=1}^{s}$, we obtain a rule η, which satisfies (i) by definition. The proof that η satisfies (ii) and (iii) can be modeled after the corresponding steps in the proof of Theorem 7.3. ∎

An obvious weakness of this resolution of the paradox of group autonomy is our requirement of the condition (b), which ensures (by virtue of Theorem 2.2) that the choice function $C^a_\tau = \zeta^\tau(\{R^a_i\}_{i\in G^\tau})$ is full rational for every $a \in A$ and every $\tau \in \{1,2,\ldots,s\}$. Within the group $\tau \in \{1,2,\ldots,s\}$, however, there is a problem of collective choice, and we saw in Chapter 3 that the collective rationality, even in the weakened form, precipitates the occurrence of Arrovian impossibility theorems. In presenting Theorem 7.5, we followed a classical "divide and conquer" principle; that is, we tried to resolve the paradox of group autonomy, assuming that the Arrovian paradox of collective choice would not intervene within the group. Work must be done in the future to find a way out from the paradox of group autonomy that is free from this restriction.

4 Equity, efficiency, and impartial justice

4.1 *Motivation behind the second resolution scheme*

Back now to individual rights and libertarian claims. We now turn to our second resolution scheme, which makes use of the information available from extended sympathy in the form of placing oneself, through an imaginary exchange of circumstances, in the position of another. In so doing, we seek for a "just" or "equitable" resolution of the Pareto libertarian paradox.

The essential idea underlying this second attempt can best be illustrated by the following quotation from Berlin (1958, pp. 54–5):

> If... the ends of men are many, and not all of them are in principle compatible with each other, then the possibility of conflict – and of tragedy – can never wholly be eliminated from human life, either personal or social. The necessity of choosing between absolute claims is then an inescapable characteristic of the human condition.... I do not want to say that individual freedom is, even in the most liberal societies, the sole, or even the dominant, criterion of social action.... The extent of a man's or a people's liberty to choose to live as they desire must be weighed against the claims of many other values, of which equality, or justice, or happiness, or security, or public order are perhaps the most obvious examples. For this reason, it cannot be unlimited.... [Respect] for the principles of justice, or shame at gross inequality of treatment, is as basic in man as the desire for liberty.

How can we formalize this suggested restriction on the "legitimate" claims of libertarian rights? A pioneering step was taken by Kelly (1976*a*; 1978, Chapter 8), who made the exercise of libertarian rights contingent on nonviolation of Suppes's grading principle of justice (1966). Unfortunately, even this restricted libertarian claim of rights, which Kelly christened the "weak just liberalism," turned out to be inconsistent with the Pareto principle. Whether or not this "impossibility of a just liberal" can be taken to mean conclusively that "introducing interpersonal comparisons is not much of a cure (in contrast with the impossibility results of the Arrow type)" (Sen, 1976, p. 228) for the Pareto libertarian impossibility theorem is debatable, however, because there are alternative ways of making use of information of the extended sympathy type in the present context. Let us now explore this relatively less cultivated area more systematically with the hope of shedding further light on the nature and significance of the Pareto libertarian paradox.

4.2 *Equity-constrained libertarian claims and Pareto efficiency*

We make use of the conceptual framework we introduced in Chapter 6, where the focus of our concern is a generalized collective choice rule Φ mapping each generalized profile $v = (u_1^v, u_2^v, \ldots, u_n^v) \in \mathscr{U}$ into a social choice function C^v on a choice space $(X, \mathscr{S})$. We shall also refer to a subjective profile $\Sigma(v) = (R_1^v, R_2^v, \ldots, R_n^v)$ corresponding to a generalized profile $v \in \mathscr{U}$, where R_i^v $(i \in N)$ is defined by (6.1). We denote by $\mathscr{U}_{ID}$ [resp. $\mathscr{U}_{CID}$] the set of all generalized profiles that satisfy the axiom of identity [resp. the axiom of complete identity].

Let us examine how our old friend, the equity-as-no-envy concept, fares in the context of the Pareto libertarian paradox. With this purpose in mind, let us define $\varepsilon_i^v(x)$ for every $v = (u_1^v, u_2^v, \ldots, u_n^v) \in \mathscr{U}$, every $i \in N$, and every $x \in X$ by

$$\varepsilon_i^v(x) = \#\{j \in N \mid u_i^v(x, j) > u_i^v(x, i)\} \tag{7.24}$$

At the risk of slight repetition, let us define, for every $S \in \mathscr{S}$, a set of no-envy equitable states in S by

$$E_q^v(S) = \{x \in S \mid \forall\, i \in N\colon \varepsilon_i^v(x) = 0\} \tag{7.25}$$

which, in turn, can be used to define an ordering R_q^v on X by

$$R_q^v = \{(x, y) \in X \times X \mid \sim [y \in E_q^v(X) \;\&\; x \notin E_q^v(X)]\} \tag{7.26}$$

Consider now the following equity-constrained libertarian claim.

Condition ECL (equity-constrained libertarian claim)
For every generalized profile $v = (u_1^v, u_2^v, \ldots, u_n^v) \in \mathscr{U}$, every $i \in N$, and every $x, y \in X$, if $(x, y) \in D_i \cap P(R_i^v)$ and $(y, x) \notin P(R_q^v)$, then $[x \in S \rightarrow y \notin C^v(S)]$ for all $S \in \mathscr{S}$, where $C^v = \Phi(v)$.

In contrast with condition SL, it is required in condition ECL that individual i's assigned libertarian right over $(x, y) \in D_i$ will be socially realized only if y is not strictly more equitable than x in the sense of no envy.

To see how this constraint can prevent the Pareto libertarian paradox from surfacing, note first that condition ECL reduces to condition SL if the generalized profile $v \in \mathscr{U}$ is such that $E_q^v(X) = \varnothing$. Suffice it to observe that we then obtain $R_q^v = X \times X$, so that $(y, x) \notin P(R_q^v)$ is vacuously true for all $x, y \in X$.

In order to provide condition ECL a fair chance of success, let $\mathscr{U}_E$ denote the set of all generalized profiles that yield nonempty no-envy equitable sets, and restrict the domain of Φ to $\mathscr{U}_E \cap \mathscr{U}_{CID}$.

Theorem 7.6
Assume that $\# X \geq 3$, and let the given rights system $D = (D_1, D_2, \ldots, D_n)$ be symmetric and nondiagonal, and assume that D_i is nonempty for at least two individuals. Then there exists no generalized collective choice rule on $\mathscr{U}_E \cap \mathscr{U}_{CID}$ that satisfies the Pareto principle (P) and the equity-constrained libertarian claim (ECL) (Suzumura, 1982, Theorem 3).

Proof: Without loss of generality, we can assume that

$$(x, y), (y, x) \in D_1 \, (x \neq y); \qquad (z, w), (w, z) \in D_2 \, (z \neq w)$$

There are three cases to be treated separately.

Case 1: $\{x, y\} = \{z, w\}$

Take any $v \in X \setminus \{x, y\}$ and consider a generalized profile $v(1) = (u_1^{v(1)}, u_2^{v(1)}, \ldots, u_n^{v(1)}) \in \mathscr{U}_{CID}$ such that $u_i^{v(1)} = u_*^{v(1)}$ for all $i \in N$ and

$$\begin{aligned} u_*^{v(1)}(y, 2) > u_*^{v(1)}(x, 1) > u_*^{v(1)}(x, 2) > u_*^{v(1)}(y, 1) \\ > u_*^{v(1)}(v, 1) = u_*^{v(1)}(v, 2) \end{aligned}$$

$$\forall i \in N \setminus \{1, 2\}: u_*^{v(1)}(x, i) = u_*^{v(1)}(x, 1) \; \& \; u_*^{v(1)}(v, i) = u_*^{v(1)}(v, 1)$$

Let $S_1 = \{x, y, z\}$. Because $E_q^{v(1)}(S_1) = \{v\}$ holds true, $v(1) \in \mathscr{U}_E \cap \mathscr{U}_{CID}$ is the case. Consider now $C^{v(1)}(S_1)$, where $C^{v(1)} = \Phi(v(1))$. By virtue of condition P and condition ECL, we obtain

$$(x, y) \in D_1 \cap P(R_1^{v(1)}) \; \& \; (y, x) \notin P(R_q^{v(1)}) \rightarrow y \notin C^{v(1)}(S_1)$$

$$(y, x) \in D_2 \cap P(R_2^{v(1)}) \; \& \; (x, y) \notin P(R_q^{v(1)}) \rightarrow x \notin C^{v(1)}(S_1)$$

and

$$(x, v) \in \bigcap_{i \in N} P(R_i^{v(1)}) \rightarrow v \notin C^{v(1)}(S_1)$$

so that we have $C^{v(1)}(S_1) = \varnothing$, a contradiction.

Case 2: $\# (\{x, y\} \cap \{z, w\}) = 1$

We can assume, without loss of generality, that $w = x$. Consider a generalized profile $v(2) = (u_1^{v(2)}, u_2^{v(2)}, \ldots, u_n^{v(2)}) \in \mathscr{U}_{CID}$, which satisfies $u_i^{v(2)} = u_*^{v(2)}$ for all $i \in N$, and

$$u_*^{v(2)}(y,2) > u_*^{v(2)}(x,1) > u_*^{v(2)}(y,1) > u_*^{v(2)}(z,1)$$
$$= u_*^{v(2)}(z,2) > u_*^{v(2)}(x,2)$$

$$\forall i \in N \setminus \{1,2\}: u_*^{v(2)}(z,i) = u_*^{v(2)}(z,1) \ \& \ u_*^{v(2)}(y,i) = u_*^{v(2)}(y,2)$$

Let $S_2 = \{x, y, z\}$. Because $E_q^{v(2)}(S_2) = \{z\}$ holds true, $v(2) \in \mathscr{U}_E \cap \mathscr{U}_{CID}$ is the case. Let us examine $C^{v(2)}(S_2)$, where $C^{v(2)} = \Phi(v(2))$. If Φ satisfies condition P and condition ECL, we obtain

$$(z,x) \in D_2 \cap P(R_2^{v(2)}) \ \& \ (x,z) \notin P(R_q^{v(2)}) \rightarrow x \notin C^{v(2)}(S_2)$$

$$(x,y) \in D_1 \cap P(R_1^{v(2)}) \ \& \ (y,x) \notin P(R_q^{v(2)}) \rightarrow y \notin C^{v(2)}(S_2)$$

and

$$(y,z) \in \bigcap_{i \in N} P(R_i^{v(2)}) \rightarrow z \notin C^{v(2)}(S_2)$$

which yield $C^{v(2)}(S_2) = \varnothing$, a contradiction.

Case 3: $\{x, y\} \cap \{z, w\} = \varnothing$

Consider a generalized profile $v(3) = (u_1^{v(3)}, u_2^{v(3)}, \ldots, u_n^{v(3)}) \in \mathscr{U}_{CID}$ such that $u_i^{v(3)} = u_*^{v(3)}$ for all $i \in N$, and

$$u_*^{v(3)}(y,2) > u_*^{v(3)}(w,2) > u_*^{v(3)}(z,2) > u_*^{v(3)}(z,1) > u_*^{v(3)}(x,1)$$
$$> u_*^{v(3)}(x,2) > u_*^{v(3)}(y,1) > u_*^{v(3)}(w,1)$$

$$\forall i \in N \setminus \{1,2\}: \begin{cases} u_*^{v(3)}(x,i) = u_*^{v(3)}(x,1) \\ u_*^{v(3)}(z,i) = u_*^{v(3)}(z,1) \\ u_*^{v(3)}(y,i) = u_*^{v(3)}(y,2) \\ u_*^{v(3)}(w,i) = u_*^{v(3)}(w,1) \end{cases}$$

Let $S_3 = \{x, y, z, w\}$. Because $E_q^{v(3)}(S_3) = \{x\}$ holds true, we obtain $v(3) \in \mathscr{U}_E \cap \mathscr{U}_{CID}$. Let us examine $C^{v(3)}(S_3)$, where $C^{v(3)} = \Phi(v(3))$. If Φ satisfies condition P and condition ECL, we obtain

$$(z,x) \in \bigcap_{i \in N} P(R_i^{v(3)}) \rightarrow x \notin C^{v(3)}(S_3)$$

$$(y,w) \in \bigcap_{i \in N} P(R_i^{v(3)}) \rightarrow w \notin C^{v(3)}(S_3)$$

$$(x,y) \in D_1 \cap P(R_1^{v(3)}) \ \& \ (y,x) \notin P(R_q^{v(3)}) \rightarrow y \notin C^{v(3)}(S_3)$$

and

$$(w,z) \in D_2 \cap P(R_2^{v(3)}) \ \& \ (z,w) \notin P(R_q^{v(3)}) \rightarrow z \notin C^{v(3)}(S_3)$$

which imply that $C^{v(3)}(S_3) = \varnothing$, a contradiction. ∎

We have thus shown that the equity-as-no-envy concept does not provide us with an equity-constrained libertarian claim that resolves the Pareto libertarian paradox. We can also show that the alternative no-envy equity concepts that we discussed in Chapter 5 do not perform any better in the context of the Pareto libertarian claims. The interested reader is referred to another source (Suzumura, 1982).

Should we then conclude from our negative result on the equity-constrained libertarian claim that this route is in fact a blind alley? We believe that the reasoned answer should be not necessarily. We now want to formulate still other ways to make libertarian claims contingent and to examine the general workability thereof.

4.3 Justice-constrained libertarian claims and Pareto efficiency

Let $\omega = (\omega_1, \omega_2, \ldots, \omega_n)$ be an n-list of the impartial principles of justice, one principle for each individual, the impartiality being construed to mean that condition IM_ω is satisfied by ω_i ($i \in N$). We shall also assume that ω_i ($i \in N$) is a complete principle of justice, so that for every generalized profile $v = (u_1^v, u_2^v, \ldots, u_n^v) \in \mathscr{U}$, $\omega_i(u_i^v)$ is an ordering on X, together forming an ethical profile $\Omega(v|\omega) = (\omega_1(u_1^v), \omega_2(u_2^v), \ldots, \omega_n(u_n^v))$.

Consider now the following three versions of the justice-constrained libertarian claims.

Condition JCL(1) [justice-constrained libertarian claim (1)]
For every admissible generalized profile $v = (u_1^v, u_2^v, \ldots, u_n^v) \in \mathscr{U}$, every $i \in N$, and every $x, y \in X$, if $(x, y) \in D_i \cap P(R_i^v)$ and $(y, x) \notin \bigcup_{j \in N} P(\omega_j(u_j^v))$ hold true, then $[x \in S \rightarrow y \notin C^v(S)]$ is implied for all $S \in \mathscr{S}$, where $C^v = \Phi(v)$.

Condition JCL(2) [justice-constrained libertarian claim (2)]
For every admissible generalized profile $v = (u_1^v, u_2^v, \ldots, u_n^v) \in \mathscr{U}$, every $i \in N$, and every $x, y \in X$, if $(x, y) \in D_i \cap P(R_i^v)$ and $(y, x) \notin P(\omega_i(u_i^v))$ hold true, then $[x \in S \rightarrow y \notin C^v(S)]$ is implied for all $S \in \mathscr{S}$, where $C^v = \Phi(v)$.

Condition JCL(3) [justice-constrained libertarian claim (3)]
For every admissible generalized profile $v = (u_1^v, u_2^v, \ldots, u_n^v) \in \mathscr{U}$, every $i \in N$, and every $x, y \in X$, if $(x, y) \in D_i \cap P(R_i^v)$ and $(y, x) \notin \bigcap_{j \in N \setminus \{i\}} P(\omega_j(u_j^v))$ hold true, then $[x \in S \rightarrow y \notin C^v(S)]$ is implied for all $S \in \mathscr{S}$, where $C^v = \Phi(v)$.

With a view toward interpreting these claims, suppose that $v = (u_1^v, u_2^v, \ldots, u_n^v) \in \mathscr{U}$, $i \in N$, and $x, y \in X$ are such that $(x, y) \in D_i \cap P(R_i^v)$ holds true. By definition, individual $i \in N$ is endowed with a right of special voice for x against y, and he wants to have his way for x. This right will be withheld in JCL(1) or in JCL(2) or in JCL(3), however, if at least one individual, whoever he may happen to be, judges y to be more just than x, or if individual i himself judges y to be more just than x, or if all individuals other than individual i himself unanimously judge y to be more just than x. It seems to us that each one of JCL(1), JCL(2), and JCL(3) has something to recommend it, and in view of the fact that

$$\forall i \in N: P(\omega_i(u_i^v)) \cup \left[\bigcap_{j \in N \setminus \{i\}} P(\omega_j(u_j^v)) \right] \subset \bigcap_{j \in N} P(\omega_j(u_j^v)) \tag{7.27}$$

is true, it is clear that JCL(1) is weaker than JCL(2) as well as JCL(3).

Before stating the central theorem of this section, we must introduce a further condition on a generalized collective choice rule that reads as follows.

Condition S (Suppes principle)
For every generalized profile $v = (u_1^v, u_2^v, \ldots, u_n^v) \in \mathscr{U}$ and every $x, y \in X$, if $(x, y) \in \bigcap_{i \in N} \omega_S(u_i^v)$ holds true, then $[x \in S \rightarrow y \notin C^v(S)]$ is implied for all $S \in \mathscr{S}$, where $C^v = \Phi(v)$.

Analytically speaking, the following theorem is the main proposition in this section.

Theorem 7.7
Let $D = (D_1, D_2, \ldots, D_n)$ be an arbitrarily given coherent rights system. There exists a rational generalized collective choice rule that satisfies the unrestricted domain (U), the Suppes principle (S), and the justice-constrained libertarian claim (1) [JCL(1)][8] (Suzumura, 1982, Theorem 7).

Proof: Take any generalized profile $v = (u_1^v, u_2^v, \ldots, u_n^v) \in \mathscr{U}$ and define a binary relation Q^v by

$$Q^v = \bigcup_{i \in N} (D_i \cap R_i^v) \tag{7.28}$$

D being coherent by assumption, there exists an ordering Q_*^v on X that satisfies

$$Q^v \subset Q_*^v \quad \text{and} \quad P(Q^v) \subset P(Q_*^v) \tag{7.29}$$

We then define R_0^v by

$$R_0^v = \{(x, y) \in X \times X \mid (y, x) \notin S_N^v \cup [P(Q_*^v) \cap \Omega_N^v]\} \tag{7.30}$$

where $S_N^v = \bigcap_{i \in N} \omega_S(u_i^v)$ and $\Omega_N^v = \bigcap_{i \in N} \omega_i(u_i^v)$. Let us show that R_0^v is complete and reflexive. Assume, to the contrary, that $(x, y) \notin R_0^v$ and $(y, x) \notin R_0^v$ for some $x, y \in X$. If (x, y) as well as

(y,x) belongs to S_N^v [resp. $P(Q_*^v) \cap \Omega_N^v$], we arrive at a contradiction of the asymmetry of S_N^v [resp. $P(Q_*^v)$]. Assume, therefore, that $(x, y) \in S_N^v$ and $(y,x) \in P(Q_*^v) \cap \Omega_N^v$ are true. Thanks to condition IM_ω, which is satisfied by each and every ω_i $(i \in N)$ by assumption, we obtain $\omega_S(u_i^v) \subset P(\omega_i(u_i^v))$ for all $i \in N$, which implies

$$S_N^v = \bigcap_{i \in N} \omega_S(u_i^v) \subset \bigcap_{i \in N} P(\omega_i(u_i^v)) \subset P(\Omega_N^v) \tag{7.31}$$

It then follows that $(x, y) \in P(\Omega_N^v)$ and $(y,x) \in \Omega_N^v$, a contradiction. Finally, the case where $(x, y) \in P(Q_*^v) \cap \Omega_N^v$ and $(y,x) \in S_N^v$ are true can be treated similarly.

The next step is to prove that

$$P(R_0^v) = S_N^v \cup [P(Q_*^v) \cap \Omega_N^v] \tag{7.32}$$

If $(x, y) \in P(R_0^v)$ is the case, then $(y,x) \notin S_N^v \cup [P(Q_*^v) \cap \Omega_N^v]$ and $(x, y) \in S_N^v \cup [P(Q_*^v) \cap \Omega_N^v]$ hold true, so that we obtain

$$P(R_0^v) \subset S_N^v \cup [P(Q_*^v) \cap \Omega_N^v] \tag{7.33}$$

To show the converse, let there be $x, y \in X$ such that $(x, y) \notin P(R_0^v)$ and $(x, y) \in S_N^v \cup [P(Q_*^v) \cap \Omega_N^v]$. We have shown already that $(x, y) \in S_N^v \cup [P(Q_*^v) \cap \Omega_N^v]$ implies $(y,x) \notin S_N^v \cup [P(Q_*^v) \cap \Omega_N^v]$, which implies $(x, y) \in P(R_0^v)$, in view of the definition of R_0^v, a contradiction.

Third, we show that R_0^v is acyclic. Assume, to the contrary, that there are $x^1, x^2, \dots, x^t$ in X such that $(x^\mu, x^{\mu+1}) \in P(R_0^v)$ $(\mu \in \{1, 2, \dots, t-1\})$ and $(x^t, x^1) \in P(R_0^v)$ hold true. If $(x^\mu, x^{\mu+1})$ $(\mu \in \{1, 2, \dots, t-1\})$ and (x^t, x^1) all belong to S_N^v [resp. $P(Q_*^v) \cap \Omega_N^v$], we arrive at a contradiction of the transitivity and asymmetry of S_N^v [resp. $P(Q_*^v) \cap \Omega_N^v$]. Mixed cases cannot be sustained either, because we have, as noted earlier, that $S_N^v \subset P(\Omega_N^v)$.

Now that R_0^v has turned out to be complete, reflexive, and acyclic,

$$C_0^v(S) = \{x \in S \mid \forall\, y \in S: (x, y) \in R_0^v\} \tag{7.34}$$

is a nonempty subset of S for every $S \in \mathcal{S}$. Associating C_0^v with the generalized profile $v = (u_1^v, u_2^v, \dots, u_n^v) \in \mathcal{U}$ we started from, we obtain a well-defined generalized collective choice rule Φ_0. By construction, Φ_0 is a rational rule with unrestricted domain.

To show that Φ_0 satisfies condition S, let $v = (u_1^v, u_2^v, \dots, u_n^v) \in \mathcal{U}$ and $x, y \in X$ be such that $(x, y) \in S_N^v$, $x \in S$, and $y \in C_0^v(S)$ hold true for some $S \in \mathcal{S}$. It then follows that $(x, y) \notin S_N^v \cup [P(Q_*^v) \cap \Omega_N^v]$, in clear contradiction of $(x, y) \in S_N^v$.

Finally, we prove that Φ_0 satisfies condition JCL(1). Suppose that there exist $v = (u_1^v, u_2^v, \ldots, u_n^v) \in \mathscr{U}$, $i \in N$, $x, y \in X$, and $S \in \mathscr{S}$ such that

$$(x, y) \in D_i \cap P(R_i^v), \quad (y, x) \notin \bigcup_{j \in N} P(\omega_j(u_j^v)), \quad x \in S, \quad y \in C_0^v(S) \tag{7.35}$$

hold true. Because ω_j is a complete principle of justice, $(y, x) \notin \bigcup_{j \in N} P(\omega_j(u_j^v))$ implies $(x, y) \in \bigcap_{j \in N} \omega_j(u_j^v) = \Omega_N^v$. By definition of Q^v, we obtain

$$(x, y) \in D_i \cap P(R_i^v) \subset D_i \cap R_i^v \subset Q^v \tag{7.36}$$

Suppose that we have $(y, x) \in Q^v$. Then we obtain $(y, x) \in D_j \cap R_j^v$ for some $j \in N$. It follows from $(x, y) \in P(R_i^v)$ and $(y, x) \in R_j^v$ that $i \neq j$, which implies that $(x, y) \in D_i$, $(y, x) \in D_j$, and $i \neq j$, in contradiction of the coherence of D. Therefore, $(y, x) \notin Q^v$ must be the case, so that we obtain $(x, y) \in P(Q^v)$. Taking (7.29) into consideration, we then obtain

$$(x, y) \in P(Q_*^v) \cap \Omega_N^v \tag{7.37}$$

On the other hand, $y \in C_0^v(S)$, $x \in S$, and (7.34) yield

$$(x, y) \notin S_N^v \cup [P(Q_*^v) \cap \Omega_N^v] \tag{7.38}$$

in contradiction of (7.37). This completes the proof. ∎

Notice now that we have

$$\forall v = (u_1^v, u_2^v, \ldots, u_n^v) \in \mathscr{U}_{ID}, \forall i \in N: P\left(\bigcap_{j \in N} R_j^v\right) \subset \omega_S(u_i^v) \tag{7.39}$$

(Sen, 1970*b*, Theorem 9*3), so that $P(\bigcap_{i \in N} R_i^v) \subset \bigcap_{i \in N} \omega_S(u_i^v)$ holds true. It then follows from Theorem 7.7 that the following possibility theorem (Suzumura, 1982, Theorem 8) on Pareto libertarianism holds true.

Theorem 7.8
Let $D = (D_1, D_2, \ldots, D_n)$ be an arbitrarily given coherent rights system. There exists a rational generalized collective choice rule on $\mathscr{U}_{ID}$ that satisfies the strong Pareto principle (SP) and the justice-constrained libertarian claim (1) [JCL(1)].[9]

We have thus established that under the axiom of identity on the admissible class of generalized profiles and the impartiality axiom on the justice principles held by each and every individual, the justice-constrained libertarian claim (1) represents a claim of rights that is compatible with the Pareto principle. A problem still remains: How broad is the escape route secured by Theorem 7.8? To this problem we now turn.

4.4 Limitations on justice-constrained libertarian claims

Before setting about pointing out the limitations of the justice-constrained libertarian claims, let us suggest a possible way to generalize Theorem 7.8. Scrutinizing the structure of our proof, it can be easily recognized that the full power of the impartiality of ω_i ($i \in N$) is nowhere needed. What is needed is that the admissible principle of justice be Paretian in that a state x that is unanimously preferred to another state y is judged to be more just than y.

Turning to the negative side of the coin, let us consider a weaker version of condition JCL(1), which goes as follows.

Condition JCL(1) [justice-constrained libertarian claim (1*)]*
For every admissible generalized profile $v = (u_1^v, u_2^v, \ldots, u_n^v) \in \mathscr{U}$, every $i \in N$, and every $x, y \in X$, if $(x, y) \in D_i \cap P(R_i^v)$ and $(y, x) \notin \bigcup_{j \in N} \omega_j(u_j^v)$ hold true, then $[x \in S \rightarrow y \notin C^v(S)]$ is implied for all $S \in \mathscr{S}$, where $C^v = \Phi(v)$.

Because $\bigcup_{j \in N} P(\omega_j(u_j^v)) \subset \bigcup_{j \in N} \omega_j(u_j^v)$ holds true, condition JCL(1*) is indeed weaker than condition JCL(1). Notice now that Theorem 7.8 makes effective use of a domain restriction in the form of the identity axiom. We now prove that if we drop this domain restriction, even the weaker condition JCL(1*) is demonstrably inconsistent with the Pareto principle.

Theorem 7.9
Assume that the rights system $D = (D_1, D_2, \ldots, D_n)$ is coherent and that, for at least two individuals, say 1 and 2,

$$\{(x, y), (y, x)\} \subset D_1 \ (x \neq y), \qquad \{(z, w), (w, z)\} \subset D_2 \ (z \neq w)$$

hold true. Assume further that $\omega_i = \omega_R$ (the Rawlsian leximin principle of justice) for all $i \in N$. Then there exists no generalized collective choice rule that satisfies the unrestricted domain (U), the Pareto principle (P), and the justice-constrained libertarian claim (1*) [JCL(1*)] (Suzumura, 1982, Theorem 9).

Proof: The rights system being coherent by assumption, we have only to consider the following two cases.

Case 1: $\#(\{x, y\} \cap \{z, w\}) = 1$

Assume, without loss of generality, that $x = w$. Consider a generalized profile $v(1) = (u_1^{v(1)}, u_2^{v(1)}, \ldots, u_n^{v(1)}) \in \mathscr{U}$ such that

$$u_1^{v(1)}(x,1) > u_1^{v(1)}(y,1) > u_1^{v(1)}(z,1) > u_1^{v(1)}(z,2) > u_1^{v(1)}(x,2) > u_1^{v(1)}(y,2)$$

$$u_2^{v(1)}(y,2) > u_2^{v(1)}(z,2) > u_2^{v(1)}(x,2) > u_2^{v(1)}(z,1) > u_2^{v(1)}(x,1) > u_2^{v(1)}(y,1)$$

$$\forall i \in N \setminus \{1,2\}: u_i^{v(1)} = u_1^{v(1)} \quad \text{on} \quad \{x,y,z\} \times \{1,2\}$$

$$\forall i \in N, \forall k \in N \setminus \{1,2\}: u_i^{v(1)}(x,k) > u_i^{v(1)}(y,k) > u_i^{v(1)}(z,k) > \max\{u_i^{v(1)}(x,i), u_i^{v(1)}(y,i), u_i^{v(1)}(z,i)\}$$

Let $S_1 = \{x, y, z\}$, and consider $C^{v(1)}(S_1)$, where $C^{v(1)} = \Phi(v(1))$. Note that we have

$$\forall i \in N: \omega_R(u_i^{v(1)}) \cap (S_1 \times S_1) = \Delta(S_1) \cup \{(z,x),(x,y),(z,y)\}$$

where $\Delta(S_1) = \{(x,x),(y,y),(z,z)\}$. Suppose that Φ satisfies condition U, condition P, and condition JCL(1*). Then we obtain

$$(x,y) \in D_1 \cap P(R_1^{v(1)}) \ \& \ (y,x) \notin \bigcup_{j \in N} \omega_R(u_j^{v(1)}) \rightarrow y \notin C^{v(1)}(S_1)$$

$$(z,x) \in D_2 \cap P(R_2^{v(1)}) \ \& \ (x,z) \notin \bigcup_{j \in N} \omega_R(u_j^{v(1)}) \rightarrow x \notin C^{v(1)}(S_1)$$

and

$$(y,z) \in \bigcap_{j \in N} P(R_j^{v(1)}) \rightarrow z \notin C^{v(1)}(S_1)$$

which imply that $C^{v(1)}(S_1) = \varnothing$, a contradiction.

Case 2: $\{x, y\} \cap \{z, w\} = \varnothing$

Consider now a generalized profile $v(2) = (u_1^{v(2)}, u_2^{v(2)}, \ldots, u_n^{v(2)}) \in \mathscr{U}$ such that

$$u_1^{v(2)}(z,1) > u_1^{v(2)}(x,1) > u_1^{v(2)}(y,1) > u_1^{v(2)}(w,1) > u_1^{v(2)}(x,2) > u_1^{v(2)}(y,2) > u_1^{v(2)}(w,2) > u_1^{v(2)}(z,2)$$

$$u_2^{v(2)}(y,2) > u_2^{v(2)}(w,2) > u_2^{v(2)}(z,2) > u_2^{v(2)}(x,2) > u_2^{v(2)}(x,1) > u_2^{v(2)}(y,1) > u_2^{v(2)}(w,1) > u_2^{v(2)}(z,1)$$

$$\forall i \in N \setminus \{1,2\}: u_i^{v(2)} = u_1^{v(2)} \quad \text{on} \quad S_2 \times \{1,2\}$$

$$\forall i \in N, \forall k \in N \setminus \{1,2\}: u_i^{v(2)}(z,k) > u_i^{v(2)}(x,k) > u_i^{v(2)}(y,k) > u_i^{v(2)}(w,k) > \max_{v \in S_2; j_1, j_2 \in \{1,2\}} u_{j_1}^{v(2)}(v, j_2)$$

where $S_2 = \{x, y, z, w\}$. Assume that Φ satisfies condition U, condition P, and condition JCL(1*), and consider $C^{v(2)}(S_2)$, where $C^{v(2)} = \Phi(v(2))$. Note that we have

$$\forall i \in N: \omega_R(u_i^{v(2)}) \cap (S_2 \times S_2) = \Delta(S_2) \cup \{(x, y), (x, w), (x, z), (y, w), (y, z), (w, z)\}$$

where $\Delta(S_2) = \{(x, x), (y, y), (z, z), (w, w)\}$. We can then verify that

$$(x, y) \in D_1 \cap P(R_1^{v(2)}) \ \&\ (y, x) \notin \bigcup_{j \in N} \omega_R(u_j^{v(2)}) \rightarrow y \notin C^{v(2)}(S_2)$$

$$(w, z) \in D_2 \cap P(R_2^{v(2)}) \ \&\ (z, w) \notin \bigcup_{j \in N} \omega_R(u_j^{v(2)}) \rightarrow z \notin C^{v(2)}(S_2)$$

$$(z, x) \in \bigcap_{j \in N} P(R_j^{v(2)}) \rightarrow x \notin C^{v(2)}(S_2)$$

and

$$(y, w) \in \bigcap_{j \in N} P(R_j^{v(2)}) \rightarrow w \notin C^{v(2)}(S_2)$$

hold true, so that we have $C^{v(2)}(S_2) = \varnothing$, a contradiction. ∎

The thrust of this theorem is that even if people are willing to make their rights-exercising contingent on nonviolation of social justice and if people agree on the relevant principle of justice, we still encounter an impossibility result if our desideratum is to design a generalized collective choice rule with an absolutely unrestricted domain.

Another way to examine the robustness of the assertion of Theorem 7.8 is to see if condition JCL(1) can be strengthened into either condition JCL(2) or condition JCL(3). That both ways are destined to lead us into an impasse is the assertion of the following proposition (Suzumura, 1982, Theorem 10).

Theorem 7.10
Assume that the rights system $D = (D_1, D_2, \ldots, D_n)$ is coherent and that $D_1 \supset \{(x, y), (y, x)\}$ $(x \neq y)$ and $D_2 \supset \{(z, w), (w, z)\}$ $(z \neq w)$. Assume further that $\omega_i = \omega_R$ holds true for all $i \in N$.

(a) There exists no generalized collective choice rule on $\mathscr{U}_{ID}$ that satisfies the Pareto principle (P) and the justice-constrained libertarian claim (2) [JCL(2)].

(b) There exists no generalized collective choice rule on $\mathscr{U}_{ID}$ that satisfies the strong Pareto principle (SP) and the justice-constrained libertarian claim (3) [JCL(3)].

Proof of (a): Assume that there exists a generalized collective choice rule Φ on $\mathscr{U}_{ID}$ that satisfies condition P and condition JCL(2).

Case 1: $\#(\{x, y\} \cap \{z, w\}) = 1$

Assume, without loss of generality, that $x = w$, and consider a generalized profile $v(1) = (u_1^{v(1)}, u_2^{v(1)}, \ldots, u_n^{v(1)}) \in \mathscr{U}_{ID}$ such that

$$u_1^{v(1)}(y,2) > u_1^{v(1)}(z,2) > u_1^{v(1)}(x,2) > u_1^{v(1)}(x,1) > u_1^{v(1)}(y,1) > u_1^{v(1)}(z,1)$$

$$u_2^{v(1)}(x,1) > u_2^{v(1)}(y,1) > u_2^{v(1)}(z,1) > u_2^{v(1)}(y,2) > u_2^{v(1)}(z,2) > u_2^{v(1)}(x,2)$$

$$\forall i \in N \setminus \{1,2\}: u_i^{v(1)} = u_1^{v(1)} \quad \text{on} \quad \{x, y, z\} \times \{1,2\}$$

$$\forall i \in N, \forall k \in N \setminus \{1,2\}: u_i^{v(1)}(y,k) > u_i^{v(1)}(z,k)$$

Let $S_1 = \{x, y, z\}$, and consider $C^{v(1)}(S_1)$, where $C^{v(1)} = \Phi(v(1))$. Note that it is the case that

$$\omega_R(u_1^{v(1)}) \cap (S_1 \times S_1) = \Delta(S_1) \cup \{(x,y),(y,z),(x,z)\}$$

and

$$\omega_R(u_2^{v(1)}) \cap (S_1 \times S_1) = \Delta(S_1) \cup \{(y,z),(z,x),(y,x)\}$$

where $\Delta(S_1) = \{(x,x),(y,y),(z,z)\}$. It then follows that

$$(x,y) \in D_1 \cap P(R_1^{v(1)}) \;\&\; (y,x) \notin P(\omega_R(u_1^{v(1)})) \to y \notin C^{v(1)}(S_1)$$

$$(z,x) \in D_2 \cap P(R_2^{v(1)}) \;\&\; (x,z) \notin P(\omega_R(u_2^{v(1)})) \to x \notin C^{v(1)}(S_1)$$

and

$$(y,z) \in \bigcap_{j \in N} P(R_j^{v(1)}) \to z \notin C^{v(1)}(S_1)$$

which imply that $C^{v(1)}(S_1) = \varnothing$, a contradiction.

Case 2: $\{x, y\} \cap \{z, w\} = \varnothing$

Consider a generalized profile $v(2) = (u_1^{v(2)}, u_2^{v(2)}, \ldots, u_n^{v(2)}) \in \mathscr{U}_{ID}$ such that

$$u_1^{v(2)}(y,2) > u_1^{v(2)}(w,2) > u_1^{v(2)}(z,2) > u_1^{v(2)}(x,2) > u_1^{v(2)}(z,1) > u_1^{v(2)}(x,1) > u_1^{v(2)}(y,1) > u_1^{v(2)}(w,1)$$

$$u_2^{v(2)}(z,1) > u_2^{v(2)}(x,1) > u_2^{v(2)}(y,1) > u_2^{v(2)}(w,1) > u_2^{v(2)}(y,2) > u_2^{v(2)}(w,2) > u_2^{v(2)}(z,2) > u_2^{v(2)}(x,2)$$

$$\forall i \in N \setminus \{1,2\}: u_i^{v(2)} = u_1^{v(2)} \quad \text{on} \quad S_2 \times \{1,2\}$$

$$\forall i \in N, \forall k \in N \setminus \{1,2\}: u_i^{v(2)}(z,k) > u_i^{v(2)}(x,k) \;\&\; u_i^{v(2)}(y,k) > u_i^{v(2)}(w,k)$$

where $S_2 = \{x, y, z, w\}$. Consider $C^{v(2)}(S_2)$, where $C^{v(2)} = \Phi(v(2))$. Note that

$$\omega_R(u_1^{v(2)}) \cap (S_2 \times S_2) = R_1^{v(2)} \cap (S_2 \times S_2)$$

and

$$\omega_R(u_2^{v(2)}) \cap (S_2 \times S_2) = R_2^{v(2)} \cap (S_2 \times S_2)$$

hold true. It then follows that

$$(x, y) \in D_1 \cap P(R_1^{v(2)}) \ \& \ (y, x) \notin P(\omega_R(u_1^{v(2)})) \rightarrow y \notin C^{v(2)}(S_2)$$

$$(w, z) \in D_2 \cap P(R_2^{v(2)}) \ \& \ (z, w) \notin P(\omega_R(u_1^{v(2)})) \rightarrow z \notin C^{v(2)}(S_2)$$

$$(z, x) \in \bigcap_{j \in N} P(R_j^{v(2)}) \rightarrow x \notin C^{v(2)}(S_2)$$

and

$$(y, w) \in \bigcap_{j \in N} P(R_j^{v(2)}) \rightarrow w \notin C^{v(2)}(S_2)$$

so that we obtain $C^{v(2)}(S_2) = \varnothing$, a contradiction. ∎

Proof of (b): Assume that Φ satisfies all the nominated conditions.

Case 1: $\#(\{x, y\} \cap \{z, w\}) = 1$

Assume that $x = w$, and consider a generalized profile $v(1) = (u_1^{v(1)}, u_2^{v(1)}, \ldots, u_n^{v(1)}) \in \mathscr{U}_{ID}$ such that

$$u_1^{v(1)}(x, 1) > u_1^{v(1)}(y, 2) > u_1^{v(1)}(y, 1) > u_1^{v(1)}(z, 2) > u_1^{v(1)}(z, 1) > u_1^{v(1)}(x, 2)$$

$$u_2^{v(1)}(y, 2) > u_2^{v(1)}(z, 2) > u_2^{v(1)}(x, 1) > u_2^{v(1)}(x, 2) > u_2^{v(1)}(y, 1) > u_2^{v(1)}(z, 1)$$

$$\forall i \in \{1, 2\}, \forall k \in N \setminus \{1, 2\}: u_i^{v(1)}(x, k) = u_i^{v(1)}(y, k) = u_i^{v(1)}(z, k) > \max\{u_1^{v(1)}(x, 1), u_2^{v(1)}(y, 2)\}$$

and

$$\forall k \in N \setminus \{1, 2\}: u_k^{v(1)}(x, 1) = u_k^{v(1)}(y, 2) > u_k^{v(1)}(y, 1) = u_k^{v(1)}(z, 2) > u_k^{v(1)}(z, 1) = u_k^{v(1)}(x, 2) = u_k^{v(1)}(x, k) = u_k^{v(1)}(y, k) = u_k^{v(1)}(z, k)$$

Note that we have

$$\omega_R(u_1^{v(1)}) \cap (S_1 \times S_1) = R_2^{v(1)} \cap (S_1 \times S_1)$$

$$\omega_R(u_2^{v(1)}) \cap (S_1 \times S_1) = R_1^{v(1)} \cap (S_1 \times S_1)$$

and

$$\forall k \in N \setminus \{1,2\}: \omega_R(u_k^{v(1)}) \cap (S_1 \times S_1) = \Delta(S_1) \cup \{(y,x),(x,z),(y,z)\}$$

where $S_1 = \{x, y, z\}$ and $\Delta(S_1) = \{(x,x),(y,y),(z,z)\}$. Consider $C^{v(1)}(S_1)$, where $C^{v(1)} = \Phi(v(1))$. We obtain

$$(x,y) \in D_1 \cap P(R_1^{v(1)}) \ \& \ (y,x) \notin \bigcap_{j \in N \setminus \{1\}} P(\omega_R(u_j^{v(1)})) \rightarrow y \notin C^{v(1)}(S_1)$$

$$(z,x) \in D_2 \cap P(R_2^{v(1)}) \ \& \ (x,z) \notin \bigcap_{j \in N \setminus \{2\}} P(\omega_R(u_j^{v(1)})) \rightarrow x \notin C^{v(1)}(S_1)$$

and

$$(y,z) \in P(R_1^{v(1)}) \cap P(R_2^{v(1)}) \cap \left[\bigcap_{j \in N \setminus \{1,2\}} R_j^{v(1)} \right] \rightarrow z \notin C^{v(1)}(S_1)$$

so that $C^{v(1)}(S_1) = \varnothing$, a contradiction.

Case 2: $\{x, y\} \cap \{z, w\} = \varnothing$

Consider a generalized profile $v(2) = (u_1^{v(2)}, u_2^{v(2)}, \ldots, u_n^{v(2)}) \in \mathscr{U}_{ID}$ such that

$$u_1^{v(2)}(z,1) > u_1^{v(2)}(x,1) > u_1^{v(2)}(y,1) > u_1^{v(2)}(w,1) > u_1^{v(2)}(y,2) > u_1^{v(2)}(w,2) > u_1^{v(2)}(z,2) > u_1^{v(2)}(x,2)$$

$$u_2^{v(2)}(y,2) > u_2^{v(2)}(w,2) > u_2^{v(2)}(z,2) > u_2^{v(2)}(x,2) > u_2^{v(2)}(z,1) > u_2^{v(2)}(x,1) > u_2^{v(2)}(y,1) > u_2^{v(2)}(w,1)$$

$$\forall i \in \{1,2\}, \forall k \in N \setminus \{1,2\}: u_i^{v(2)}(x,k) = u_i^{v(2)}(y,k) = u_i^{v(2)}(z,k) = u_i^{v(2)}(w,k) > \max\{u_1^{v(2)}(z,1), u_2^{v(2)}(y,2)\}$$

and

$$\begin{aligned}\forall k \in N \setminus \{1,2\}: u_k^{v(2)}&(z,1) \\ &= u_k^{v(2)}(y,2) > u_k^{v(2)}(x,1) \\ &= u_k^{v(2)}(w,2) > u_k^{v(2)}(y,1) \\ &= u_k^{v(2)}(z,2) > u_k^{v(2)}(w,1) \\ &= u_k^{v(2)}(x,2) > u_k^{v(2)}(x,k) \\ &= u_k^{v(2)}(y,k) = u_k^{v(2)}(z,k) = u_k^{v(2)}(w,k)\end{aligned}$$

It then follows that

$$\omega_R(u_1^{v(2)}) \cap (S_2 \times S_2) = R_2^{v(2)} \cap (S_2 \times S_2)$$

$$\omega_R(u_2^{v(2)}) \cap (S_2 \times S_2) = R_1^{v(2)} \cap (S_2 \times S_2)$$

$$\forall k \in N \setminus \{1,2\}: \omega_R(u_k^{v(2)}) \cap (S_2 \times S_2)$$
$$= \Delta(S_2) \cup \{(y,z),(z,y),(y,x),(y,w),(z,x),(z,w),(x,w),(w,x)\}$$

where $S_2 = \{x, y, z, w\}$ and $\Delta(S_2) = \{(x,x),(y,y),(z,z),(w,w)\}$. Let $C^{v(2)} = \Phi(v(2))$, and consider $C^{v(2)}(S_2)$. By virtue of condition SP and condition JCL(3), we obtain

$$(x, y) \in D_1 \cap P(R_1^{v(2)}) \;\&\; (y,x) \notin \bigcap_{j \in N \setminus \{1\}} P(\omega_R(u_j^{v(2)}))$$
$$\rightarrow y \notin C^{v(2)}(S_2)$$

$$(w, z) \in D_2 \cap P(R_2^{v(2)}) \;\&\; (z,w) \notin \bigcap_{j \in N \setminus \{2\}} P(\omega_R(u_j^{v(2)}))$$
$$\rightarrow z \notin C^{v(2)}(S_2)$$

$$(z, x) \in P(R_1^{v(2)}) \cap P(R_2^{v(2)}) \cap \left[\bigcap_{j \in N \setminus \{1,2\}} R_j^{v(2)}\right]$$
$$\rightarrow x \notin C^{v(2)}(S_2)$$

and

$$(y, w) \in P(R_1^{v(2)}) \cap P(R_2^{v(2)}) \cap \left[\bigcap_{j \in N \setminus \{1,2\}} R_j^{v(2)}\right] \rightarrow w \notin C^{v(2)}(S_2)$$

so that $C^{v(2)}(S_2) = \varnothing$, a contradiction. ∎

Putting all the pieces together, we should emphasize the fairly weak nature of Theorem 7.8. Formally speaking, it is a possibility theorem, but it is thickly surrounded by obstacles that defy any attempt to generalize the moral thereof. Notice, however, that the analysis leading to this frail possibility theorem does seem to help us better understand the nature of the Pareto libertarian paradox.

5 Decomposable rights system and libertarian claims

5.1 Reflections on the coherence of the rights system

Back now to our previous conceptual framework in which we base our analysis on the preference orderings on X. Let us have a second look at condition SL. A salient feature of this formulation of the libertarian claim of rights is that, apart from our interpretation, there is nothing in the formal structure thereof that makes the difference between x and y, where $(x, y) \in D_i$ for some $i \in N$, to be individual i's purely personal concern. A reformulation of the libertarian claim of rights due to Gibbard (1974) is of particular importance in this context. In this section we shall examine several problems that come to the fore when we reformulate libertarian rights along his line.

The gist of the Gibbardian libertarian claim is that each individual should be assured of his own way in determining certain "personal" features of the world. In formalizing this intuitive idea, the social state is now construed to be a list of impersonal and personal features of the world. Therefore, let X_0 and X_i $(i \in N)$ be, respectively, the set of all impersonal features of the world and the set of all personal features of individual i. The set of all social states X is now represented by

$$X = X_0 \times X_1 \times \cdots \times X_n$$

It will be assumed that X_0 and X_i $(i \in N)$ are finite sets with at least two elements each.

Several notational conventions will now be introduced. For each $i \in N$ and each $x = (x_0, x_1, \ldots, x_n) \in X$, we denote

$$x_{)i(} = (x_0, x_1, \ldots, x_{i-1}, x_{i+1}, \ldots, x_n)$$

and

$$X_{)i(} = X_0 \times X_1 \times \cdots \times X_{i-1} \times X_{i+1} \times \cdots \times X_n$$

Furthermore, for each $x_i \in X_i$ $(i \in N)$ and each $z = (z_0, z_1, \ldots, z_{i-1}, z_{i+1}, \ldots, z_n) \in X_{)i(}$ $(i \in N)$, we denote

$$(x_i; z) = (z_0, z_1, \ldots, z_{i-1}, x_i, z_{i+1}, \ldots, z_n)$$

Let us now define an n-list of the subsets of $X \times X$, $D' = (D'_1, D'_2, \ldots, D'_n)$, by

$$D'_i = \{(x, y) \in X \times X \mid x_{)i(} = y_{)i(}\} \qquad (i \in N)$$

By definition, $(x, y) \in D'_i$ holds true if and only if x and y can possibly differ only in the specification of individual i's personal feature. In what follows, D' will be referred to as the *Gibbardian* or the *decomposable rights system*.

The first point to be made on the decomposable rights system D' is that it is always incoherent. To make this point crystal clear, let us consider the following example (Gibbard, 1974, p. 389; Sen, 1976, pp. 234–5).

Example 7.4
Ian and John have two options each, green (G) and red (R), for the color of their clothes. Every other features of the world being fixed, there are four

possible social states, (G, G), (G, R), (R, G), and (R, R), where the first index refers to the color of Ian's clothes and the second to that of John's clothes. In this situation, the decomposable rights system $D' = (D'_I, D'_J)$ is such that

$$D'_I = \{((G,G),(R,G)),((R,G),(G,G)),\\ ((G,R),(R,R)),((R,R),(G,R))\}$$

and

$$D'_J = \{((G,G),(G,R)),((G,R),(G,G)),\\ ((R,G),(R,R)),((R,R),(R,G))\}$$

It is clear that D' is incoherent, because we have

$$((G,G),(R,G)) \in D'_I, \qquad ((R,G),(R,R)) \in D'_J$$

$$((R,R),(G,R)) \in D'_I, \qquad ((G,R),(G,G)) \in D'_J$$

Consider now the following profile:

Ian: $(G,G),(R,G),(R,R),(G,R)$

John: $(R,G),(R,R),(G,R),(G,G)$

If we require our rule to realize the decomposable rights system D', then $C = F(R_I, R_J)$ performs on $S = \{(G, G), (G, R), (R, G), (R, R)\}$ as follows:

$$((G,G),(R,G)) \in D'_I \cap P(R_I) \rightarrow (R,G) \notin C(S)$$

$$((R,G),(R,R)) \in D'_J \cap P(R_J) \rightarrow (R,R) \notin C(S)$$

$$((R,R),(G,R)) \in D'_I \cap P(R_I) \rightarrow (G,R) \notin C(S)$$

and

$$((G,R),(G,G)) \in D'_J \cap P(R_J) \rightarrow (G,G) \notin C(S)$$

which implies that $C(S) = \varnothing$. ▮

Let us emphasize that the problem exposed by the incoherence of the decomposable rights system D' is twofold. First, a libertarian claim to the effect that the collective choice rule should realize the decomposable rights system D' turns out to be untenable (given the requirement of unrestricted applicability of the rule) *without invoking the Pareto principle.* In addition, there is a second problem: The resolution schemes we have presented thus far presuppose coherence of the rights system, so that (prima facie, at least) they do not apply to the decomposable rights system. Because the intuitive justification of the decomposable rights system is very appealing, we must somehow cope with this difficulty.

5.2 *Gibbard's resolution scheme revisited*

Gibbard's own resolution scheme, which we discussed briefly in Section 1 of this chapter, does apply to the decomposable rights system, and it is worthwhile to take a closer look at his proposal.

There are three libertarian claims that Gibbard (1974) discussed, the third of which represents his proposed resolution for the Pareto libertarian paradox. The first libertarian claim is a naive claim to the effect that the collective choice rule should realize the decomposable rights system.

Condition GL(1) (Gibbard's first libertarian claim)
For every profile $a = (R_1^a, R_2^a, \ldots, R_n^a) \in A$, every $i \in N$, and every $x, y \in X$, if $(x, y) \in D_i' \cap P(R_i^a)$ holds true, then $[x \in S \rightarrow y \notin C^a(S)]$ must be the case, where $C^a = F(a)$, for all $S \in \mathscr{S}$.

It is unfortunately the case that there exists no rule that satisfies this naive libertarian claim of rights and the unrestricted domain condition. This is the assertion of Gibbard's first impossibility theorem (Gibbard, 1974, Theorem 1), the essence of which was captured by Example 7.4.

Before turning to Gibbard's second libertarian claim, it will be useful to formulate two versions of the Pareto principle.

Condition EP (exclusion Pareto principle)
For every profile $a = (R_1^a, R_2^a, \ldots, R_n^a) \in A$ and every $x, y \in X$, if $(x, y) \in \bigcap_{i \in N} P(R_i^a)$ holds true, then $[x \in S \rightarrow y \notin C^a(S)]$ is the case, where $C^a = F(a)$, for all $S \in \mathscr{S}$.

Condition IP (inclusion Pareto principle)
For every profile $a = (R_1^a, R_2^a, \ldots, R_n^a) \in A$ and every $x, y \in X$, if $(x, y) \in \bigcap_{i \in N} P(R_i^a)$ holds true, then $[\{x \in S \ \& \ y \in C^a(S)\} \rightarrow x \in C^a(S)]$ is the case, where $C^a = F(a)$, for all $S \in \mathscr{S}$.

To interpret these conditions, suppose that everyone in the society strictly prefers x to y. Then condition EP requires that the rule prohibit y to be chosen from every environment where x is available, and condition IP requires that the rule be such that x is chosen from every environment where x is available and y is chosen. It is clear that condition EP, which is nothing other than our old friend condition P, is a stronger requirement on a rule than is condition IP.[10]

Gibbard's second libertarian claim reads as follows.

Condition GL(2) (Gibbard's second libertarian claim)
For every profile $a = (R_1^a, R_2^a, \ldots, R_n^a) \in A$, every $i \in N$, and every $x, y \in X$, if $(x, y) \in D_i' \cap P(R_i^a)$ and $((x_i; z), (y_i; z)) \in P(R_i^a)$ for all $z \in X_{)i(}$ hold true, then $[x \in S \rightarrow y \notin C^a(S)]$ is the case, where $C^a = F(a)$, for all $S \in \mathscr{S}$.

In condition GL(1) it is required that the collective choice rule allow each and every individual to exercise his endowed right $(x, y) \in D'_i$ whenever he happens to prefer x to y. In contrast, condition GL(2) does not necessarily allow individuals' de facto preferences to rule the roost. It is required in condition GL(2) that the rule protect the right $(x, y) \in D'_i$ only when the ith individual prefers the distinguishing feature x_i of x unconditionally to the corresponding feature y_i of y. Clearly, condition GL(2) represents a milder libertarian claim than condition GL(1). Nevertheless, there exists no collective choice rule that satisfies condition U, condition EP, and condition GL(2), which is the second impossibility theorem due to Gibbard (1974, Theorem 2). The following theorem (Suzumura, 1980*b*, Theorem 1) is a slight generalization thereof.

Theorem 7.11
There exists no collective choice rule that satisfies the unrestricted domain (U), the inclusion Pareto condition (IP), and Gibbard's second libertarian claim [GL(2)].

Proof: Suppose that there exists a rule satisfying all the nominated conditions. Take any $x_0^* \in X_0$ and $x_i^* \in X_i$ $(i \in N \setminus \{1,2\})$ and fix them throughout this proof. Take $x_i, x'_i \in X_i$ $(x_i \neq x'_i)$ for $i = 1,2$, and define

$$x^1 = (x_0^*, x_1, x_2, x_3^*, \ldots, x_n^*)$$

$$x^2 = (x_0^*, x_1, x'_2, x_3^*, \ldots, x_n^*)$$

$$x^3 = (x_0^*, x'_1, x_2, x_3^*, \ldots, x_n^*)$$

and

$$x^4 = (x_0^*, x'_1, x'_2, x_3^*, \ldots, x_n^*)$$

Let $S = \{x^1, x^2, x^3, x^4\} \in \mathscr{S}$, and consider a profile $a = (R_1^a, R_2^a, \ldots, R_n^a) \in A$ that satisfies

$R_1^a(S)$: x^1, x^3, x^2, x^4

$R_2^a(S)$: x^4, x^3, x^2, x^1

and, for all $i \in N \setminus \{1,2\}$,

$R_i^a(\{x^2, x^3\})$: x^3, x^2

Clearly, $(x^1, x^3) \in D'_1$, $(x^2, x^4) \in D'_1$, and $(x^2, x^1) \in D'_2$ hold true, and individual 1 prefers x_1 to x'_1 unconditionally, and individual 2 prefers x'_2 to x_2 unconditionally. Therefore, condition GL(2) implies $x^3 \notin C^a(S)$, $x^4 \notin C^a(S)$, and $x^1 \notin C^a(S)$, where $C^a = F(a)$. Suppose now that $x^2 \in C^a(S)$ holds true. Then we have $(x^3, x^2) \in \bigcap_{i \in N} P(R_i^a)$,

$x^3 \in S$, and $x^2 \in C^a(S)$, so that condition IP requires that $x^3 \in C^a(S)$, which contradicts $x^3 \notin C^a(S)$. Therefore, we must have $x^2 \notin C^a(S)$, so that $C^a(S) = \emptyset$, a contradiction. ∎

A salient common feature of conditions GL(1) and GL(2) deserves particular attention. It is supposed that the ith individual's right is exercised in complete neglect of repercussion from the rest of society, guided solely by the individual rational calculus. From this point of view, the gist of the Gibbardian impossibility theorems mentioned thus far can be interpreted as failure of isolated rational rights-exercising.

An ingenious proposal that is crystallized in Gibbard's third libertarian claim is to make the individual's libertarian rights alienable in cases where the exercise of his libertarian rights brings him into a situation he likes no better than what would otherwise have been brought about. At the risk of slight overlapping with Section 1.7 of this chapter, let us reiterate Gibbard's reasoning, which goes as follows. Given a profile $a = (R_1^a, R_2^a, \ldots, R_n^a) \in A$ and an environment $S \in \mathscr{S}$, the individual has the will as well as the right to exclude y from $C^a(S)$, where $C^a = F(a)$, if $x \in S$ and $(x, y) \in D_i' \cap P(R_i^a)$ hold true, but his right for the pair (x, y) had better be waived if there exists a sequence $\{y_1, y_2, \ldots, y_\lambda\}$ in S such that

$$y_\lambda = x, (y, y_1) \in R_i^a \;\&\; y \neq y_1 \tag{7.40}$$

and

$$(\forall t \in \{1, 2, \ldots, \lambda - 1\}):$$

$$(y_t, y_{t+1}) \in \left(\bigcap_{j \in N} P(R_j^a) \right) \cup \left(\bigcup_{j \in N \setminus \{i\}} [D_j' \cap P(R_j^a)] \right) \tag{7.41}$$

hold true.

Let us define a subset $W_i(a|S)$ of D_i', to be called the *waiver set*, by $(x, y) \in W_i(a|S)$ if and only if (7.40) and (7.41) hold true for some sequence $\{y_\mu\}_{\mu=1}^{\lambda}$ in S. We are now ready to introduce Gibbard's third libertarian claim.

Condition GL(3) (Gibbard's third libertarian claim)
For every profile $a = (R_1^a, R_2^a, \ldots, R_n^a) \in A$, every $S \in \mathscr{S}$, every $i \in N$, and every $x, y \in X$, if $(x, y) \in D_i' \cap P(R_i^a)$ and $(x, y) \notin W_i(a|S)$ hold true, then $[x \in S \rightarrow y \notin C^a(S)]$ is true, where $C^a = F(a)$.

Clearly, GL(3) is a libertarian claim that differs essentially from GL(1) as well as from GL(2). It is explicitly recognized in GL(3) that an individual's rights-exercising can induce unfavorable responses by others that may well nullify the benefit that motivated the initial exercising. Gibbard has shown that condition GL(3) represents a Pareto-consistent libertarian claim; that is, there exists a collective choice rule that satisfies the unrestricted domain, condition EP, and condition GL(3) (Gibbard, 1974, Theorem 4).

Attractive though Gibbard's proposed libertarian claim and the resolution of the Pareto libertarian paradox based thereupon, it should be instructive to call the reader's attention to the subtlety of Gibbard's success. The best way to explain it is to examine Kelly's alleged "flaws" (1976*b*; 1978, Chapter 9) in Gibbard's definition of a rights-waiving rule and his revised libertarian claims.[11]

Let us begin with Kelly's first proposed revision. For any profile $a = (R_1^a, R_2^a, \ldots, R_n^a) \in A$ and any set $S \in \mathscr{S}$ of available states, an individual $i \in N$ is said to waive his right for $(x, y) \in D_i'$; that is, $(x, y) \in W_i^*(a|S)$ holds true if and only if there exists a sequence $\{y_1, y_2, \ldots, y_\lambda\}$ in S such that

$$y_\lambda = x \;\&\; (y, y_1) \in P(R_i^a) \tag{7.42}$$

and (7.41) hold true. Then the first revised libertarian claim reads as follows.

Condition KL(1) (Kelly's first libertarian claim)
For every profile $a = (R_1^a, R_2^a, \ldots, R_n^a) \in A$, every $S \in \mathscr{S}$, every $i \in N$, and every $x, y \in X$, if $(x, y) \in D_i' \cap P(R_i^a)$ and $(x, y) \notin W_i^*(a|S)$ hold true, then $[x \in S \rightarrow y \notin C^a(S)]$ is implied, where $C^a = F(a)$.

Clearly, the only difference between condition GL(3) and condition KL(1) lies in the contrast between (7.40) and (7.42). Kelly's motivation behind this revision is that "in forcing the move from y to x by exercising $[(x, y) \in D_i'$, individual $i]$ does not seem to have gotten into trouble if he is forced in the end to take a y_1 where he is indifferent between y_1 and y. Waiving might be appropriate for a cautious exerciser if $[(y, y_1) \in P(R_i^a)]$ for some [sequence $\{y_1, y_2, \ldots, y_\lambda\}$], but not if only $[(y, y_1) \in R_i^a$ as in (7.40)]" (Kelly, 1976*b*, p. 14; 1978, pp. 146–7).

Going one step further, Kelly proposes his second revised libertarian claim. Suppose that a profile $a = (R_1^a, R_2^a, \ldots, R_n^a) \in A$ and a set $S \in \mathscr{S}$ of available states are given. This time, individual $i \in N$ is supposed to waive his right for $(x, y) \in D_i'$; that is, $(x, y) \in W_i^{**}(a|S)$ holds true if and only if the following two conditions are satisfied:

(a) There exists a sequence $\{y_1, y_2, \ldots, y_\lambda\}$ in S such that

$$y_\lambda = x \;\&\; (y, y_1) \in P(R_i^a) \tag{7.43}$$

and

$$\forall t \in \{1, 2, \ldots, \lambda - 1\}:$$

$$(y_t, y_{t+1}) \in \left(\bigcap_{j \in N} P(R_j^a)\right) \cup \left(\bigcup_{j \in N \setminus \{i\}} [D_j' \cap P(R_j^a)]\right) \tag{7.44}$$

(b) For every sequence $\{z_1, z_2, \ldots, z_{\lambda^*}\}$ in S such that

$$z_{\lambda^*} = y_1 \ \& \ (z_1, y) \in P(R_i^a) \tag{7.45}$$

and

$$\forall t \in \{1, 2, \ldots, \lambda^* - 1\}:$$

$$(z_t, z_{t+1}) \in \left(\bigcap_{j \in N} P(R_j^a) \right) \cup \left(\bigcup_{j \in N} [D'_j \cap P(R_j^a)] \right) \tag{7.46}$$

there exists a sequence $\{w_1, w_2, \ldots, w_{\lambda^{**}}\}$ in S such that

$$w_{\lambda^{**}} = z_1 \ \& \ (y, w_1) \in P(R_i^a) \tag{7.47}$$

and

$$\forall t \in \{1, 2, \ldots, \lambda^{**} - 1\}:$$

$$(w_t, w_{t+1}) \in \left(\bigcap_{j \in N} P(R_j^a) \right) \cup \left(\bigcup_{j \in N \setminus \{i\}} [D'_j \cap P(R_j^a)] \right) \tag{7.48}$$

The second revised libertarian claim now reads as follows.

Condition KL(2) (Kelly's second libertarian claim)
For every profile $a = (R_1^a, R_2^a, \ldots, R_n^a) \in A$, every set $S \in \mathscr{S}$ of available states, every $i \in N$, and every $x, y \in X$, if $(x, y) \in D'_i \cap P(R_i^a)$ and $(x, y) \notin W_i^{**}(a|S)$ hold true, then $[x \in S \rightarrow y \notin C^a(S)]$ is implied, where $C^a = F(a)$.

An obvious difference between condition KL(1) and condition KL(2) is that condition (b) is added in the definition of $W_i^{**}(a|S)$, which requires that any sequence $\{z_1, z_2, \ldots, z_{\lambda^*}\}$ that seems to repair in the eyes of individual i the damage caused to him by a sequence $\{y_1, y_2, \ldots, y_\lambda\}$ will be made ineffective by some other sequence $\{w_1, w_2, \ldots, w_{\lambda^{**}}\}$ that is not under i's control.

Taken by themselves, these proposed revisions may seem to be fairly persuasive, and Kelly (1976*b*, p. 144; 1978, p. 148) asserts that "[they cause] no significant changes in the theorems that make up Gibbard's libertarian claim." However, the truth is that Kelly's reasonable-looking revisions to Gibbard's libertarian claim change it into standards for individual liberty that cannot possibly be met. Indeed, we can prove the following impossibility theorems.

Theorem 7.12
There exists no collective choice rule that satisfies the unrestricted domain (U) and Kelly's first libertarian claim [KL(1)] (Suzumura, 1980*b*, Theorem 2).

Theorem 7.13
There exists no collective choice rule that satisfies the unrestricted domain (U) and Kelly's second libertarian claim [KL(2)] (Suzumura, 1980*b*, Theorem 3).

To prove these theorems, note first that for every profile $a = (R_1^a, R_2^a, \ldots, R_n^a) \in A$ and every $S \in \mathscr{S}$, the following set-theoretic inclusions are true:

$$\forall i \in N: W_i^{**}(a|S) \subset W_i^{*}(a|S) \subset W_i(a|S) \tag{7.49}$$

Clearly, then, condition KL(2) is a stronger libertarian claim than condition KL(1), so that we have only to prove Theorem 7.12, Theorem 7.13 being a corollary thereof.

Proof of Theorem 7.12: Suppose that F is a collective choice rule that satisfies condition KL(1) and condition U. Let $S = \{x^1, x^2, x^3, x^4\}$ be defined as in the proof of Theorem 7.11, and let a profile $a = (R_1^a, R_2^a, \ldots, R_n^a) \in A$ be such that

$R_1^a(S)$: $x^1, x^4, [x^2, x^3]$

$R_2^a(S)$: $x^3, x^2, [x^1, x^4]$

We impose no restriction on R_i^a for $i \in N \setminus \{1,2\}$ whatsoever. Clearly, $(x^1, x^3) \in D_1'$, $(x^4, x^2) \in D_1'$, $(x^3, x^4) \in D_2'$, and $(x^2, x^1) \in D_2'$ hold true. No other individual has rights over these pairs of states. Consider $(x^1, x^3) \in D_1' \cap P(R_1^a)$. The worst that can happen to individual 1 after his exercise of $(x^1, x^3) \in D_1'$ is the counterexercise by individual 2 of $(x^2, x^1) \in D_2'$, in view of $(x^2, x^1) \in P(R_2^a)$. Note that there is no state in S that strictly dominates x^1 in the sense of Pareto. Because x^2 and x^3 are indifferent to individual 1 and $x^2 \neq x^3$, condition GL(3) will let individual 1 waive his right over (x^1, x^3), but condition KL(1) does allow individual 1 to exercise his right over (x^1, x^3): $(x^1, x^3) \in W_1(a|S) \setminus W_1^*(a|S)$. Similar reasoning leads us to $(x^4, x^2) \in W_1(a|S) \setminus W_1^*(a|S)$, $(x^3, x^4) \in W_2(a|S) \setminus W_2^*(a|S)$, and $(x^2, x^1) \in W_2(a|S) \setminus W_2^*(a|S)$. By virtue of condition KL(1), it then follows that $C^a(S) = \varnothing$, a contradiction. ▮

Kelly's first revised libertarian claim thus brings back an impossibility. A fortiori, his second (and stronger) revised libertarian claim is inconsistent with the existence of a universally applicable collective choice rule. One may thereby be tempted to conclude that the system of alienable rights is something like fragile glasswork that is in danger of being smashed to pieces while one is giving it its finishing touch. To be fair, however, one should examine whether or not the finishing touch is an appropriate one.

Back, then, to the contrast between condition GL(3) and condition KL(1), that is, the contrast between (7.40) and (7.42). According to Kelly, stipulation (7.42) is recommended in place of (7.40) because, in forcing the move from y to x by exercising $(x, y) \in D_i'$, individual i does not lose anything even if he is forced in the end to take a y_1 such that $(y, y_1) \in I(R_i^a)$ and $y \neq y_1$. Note, however, that he does not gain anything either. Note also that the rights-exercising in Gibbard's system places heavy demands on the gathering and processing of information (Kelly, 1976*b*, p. 141; 1978, p. 146), so that rights-exercising will be unwise unless it will yield a positive gain. This argument, if accepted, would favor (7.40) rather than (7.42), and it would necessitate the following modification of condition KL(2). Given a profile $a = (R_1^a, R_2^a, \ldots, R_n^a) \in A$ and a set $S \in \mathscr{S}$ of available states, let the waiver set $W_i^0(a|S)$ be defined by $(x, y) \in W_i^0(a|S)$ if and only if the following two conditions are satisfied:

(a) There exists a sequence $\{y_1, y_2, \ldots, y_\lambda\}$ in S such that

$$y_\lambda = x, (y, y_1) \in R_i^a \;\&\; y \neq y_1 \tag{7.50}$$

and

$$\forall t \in \{1, 2, \ldots, \lambda - 1\}:$$

$$(y_t, y_{t+1}) \in \left(\bigcap_{j \in N} P(R_j^a) \right) \cup \left(\bigcup_{j \in N \setminus \{i\}} [D_j' \cap P(R_j^a)] \right) \tag{7.51}$$

(b) For any sequence $\{z_1, z_2, \ldots, z_{\lambda^*}\}$ in S such that

$$z_{\lambda^*} = y_1 \;\&\; [(z_1, y) \in P(R_i^a) \vee z_1 = y] \tag{7.52}$$

and

$$\forall t \in \{1, 2, \ldots, \lambda^* - 1\}:$$

$$(z_t, z_{t+1}) \in \left(\bigcap_{j \in N} P(R_j^a) \right) \cup \left(\bigcup_{j \in N} [D_j' \cap P(R_j^a)] \right) \tag{7.53}$$

there exists a sequence $\{w_1, w_2, \ldots, w_{\lambda^{**}}\}$ in S such that

$$w_{\lambda^{**}} = z_1, (y, w_1) \in R_i^a \;\&\; y \neq w_1 \tag{7.54}$$

and

$$\forall t \in \{1, 2, \ldots, \lambda^{**} - 1\}:$$

$$(w_t, w_{t+1}) \in \left(\bigcap_{j \in N} P(R_j^a) \right) \cup \left(\bigcup_{j \in N \setminus \{i\}} [D_j' \cap P(R_j^a)] \right) \tag{7.55}$$

We can now put forward the following libertarian claim of rights.

Condition GKL(1) (Gibbard–Kelly first libertarian claim)
For every profile $a = (R_1^a, R_2^a, \ldots, R_n^a) \in A$, every set $S \in \mathscr{S}$ of available states, every $i \in N$, and every $x, y \in X$, if $(x, y) \in D_i' \cap P(R_i^a)$ and $(x, y) \notin W_i^0(a|S)$ hold true, then $[x \in S \rightarrow y \notin C^a(S)]$ is implied, where $C^a = F(a)$.

How does condition GKL(1) fare in the context of a universal collective choice rule? That it fares no better than condition KL(1) and condition KL(2) is the verdict of the following theorem (Suzumura, 1980*b*, Theorem 4).

Theorem 7.14
There exists no collective choice rule that satisfies the unrestricted domain (U) and the Gibbard–Kelly first libertarian claim [GKL(1)].

Proof: Suppose that there exists a collective choice rule F that satisfies condition U and condition GKL(1). Let $S = \{x^1, x^2, x^3, x^4\} \in \mathscr{S}$ and $a = (R_1^a, R_2^a, \ldots, R_n^a) \in A$ be the same as in the proof of Theorem 7.10. Consider $(x^1, x^3) \in D_1' \cap P(R_1^a)$. The worst situation that individual 1's exercise of $(x^1, x^3) \in D_1'$ can induce is the counterexercise by individual 2 of $(x^2, x^1) \in D_2'$, in view of $(x^2, x^1) \in P(R_2^a)$. Individual 1 can then exercise $(x^4, x^2) \in D_1' \cap P(R_1^a)$ to secure x^4, which he prefers to x^3. Is there any nullifying sequence? The worst that could happen to individual 1 is the exercise by individual 2 of $(x^3, x^4) \in D_2'$, which does not require individual 1 to waive his right $(x^1, x^3) \in D_1'$, according to the definition of $W_1^0(a|S)$.[12] Therefore, condition GKL(1) ensures that $x^3 \notin C^a(S)$. By the same token, we can verify that

$$[(x^4, x^2) \in D_1' \cap P(R_1^a) \ \& \ (x^4, x^2) \notin W_1^0(a|S)] \rightarrow x^2 \notin C^a(S)$$

$$[(x^2, x^1) \in D_2' \cap P(R_2^a) \ \& \ (x^2, x^1) \notin W_2^0(a|S)] \rightarrow x^1 \notin C^a(S)$$

and

$$[(x^3, x^4) \in D_2' \cap P(R_2^a) \ \& \ (x^3, x^4) \notin W_2^0(a|S)] \rightarrow x^4 \notin C^a(S)$$

so that we obtain $C^a(S) = \varnothing$, a contradiction. ∎

If we examine the profile that we used in proving Theorem 7.12, Theorem 7.13, and Theorem 7.14, it turns out that both individuals 1 and 2 are expressing preferences that are conditional on the other's selection of his personal features: Individual 1 prefers x_1 to x_1' if individual 2 has x_2, whereas he prefers x_1' to x_1 if individual 2's choice is x_2', and vice versa. Presumably it is too much to ask for the existence of a universal collective choice rule that protects the individual's mere conditional preferences. On reflection, we can only require the existence of a rule that protects the individual's libertarian rights so far as the relevant individual expresses unconditional preference for his personal features.

Let us now define a subset $N(a|S)$ of N, given a profile $a = (R_1^a, R_2^a, \ldots, R_n^a) \in A$ and a set $S \in \mathscr{S}$ of available states, as a set of individuals who have unconditional preferences; that is $i \in N(a|S)$ holds true if and only if

$$(x, y) \in D_i' \cap (S \times S) \cap P(R_i^a) \tag{7.56}$$

always implies that

$$\forall z_{)i(} \in X_{)i(}: (x_i; z_{)i(}), (y_i; z_{)i(}) \in S \to ((x_i; z_{)i(}), (y_i; z_{)i(})) \in P(R_i^a) \tag{7.57}$$

holds true.

We can then define a new waiver set $W_i^{oo}(a|S)$ by $(x, y) \in W_i^{oo}(a|S)$ if and only if either $i \in N \setminus N(a|S)$ or the following two conditions hold true:

(a) There exists a sequence $\{y_1, y_2, \ldots, y_\lambda\}$ in S such that

$$y_\lambda = x, (y, y_1) \in R_i^a \ \& \ y \neq y_1$$

and

$$\forall t \in \{1, 2, \ldots, \lambda - 1\}:$$

$$(y_t, y_{t+1}) \in \left(\bigcap_{j \in N} P(R_j^a) \right) \cup \left(\bigcup_{j \in N(a|S) \setminus \{i\}} [D_j' \cap P(R_j^a)] \right)$$

(b) For any sequence $\{z_1, z_2, \ldots, z_{\lambda^*}\}$ in S such that

$$z_{\lambda^*} = y_1 \ \& \ [(z_1, y) \in P(R_i^a) \vee z_1 = y]$$

and

$$\forall t \in \{1, 2, \ldots, \lambda^* - 1\}:$$

$$(z_t, z_{t+1}) \in \left(\bigcap_{j \in N} P(R_j^a) \right) \cup \left(\bigcup_{j \in N(a|S)} [D_j' \cap P(R_j^a)] \right)$$

there exists a sequence $\{w_1, w_2, \ldots, w_{\lambda^{**}}\}$ in S such that

$$w_{\lambda^{**}} = z_1, (y, w_1) \in R_i^a \ \& \ y \neq w_1$$

and

$$\forall t \in \{1, 2, \ldots, \lambda^{**} - 1\}:$$

$$(w_t, w_{t+1}) \in \left(\bigcap_{j \in N} P(R_j^a) \right) \cup \left(\bigcup_{j \in N(a|S) \setminus \{i\}} [D_j' \cap P(R_j^a)] \right)$$

We are now ready to formulate the final version of the libertarian claim in the spirit of Gibbard and Kelly.

Condition GKL(2) (Gibbard–Kelly second libertarian claim)
For every profile $a = (R_1^a, R_2^a, \dots, R_n^a) \in A$, every set $S \in \mathscr{S}$ of available states, every $i \in N$, and every $x, y \in X$, if $(x, y) \in D_i' \cap P(R_i^a)$ and $(x, y) \notin W_i^{00}(a|S)$ hold true, then $[x \in S \to y \notin C^a(S)]$ is implied, where $C^a = F(a)$.

Clearly, condition GKL(2) is weaker than condition GKL(1). Unfortunately, this modest version of the libertarian claim still cannot break the impasse, as we show in the following theorem.

Theorem 7.15
There exists no collective choice rule that satisfies the unrestricted domain (U), the inclusion Pareto condition (IP), and the Gibbard–Kelly second libertarian claim [GKL(2)].

Proof: Suppose that there exists a collective choice rule F that satisfies all the nominated conditions. Take any $x_i^* \in X_i$ ($i \in N \setminus \{1,2\}$) and fix them throughout the rest of this proof. Take $x_i, x_i' \in X_i$ ($x_i \neq x_i'$) for $i \in \{0, 1, 2\}$, and define

$$x^0 = (x_0, x_1, x_2', x_3^*, \dots, x_n^*)$$

$$x^1 = (x_0, x_1, x_2, x_3^*, \dots, x_n^*)$$

$$x^2 = (x_0', x_1, x_2, x_3^*, \dots, x_n^*)$$

$$x^3 = (x_0, x_1', x_2, x_3^*, \dots, x_n^*)$$

and

$$x^4 = (x_0', x_1', x_2, x_3^*, \dots, x_n^*)$$

Let $S = \{x^0, x^1, x^2, x^3, x^4\} \in \mathscr{S}$, and let a profile $a = (R_1^a, R_2^a, \dots, R_n^a) \in A$ be such that

$R_1^a(S)$: x^1, x^3, x^2, x^4, x^0

$R_2^a(S)$: x^3, x^2, x^0, x^4, x^1

and, for all $i \in N \setminus \{1, 2\}$,

$R_i^a(\{x^0, x^2, x^3\})$: x^3, x^2, x^0

By definition, we have $(x^1, x^3) \in D_1'$, $(x^2, x^4) \in D_1'$, and $(x^0, x^1) \in D_2'$. It is easy to see that individual 1 prefers x_1 to x_1' unconditionally, and individual 2 prefers x_2' to x_2 unconditionally.

Note that the worst contingency that can be induced by the exercise of $(x^1, x^3) \in D'_1$ is the counterexercise of $(x^0, x^1) \in D'_2$ by individual 2. Because $(x^3, x^0) \in \bigcap_{i \in N} P(R_i^a)$ holds true and there exists no nullifying sequence in S, we obtain $(x^1, x^3) \notin W_1^{00}(a|S)$. It then follows that

$$[(x^1, x^3) \in D'_1 \cap P(R_1^a) \ \&\ (x^1, x^3) \notin W_1^{00}(a|S)] \rightarrow x^3 \notin C^a(S)$$

where $C^a = F(a)$. We can similarly verify that

$$[(x^2, x^4) \in D'_1 \cap P(R_1^a) \ \&\ (x^2, x^4) \notin W_1^{00}(a|S)] \rightarrow x^4 \notin C^a(S)$$

and

$$[(x^0, x^1) \in D'_2 \cap P(R_2^a) \ \&\ (x^0, x^1) \notin W_2^{00}(a|S)] \rightarrow x^1 \notin C^a(S)$$

hold true.

Finally, we invoke condition IP. Suppose that $x^2 \in C^a(S)$ is true. Then $(x^3, x^2) \in \bigcap_{i \in N} P(R_i^a)$, $x^3 \in S$, and $x^2 \in C^a(S)$ yield $x^3 \in C^a(S)$ by virtue of condition IP, a contradiction. Therefore, $x^2 \notin C^a(S)$ is true. Suppose now that $x^0 \in C^a(S)$. Then $(x^2, x^0) \in \bigcap_{i \in N} P(R_i^a)$, $x^2 \in S$, and $x^0 \in C^a(S)$ must imply $x^2 \in C^a(S)$, which is a contradiction again. Therefore, we must admit that $x^0 \notin C^a(S)$, so that $C^a(S) = \varnothing$, a contradiction. ∎

5.3 *Possibility theorems in the presence of the decomposable rights system*

Stocktaking may be in order before we proceed. Our resolution schemes discussed in Sections 2 and 4 of this chapter are based on the coherence of the rights system and, as such, appear to be inapplicable to the decomposable rights system. Gibbard's alienable rights system does apply to the decomposable rights system, but it is surrounded by several negative results that crop up when we slightly modify Gibbard's system along the line suggested by Kelly (1976*b*; 1978, Chapter 9). Indeed, Gibbard's system of alienable rights in the revised version proposed by Kelly represents a standard for individual liberty that cannot be met by any universal collective choice rule, as we have shown. How, then, should we proceed with the decomposable rights system?

In what follows, we should like to show that our resolution schemes can be adapted in such a way as to be applicable to the decomposable rights system, even if they were originally constructed on the assumption of coherence of the rights system. The essential point of this modification is to make the individual's libertarian rights contingent on his unconditional preference for his personal feature alternatives, just as in condition GL(2).

Let us begin with our first resolution scheme, as introduced in Section 2. For any profile $a = (R_1^a, R_2^a, \ldots, R_n^a) \in A$ and any $i \in N$, we define a relation $\bar{Q}_i^a$ by

$$\bar{Q}_i^a = \{(x, y) \in D_i' | \forall z \in X_{)i(}: ((x_i; z), (y_i; z)) \in P(R_i^a)\} \tag{7.58}$$

In words, $(x, y) \in \bar{Q}_i^a$ holds true if and only if x and y differ only in the personal feature of individual i and individual i prefers the distinguishing feature x_i of x unconditionally to the corresponding feature y_i of y. Let $\bar{Q}^a$ be defined by

$$\bar{Q}^a = \bigcup_{i \in N} \bar{Q}_i^a \tag{7.59}$$

Lemma 7.1
For every profile $a = (R_1^a, R_2^a, \ldots, R_n^a) \in A$, $\bar{Q}^a$ is a coherent binary relation on X.

Proof: Suppose, to the contrary, that there exist $a = (R_1^a, R_2^a, \ldots, R_n^a) \in A$ and $\{x^1, x^2, \ldots, x^t\} \in \mathscr{S}$ such that $(x^1, x^2) \in P(\bar{Q}^a)$, $(x^\mu, x^{\mu+1}) \in \bar{Q}^a$ for all $\mu \in \{2, 3, \ldots, t-1\}$, and $(x^t, x^1) \in \bar{Q}^a$ hold true. By construction of $\bar{Q}^a$, there exists an $i \in N$ such that

$$(x^1, x^2) \in D_i' \tag{7.60}$$

and

$$\forall z \in X_{)i(}: ((x_i^1; z), (x_i^2; z)) \in P(R_i^a) \tag{7.61}$$

are satisfied. Corresponding to a sequence $\{x^\mu\}_{\mu=1}^t$, we now define a sequence $\{x_*^\mu\}_{\mu=1}^t$ by

$$\forall \mu \in \{1, 2, \ldots, t\}: x_*^\mu = (x_i^\mu; x_{)i(}^1) \tag{7.62}$$

By virtue of (7.61), we obtain

$$(x_*^1, x_*^2) \in P(R_i^a) \tag{7.63}$$

We show that

$$\forall \mu \in \{2, 3, \ldots, t-1\}: (x_*^\mu, x_*^{\mu+1}) \in R_i^a \;\&\; (x_*^t, x_*^1) \in R_i^a \tag{7.64}$$

holds true. Take any $\mu \in \{2, 3, \ldots, t-1\}$. Because $(x^\mu, x^{\mu+1}) \in \bar{Q}^a$ is the case, if $x_{)i(}^\mu \neq x_{)i(}^{\mu+1}$ is true, then $x_{)j(}^\mu = x_{)j(}^{\mu+1}$ must be the case for some $j \in N \setminus \{i\}$. It is clear that $i \neq j$, so that $x_i^\mu = x_i^{\mu+1}$ is true. By (7.62) we then obtain $x_*^\mu = x_*^{\mu+1}$. On the other hand, if $x_{)i(}^\mu = x_{)i(}^{\mu+1}$ holds true, then

$$\forall z \in X_{)i(}: ((x_i^\mu; z), (x_i^{\mu+1}; z)) \in P(R_i^a) \tag{7.65}$$

holds true. Letting $z = x^1_{)i($ in (7.65), we obtain $(x^{\mu}_{*}, x^{\mu+1}_{*}) \in P(R^a_i)$. We can similarly prove that $(x^t_{*}, x^1_{*}) \in R^a_i$ is true.

Now that (7.64) is true, we can invoke (7.63) to conclude that R^a_i cannot be consistent, a contradiction. ∎

$\bar{Q}^a$ being coherent, there exists an ordering $\bar{R}$ that extends $\bar{Q}^a$ by virtue of Theorem A(5) in the Appendix to Chapter 1. Let $\bar{\mathscr{R}}^a$ denote the set of all ordering extensions of $\bar{Q}^a$. Let us call an individual $j \in N$ to be a *liberal* (*G*) if and only if

$$\exists \bar{R} \in \bar{\mathscr{R}}^a: \bar{R}^{0a}_j = R^a_j \cap \bar{R} \tag{7.66}$$

holds true, where $\bar{R}^{0a}_j$ denotes a transitive subrelation of R^a_j that individual j wants to count in social choice. In words, individual j is a liberal(G) if and only if he claims only those parts of his preferences to count that are compatible with others' unconditional preferences over their personal features.

We are now ready to present the following possibility theorem (Suzumura, 1978, Theorem 2) on the decomposable rights system.

Theorem 7.16
If there exists at least one liberal(G) individual in the society, then there exists a rational collective choice rule satisfying the unrestricted domain (U), Gibbard's second libertarian claim [GL(2)], and the conditional Pareto principle (CP).

Sketch of proof: Let $D' = (D'_1, D'_2, \ldots, D'_n)$ be the decomposable rights system, and take any profile $a = (R^a_1, R^a_2, \ldots, R^a_n) \in A$. Let N'_1 denote the set of all liberal(G) individuals, which is nonempty by assumption. Let

$$\bar{R}^{0a}_i = \begin{cases} \exists \bar{R}^i \in \bar{\mathscr{R}}^a: R^a_i \cap \bar{R}^i & \text{if } i \in N'_1 \\ R^a_i & \text{otherwise} \end{cases} \tag{7.67}$$

and define

$$\bar{R}^a_0 = \{(x, y) \in X \times X \mid (y, x) \notin \bar{P} \cup P(\bar{R}^{0a})\} \tag{7.68}$$

where $\bar{R}^{0a} = \bigcap_{i \in N} \bar{R}^{0a}_i$ and $\bar{P} = \bigcap_{i \in N'_1} P(\bar{R}^i)$. We can easily verify that

$$P(\bar{R}^a_0) = \bar{P} \cup P(\bar{R}^{0a}) \tag{7.69}$$

holds true. Furthermore, $\bar{R}^a_0$ is complete, reflexive, and acyclic. Therefore, a function $\bar{C}^a_0$ on $\mathscr{S}$ that is defined by $\bar{C}^a_0(S) = G(S, \bar{R}^a_0)$ for all $S \in \mathscr{S}$ is a rational choice function on a choice space $(X, \mathscr{S})$.

Associating this $\bar{C}_0^a$ with the profile $a = (R_1^a, R_2^a, \ldots, R_n^a) \in A$, we obtain a rational collective choice rule. That this rule satisfies condition CP can be proved as in the proof of Theorem 7.3.

What remains to be verified is that this rule satisfies condition GL(2). Suppose that there exist $i \in N$, $(x, y) \in D_i'$, and $S \in \mathcal{S}$ such that $x \in S$, $y \in C_0^a(S)$, and $((x_i; z), (y_i; z)) \in P(R_i^a)$ for all $z \in X_{)i(}$. By definition, we then have $(x, y) \in \bar{Q}_i^a \subset \bar{Q}^a$ and $(y, x) \in \bar{R}_0^a$. In view of (7.68), it then follows that $(x, y) \notin \bar{P} \cup P(\bar{R}^{0a})$ holds true. By virtue of the definition of $\bar{\mathscr{R}}^a$, we have $P(\bar{Q}^a) \subset \bigcap_{i \in N_i^*} P(\bar{R}^i) = \bar{P}$, so that if we can show that $(x, y) \in P(\bar{Q}^a)$, we obtain a contradiction, and we are home. Assume, therefore, that $(y, x) \in \bar{Q}^a$, so that $(y, x) \in \bar{Q}_j^a$ holds true for some $j \in N$. If $i = j$ is true, this contradicts the asymmetry of $P(\bar{R}_i^a)$, whereas if $i \neq j$ is the case, this contradicts the way D_i' and D_j' are defined. ▮

To exemplify how this resolution scheme works, let us apply it to a slightly modified version of Example 7.4. Let the decomposable rights system $D' = (D_I', D_J')$ be as before, and consider the following profile:

Ian: $(G, G), (R, G), (G, R), (R, R)$

John: $(R, R), (R, G), (G, R), (G, G)$

That is, Ian prefers G to R unconditionally, and John prefers R to G unconditionally. Corresponding to this rights system and a profile, we obtain

$$\bar{Q}_I = \{((R, R), (R, G)), ((G, R), (R, R))\}$$

and

$$\bar{Q}_J = \{((R, R), (R, G)), ((G, R), (G, G))\}$$

An ordering extension $\bar{R}$ of $Q_I \cup Q_J$ is then given by

$$\bar{R}: (G, R), (R, R), (G, G), (R, G)$$

Suppose that Ian is liberal(G), but John is not, so that

$$\bar{R}_I^0 = \bar{R} \cap R_I = \Delta_X \cup \{((G, R), (R, R)), ((G, G), (R, G))\}$$

where $\Delta_X = \{((G, G), (G, G)), ((G, R), (G, R)), ((R, G), (R, G)), ((R, R), (R, R))\}$ and $\bar{R}_J^0 = \bar{R}_J$, yielding $\bar{R}^0 = \Delta_X$. We then obtain

$$\bar{R}_0 = \Delta_X \cup \{((G, R), (R, R)), ((G, R), (G, G)), ((G, R), (R, G)), ((R, R), (G, G)), ((R, R), (R, G)), ((G, G), (R, G))\}$$

so that

$$G(\{(G,G),(G,R),(R,G),(R,R)\},\bar{R}_0) = \{(G,R)\}$$

Therefore, our solution to this conflict situation is to let people choose whatever color they unconditionally prefer. This conclusion remains intact if it is John rather than Ian who is liberal(G).

Let us now turn to the second resolution scheme, which we discussed in Section 4. To show that it can also be made applicable to the decomposable rights system, take any generalized profile $v = (u_1^v, u_2^v, \ldots, u_n^v) \in \mathscr{U}$ and any $i \in N$, and define $\bar{Q}_i^v$ by

$$\bar{Q}_i^v = \{(x, y) \in D_i' | \forall z \in X_{)i(}: ((x_i; z), (y_i; z)) \in P(R_i^v)\} \quad (7.70)$$

where R_i^v is the subjective preference ordering corresponding to u_i^v. We now modify condition JCL(1) as follows.

*Condition JCL(1**) [justice-constrained libertarian claim (1**)]*
For every admissible generalized profile $v = (u_1^v, u_2^v, \ldots, u_n^v) \in \mathscr{U}$, every $i \in N$, and every $x, y \in X$, if $(x, y) \in \bar{Q}_i^v$ and $(y, x) \notin \bigcup_{j \in N} P(\omega_j(u_j^v))$ hold true, then $[x \in S \rightarrow y \notin C^v(S)]$ is implied, where $C^v = \Phi(v)$, for all $S \in \mathscr{S}$.

We can now assert that Theorem 7.7 and Theorem 7.8 hold true for the decomposable rights system as well, if only we replace condition JCL(1) by condition JCL(1**). The only place where the proof of Theorem 7.7 needs modification is that we should replace Q^v in (7.28) by $\bar{Q}^v = \bigcup_{i \in N} \bar{Q}_i^v$, where $\bar{Q}_i^v$ is defined by (7.70). Therefore, we obtain the following:

Theorem 7.17
There exists a rational generalized collective choice rule on $\mathscr{U}_{ID}$ that satisfies the strong Pareto principle (SP) and the justice-constrained libertarian claim (1**) [JCL(1**)].

6 Concluding remarks

The possible conflict between libertarian claims and democratic values is deep and difficult to resolve. Sen (1970*a*; 1970*b*, Chapter 6*) and Gibbard (1974) have uncovered this conflict in a particularly illuminating way in the framework of social choice theory. It has been shown that unadulterated exercise of individuals' libertarian rights, coupled with mechanical use of the Pareto principle, can disqualify all collective choice rules unless we renounce the general applicability of the rule. The Pareto libertarian paradox can be given a different interpretation with no less regrettable consequences if we use the term "individual" to mean not necessarily a human individual but a social group within a society. The paradox then suggests the impossibility of assigning certain amounts of autonomy over some spheres of decision making to each social group.

In this chapter we have discussed two resolution schemes for these paradoxes. The first scheme is based on the intuitive concept of a liberal individual who agrees that some parts of his preferences should not count in the social choice over others' protected spheres. It has been shown that the existence of such a liberal individual plays a vital role in reconciling the Pareto principle with the minimal amount of personal liberty. The second scheme starts from the idea that the protection of the certain amount of personal liberty is a value to be weighed against many other values, including human equality and social justice, that are also basic in people. We have shown that if the rights-exercising is restricted by impartial justice considerations, the libertarian claims thus constrained turn out to be compatible with the Pareto principle.

There seem to exist some cases in which the conflict in question should be resolved by letting libertarian claims prevail over the Pareto principle. There also seem to exist some other cases in which the appeal to social justice or equality of treatment does make important sense, and it is interesting to see whether or not the appeal to social justice, if systematically pursued, provides us with a workable way out of the Pareto libertarian paradox in such cases. Although these two approaches differ in their informational basis, as well as in the class of situations in which they yield reasonable outcomes, they seem to tell a common general moral to the effect that in order to guarantee a minimal amount of personal liberty or group autonomy, it is necessary that there prevail an individual (or group) attitude of respect and care for one another's equal liberty and for the realization of social justice in the conflict situation.

A final remark seems to be in order. We began our analysis in this chapter with a premise that a boundary must be drawn between the sphere of private life and that of public authority, and each individual should have an inviolability of some extent of personal liberty within his private sphere. But how and where should this boundary be drawn? This question is difficult to answer in the vacuum, because individuals are so highly interdependent that any individual activity can hardly be so exclusively private as to be totally independent of the lives of others. It seems to be too naive to hope that a single formula can, in principle, be found that can determine the boundaries once and for all. To the extent that our analysis has nothing to say about the rules or commandments that determine the boundaries, it is a partial analysis of the problem of a libertarian social choice rule. But the part of the problem that we do analyze seems to be an important part, and it is not clear how much further we can go beyond

Berlin, who wrote that "what these rules or commandments will have in common is that they are accepted so widely, and are grounded so deeply in the actual nature of men as they have developed through history, as to be, by now, an essential part of what we mean by being a normal human being" (Berlin, 1958, p. 50). This is one of the problems in social choice theory where an innovative idea is very much hoped for.

CHAPTER 8

Epilogue

> [L]et not then my readers imagine that I dare flatter myself with having seen what I think is so difficult to discover. I have opened some arguments; I have risked some conjectures; but not so much from any hopes of being able to solve the question, as with a view of throwing upon it some light, and giving a true statement of it. Others may with great facility penetrate further in the same road, but none will find it an easy matter to get the end of it.
>
> Jean-Jacques Rousseau*

In concluding this study, a few general observations that might shed further light on the nature of our problem may be in order. We would also like to add some qualifications on the analysis presented in this work.

Many reputable welfare economists have been strenuously denying the relevance of Arrovian impossibility theorems to welfare economics. Some of them have gone as far as to purge social choice theory altogether from the sacred realm of economics.[1] Although we are in full agreement with Arrow's response (1963, p. 108) to the effect that "one can hardly think of a less interesting question about [Arrow's] theorem than whether it falls on one side or another of an arbitrary boundary separating intellectual provinces," the reason for which Arrow's result has been denied any legitimacy in welfare economics is worth our examination, which seems to bring about an important clarification.

According to Little (1952, pp. 423–4):

> Bergson's welfare function [in the traditional welfare economics] was meant as a "process or rule" which would indicate the best economic state as a function of a changing environment (i.e., changing sets of possibilities defined by different economic transformation functions), the individuals' tastes being given.... If tastes change, we may expect a new ordering of all the conceivable states; but we do not require that the difference between the new and the old ordering should bear any particular relation to the changes of taste which have occurred. We have, so to speak, a new world and a new order; and we do not demand correspondence

* J.-J. Rousseau, *Discourse on the Origin and Foundation of Inequality among Mankind* (English translation by L. G. Crocker). New York: Washington Square Press, 1964, p. 168.

between the change in the world and the change in the order.... Traditionally, tastes are given; indeed, one might almost say that the given individuals are traditionally defined as the possessors of the given tastes and that no sense is attached to the notion of given individuals with changing tastes.[2]

Formally speaking, this is an argument that goes against the unrestricted domain condition that we have required throughout this work.[3] In view of Little's emphatic denial of this condition, it may not be out of place to recapitulate our case for this condition.

Recollect that in the primordial stage of rule selection, where the "veil of ignorance" prevails, no one knows his natural gift, social position, wealth, and other natural as well as social contingencies, but everyone knows that the rule chosen now will be binding indefinitely on future contingencies. One need not be a slavish materialist to acknowledge that the personal and social luck of an individual almost inevitably affects his view on the society; hence, individual preferences are contingent on future realization of the natural and social luck that is hidden behind the veil of ignorance in the primordial stage. This being the case, the assumption of an unrestricted domain for a rule to be chosen seems to follow quite naturally from our problem-setting itself. Let us emphasize that there are two essential components in this argument: Unavoidable uncertainty about future contingencies and a firm commitment in advance to a rule for conflict resolution. To the extent that these two features are recognized to be at all important, the unrestricted domain condition seems to be on rather firm ground.[4]

Throughout this work we have assumed that a group of free individuals are to decide among themselves a collective choice rule once and for all in the primordial stage of rule selection. In reality, however, everyone is born in a world where the constitutional rules are already established and have their (possibly long) history. It seems clear, therefore, that the primordial stage of rule selection as we have conceptualized it is in fact a state "which, if ever it did, does not now, and in all probability never will exist" (Rousseau, 1964, p. 169). How, then, can we justify this theoretical device in the first place?

Our plea is the same as that of Rousseau (1964, p. 169) in justifying his state of nature: It is a state "of which ... it is absolutely necessary to have just notions to judge properly of our present state." That is to say, a rule that can be chosen and unanimously acknowledged to be fair in the hypothetical primordial stage, if there is any such rule, will serve as a standard of reference "to judge properly of our present state."

In trying to circumvent several impossibility theorems in social choice theory that send unambiguous signals that our conceptual framework is in need of reexamination, we have introduced a series of concepts that are, strictly speaking, beyond the traditional confines of individualism and ordinalism. We have also taken recourse to intersituational comparisons of welfare in the form of extended sympathy. In this framework, we ask each individual to place himself in the position of others through an imaginary exchange of circumstances, thereby participating in others' feelings, so as to rank the welfare position of Mr. *A* in social state *x* vis-à-vis that of Mr. *B* in social state *y*. This participation in the feelings of others by means of imaginary identification of oneself with others is what Adam Smith (1759) – and some other moral philosophers – have called sympathy,[5] which is because this approach in social choice theory is called the extended sympathy approach. It deserves emphasis that sympathy serves in this approach as the *principle of communication between individuals* (Morrow, 1923, p. 29) that will bring about coordination of the interests of the various individuals through mutual adaptation of the individuals' claims.

Incidentally, it might be asked whether or not the ignorance assumption in the primordial stage of rule selection (which prevents anyone from knowing others' personality characteristics and social contingencies) and the extended sympathy approach (in which we ask each individual to place himself in the positions of others by imaginary exchange of circumstances) are compatible in the first place. To solve this problem, we have only to recall that in the primordial stage of rule selection we are concerned with the design of the rule itself, and we do not need to know what informational input the rule requires for its actual application, whereas when the selected rule is invoked in order to resolve the conflict situation, the veil of ignorance is already lifted, and we are free to gather as much relevant information as the rule requires. There is, in principle, no contradiction here.

On reflection, it might be recognized that our possibility theorems presented in this work have always replaced an unadulterated "pure" principle of social choice by a constrained version thereof, the constraint in question being formulated in terms of nonpaternalistic and impartial concern for equality of treatment and/or realization of social justice in conflict resolution. Concepts such as the equity-constrained binary Pareto principle, Pareto-constrained ethical majoritarianism, justice-constrained subjective majoritarianism, the concept of liberal and liberal(G) individuals, and justice-constrained libertarian claims were introduced in an attempt to crystallize this common thread formally. Presumably we can conclude our analysis by suggesting that the factors that are ultimately responsible for the stability of the voluntary association of free individuals are the individual's sympathy, care for one another's well-being, and respect for one another's equal liberty and rights. On reflection, this seems to be as it should naturally be, and our analysis has served its purpose if it contributes to bring this point home.

Finally, let us remember that "once a machinery for making social choices from individual tastes is established, individuals will find it profitable, from a rational point of view, to misrepresent their tastes by their actions. [Therefore] even in a case where it is possible to construct a procedure showing how to aggregate individual tastes into a consistent preference pattern, there still remains the problem of devising rules of the game so that individuals will actually express their true tastes even when they are acting rationally" (Arrow, 1963, p. 7). In this work we have been solely concerned with the design of "a machinery for making social choice from individual tastes," in neglect of what has become known as the problem of implementation of collective choice rules. We just hope that our deliberate division of labor will be somehow justified.[6]

Notes

Chapter 1: Prologue

1 Pathological performances of the hypothetical compensation principles have been uncovered by Scitovsky (1941), Samuelson (1950*a*), Gorman (1955), Graaff (1957), Mishan (1960), and Chipman and Moore (1971, 1973, 1978), among others. See also Suzumura (1980*a*) for our evaluation of these and related welfare criteria.

2 Let us emphasize that although the concept of the primordial stage of rule selection, where the "veil of ignorance" described by Rawls (1962, pp. 138–9; 1968, pp. 52 and 70; 1971, pp. 12, 18–19, and 141–2) prevents everyone from being advantaged or disadvantaged by the natural and/or social hazards, is an idealized theoretical device that enables individuals to think about a rule from the general and impartial viewpoint, there is nothing particularly fictitious about it. Indeed, it is a common feature of the constitutional choice, namely the choice among alternative constitutional rules that, once chosen, will operate over an indefinite future, that each and every individual participating in the selection process will be unsure about just how the chosen rule will affect the individual's future self-interests given the uncertainty of the future prospects.

As Rawls (1974, p. 145) himself observed, "the idea that economists may find most useful in contract theory is that of the original position," and, indeed, we are deeply indebted to Rawls's ingenious idea in formulating the primordial stage of rule selection. For detailed examinations of the Rawlsian theory, the reader is referred to Alexander (1974), Arrow (1973), Barry (1973), Daniels (1975), Gordon (1976), Harsanyi (1975), and Wolff (1977), among many others.

3 In our treatment of the problem of rule selection, we have followed, in effect, what Plott (1972) called the "ethics approach" to the problem of choosing political processes. The other approach identified by Plott, which he attributed to Buchanan and Tullock (1962), "views the individual as choosing among rules according to a direct calculation as to which rule affords him the best advantage" (Plott, 1972, p. 87). For some conceptual difficulties of this alternative approach, the reader is referred to Plott's lucid argument.

It would also be illuminating to compare our view on rule selection with that of Kemp (1953–4), which goes as follows: "To decide upon the reasonableness of a particular condition or set of conditions an individual must know the likely outcome for him of submission to those conditions. This knowledge can be acquired only from a consideration of the limited number of choice situations likely to appear in the near future. Without some knowledge of the alternatives likely to face the community during his expected lifetime, and of the preferences of other members of the community during that period, an individual cannot ascertain the implications for him of a set of conditions.... At any moment the community is faced, not with all conceivable alternatives, but with a few of the attainable alternatives. Only the latter, and those likely to become attainable in the near future, are relevant to the selection of a social choice procedure; only in the light of particular choice situations can an individual appraise a condition or set of conditions.... The implication of this discussion is that the conditions upon which individuals might agree, and the choice procedures satisfying those conditions, should change from choice situation to choice situation" (Kemp, 1953–4, p. 241). It seems to us that Kemp's argument, which might well be a legitimate one in a short-run policy choice context within an existing constitutional setup, is totally inappropriate in a constitutional choice context. In the latter context, the veil-of-ignorance assumption does seem to give appropriate expression to the unavoidable uncertainty of the distant future, over which the rule chosen now will continue to determine social decisions.

4 This short list enumerates only those properties of a binary relation that actually play some role in this book. For these and other related properties, the interested reader is referred to Arrow (1963), Berge (1963), Birkhoff (1967), Birkhoff and MacLane (1965), Chipman (1971), Debreu (1959), Fishburn (1970*c*, 1970*e*, 1972, 1973), Halmos (1960), Kelley (1955), Pattanaik (1971), Sen (1970*b*), and von Neumann and Morgenstern (1953).

5 Because consistency, having been first introduced by Suzumura (1976*b*), may be somewhat unfamiliar, we provide three clarifying comments:

1. Consistency lies strictly in between transitivity and acyclicity. To verify this, let $X = \{x, y, z\}$ and define

$$R^1 = \{(x, y), (y, z), (z, y)\}$$

and

$$R^2 = \{(x, y), (y, z), (z, y), (x, z), (z, x)\}$$

Clearly, R^1 is consistent but not transitive, whereas R^2 is acyclic but not consistent.

2. The discrepancy between transitivity and consistency disappears, however, if R is complete and reflexive. To verify this assertion, suppose that R is complete and reflexive but not transitive. Then there exist x, y, and z such that $(x, y) \in R$, $(y, z) \in R$, and $(x, z) \notin R$. By virtue of reflexivity of R, $x \neq z$ must be the case. R being complete and reflexive, we then obtain that $(z, x) \in P(R)$, $(x, y) \in R$, and $(y, z) \in R$, so that R fails to be consistent. We may therefore assert that *a complete and reflexive binary relation is consistent if and only if it is transitive.*

3. Champernowne (1969, Chapter 2) introduced an interesting concept of consistent preference (or probability) relations that is similar to, but distinct from, ours. We say that a t-tuple of options $(x^1, x^2, \ldots, x^t)$ is a *C-cycle* of order t if and only if we have $(x^1, x^2) \in P(R) \cup N(R)$, $(x^\tau, x^{\tau+1}) \in R$ $(\tau = 2, 3, \ldots, t-1)$, and $(x^t, x^1) \in R$, where $(x, y) \in N(R)$ if and only if $(x, y) \notin R$ and $(y, x) \notin R$ hold true. R is said to be *Champernowne-consistent* if and only if there exists no C-cycle of any finite order. Unfortunately it is the case that *R is Champernowne-consistent if and only if it is transitive.* It is obvious that transitivity implies Champernowne consistency, so that we have only to establish the converse. Suppose that R is not

transitive. Then we have $(x, y) \in R$, $(y, z) \in R$, and $(x, z) \notin R$ for some $x, y, z \in X$. It then follows that

$$(z, x) \in P(R) \cup N(R), (x, y) \in R, \quad \text{and} \quad (y, z) \in R$$

so that $\{z, x, y\}$ is a C-cycle of order 3. Therefore, R is not Champernowne-consistent, as was to be proved.

6 Formal proof of this well-known fact may be found, for example, in the work of Arrow (1963, p. 41, fn. 13).

7 Further interesting properties of the transitive closure have been discussed in detail by Fishburn (1972). See also Herzberger (1973), who called the transitive closure of R the *ancestral* thereof.

8 Stricıly peaking, Szpilrajn (1930) was concerned with strict partial orderings (which are irreflexive and transitive) rather than quasi orderings, but the corresponding theorem on quasi orderings is a direct descendant of his result, so that we can legitimately impute Theorem A(4) to him.

9 The axiom of choice asserts that *for any nonempty collection $\mathscr{A}$ of nonempty sets there exists a single-valued mapping γ defined on $\mathscr{A}$ that assigns to each set $A \in \mathscr{A}$ an element $\gamma(A) \in A$*. The mapping γ is called a *selector* for $\mathscr{A}$, the existence of which may be considered a result of selecting, for each set $A \in \mathscr{A}$, an element in A. If $\mathscr{A}$ consists only of a finite number of sets, the existence of a selector for $\mathscr{A}$ is beyond any dispute. The axiom of choice is an assumption that guarantees the existence of a selector for $\mathscr{A}$ containing an infinite number of sets. On the meaning of and the plea for this axiom, the reader is referred to Halmos (1960, Section 15) and Kelley (1955, Chapter 0).

Chapter 2: Rational choice and revealed preference

1 On this and related problems, the reader is referred to Armstrong (1948), Chipman (1971), Fishburn (1970*c*, 1970*e*), Herzberger (1973), and Luce (1956), among others.

2 Other than the formal requirement that states are mutually exclusive and jointly exhaustive, the concept of a state is left unspecified.

3 Note, however, that the subtle difference between M-rationality and G-rationality evaporates if a G-rationalization R of C on $(X, \mathscr{S})$ is complete and reflexive. We have only to note that

$$\forall S \in \mathscr{S}: C(S) = G(S, R) = M(S, R)$$

holds true in this case by virtue of Theorem A(2) in the Appendix to Chapter 1.

4 Care should be taken with the difference between (2.1) and the requirement that

$$\forall S \in \mathscr{S}, \exists R \subset X \times X: C(S) = G(S, R) \tag{2.1*}$$

Clearly (2.1*) is always true. We have only to define R_S, given an $S \in \mathscr{S}$, by putting together all states in $C(S)$ and all states in $S \setminus C(S)$, respectively, and declaring any state in $C(S)$ to be better than any state in $S \setminus C(S)$, while declaring universal indifference within each of $C(S)$ and $S \setminus C(S)$. Our concept of rational choice is not (2.1*) but (2.1), which is not always true, as asserted.

5 We use the following conventions concerning inequalities between two l-vectors $x = (x_1, x_2, \ldots, x_l)$ and $y = (y_1, y_2, \ldots, y_l)$:

$$x \gg y \leftrightarrow x_i > y_i \quad (i = 1, 2, \ldots, l)$$

$$x \geq y \leftrightarrow x_i \geq y_i \quad (i = 1, 2, \ldots, l)$$

$$x > y \leftrightarrow x \geq y \ \& \ x \neq y$$

We denote by $x \cdot y$ the inner product between x and y, which is defined by

$$x \cdot y = \sum_{i=1}^{l} x_i y_i$$

6 Strictly speaking, $h(B(p, M))$ is a singleton subset of $B(p, M)$ rather than an element thereof. However, nothing of substance will be gained by being pedantic in our choice of words in the present context.

7 $T(R_C)$ and $T(R_C^*)$ are the transitive closure of R_C and that of R_C^*, respectively. See the Appendix to Chapter 1 for the definition of the transitive closure.

8 Two clarifying remarks are in order here:

(i) If we define R_h and R_h^* by

$$(x, y) \in R_h \leftrightarrow \exists B(p, M) \in \mathscr{B}: \begin{cases} x = h(B(p, M)) \\ \& \\ y \in B(p, M) \end{cases}$$

and

$$(x, y) \in R_h^* \leftrightarrow \exists B(p, M) \in \mathscr{B}: \begin{cases} x = h(B(p, M)) \\ \& \\ y \in B(p, M) \setminus \{h(B(p, M))\} \end{cases}$$

then Samuelson's weak postulate may be stated as

$$\forall x, y \in X: (x, y) \in R_h^* \rightarrow (y, x) \notin R_h$$

Similarly, Samuelson's strong postulate and Houthakker's semitransitivity axiom may be stated, respectively, as

$$\forall x, y \in X: (x, y) \in T(R_h^*) \rightarrow (y, x) \notin R_h$$

and

$$\forall x, y \in X: (x, y) \in T(R_h) \rightarrow (y, x) \notin R_h^*$$

(ii) It was Richter (1966, p. 637) who maintained that "the revealed preference notions employed in [the weak axiom of Samuelson and the strong axiom of Houthakker] are relevant only to the special case of competitive consumers, so that axioms also have meaning only in that limited context." However, these axioms can be and have been generalized beyond the narrow confinement of competitive consumers. Indeed, Richter (1971) himself defined the weak and the strong axioms for a *single-valued* choice function. Furthermore, there seems to be no reason that we should not go one step further and consider these axioms in terms of a *set-valued* choice function.

9 This corresponds to condition F3 stipulated by Herzberger (1973, p. 191), according to whom a choice function C on $(X, \mathscr{S})$ is called *regular* if it satisfies finite additivity along with a condition that $\{x\} \in \mathscr{S}$ for all $x \in X$.

10 Arrow (1959, Theorem 3). For the validity of this theorem (and some of the subsequent ones), the assumption that C has a choice space $(X, \mathscr{S}_F)$ is overly strong. It suffices that the domain $\mathscr{S}$ of C contains all pairs and all triples taken from X, as can easily be observed from the proof. However, some of the later theorems in this chapter do require the full power of the assumption that $\mathscr{S} = \mathscr{S}_F$, and it does not seem to be highly rewarding to seek minor generality here.

11 In the proof of Theorem 2.2, we have shown that (2.18) implies (2.19). In that proof we did not use transitivity of R; neither did we use the domain restriction $\mathscr{S} = \mathscr{S}_F$, so that we have in effect proved that the rational choice function satisfies Chernoff's axiom.

12 In Sen's (1970*b*, p. 17) phrase, "[Chernoff's axiom] states that if the world champion in some game is a Pakistani, then he must also be the champion in Pakistan."

13 Note that, thanks to Theorem 2.5, we can talk about path independence per se without ambiguity.

14 This property does not apply to a choice function with general domain, as Example 7 in Appendix B establishes.

15 Intuitively speaking, C on $(X, \mathscr{S})$ is an R-cut; i.e., $C = C^R_{cu}$, just when $x \in C(S)$ holds true if and only if, judged by R, x is at least as good as *some* state actually chosen by C from S for every $S \in \mathscr{S}$.

16 In words, C on $(X, \mathscr{S})$ is an R-solution, i.e., $C = C^R_{so}$, just when $x \in C(S)$ holds true if and only if, judged by R, x is at least as good as *every* state actually chosen by C from S for every $S \in \mathscr{S}$.

17 C on $(X, \mathscr{S})$ is an R-core, i.e., $C = C^R_{co}$, if and only if

$$\forall S \in \mathscr{S}: C(S) = G(S, R)$$

holds true so that $C(S)$ consists of and only of the R-greatest points in S for every $S \in \mathscr{S}$.

18 Similarly, C being a $T(R_C)$-cut is equivalent to the strong congruence axiom.

19 Scrutinizing the structure of this proof, we can verify that the domain condition $\mathscr{S} = \mathscr{S}_F$ is used only when we invoke Theorem 2.9. Therefore, it is generally true that a choice function C on $(X, \mathscr{S})$ is rational if and only if C is an R_C-core, i.e., $C = C^{R_C}_{co}$. This fact was proved by Richter (1971, Theorem 2) as well as by Wilson (1970, Theorem 3).

20 Here again we do not make any use of the domain restriction $\mathscr{S} = \mathscr{S}_F$, and the equivalence of Arrow's and Chernoff's axioms for a *single-valued* choice function is valid quite generally.

21 The converse of this proposition does not hold in general, as Example 8 in Appendix B establishes.

22 This axiom also appeared as Postulate 5* in the work of Chernoff (1954, p. 430), along with what we have called Chernoff's axiom, the latter being called Postulate 4 by Chernoff (1954, p. 429).
23 This argument was communicated to me by Dennis Packard. See also Bordes (1979) and Richelson (1978) for further discussion.
24 The converse of this proposition is negated by Examples 9 and 10 in Appendix B.
25 Examples 11 and 12 in Appendix B negate the general reversibility of this proposition.
26 The converse of this proposition is not true in general, as Example 12 makes clear.
27 Of course, a single-headed arrow can become reversible in the presence of some special features of a choice function. For instance, *in the presence of Chernoff's axiom, the superset axiom and Nash's axiom are equivalent*. [Note that NA implies SUA in general, so that we have only to verify that, coupled with CA, SUA implies NA. Let $S_1, S_2 \in \mathscr{S}$ be such that $S_1 \subset S_2$ and $C(S_2) \subset S_1$. Because $S_1 \cap C(S_2) \neq \varnothing$, we have $S_1 \cap C(S_2) = C(S_2) \subset C(S_1)$, by virtue of CA. SUA then ensures that $C(S_1) = C(S_2)$, as is required by NA.] It is also the case that *Nash's axiom and Arrow's axiom are equivalent for a single-valued choice function*. [We have only to prove that NA then implies AA. Let S_1 and S_2 in $\mathscr{S}$ be such that $S_1 \subset S_2$ and $S_1 \cap C(S_2) \neq \varnothing$. $C(S_2)$ being a singleton set, we must have $C(S_2) \cap S_1 = C(S_2)$, which implies that $C(S_1) = C(S_2) = S_1 \cap C(S_2)$, as was to be verified.] Because we do not have occasion to make use of these special results in the rest of this book, we shall not explore them further.
28 See Simon (1978, p. 2) (italics added).
29 The converse of this proposition is negated by Example 13 in Appendix B.
30 The strong axiom is not necessary for a choice function with the general domain to be quasi-transitive rational. This fact is established by Example 14 in Appendix B.
31 The converse of this theorem does not hold true, as Examples 15 and 16 in Appendix B unambiguously establish.
32 We have only to refer to Example 16 in Appendix B in order to negate the converse of this theorem.
33 Example 17 in Appendix B shows that SA(H) is not necessary for R_C^* to be acyclic; neither is it necessary for C to obey WA.
34 For the sake of completeness, we present several counterexamples in Appendix B that negate some plausible reversibility conjectures. See Examples 18 to 21.

Chapter 3: Arrovian impossibility theorems

1 Samuelson's assertion to the effect that "if the [social preference] ordering is transitive, it *automatically* satisfies the condition called 'independence of irrelevant alternatives'" (Samuelson, 1967, p. 43) seems to be a good case in point. How can we otherwise make any meaningful sense of this statement?
2 For some (apparent and/or real) weakenings of the condition I, the reader is referred to Blau (1971) and Hansson (1973). Useful clarifications of the meaning

of the condition I have also been put forward by Johansen (1969), Luce and Raiffa (1957), Ray (1973), and Sen (1970*b*), among others.

3 In the currently prevailing version of his impossibility theorem, Arrow (1963, p. 76) endorses a weak variant of this principle, which requires that if every individual prefers a state x to another state y, then so should society. In the first version of his theorem, presented in the first edition of this work, which appeared in 1951, Arrow did not assign an independent role to this condition. Instead, he derived it from the combination of other, supposedly more basic, axioms on his social welfare function. See Consequence 3 in Arrow (1963, p. 54).

4 In particular, a full rational collective choice rule satisfies the binary version of each Pareto principle if and only if it satisfies the general version thereof.

5 Gibbard's original definition was phrased in terms of a social preference relation rather than a social choice function. But the definition in the text seems to capture faithfully the essence of Gibbard's concept.

6 Applying the convention introduced in the Appendix to Chapter 1, profiles will be written horizontally, with more preferred alternatives to the left of the less preferred, indifference, if any, being indicated by square brackets. Parentheses embracing two or more states indicate that there is no restriction whatsoever on the ranking of these states vis-à-vis each other. Take, for example, R_i^a for $i \in N \backslash V$. It is here stipulated that the restriction of R_i^a on S is such that y is preferred to x^* as well as to y^*, and both of x^* and y^* are ranked higher than x, with the relative ranking between x^* and y^* being left completely unspecified.

7 A $V \in \mathscr{D}_F$ is a smallest element of $\mathscr{D}_F$ if and only if $\# V^* < \# V$ implies $V^* \notin \mathscr{D}_F$. Such V will be called a smallest decisive set for F.

8 Condition PR was first introduced by May (1952) in his axiomatization of the simple majority decision rule, which we shall discuss in Chapter 4.

9 The two sets $V_1(\lambda)$ and $V_2(\lambda)$ in (b3) need not necessarily be disjoint; this can be exemplified as follows: Let $N = \{1, 2, 3\}$, and let a rule F be defined by $\{x\} = C^a(\{x, y\})$ if $[(x, y) \in P(R_1^a \cap R_2^a)$ & $(y, x) \in P(R_2^a \cap R_3^a)]$, and by $y \in C^a(\{x, y\})$ otherwise, where $C^a = F(a)$. It is easy to verify that each member of $\{1, 2\}$ is blocking for F and each member of $\{2, 3\}$ is inversely blocking for F in this case.

10 Suppose that individuals prefer x to y unanimously. Then a rule satisfying PD chooses either x or y, but not both, from $\{x, y\} \in \mathscr{S}$.

11 In this formulation, f corresponds precisely to what Arrow (1950, 1963) called a *social welfare function*.

12 According to Plott (1973, pp. 1077–8), "the question 'why rational social choice?' is seldom discussed. Then, when the issue is raised, there is a remarkable tendency for writers to 'talk past' each other. It is as though each writer finds the answer so 'obvious' that he feels little need to be clear on the subject. Consequently, many potentially serious disagreements never surface." It was Plott who greatly contributed to uncovering potentially serious disagreements among social choice theorists, as did Sen (1977*a*).

13 Indeed, full rationality, quasi-transitive rationality, and acyclic rationality can also be argued for by having recourse to their characterization in terms of various choice-consistency axioms that we expounded in Chapter 2.

14 Because $\mathscr{S}$ contains all singletons and pair-sets taken from X, it is clearly the case that R^C is reflexive and transitive. Therefore, C being base-transitive is equivalent to R^C being an ordering.
15 In essence, this theorem is due to Mas-Colell and Sonnenschein (1972). They required quasi-transitive rationality, but their proof did not in fact use the full power of this requirement.
16 Arrow's justification (1963, pp. 26–7) of his independence-of-irrelevant-alternatives axiom is obviously instead an argument for this condition and, as such, is rather forceful.
17 Examinations and defenses of the simple majority decision rule have been presented by Riemer (1951–2), May (1952), Dahl (1956), and Downs (1961), among many others. Chapter 4 will be devoted to formal examination of this rule.
18 In order to see this, we have only to constrict Example 4.1 by decreasing the numbers of states and of individuals and see if it comes to conflict with base triple acyclicity. That it does not can be easily verified.
19 The reader is referred to our argument in favor of U and I in Section 1.2 of this chapter.

Chapter 4: Simple majority rule and extensions

1 Let Π_N denote the set of all permutations on N. We say that $a = (R_1^a, R_2^a, \ldots, R_n^a) \in A$ is a reordering of $b = (R_1^b, R_2^b, \ldots, R_n^b) \in A$ if and only if there exists a $\pi \in \Pi_N$ satisfying $R_{\pi(i)}^a = R_i^b$ for all $i \in N$.
2 See, however, a detailed critical examination of these impartiality conditions by Campbell and Fishburn (1980).
3 Another remarkable theorem on the performance of the SMD rule due to Rae (1969) and Taylor (1969) is also quite revealing. According to their result, the SMD rule is the unique decision rule that minimizes the probability that a typical member will support an alternative that the community rejects, or will oppose an alternative that the community accepts, if he assumes that future preferences are unknown and the members vote (for or against) independently.
4 In the literature on the SMD rulę, a slightly modified version of the Condorcet function plays a vital role. For any profile $a \in A$, let the *quasi Condorcet function* C_{**}^a be defined on a choice space $(X, \mathscr{S})$ by

$$\forall S \in \mathscr{S}: C_{**}^a(S) = G(S, M^a)$$

In general, C_{**}^a is not necessarily a choice function, because we can well have $C_{**}^a(S) = \varnothing$ for some $a \in A$ and some $S \in \mathscr{S}$. There are many works in the social choice literature on the conditions on the class of profiles under which the modified Condorcet function C_{**}^a becomes a well-defined choice function on a choice space $(X, \mathscr{S})$. See, among many others, Arrow (1963), Black (1958), Craven (1971), Dummett and Farquharson (1961), Fishburn (1971*b*, 1973, 1974*b*), Pattanaik (1971), Sen (1969, 1970*b*), and Vickrey (1960). In this book, however, we are not concerned with that investigation, and we shall retain the condition U throughout, the reason being our exclusive concern with the problem of rule design in the primordial stage of ignorance.

5 Extensive studies of the Condorcet criterion have been made by Black (1958) and Fishburn (1973, Chapter 12). Important contributions on the Condorcet extensions of the SMD rule include those of Black (1958), Fishburn (1973, Chapter 13; 1977), and Goodman (1954), and the positional (non-Condorcet) extensions have been analyzed by Black (1958, 1976), Fine and Fine (1974), Fishburn (1973, Chapter 13), Gärdenfors (1973), Grazia (1953), Hansson (1973), and Young (1974).

6 In this generalization we follow Black (1958, 1976), Fishburn (1973), and Luce and Raiffa (1957, p. 358).

7 An axiomatization of the Borda rule has been provided by Young (1974).

8 We did not have access to Copeland's original paper. His proposed choice procedure has been discussed in detail by Fishburn (1973, 1977), Goodman (1954), and Luce and Raiffa (1957, p. 358).

9 When $n = \# N$ is even, the strong Pareto principle (SP) can be replaced by the weaker Pareto principle (P), as can easily be ascertained by examining the proof of Theorem 4.3.

10 This condition is due originally to Fishburn (1977).

11 This is the famous "voting paradox" situation; see Arrow (1963, p. 3).

12 This TCM rule corresponds to what Sen (1983) has aptly called the Weak Closure Maximality, his Strong Closure Maximality corresponding to the closely related rule proposed originally by Schwartz (1972). The contrast and similarity between these transitive closure rules are clarified by Bordes (1976, 1979), Kalai and associates (1976), and Kalai and Schmeidler (1977), who also give interesting related results.

13 As a matter of fact, a slightly stronger assertion can be made. Consider the following variant of the Condorcet condition that is due to Smith (1973):

Condition SC (Smith's Condorcet condition): For every profile $a = (R_1^a, R_2^a, \ldots, R_n^a) \in A$ and every $S \in \mathcal{S}$, if S can be partitioned into two non-empty subsets S_1 and S_2 in such a way that $(x, y) \in P(M^a)$ holds true for all $x \in S_1$ and $y \in S_2$, then $C^a(S) \cap S_2 = \varnothing$.

Note that the Condorcet criterion discussed in the text is a special case in which S_1 is a singleton set. We can show that the TCM rule satisfies this "most compelling extension of the basic [Condorcet] principle" (Fishburn, 1977, p. 479). To verify this assertion, let a, S_1, and S_2 be as stated in condition SC. Take any $x \in S_1$ and $y \in C_{TM}^a(S)$. By definition, there exist $z^1, z^2, \ldots, z^t \in S$ satisfying $y = z^1$, $(z^\tau, z^{\tau+1}) \in M^a$ for all $\tau \in \{1, 2, \ldots, t-1\}$, $z^t = x$. Because $z^t = x \in S_1$ holds true by assumption, $z^{t-1} \in S_1$ must be the case, which initiates backward induction to yield $y = z^1 \in S_1$ eventually. Therefore, we obtain $C_{TM}^a(S) \subset S_1$, namely, $C_{TM}^a(S) \cap S_2 = \varnothing$, as desired.

On reflection, the Copeland rule can also be shown to satisfy condition SC, as was noted by Fishburn (1977).

14 We can locate the gulf between the possibility and impossibility results a bit more sharply. Consider the following two revealed preference axioms, both of

which essentially require that the preferences revealed in *binary* choice situations never be contradicted in *nonbinary* choice situations.

Condition RP(1)

$$\forall x, y \in X: [\{x\} = C(\{x, y\}) \rightarrow \forall S \in \mathscr{S}: (x \in S \rightarrow y \notin C(S))]$$

Condition RP(2)

$$\forall x, y \in X: [\{x\} = C(\{x, y\}) \rightarrow \forall S \in \mathscr{S}: (x \in S \setminus C(S) \rightarrow y \notin C(S))]$$

It is easy to prove that CA (Chernoff's axiom) implies RP(1), which in turn implies RP(2) as well as BTA (base triple acyclicity), and that DCA (dual Chernoff axiom) implies RP(2); for proofs, see Suzumura (1976*b*, pp. 388–9). We can then assert the following result: (a) Assume that $\# X \geq 3$ and $n = \# N \geq 4$. Then there exists no collective choice rule that satisfies U, RP(1), BI, BP, and PR without admitting the existence of a vetoer. (b) There exists a collective choice rule satisfying all of U, RP(2), BI, BP, and PR without admitting the existence of a vetoer.

Note that the impossibility in (a) is turned into the possibility in (b) by *weakening* RP(1) into RP(2). A rather subtle difference between RP(1) and RP(2) is squarely responsible for such a great contrast in implications.

15 Note that Examples 4.2 and 4.4 are enough to assert that F_β and F_γ do not necessarily satisfy even a single choice-consistency axiom appearing in Figure 2.2.

16 Suppose that the even-chance random mechanism is used to single out the final choice from the set $\{x, y, z\}$, and consider an individual whose von Neumann–Morgenstern utility function v exhibits risk aversion. The even-chance lottery with prizes x, y, and z gives him the expected utility of

$$\tfrac{2}{3} \cdot v(\tfrac{1}{2}) + \tfrac{1}{3} \cdot v(0)$$

which is smaller than $v(\frac{1}{3})$ provided by the certain choice of w. Therefore, a risk-averting individual will not voluntarily agree to adopt such a conflict resolution rule in the primordial game of rule selection, as claimed.

17 The voting-by-veto approach has been vigorously explored by Mueller (1979*a*; 1979*b*, Chapter 4), Moulin (1981), and others. The fairness-as-no-envy approach has been extensively cultivated in the particular context of resource allocation problems by Crawford (1979), Daniel (1975, 1978), Feldman and Kirman (1974), Feldman and Weiman (1979), Foley (1967), Goldman and Sussangkarn (1978, 1980), Otsuki (1981), Pazner (1976, 1977), Pazner and Schmeidler (1974, 1976, 1978), Schmeidler and Vind (1972), Svensson (1977), Thomson (1980*a*, 1980*b*), Varian (1974, 1975, 1976), and others.

18 In the Appendix to Chapter 1 we asserted that any nonempty finite set S has an R-greatest point if R is reflexive, complete, and acyclic. Likewise, we can assert that any nonempty finite set S has an R-smallest point if R is reflexive, complete, and acyclic.

Chapter 5: The fairness-as-no-envy approach in social choice theory

1 This dilemma was first exposed by Pazner and Schmeidler (1974). See also Varian (1974, 1975, 1976).

2 Several variants of the no-envy equity concept have been succinctly surveyed and critically evaluated by Pazner (1977) and Sen (1983, Section 5).

3 Despite Socrates' rather harsh treatment, an impatient accusation by Thrasymachus to the following effect seems to command our more serious concern: "I say that if you want really to know what justice is, you should not only ask but answer, and you should not seek honour to yourself from the refutation of an opponent, but have your own answer; for there is many a one who can ask and cannot answer" [*The Dialogues of Plato* (translated into English with analyses and introductions by B. Jowett), Vol. III, 3rd edition. London: Oxford University Press, 1892, pp. 12–13].

4 The definition (5.8) seems to correspond precisely to what Adam Smith (1759, p. 317) meant by sympathy when he wrote that: "Though sympathy is very properly said to arise from an imaginary change of situations with the person principally concerned, yet this imaginary change is not supposed to happen to me in my own person and character, but in that of the person with whom I sympathize. When I condole with you for the loss of your only son, in order to enter into your grief I do not consider what I, a person of such a character and profession, should suffer, if I had a son, and if that son was unfortunately to die: but I consider what I should suffer if I was really you, and I not only change circumstances with you, but I change persons and characters. My grief, therefore, is entirely upon your account, and not in the least upon my own."

5 The following passage from Smith (1759, pp. 22–3) seems to serve as a very apt explanation of what is involved in the axiom of identity: "What [the sympathetic spectator] feel[s] will, indeed, always be in some respects different from what [the person principally concerned] feels, and compassion can never be exactly the same with original sorrow; because the secret consciousness that the change of situations, from which the sympathetic sentiment arises, is but imaginary, not only lowers it in degree, but in some measure varies it in kind, and gives it a quite different modification. These two sentiments, however, may, it is evident, have such a correspondence with one another, as is sufficient for the harmony of society. Though they will never be unisons, they may be concords, and this is all that is wanted or required."

6 We have shown in effect that the apparent conceptual difference between the Foley and Pazner fairness concepts evaporates for any extended profile satisfying the axiom of identity. This may puzzle some readers, because if we confine our attention to only the interpersonal exchange of commodity bundles, examples abound showing the discrepancy between the two. Let us stress that we are concerned here with the totality of the individual's welfare position in the society, and our conclusion should be understood with this broader context in mind.

7 Written more explicitly,

$$\beta(S_0) = (\tilde{R}_1^{\beta}(S_0 \times N), \tilde{R}_2^{\beta}(S_0 \times N), \ldots, \tilde{R}_n^{\beta}(S_0 \times N))$$

8 Note that $C_{GS}^{\alpha}(S)$ is nothing other than the set of all $T(Q^{\alpha})$-maximal states in S.

9 Note also that Ψ_{GS} satisfies what can be called the *inclusion Pareto condition*, which requires the following: If an extended profile $\alpha \in \mathscr{A}$ and $x, y \in X$ are such that $(x, y) \in \bigcap_{i \in N} P(R_i^{\alpha})$, then $[\{x \in S \;\&\; y \in C^{\alpha}(S)\} \rightarrow x \in C^{\alpha}(S)]$ for all $S \in \mathscr{S}$,

where $C^{\alpha} = \Psi(\alpha)$. The proof of this assertion is in effect contained in step 2 of the proof of Theorem 5.5.

10 Indeed, Ψ_{*} satisfies the unrestricted domain condition (EU), the independence condition (EI), the anonymity condition (EAN), and the stability axiom (ST) as well, although it fails to satisfy the conditional binary exclusion Pareto condition (CBEP).

11 Unlike Ψ_{GS}, however, Ψ_{ε} does not necessarily satisfy the fairness inclusion condition, as we can easily exemplify.

Chapter 6: Impartiality and extended sympathy

1 Suppes's *grading principle of justice* (1966) is the asymmetric part of $\omega_S(u)$ for every generalized utility function u.

2 In Chapter 5 we made use of a lexicographic ordering $>_L$ that orders $E^{(n)}$ by rearranging the components of each $v \in E^{(n)}$ in decreasing order, whereas $>_L^*$ orders $E^{(n)}$ by rearranging the components of each $v \in E^{(n)}$ in increasing order.

3 A principle of justice characterized here can be called a Rawlsian, but it may not correspond to Rawls's theory of justice (1971) in several important respects. Note, in particular, that Rawls maintains that people's values – preferences – are not to be used in assessing the justice or injustice of the institutions, because people's values are derivative from the very institution we want to bring under scrutiny: "The conceptions of the good that individuals form depend in part on their natural abilities and the way these are shaped and realized by social and other contingencies" (Rawls, 1975, p. 552). Instead, he bases his theory of justice on the concept of the *primary goods,* which consist of "rights and liberties, opportunities and powers, income and wealth" (Rawls, 1971, p. 92), together with a person's self-respect. Note, however, that a serious problem of measuring these heterogeneous primary goods and amalgamating them into an interpersonally commensurable *index of primary goods* is not discussed by Rawls. Furthermore, we are in full recognition that people's values are conditioned by natural and social contingencies. Indeed, this is why we are posing the problem of rule design in the primordial stage of ignorance. The reader is referred back to Chapter 1 on this point.

For useful general discussions on several aspects of Rawls's theory of justice, the interested reader is referred to Alexander (1974), Arrow (1973), Barry (1973), Buchanan (1975), Daniels (1975), Dworkin (1973), Gordon (1976), Hare (1973), Lyons (1972), and Rawls (1962, 1963, 1967, 1968, 1971, 1975).

4 Sen (1973*a*) has introduced a weak version of this axiom in the income distributional context, and Hammond (1976) has generalized it into the condition SHE_{ω}.

5 See Maskin (1978) for an alternative axiomatization of ω_B that enumerates among the characterizing axioms a requirement of the continuity of justice judgments.

6 For the truth of this theorem, we need not take recourse to the full force of condition SP and condition JU. It does not seem to be highly rewarding, however, to squeeze out redundancy from the statement of this simple proposition.

7 It is true that this argument is valid only when $(v, S) \in \mathscr{U}_{ID} \times \mathscr{S}$ is such that $C_{\varepsilon}^{v}(S) \cap C_{\sigma\sigma}^{v}(S) \neq \varnothing$. If it so happens that $C_{\varepsilon}^{v}(S) \cap C_{\sigma\sigma}^{v}(S) = \varnothing$, the case against $C_{\sigma\sigma}^{v}(S)$ is that much strengthened, not weakened, because every alternative in $C_{\sigma\sigma}^{v}(S)$ is then justice-dominated by definition. To assume that $C_{\varepsilon}^{v}(S) \cap C_{\sigma\sigma}^{v}(S) \neq \varnothing$ is therefore to give $C_{\sigma\sigma}^{v}(S)$ a fair chance in the contest against $C_{\sigma\varepsilon}^{v}(S)$, in which the performance of $C_{\sigma\varepsilon}^{v}(S)$ supersedes that of $C_{\sigma\sigma}^{v}(S)$, as asserted.

Chapter 7: Individual rights and libertarian claims

1 On the various shades of libertarian ideals, the reader is referred to Berlin (1958), Buchanan (1975), Cranston (1967), Dasgupta (1980), Hayek (1960), Mill (1859), Nozick (1974), and Rawls (1971), among many others.

2 Farrell (1976, Section 6) proposed another resolution scheme as well, which he called the *liberal partition*. On this and other proposals that we do not discuss in this chapter, Sen (1976, 1983) should be consulted.

3 "Given any $[(u, v) \in D_i]$, for each $j \neq i$ who has a preference between u and v, *raise the less preferred to the indifference class of the more preferred*, so producing a new preference ordering for j" (Farrell, 1976, p. 5, italics added).

4 This is certainly not to deny the importance of Farrell's analysis on the internal consistency of the rights system. Indeed, our positive analysis in this chapter owes much to his seminal work.

5 A possible interpretation of this example is provided by Sen's work-choice case (1976, p. 222). Sen himself used this example to criticize Blau's scheme as well as Gibbard's scheme on ethical grounds, and we use the same example to show that Gibbard's scheme has an unpalatable feature of basing the resolution of the Pareto libertarian paradox on people's mistakes.

6 Some other features of Gibbard's scheme have been discussed in detail by Kelly (1976; 1978, Chapter 9) and Sen (1976). We shall have more to say on this scheme in Section 5 of this chapter.

7 Thanks are due to Peter Hammond for his comments on this point. Note that for a given profile $a = (R_1^a, R_2^a, \ldots, R_n^a) \in A$, there may well be multiple ordering extensions of Q^a, and the outcome of applying our resolution scheme may occasionally depend on which ordering extension we choose.

8 In private correspondence, D. Austen–Smith has kindly informed me that a much simpler proof of the *compatibility* between condition SP and condition JCL(1) can be constructed. This is undoubtedly a useful observation, but the method of proof we used in establishing Theorem 7.8 enables us to assert that a *rational* collective choice rule can be constructed in such a way as to satisfy condition SP as well as condition JCL(1).

9 This proposition generalizes a corollary to Theorem 3 of Suzumura (1978). Our previous result essentially assumed that the admissible profiles satisfy the axiom of complete identity and that the maximin principle of justice is unanimously accepted by all individuals.

10 It might be of some interest to present a concrete collective choice rule that satisfies condition IP but does not satisfy condition EP. The simplest possible

example is a rule that assigns to each and every profile $a = (R_1^a, R_2^a, \ldots, R_n^a) \in A$ a choice function C^a such that $C^a(S) = S$ for all $S \in \mathscr{S}$. A more meaningful example is provided by transitive closure of the SMD rule, which we discussed in Chapter 4.

In Chapter 3, condition IP was introduced under the name of the weak Pareto principle. It is for mnemonic convenience that we use a different name in this chapter.

11 Kelly (1976*b*; 1978, Chapter 9) proposed the third revised libertarian claim as well, but from the point of view of our current analysis, it is unnecessary to get into this complicated proposal.

12 Two clarifying comments may be in order here. First, from x^2, something else may happen [besides individual 1 exercising his right $(x^4, x^2) \in D_1']$ if the Pareto dominance relation is weakened from $\bigcap_{i \in N} P(R_i^a)$ to $P(\bigcap_{i \in N} R_i^a)$. That is to say, if $(x^3, x^2) \in R_i^a$ for all $i \in N \setminus \{1, 2\}$ and if in (7.51), (7.53), and (7.55) all instances of $\bigcap_{i \in N} P(R_i^a)$ are replaced by $P(\bigcap_{i \in N} R_i^a)$, x^3 might be picked over x^2 by the Pareto dominance. It is clear, however, that this possibility does not affect our conclusion that $(x^1, x^3) \notin W_1^0(a|S)$. Second, in arriving at the conclusion that $(x^1, x^3) \notin W_1^0(a|S)$, we have followed the "path" $x^3 \to x^1 \to x^2 \to x^4 \to x^3$ generated by the successive rights-exercising of individuals 1 and 2. That is, we started from x^3 and came back to x^3 again! It might be asked: Why don't we let individual 1 waive his right $(x^1, x^3) \in D_1'$ in this case? Put differently, why do we stipulate the condition $y \neq y_1$ in (7.50)? The reason is that there exists an important difference between (a) the travel from x^3 (via a sequence of states) back to x^3 again and (b) the travel from x^3 to an $x^* \in S$ such that $(x^3, x^*) \in I(R_1)$. In the former case, individual 1 comes back to x^3 without losing his right over x^3, whereas in the latter case, individual 1 may well be stuck at x^* without having any right over x^*. This is also the reason we modified (7.45) into (7.52).

13 Elsewhere (Suzumura, 1980*b*, Theorem 5) we have required that $n = \#N \geq 3$. Thanks are due Wulf Gaertner, who pointed out that this assumption can be discarded.

Chapter 8: Epilogue

1 To witness, let us cite several representative passages from various authors: "Arrow's theorem is in my opinion unrelated to welfare economics" (Bergson, 1966, p. 76). "Arrow's work has no relevance to the traditional theory of welfare economics, which culminates in the Bergson–Samuelson formulation" (Little, 1952, p. 425). "The Arrow result is much more a contribution to the infant discipline of mathematical politics than to the traditional mathematical theory of welfare economics. I export Arrow from economics to politics because I do not believe that he has proved the impossibility of the traditional Bergson welfare function of economics" (Samuelson, 1967, p. 42).

2 Samuelson made the same point when he asserted that "for Bergson, one and only one of the ... possible patterns of individuals' orderings is needed. It could be *any* one, but it is *only* one. From *it* (not from each of them all) comes a social ordering.... The only Axiom restricting a Bergson Social Welfare Function (of

individualistic type) is a 'tree' property of Pareto-optimality type" (Samuelson, 1967, pp. 48–9).

3 As a matter of fact, Little's cited argument acts counter to some other Arrovian conditions such as independence and nondictatorship as well. We need not discuss this side of the coin in detail, however, because these other conditions are more easily defensible and are defended in Chapter 3.

4 In disputing the applicability of Arrow's impossibility theorem to the Bergson social welfare function, the cited passage of Little emphasized that the Bergson function is based on one profile only, in contradistinction to Arrow's unrestricted domain condition. Notice, however, that the recent results of Kemp and Ng (1976), Parks (1976*a*), and Pollak (1979) have shown that there exist single-profile analogues of the Arrovian impossibility theorems, so that the single-profile feature of the Bergson–Samuelson framework is not a sure-fire guarantee against the disease of the logical contradiction uncovered by Arrow.

5 See T. D. Campbell (1971), Macfie (1967), and Morrow (1923), among others.

6 There is already a voluminous literature on the problem of implementation of collective choice rules. The interested reader is referred to Blair (1981), Dasgupta and associates (1979), Dummett and Farquharson (1961), Farquharson (1969), Gibbard (1973, 1977, 1978), Hurwicz (1972), Hurwicz and Schmeidler (1978), Maskin (1979), Pattanaik (1978), Peleg (1978*b*), Satterthwaite (1975), Sen (1979*a*), and Vickrey (1960), among many others.

Bibliography

Alchian, A. A. 1953. "The Meaning of Utility Measurement." *American Economic Review* 43:26–50.

Alexander, S. S. 1974. "Social Evaluation through Notional Choice." *Quarterly Journal of Economics* 88:597–624.

Armstrong, W. E. 1948. "Uncertainty and the Utility Functions." *Economic Journal* 58:1–10.

Arrow, K. J. 1950. "A Difficulty in the Concept of Social Welfare." *Journal of Political Economy* 58:328–46.

1951. "Little's Critique of Welfare Economics." *American Economic Review* 41:923–34.

1959. "Rational Choice Functions and Orderings." *Economica* (N. S.) 26:121–7.

1963. *Social Choice and Individual Values*, 2nd edition. New York: Wiley.

1967*a*. "Public and Private Values." In: *Human Values and Economic Policy*, edited by S. Hook. New York University Press, pp. 3–21.

1967*b*. "The Place of Moral Obligation in Preference Systems." In: *Human Values and Economic Policy*, edited by S. Hook. New York University Press, pp. 117–19.

1967*c*. "Values and Collective Decision-Making." In: *Philosophy, Politics and Society*, 3rd ser., edited by P. Laslett and W. G. Runciman. New York: Barnes & Noble, pp. 215–32.

1973. "Some Ordinalist-Utilitarian Notes on Rawls's Theory of Justice." *Journal of Philosophy* 70:245–63.

1974. "General Economic Equilibrium: Purpose, Analytic Techniques, Collective Choice." *American Economic Review* 64:253–72.

1977*a*. "Extended Sympathy and the Possibility of Social Choice." *American Economic Review, Papers and Proceedings* 67:219–25.

1977*b*. "Current Developments in the Theory of Social Choice." *Social Research* 44:607–22.

Austen-Smith, D. 1981. "Necessary and Sufficient Conditions for Libertarian Collective Choice Rules." Discussion Paper No. 70, Department of Economics and Related Studies, University of York.

Barone, E. 1908. "Il ministro della produzione nello stato collectivista." *Giornale degli economisti e rivista di statistica* 37:267–93, 391–414. English translation: 1935. "The Ministry of Production in the Collectivist State." In: *Collectivist Economic Planning*, edited by F. A. von Hayek. London: Routledge, pp. 245–90.

Barry, B. 1973. *The Liberal Theory of Justice*. Oxford: Clarendon Press.

Batra, R. N., and P. K. Pattanaik. 1972. "On Some Suggestions for Having Non-Binary Social Choice Functions." *Theory and Decision* 3:1–11.

Berge, C. 1963. *Topological Spaces.* London: Oliver and Boyd.
Bergson, A. 1938. "A Reformulation of Certain Aspects of Welfare Economics." *Quarterly Journal of Economics* 52:310–34.
1954. "On the Concept of Social Welfare." *Quarterly Journal of Economics* 68:233–52.
1966. *Essays in Normative Economics.* Cambridge, Mass.: Harvard University Press.
Berlin, I. 1958. *Two Concepts of Liberty.* Oxford University Press.
Binmore, K. G. 1976. "Social Choice and Parties." *Review of Economic Studies* 43:459–64.
Birkhoff, G. 1967. *Lattice Theory,* 3rd edition. Providence, R. I.: American Mathematical Society.
Birkhoff, G., and S. MacLane. 1965. *A Survey of Modern Algebra,* 3rd edition. New York: Macmillan.
Black, D. 1958. *The Theory of Committees and Elections.* Cambridge University Press.
1969. "On Arrow's Impossibility Theorem." *Journal of Law and Economics* 12:227–48.
1976. "Partial Justification of the Borda Count." *Public Choice* 28:1–15.
Blackorby, C., and D. Donaldson. 1976. "Utility vs Equity: Some Plausible Quasi-Orderings." *Journal of Public Economics* 7:365–81.
Blair, D. H. 1981. "On the Ubiquity of Strategic Voting Opportunities." *International Economic Review* 22:649–55.
Blair, D. H., G. Bordes, J. S. Kelly, and K. Suzumura. 1976. "Impossibility Theorems without Collective Rationality." *Journal of Economic Theory* 13:361–79.
Blair, D. H., and R. A. Pollak. 1979. "Collective Rationality and Dictatorship: The Scope of the Arrow Theorem." *Journal of Economic Theory* 21:186–94.
Blau, J. H. 1957. "The Existence of Social Welfare Functions." *Econometrica* 25:302–13.
1971. "Arrow's Theorem with Weak Independence." *Economica* (N. S.) 38:413–20.
1972. "A Direct Proof of Arrow's Theorem." *Econometrica* 40:61–7.
1975. "Liberal Values and Independence." *Review of Economic Studies* 42:395–401.
Bordes, G. 1976. "Consistency, Rationality and Collective Choice." *Review of Economic Studies* 43:451–7.
1979. "Some More Results on Consistency, Rationality and Collective Choice." In: *Revelation and Aggregation of Preferences,* edited by J.-J. Laffont. Amsterdam: North Holland, pp. 175–97.
Bordes, G., and M. Salles. 1978. "Sur l'Impossibilité des Fonctions de Décision Collective: Un Commentaire et un Résultat." *Revue d'Economie Politique* 88:442–8.
Breyer, F. 1977. "The Liberal Paradox, Decisiveness over Issues, and Domain Restrictions." *Zeitschrift für Nationalökonomie* 37:45–60.
1980. "Empathy and Respect for the Rights of Others." *Zeitschrift für Nationalökonomie* 40:59–64.

Brown, D. J. 1974. "An Approximate Solution to Arrow's Problem." *Journal of Economic Theory* 9:375–83.

1975. "Aggregation of Preferences." *Quarterly Journal of Economics* 89:456–69.

Bryce, J. 1924. *Modern Democracies*. New York: Macmillan.

Buchanan, J. M. 1954*a*. "Social Choice, Democracy, and Free Markets." *Journal of Political Economy* 62:114–23.

1954*b*. "Individual Choice in Voting and the Market." *Journal of Political Economy* 62:334–43.

1975. *The Limits of Liberty*. University of Chicago Press.

Buchanan, J. M., and G. Tullock. 1962. *The Calculus of Consent*. Ann Arbor: University of Michigan Press.

Campbell, D. E. 1976. "Democratic Preference Functions." *Journal of Economic Theory* 12:259–72.

1978*a*. "Realization of Choice Functions." *Econometrica* 46:171–80.

1978*b*. "Rationality from a Computational Standpoint." *Theory and Decision* 9:255–66.

1980. "Algorithms for Social Choice Functions." *Review of Economic Studies* 47:617–27.

Campbell, D. E., and P. C. Fishburn. 1980. "Anonymity Conditions in Social Choice Theory." *Theory and Decision* 12:21–39.

Campbell, T. D. 1971. *Adam Smith's Science of Morals*. London: George Allen & Unwin.

Champernowne, D. G. 1969. *Uncertainty and Estimation in Economics, Vol. I.* San Francisco: Holden-Day.

Chernoff, H. 1954. "Rational Selection of Decision Functions." *Econometrica* 22:422–43.

Chipman, J. S. 1971. "Consumption Theory without Transitive Indifference." In: *Preferences, Utility, and Demand,* edited by J. S. Chipman, L. Hurwicz, M. K. Richter, and H. F. Sonnenschein. New York: Harcourt Brace Jovanovich, pp. 224–53.

1976. "The Paretian Heritage." *Revue européenee des sciences sociales et Cahiers Vilfredo Pareto* 14:65–171.

Chipman, J. S., and J. C. Moore. 1971. "The Compensation Principle in Welfare Economics." In: *Papers in Quantitative Economics, II,* edited by A. M. Zarley. Lawrence: University of Kansas Press, pp. 1–77.

1973. "Aggregate Demand, Real National Income, and the Compensation Principle." *International Economic Review* 14:153–81.

1978. "The New Welfare Economics 1939–1974." *International Economic Review* 19:547–84.

Cranston, M. 1967. *Freedom – A New Analysis,* 3rd edition. London: Longmans.

Craven, J. 1971. "Majority Voting and Social Choice." *Review of Economic Studies* 38:265–7.

Crawford, V. P. 1979. "A Procedure for Generating Pareto-Efficient Egalitarian-Equivalent Allocations." *Econometrica* 47:49–60.

Crawford, V. P., and W. P. Heller. 1979. "Fair Division and Indivisible Commodities" *Journal of Economic Theory* 21:10–27.

Dahl, R. A. 1956. *A Preface to Democratic Theory.* University of Chicago Press.
Daniel, T. E. 1975. "A Revised Concept of Distributional Equity." *Journal of Economic Theory* 11:94–109.
1978. "Pitfalls in the Theory of Fairness – Comment." *Journal of Economic Theory* 19:561–4.
Daniels, N. (editor). 1975. *Reading Rawls: Critical Studies of a Theory of Justice.* Oxford: Basil Blackwell.
Dasgupta, P. 1980. "Decentralization and Rights." *Economica* (N. S.) 47:107–24.
Dasgupta, P., P. J. Hammond, and E. Maskin. 1979. "The Implementation of Social Choice Rules: Some General Results on Incentive Compatibility." *Review of Economic Studies* 46:185–216.
d'Aspremont, C., and L. Gevers. 1977. "Equity and the Informational Basis of Collective Choice." *Review of Economic Studies* 44:199–209.
Deb, R. 1977. "On Schwartz's Rule." *Journal of Economic Theory* 16:103–10.
1981. "*k*-Monotone Social Decision Functions and the Veto." *Econometrica* 49:899–909.
Debreu, G. 1959. *Theory of Value.* New York: Wiley.
Deschamps, R., and L. Gevers. 1978. "Leximin and Utilitarian Rules: A Joint Characterization." *Journal of Economic Theory* 17:143–63.
Diamond, P. A. 1967. "Cardinal Welfare, Individualistic Ethics, and Interpersonal Comparison of Utility: Comment." *Journal of Political Economy* 75:765–6.
Downs, A. 1957. *An Economic Theory of Democracy.* New York: Harper & Row.
1961. "In Defence of Majority Voting." *Journal of Political Economy* 69: 192–9.
Dummett, M., and R. Farquharson. 1961. "Stability in Voting." *Econometrica* 29:33–43.
Dworkin, R. 1973. "The Original Position." *University of Chicago Law Review* 40:500–33. Reprinted in Daniels (1975, pp. 16–53).
Farquharson, R. 1969. *Theory of Voting.* Oxford: Basil Blackwell.
Farrell, M. J. 1976. "Liberalism in the Theory of Social Choice." *Review of Economic Studies* 43:3–10.
Feldman, A. M. 1974. "A Very Unsubtle Version of Arrow's Impossibility Theorem." *Economic Inquiry* 12:534–46.
1980. *Welfare Economics and Social Choice Theory.* Boston: Martinus Nijhoff.
Feldman, A., and A. Kirman. 1974. "Fairness and Envy." *American Economic Review* 64:995–1005.
Feldman, A., and D. Weiman. 1979. "Envy, Wealth, and Class Hierarchies." *Journal of Public Economics* 11:81–91.
Ferejohn, J. A. 1978. "The Distribution of Rights in Society." In: *Decision Theory and Social Ethics,* edited by H. W. Gottinger and W. Leinfellner. Dordrecht: D. Reidel, pp. 119–31.
Ferejohn, J. A., and D. M. Grether. 1977*a*. "Weak Path Independence." *Journal of Economic Theory* 14:19–31.
1977*b*. "Some New Impossibility Theorems." *Public Choice* 30:35–42.
Fine, B. 1975. "Individual Liberalism in a Paretian Society." *Journal of Political Economy* 83:1277–81.

Fine, B., and K. Fine. 1974. "Social Choice and Individual Ranking." *Review of Economic Studies* 41:303–22, 459–75.

Fishburn, P. C. 1970*a*. "Arrow's Impossibility Theorem: Concise Proof and Infinite Voters." *Journal of Economic Theory* 2:103–6.

1970*b*. "Comments on Hansson's 'Group Preferences'." *Econometrica* 38:933–5.

1970*c*. "Intransitive Indifference in Preference Theory: A Survey." *Operations Research* 18:207–28.

1970*d*. "The Irrationality of Transitivity in Social Choice." *Behavioral Science* 15:119–23.

1970*e*. *Utility Theory for Decision Making*. New York: Wiley.

1971*a*. "Should Social Choice be Based on Binary Comparisons?" *Journal of Mathematical Sociology* 1:133–42.

1971*b*. "A Comparative Analysis of Group Decision Methods." *Behavioral Science* 16:538–44.

1972. *Mathematics of Decision Theory*. The Hague: Mouton.

1973. *The Theory of Social Choice*. Princeton University Press.

1974*a*. "On Collective Rationality and a Generalized Impossibility Theorem." *Review of Economic Studies* 41:445–57.

1974*b*. "Paradoxes of Voting." *American Political Science Review* 68:537–46.

1974*c*. "Social Choice Functions." *SIAM Review* 16:63–90.

1974*d*. "Subset Choice Conditions and the Computation of Social Choice Sets." *Quarterly Journal of Economics* 88:320–9.

1974*e*. "Impossibility Theorems without the Social Completeness Axiom." *Econometrica* 42:695–704.

1977. "Condorcet Social Choice Functions." *SIAM Journal of Applied Mathematics* 33:469–89.

Fishburn, P. C., and W. V. Gehrlein. 1977. "Collective Rationality versus Distribution of Power for Binary Social Choice Functions." *Journal of Economic Theory* 15:72–91.

Fleming, J. M. 1952. "A Cardinal Concept of Welfare." *Quarterly Journal of Economics* 66:366–84.

1957. "Cardinal Welfare and Individualistic Ethics: A Comment." *Journal of Political Economy* 65:355–7.

Foley, D. 1967. "Resource Allocation and the Public Sector." *Yale Economic Essays* 7:45–98.

Fountain, J., and K. Suzumura. 1982. "Collective Choice Rules Without the Pareto Principle." *International Economic Review* 23:299–308.

Gaertner, W., and L. Krüger. 1981. "Self-Supporting Preferences and Individual Rights: The Possibility of Paretian Libertarianism." *Economica* (N. S.) 41:17–28.

Gärdenfors, P. 1973. "Positionalist Voting Functions." *Theory and Decision* 4:1–24.

Gevers, L. 1979. "On Interpersonal Comparability and Social Welfare Orderings." *Econometrica* 47:75–89.

Gibbard, A. 1969. "Social Choice and the Arrow Conditions." Unpublished manuscript.

1973. "Manipulation of Voting Schemes: A General Result." *Econometrica* 41:587–601.

1974. "A Pareto-Consistent Libertarian Claim." *Journal of Economic Theory* 7:388–410.

1977. "Manipulation of Schemes that Mix Voting with Chance." *Econometrica* 45:665–81.

1978. "Straightforwardness of Game Forms with Lotteries." *Econometrica* 46:595–614.

1979. "Disparate Goods and Rawls' Difference Principle: A Social Choice Theoretic Treatment." *Theory and Decision* 11:267–88.

Goldman, S. M., and C. Sussangkarn. 1978. "On the Concept of Fairness." *Journal of Economic Theory* 19:210–16.

1980. "On Equity and Efficiency." *Journal of Economic Theory* 5:29–31.

Goodman, L. A. 1954. "On Methods of Amalgamation." In: *Decision Processes*, edited by R. M. Thrall, C. H. Coombs, and R. L. Davis. New York: Wiley, pp. 39–48.

Goodman, L. A., and H. Markowitz. 1952. "Social Welfare Functions Based on Individual Rankings." *American Journal of Sociology* 58:257–62.

Gordon, S. 1976. "The New Contractarians." *Journal of Political Economy* 84:573–90.

Gorman, W. M. 1955. "The Intransitivity of Certain Criteria Used in Welfare Economics." *Oxford Economic Papers* 7:25–35.

Graaff, J. de V. 1957. *Theoretical Welfare Economics*. Cambridge University Press.

1977. "Equity and Efficiency as Components of the General Welfare." *South African Journal of Economics* 45:362–75.

Grazia, A. de. 1953. "Mathematical Derivation of an Election System." *Isis* 44:42–51.

Guha, A. S. 1972. "Neutrality, Monotonicity, and the Right of Veto." *Econometrica* 40:821–6.

Guilbaud, G. T. 1966. "Theories of the General Interest, and the Logical Problem of Aggregation." In: *Readings in Mathematical Social Science*, edited by P. F. Lazarsfeld and N. W. Henry. Chicago: Science Research Associates, pp. 262–307.

Halmos, P. R. 1960. *Naive Set Theory*. New York: Van Nostrand Reinhold.

Hammond, P. J. 1976. "Equity, Arrow's Conditions, and Rawls' Difference Principle." *Econometrica* 44:793–804.

1979. "Equity in Two Person Situations: Some Consequences." *Econometrica* 47:1127–35.

Hansson, B. 1968. "Choice Structures and Preference Relations." *Synthese* 18:433–58.

1969*a*. "Group Preferences." *Econometrica* 37:50–4.

1969*b*. "Voting and Group Decision Function." *Synthese* 20:526–37.

1973. "The Independence Condition in the Theory of Social Choice." *Theory and Decision* 4:25–49.

1976. "The Existence of Group Preference Functions." *Public Choice* 28:89–98.

Hare, R. M. 1973. "Rawls' Theory of Justice." *Philosophical Quarterly* 23:144–55, 241–52. Reprinted in Daniels (1975, pp. 81–107).

Harsanyi, J. C. 1953. "Cardinal Utility in Welfare Economics and in the Theory of Risk-Taking." *Journal of Political Economy* 61:434–5.

1955. "Cardinal Welfare, Individualistic Ethics, and Interpersonal Comparisons of Utility." *Journal of Political Economy* 63:309–21.

1975. "Can the Maximin Principle Serve as a Basis for Morality? A Critique of John Rawls's Theory." *American Political Science Review* 69:594–606.

1977. *Rational Behavior and Bargaining Equilibrium in Games and Social Situations.* Cambridge University Press.

1978. "Bayesian Decision Theory and Utilitarian Ethics." *American Economic Review, Papers and Proceedings* 68:223–8.

1979. "Bayesian Decision Theory, Rule Utilitarianism, and Arrow's Impossibility Theorem." *Theory and Decision* 11:289–317.

Hayek, F. A. 1948. *Individualism and Economic Order,* University of Chicago Press.

1960. *The Constitution of Liberty,* University of Chicago Press.

Heinberg, J. G. 1926. "History of the Majority Principle." *American Political Science Review* 20:52–68.

1932. "Theories of Majority Rule." *American Political Science Review* 26:452–69.

Heiner, R. A. 1981*a*. "Length and Cycle Equalization." *Journal of Economic Theory* 25:101–30.

1981*b*. "The Collective Decision Problem, and a Theory of Preference." *Economic Inquiry* 19:297–332.

Herzberger, H. G. 1973. "Ordinal Preference and Rational Choice." *Econometrica* 41:187–237.

Hicks, J. R. 1939. "The Foundations of Welfare Economics." *Economic Journal* 49:696–712.

1940. "The Valuation of the Social Income." *Economica* (N. S.) 7:105–24.

1941. "The Rehabilitation of Consumers' Surplus." *Review of Economic Studies* 8:108–16.

1946. *Value and Capital,* 2nd edition. Oxford University Press.

Houthakker, H. S. 1950. "Revealed Preference and the Utility Function." *Economica* (N. S.) 17:159–74.

1965. "On the Logic of Preference and Choice." In: *Contributions to Logic and Methodology in Honour of J. M. Bochenski,* edited by Anna-Teresa Tymieniecka. Amsterdam: North Holland, pp. 193–205.

Howard, N. 1971. *Paradoxes of Rationality: Theory of Metagames and Political Behavior*. Cambridge, Mass.: MIT Press.

Hurwicz, L. 1972. "On Informationally Decentralized Systems." In: *Decision and Organization,* edited by R. Radner and B. McGuire. Amsterdam: North Holland, pp. 297–336.

Hurwicz, L., and D. Schmeidler. 1978. "Construction of Outcome Functions Guaranteeing Existence and Pareto Optimality of Nash Equilibria." *Econometrica* 46:1447–74.

Inada, K. 1955. "Alternative Incompatible Conditions for a Social Welfare Function." *Econometrica* 23:396–9.

1971. "Social Welfare Functions and Social Indifference Surfaces." *Econometrica* 39:599–623.

Jamison, D. T., and L. J. Lau. 1973. "Semiorders and the Theory of Choice." *Econometrica* 41:901–12.

1975. "Semiorders and the Theory of Choice: A Correction." *Econometrica* 43:979–80.

Jefferson, T. 1801. "First Inaugural Address." Reprinted 1897 in: *The Writings of Thomas Jefferson,* edited by P. L. Ford, Vol. VIII. New York: G. P. Putnam, p. 2.

Johansen, L. 1969. "An Examination of the Relevance of Kenneth Arrow's General Possibility Theorem for Economic Planning." *Economics of Planning* 9:5–41.

Kalai, E., E. A. Pazner, and D. Schmeidler. 1976. "Collective Choice Correspondences as Admissible Outcomes of Social Bargaining Processes." *Econometrica* 44:233–40.

Kalai, E., and D. Schmeidler. 1977. "An Admissible Set Occurring in Various Bargaining Situations." *Journal of Economic Theory* 14:402–11.

Kaldor, N. 1939. "Welfare Propositions in Economics and Interpersonal Comparisons of Utility." *Economic Journal* 49:549–52.

Kaneko, M., and K. Nakamura. 1979. "The Nash Social Welfare Function." *Econometrica* 47:423–35.

Karni, E. 1978. "Collective Rationality, Unanimity and Liberal Ethics." *Review of Economic Studies* 45:571–4.

Kelley, J. L. 1955. *General Topology.* Princeton, N. J.: D. Van Nostrand.

Kelly, J. S. 1976*a.* "The Impossibility of a Just Liberal." *Economica* (N. S.) 43:67–75.

1976*b.* "Rights Exercising and a Pareto-Consistent Libertarian Claim." *Journal of Economic Theory* 13:138–53.

1978. *Arrow Impossibility Theorems.* New York: Academic Press.

Kemp, M. C. 1953–4. "Arrow's General Possibility Theorem." *Review of Economic Studies* 21:240–3.

Kemp, M. C., and Y. K. Ng. 1976. "On the Existence of Social Welfare Functions, Social Orderings and Social Decision Functions." *Economica* (N. S.) 43:59–66.

Kendall, W., and G. C. Carey. 1968. "The 'Intensity' Problem and Democratic Theory." *American Political Science Review* 62:5–24.

Kim, K. H., and F. W. Roush. 1980. "Binary Social Welfare Functions." *Journal of Economic Theory* 23:416–19.

Kirman, A. P., and D. Sondermann. 1972. "Arrow's Theorem, Many Agents, and Invisible Dictators." *Journal of Economic Theory* 5:267–77.

Kleinberg, N. L. 1980. "Fair Allocations and Equal Incomes." *Journal of Economic Theory* 23:189–200.

Little, I. M. D. 1952. "Social Choice and Individual Values." *Journal of Political Economy* 60:422–32.

1957. *A Critique of Welfare Economics,* 2nd edition. Oxford University Press.

Luce, R. D. 1956. "Semiorders and the Theory of Utility Discrimination." *Econometrica* 24:178–91.

Luce, R. D., and H. Raiffa. 1957. *Games and Decisions.* New York: Wiley.

Lyons, D. 1972. "Rawls Versus Utilitarianism." *Journal of Philosophy* 69:535–45.

Macfie, A. L. 1967. *The Individual in Society: Papers on Adam Smith.* London: George Allen & Unwin.

Machlup, F. 1969. "Liberalism and the Choice of Freedoms." In: *Roads to Freedom,* edited by E. Streissler. London: Routledge & Kegan Paul, pp. 117–46.

Mas-Colell, A., and H. Sonnenschein. 1972. "General Possibility Theorems for Group Decisions." *Review of Economic Studies* 39:185–92.

Maskin, E. 1978. "A Theorem on Utilitarianism." *Review of Economic Studies* 45:93–6.

1979. "Implementation and Strong Nash-Equilibrium." In: *Aggregation and Revelation of Preferences,* edited by J.-J. Laffont. Amsterdam: North Holland, pp. 433–9.

May, K. O. 1952. "A Set of Independent Necessary and Sufficient Conditions for Simple Majority Decision." *Econometrica* 20:680–4.

Mill, J. S. 1859. *On Liberty,* London: Parker. Reprinted 1977 in: *The Collected Works of John Stuart Mill, Vol. XVIII,* edited by J. M. Robson. University of Toronto Press.

Mirkin, B. G. 1979. *Group Choice,* edited and introduced by P. C. Fishburn. Washington, D.C.: V. H. Winston & Sons.

1981. "Federations and Transitive Group Choice." *Mathematical Social Sciences* 2:35–8.

Mishan, E. J. 1960. "A Survey of Welfare Economics, 1939–1959." *Economic Journal* 70:197–265.

1965. "The Recent Debate on Welfare Criteria." *Oxford Economic Papers* 17:219–36.

1969. *Welfare Economics: An Assessment.* Amsterdam: North Holland.

1980. "The New Welfare Economics: An Alternative View." *International Economic Review* 21:671–705.

Morrow, G. 1923. *The Ethical and Economic Theories of Adam Smith.* New York: Longmans Green.

Moulin, H. 1981. "The Proportional Veto Principle." *Review of Economic Studies* 48:407–16.

Mueller, D. C. 1979*a*. "Voting by Veto." *Journal of Public Economics* 10:57–75.

1979*b*. *Public Choice.* Cambridge University Press.

Murakami, Y. 1961. "A Note on the General Possibility Theorem of the Social Welfare Function." *Econometrica* 29:244–6.

1968. *Logic and Social Choice.* London: Routledge & Kegan Paul.

Nakamura, K. 1975. "The Core of a Simple Game with Ordinal Preferences." *International Journal of Game Theory* 4:95–104.

1979. "The Vetoers in a Simple Game with Ordinal Preferences." *International Journal of Game Theory* 8:55–61.

1981. *Game Theory and Social Choice,* edited by M. Suzuki. Tokyo: Keiso Shuppan Service Centre.

Nash, J. F. 1950. "The Bargaining Problem." *Econometrica* 18:155–62.

Nozick, R. 1974. *Anarchy, State, and Utopia.* Oxford: Basil Blackwell.

Osborne, D. K. 1975. "On Liberalism and the Pareto Principle." *Journal of Political Economy* 83:1283–7.

Otsuki, M. 1981. "On Distribution According to Labour – A Concept of Fairness in Production Economies." *Review of Economic Studies* 47:945–58.

Packard, D. J. 1977. "A Proposed Solution to the Voters Preference Aggregation Problem." *Theory and Decision* 8:255–64.

Packard, D. J., and R. A. Heiner. 1977. "Ranking Functions and Independence Conditions." *Journal of Economic Theory* 16:84–102.

Packel, E. 1981. "Social Decision Functions and Strongly Decisive Sets." *Review of Economic Studies* 48:343–9.

Pareto, V. 1909. *Manuel d'Économie Politique*. Paris: Girard & Briere. English translation, 1971. *Manual of Political Economy*. London: Macmillan.

Parks, R. P. 1976*a*. "An Impossibility Theorem for Fixed Preferences: A Dictatorial Bergson-Samuelson Welfare Function." *Review of Economic Studies* 43:447–50.

1976*b*. "Further Results on Path Independence, Quasitransitivity, and Social Choice." *Public Choice* 26:75–87.

Pattanaik, P. K. 1968. "Risk, Impersonality, and the Social Welfare Function." *Journal of Political Economy* 76:1152–69.

1971. *Voting and Collective Choice*. Cambridge University Press.

1978. *Strategy and Group Choice*. Amsterdam: North Holland.

Pazner, E. A. 1976. "Recent Thinking on Economic Justice." *Journal of Peace Science* 2:143–57.

1977. "Pitfalls in the Theory of Fairness." *Journal of Economic Theory* 14:458–66.

Pazner, E. A., and D. Schmeidler. 1974. "A Difficulty in the Concept of Fairness." *Review of Economic Studies* 41:441–3.

1976. "Social Contract Theory and Ordinal Distributive Equity." *Journal of Public Economics* 5:261–8.

1978. "Egalitarian Equivalent Allocations: A New Concept of Economic Equity." *Quarterly Journal of Economics* 92:671–88.

Peleg, B. 1978*a*. "Representation of Simple Games by Social Choice Functions." *International Journal of Game Theory* 7:81–4.

1978*b*. "Consistent Voting Systems." *Econometrica* 46:153–61.

Phelps, E. S. 1977. "Recent Developments in Welfare Economics: Justice et Equite." In: *Frontiers of Quantitative Economics, Vol. IIIB*, edited by M. D. Intriligator, Amsterdam: North Holland, pp. 703–30.

Plott, C. R. 1972. "Individual Choice of a Political-Economic Process." In: *Probability Models of Collective Decision Making*, edited by R. G. Niemi and H. F. Weisberg. Columbus, Ohio: Merrill Publishing.

1973. "Path Independence, Rationality, and Social Choice." *Econometrica* 41:1075–91.

1976. "Axiomatic Social Choice Theory: An Overview and Interpretation." *American Journal of Political Science* 20:511–96.

1978. "Rawls's Theory of Justice: An Impossibility Result." In: *Decision Theory and Social Ethics, Issues in Social Choice*, edited by H. W. Gottinger and W. Leinfellner. Dordrecht: D. Reidel, pp. 201–14.

Pollak, R. A. 1979. "Bergson–Samuelson Social Welfare Functions and the Theory of Social Choice." *Quarterly Journal of Economics* 93:73–90.

Radner, R., and J. Marschak. 1954. "Note on Some Proposed Decision Criteria." In: *Decision Processes,* edited by R. M. Thrall, C. H. Coombs, and R. L. Davis. New York: Wiley, pp. 61–8.

Rae, D. 1969. "Decision-Rules and Individual Values in Constitutional Choice." *American Political Science Review* 63:40–56.

Rawls, J. 1962: "Justice as Fairness." In: *Philosophy, Politics and Society,* 2nd ser., edited by P. Laslett and W. G. Runciman. Oxford: Basil Blackwell, pp. 132–57.

1963. "Constitutional Liberty and the Concept of Justice." In: *Nomos VI: Justice,* edited by C. J. Friedrich and J. W. Chapman. New York: Atherton Press, pp. 98–125.

1967. "Distributive Justice." In: *Philosophy, Politics and Society,* 3rd ser., edited by P. Laslett and W. G. Runciman. Oxford: Basil Blackwell, pp. 58–82.

1968. "Distributive Justice: Some Addenda." *Natural Law Forum* 13:51–71.

1971. *A Theory of Justice.* Cambridge, Mass.: Harvard University Press.

1974. "Some Reasons for the Maximin Criterion." *American Economic Review, Papers and Proceedings* 64:141–6.

1975. "Fairness to Goodness." *Philosophical Review* 84:536–54.

Ray, P. 1973. "Independence of Irrelevant Alternatives." *Econometrica* 41:987–91.

Richelson, J. T. 1978. "Some Further Results on Consistency, Rationality and Collective Choice." *Review of Economic Studies* 45:343–6.

Richter, M. K. 1966. "Revealed Preference Theory." *Econometrica* 34:635–45.

1971. "Rational Choice." In: *Preferences, Utility, and Demand,* edited by J. S. Chipman, L. Hurwicz, M. K. Richter, and H. F. Sonnenschein. New York: Harcourt Brace Jovanovich, pp. 27–58.

Riemer, N. 1951–2. "The Case for Bare Majority Rule." *Ethics* 62:16–32.

Riker, W. H., and P. C. Ordeshook. 1973. *An Introduction to Positive Political Theory.* Englewood Cliffs, N.J.: Prentice-Hall.

Robbins, L. 1935. *An Essay on the Nature and Significance of Economic Science,* 2nd edition. London: Macmillan.

Roberts, K. W. S. 1980*a*. "Possibility Theorems with Interpersonally Comparable Welfare Levels." *Review of Economic Studies* 47:409–20.

1980*b*. "Interpersonal Comparability and Social Choice Theory." *Review of Economic Studies* 47:421–39.

Rousseau, J.-J. 1964. *Discourse on the Origin and Foundation of Inequality among Mankind,* translated by L. G. Crocker. New York: Washington Square Press.

Rowley, C. K. 1978. "Liberalism and Collective Choice: A Return to Reality?" *The Manchester School of Economic and Social Studies* 46:224–51.

Rowley, C. K., and A. T. Peacock. 1975. *Welfare Economics: A Liberal Restatement.* London: Martin Robertson.

Samuelson, P. A. 1938. "A Note on the Pure Theory of Consumer's Behavior." *Economica* (N. S.) 5:61-71.

1947. *Foundations of Economic Analysis.* Cambridge, Mass.: Harvard University Press.

1948. "Consumption Theory in Terms of Revealed Preference." *Economica* (N. S.) 15:243–53.

1950*a*. "Evaluation of Real National Income." *Oxford Economic Papers* 2:1–29.

1950*b*. "The Problem of Integrability in Utility Theory." *Economica* (N. S.) 17:355–81.
1967. "Arrow's Mathematical Politics." In: *Human Values and Economic Policy*, edited by S. Hook. New York University Press, pp. 41–51.
1977. "Reaffirming the Existence of 'Reasonable' Bergson-Samuelson Social Welfare Functions." *Economica* (N. S.) 44:81–8.
Satterthwaite, M. A. 1975. "Strategy-Proofness and Arrow's Conditions: Existence and Correspondence Theorems for Voting Procedures and Social Welfare Functions." *Journal of Economic Theory* 10:187–217.
Schick, F. 1969. "Arrow's Proof and the Logic of Preference." *Philosophy of Science* 36:127–44.
Schmeidler, D., and K. Vind. 1972. "Fair Net Trades." *Econometrica* 40:637–42.
Schwartz, T. 1972. "Rationality and the Myth of the Maximum." *Noûs* 7:97–117.
1976. "Choice Functions, 'Rationality' Conditions, and Variations of the Weak Axiom of Revealed Preference." *Journal of Economic Theory* 13:414–27.
1981. "The Universal-Instability Theorem." *Public Choice* 37:487–501.
Scitovsky, T. 1941. "A Note on Welfare Propositions in Economics." *Review of Economic Studies* 9:77–88.
Seidl, C. 1975. "On Liberal Values." *Zeitschrift für Nationalökonomie* 35:257–92.
Sen, A. K. 1969. "Quasi-Transitivity, Rational Choice and Collective Decision." *Review of Economic Studies* 36:381–93.
1970*a*. "The Impossibility of a Paretian Liberal." *Journal of Political Economy* 78:152–7.
1970*b*. *Collective Choice and Social Welfare*. San Francisco: Holden-Day.
1971. "Choice Functions and Revealed Preference." *Review of Economic Studies* 38:307–17.
1973*a*. *On Economic Inequality*. Oxford University Press.
1973*b*. "Behaviour and the Concept of Preference." *Economica* (N. S.) 40:241–59.
1976. "Liberty, Unanimity and Rights." *Economica* (N. S.) 43:217–45.
1977*a*. "Social Choice Theory: A Re-Examination." *Econometrica* 45:53–89.
1977*b*. "Rational Fools: A Critique of the Behavioral Foundations of Economic Theory." *Philosophy and Public Affairs* 6:317–44.
1977*c*. "On Weights and Measures: Informational Constraints in Social Welfare Analysis." *Econometrica* 45:1539–72.
1979*a*. "Strategies and Revelation: Informational Constraints in Public Decisions." In: *Aggregation and Revelation of Preferences*, edited by J.-J. Laffont. Amsterdam: North Holland, pp.13–28.
1979*b*. "Interpersonal Comparisons of Welfare." In: *Economics and Human Welfare*, edited by M. J. Boskin. New York: Academic Press, pp. 183–201.
1979*c*. "Personal Utilities and Public Judgements: Or What's Wrong with Welfare Economics?" *Economic Journal* 89:537–58.
1982. *Choice, Welfare and Measurement*. Oxford: Basil Blackwell.
1983. "Social Choice Theory." In: *Handbook of Mathematical Economics, III*, edited by K. J. Arrow and M. Intriligator. Amsterdam: North Holland.
Simon, H. A. 1978. "Rationality as Process and as Product of Thought." *American Economic Review, Papers and Proceedings* 68:1–16.

Smith, A. 1759. *The Theory of Moral Sentiments.* London: printed for A. Millar, in the Strand, and A. Kincaid and J. Bell, in Edinburgh. Reprinted 1969: New Rochelle, N.Y.: Arlington House.

Smith, J. H. 1973. "Aggregation of Preferences with Variable Electorate." *Econometrica* 41:1027–41.

Stevens, D. N., and J. E. Foster. 1978. "The Possibility of Democratic Pluralism." *Economica* (N. S.) 45:401–6.

Strasnick, S. 1976*a*. "Social Choice and the Derivation of Rawls's Difference Principle." *Journal of Philosophy* 73:85–99.

1976*b*. "The Problem of Social Choice: Arrow to Rawls." *Philosophy and Public Affairs* 5:241–73.

1977. "Ordinality and the Spirit of the Justified Dictator." *Social Research* 44:668–90.

1979*a*. "Extended Sympathy Comparisons and the Basis of Social Choice." *Theory and Decision* 10:311–28.

1979*b*. "Neo-Utilitarian Ethics and the Ordinal Representation Assumption." Department of Philosophy, Stanford University.

Sugden, R. 1978. "Social Choice and Individual Liberty." In: *Contemporary Economic Analysis,* edited by M. Artis and A. R. Nobay. London: Croom Helm, pp. 243–71.

Suppes, P. 1966. "Some Formal Models of Grading Principles." *Synthese* 6:284–306.

Suzumura, K. 1976*a*. "Rational Choice and Revealed Preference." *Review of Economic Studies* 43:149–58.

1976*b*. "Remarks on the Theory of Collective Choice." *Economica* (N. S.) 43:381–90.

1977. "Houthakker's Axiom in the Theory of Rational Choice." *Journal of Economic Theory* 14:284–90.

1978. "On the Consistency of Libertarian Claims." *Review of Economic Studies* 45:329–42.

1979. "On the Consistency of Libertarian Claims: A Correction." *Review of Economic Studies* 46:743.

1980*a*. "On Distributional Value Judgements and Piecemeal Welfare Criteria." *Economica* (N.S.) 47:125–39.

1980*b*. "Liberal Paradox and the Voluntary Exchange of Rights-Exercising." *Journal of Economic Theory* 22:407–22.

1981*a*. "On the Possibility of 'Fair' Collective Choice Rule." *International Economic Review* 22:307–20.

1981*b*. "On Pareto-Efficiency and the No-Envy Concept of Equity." *Journal of Economic Theory* 25:367–79.

1982. "Equity, Efficiency and Rights in Social Choice." *Mathematical Social Sciences* 3:131–55.

1983. "Resolving Conflicting Views of Justice in Social Choice." Discussion Paper No. 156, Kyoto Institute of Economic Research. In: *Social Choice and Welfare,* edited by P. K. Pattanaik and M. Salles. Amsterdam: North Holland, pp. 125–49.

Svensson, L.-G. 1977. *Social Justice and Fair Distributions.* Lund: Lund Economic Studies.

Szpilrajn, E. 1930. "Sur l'Extension de l'Ordre Partiel." *Fundamenta Mathematicae* 16:386–9.

Taylor, M. 1969. "Proof of a Theorem on Majority Rule." *Behavioral Science* 14:228–31.

Thomson, W. 1980*a*. "Equity in Exchange Economies." Discussion Paper No. 80–134, Department of Economics, University of Minnesota.

1980*b*. "Anonymity and Equity." Discussion Paper No. 791, Harvard Institute of Economic Research, Harvard University.

Uzawa, H. 1957. "Note on Preference and Axioms of Choice." *Annals of the Institute of Statistical Mathematics* 8:35–40.

1971. "Preference and Rational Choice in the Theory of Consumption." In: *Preferences, Utility, and Demand,* edited by J. S. Chipman, L. Hurwicz, M. K. Richter, and H. F. Sonnenschein. New York: Harcourt Brace Jovanovich, pp. 7–28.

Varian, H. R. 1974. "Equity, Envy, and Efficiency." *Journal of Economic Theory* 9:63–91.

1975. "Distributive Justice, Welfare Economics, and the Theory of Fairness." *Philosophy and Public Affairs* 4:223–47.

1976. "Two Problems in the Theory of Fairness." *Journal of Economic Theory* 5:249–60.

Vickrey, W. 1960. "Utility, Strategy, and Social Decision Rules." *Quarterly Journal of Economics* 74:507–35.

1977. "Economic Rationality and Social Choice." *Social Research* 44:691–707.

von Neumann, J., and O. Morgenstern. 1953. *Theory of Games and Economic Behavior,* 3rd edition. Princeton University Press.

Wilson, R. B. 1970. "The Finer Structure of Revealed Preference." *Journal of Economic Theory* 2:348–53.

1972*a*. "The Game-Theoretic Structure of Arrow's General Possibility Theorem." *Journal of Economic Theory* 5:14–20.

1972*b*. "Social Choice Theory without the Pareto Principle." *Journal of Economic Theory* 5:478–86.

1975. "On the Theory of Aggregation." *Journal of Economic Theory* 10:89–99.

Wolff, R. P. 1977. *Understanding Rawls: A Reconstruction and Critique of a Theory of Justice,* Princeton University Press.

Wriglesworth, J. L. 1981. "Solutions to the Gibbard and Sen Paradoxes Using Information Available from Interpersonal Comparisons." Lincoln College, Oxford University.

Yaari, M. E. 1981. "Rawls, Edgeworth, Shapley, Nash: Theories of Distributive Justice Re-examined." *Journal of Economic Theory* 24:1–39.

Young, H. P. 1974. "An Axiomatization of Borda's Rule." *Journal of Economic Theory* 9:43–52.

Index